Affective Communities in World Politics

Emotions underpin how political communities are formed and function. Nowhere is this more pronounced than in times of trauma. The emotions associated with suffering caused by war, terrorism, natural disasters, famine and poverty can play a pivotal role in shaping communities and orientating their politics. But until recently the political roles of emotions have received only scant attention.

This book contributes to burgeoning literatures on emotions and international relations by investigating how "affective communities" emerge after trauma. Drawing on several case studies and an unusually broad set of interdisciplinary sources, the book examines the role played by representations – from media images to historical narratives and political speeches. Representations of traumatic events are crucial, the book argues, because they generate socially embedded emotional meanings, which, in turn, enable direct victims and distant witnesses to share the injury – as well as the associated loss – in a manner that affirms a particular notion of collective identity. While ensuing political orders often re-establish old patterns, traumatic events can also generate new "emotional cultures" that genuinely transform national and transnational communities.

EMMA HUTCHISON is a RESEARCH FELLOW in the School of Political Science and International Studies at the University of Queensland, Australia. Her work focuses on emotions and trauma in world politics, particularly in relation to security, humanitarianism and international aid. She has published widely on these and related topics in scholarly books and international journals, including *International Theory*, *International Political Sociology*, *Review of International Studies*, and the *European Journal of Social Theory*.

CAMBRIDGE STUDIES IN INTERNATIONAL RELATIONS: 140

Affective Communities in World Politics

Cambridge Studies in International Relations is a joint initiative of Cambridge University Press and the British International Studies Association (BISA). The series aims to publish the best new scholarship in international studies, irrespective of subject matter, methodological approach or theoretical perspective. The series seeks to bring the latest theoretical work in International Relations to bear on the most important problems and issues in global politics.

CAMBRIDGE STUDIES IN INTERNATIONAL RELATIONS

139 Patricia Owens
Economy of force
Counterinsurgency and the historical rise of the social

138 Ronald R. Krebs
Narrative and the making of US national security

137 Andrew Phillips and J. C. Sharman
International order in diversity
War, trade and rule in the Indian Ocean

136 Ole Jacob Sending, Vincent Pouliot and Iver B. Neumann
Diplomacy and the making of world politics

135 Barry Buzan and George Lawson
The global transformation
History, modernity and the making of international relations

134 Heather Elko McKibben
State strategies in international bargaining
Play by the rules or change them?

133 Janina Dill
Legitimate targets?
Social construction, international law, and US bombing

132 Nuno P. Monteiro
Theory of unipolar politics

131 Jonathan D. Caverley
Democratic militarism
Voting, wealth, and war

130 David Jason Karp
Responsibility for human rights
Transnational corporations in imperfect states

129 Friedrich Kratochwil
The status of law in world society
Meditations on the role and rule of law

Series list continues after index

Affective Communities in World Politics

Collective Emotions after Trauma

EMMA HUTCHISON

CAMBRIDGE
UNIVERSITY PRESS

CAMBRIDGE
UNIVERSITY PRESS

University Printing House, Cambridge CB2 8BS, United Kingdom

Cambridge University Press is part of the University of Cambridge.

It furthers the University's mission by disseminating knowledge in the pursuit of education, learning and research at the highest international levels of excellence.

www.cambridge.org
Information on this title: www.cambridge.org/9781107095014

First published 2016

A catalogue record for this publication is available from the British Library

Library of Congress Cataloguing in Publication data
Names: Hutchison, Emma, 1980– author.
Title: Affective communities in world politics : collective emotions after trauma / Emma Hutchison, the University of Queensland.
Description: New York : Cambridge University Press, 2016. | Series: Cambridge studies in international relations ; 140 | Includes bibliographical references and index.
Identifiers: LCCN 2015042957 | ISBN 9781107095014 (hardback) Subjects: LCSH: Political psychology. | Emotions – Political aspects. | Psychic trauma – Political aspects. | Group identity – Political aspects. | International relations – Psychological aspects. | BISAC: POLITICAL SCIENCE / International Relations / General.
Classification: LCC JA74.5.H86 2016 | DDC 327.101/9–dc23
LC record available at http://lccn.loc.gov/2015042957

ISBN 978-1-107-09501-4 Hardback

For my family

Contents

Figures and tables

Preface

This book contributes to burgeoning literature on emotions and international relations by investigating how "affective communities" emerge after traumatic events. While trauma is frequently conceptualized as an individual, isolating experience, this book examines how representations – from media images to historical narratives and political speeches – make traumatic events collectively meaningful. Representations are crucial, the book argues, because they mobilize socially embedded emotional meanings, which, in turn, enable direct victims and witnesses to share the injury and loss in a manner that affirms a particular collective sense of identity. Representations of trauma can thus help to constitute bonds between individuals. They illuminate how and to whom individuals feel emotionally attached. While emotions mobilized after trauma often re-establish prevailing political orders and patterns, traumatic events can also generate new "emotional cultures" that genuinely transform national and transnational communities. The communities that ensue can be conceived of as "affective communities" in so far as they are necessarily constituted through, and distinguished by, social, collective forms of feeling.

One fundamental premise therefore focuses my inquiry: emotions permeate the complex, overlapping social structures that undergird decision making and collective action in world politics. Emotions are a fundamental, unavoidable and inherent dimension of human life, and thus of all social and political life. However, world politics has been traditionally perceived as a realm where, above all, precision, instrumentality and hence a technical, calculated, emotional-less rationality must necessarily prevail. Numerous scholars meanwhile show that the vision of an emotion-free rationality is a chimera. Rationality necessarily contains emotions, just as thinking does feeling. Emotions cannot be removed from political decision making, because emotions exist at the core of human life. Even if we try to hold our emotions at bay, they have always already shaded our inner-most thoughts and perceptions of the world around us. But these seemingly individual emotions are always already collective and political. Emotions are embedded in and structured by particular social systems and, as such, are interwoven with the dominant interests, values and aspirations of those systems.

An investigation into the emotional underpinnings of political communities is important to international relations because it helps us to understand what motivates and drives political actors. This is as much the case with individuals, such as political leaders or diplomats, as it is with collectives, such as states or social movements. Understanding that emotions lie beneath all political perceptions provides important signals and critical clues as to why particular international actors respond and behave in the ways that they do. While this book examines the dynamics at stake in times of trauma, the ensuing implications are much broader. Emotions permeate all political events and issues. Individuals and political communities attribute meaning, value and priority to political phenomena by drawing upon socially cultivated affective and emotional dispositions.

Revealing that emotions are situated at the core of political perceptions and behaviors is thus significant because it assists scholars and analysts to puzzle together how particular political situations come to be. Emotions tell us things. While they are often hidden and inaudible, neglected and refuted, when uncovered and taken seriously, the political insights they provide are invaluable for analyzing politics and policy and for ascertaining what strategy might be best formulated next.

My argument regarding the links between emotions and political communities goes against some strands of international relations scholarship, particularly those who are concerned that such a move may "anthropomorphize" the state. It is true that attributing state actions with emotions and emotionality can be fraught. But, to me, it is a commonsensical proposition. Once we appreciate the "situatedness" of emotions, it becomes apparent that communities of all sizes provide an anchor to become attached to and potentially motivated by. To claim that political collectives – including nation-states and even international and transnational organizations – act in part on socially attuned emotions is merely to invoke the argument that it is exactly within such collective social structures that our emotions take on shape and meaning. This is not to claim that emotions within these structures and ensuing communities are homogenous, or that individual allegiances do not overlap to constitute different, intersecting, potentially contradictory "affective communities." It is merely to argue that in particular circumstances, and through particular activating representations or frames, emotions can be mobilized in ways that make possible collective, political ends. Emotions can become receptacles of political agency and power. Emotions can help to affect political change, or they can be summoned in service of the status quo, for what may be for the better or for the worse. An appreciation of how such collective emotions operate – how emotions can become entrenched or act as sites of resistance – has in this way direct implications for how scholars and practitioners engage and try to resolve some of the world's most pressing political, security and ethical problems.

Acknowledgments

Writing this book has been as much a part of a personal search to understand trauma as it has been a scholarly one. Formally, it began some time ago, as my PhD dissertation, but my ruminating about trauma, emotions and community started long before this, as a consequence of my own experiences. In one sense, even to me, what I have endured seems very different from the political trauma I examine in this book. I am reluctant even to label my own experiences "trauma." Yet, in another sense, there are synergies that suggest that the boundaries between my life and my research are not so black and white. This book would not be what it is without the intersection between the two.

Relatively young – aged eighteen – I was diagnosed with a chronic health condition that, quite literally, made me see the world anew. It was end-stage renal failure, and I was given twelve months until I would need to start dialysis. It was to be only three. The seamless, carefree vision of reality as I knew it was over. Like the instances of political trauma I write of, normal life was replaced with one filled with uncertainty, contingency and doubt. Over the next few years, until I received and fully adjusted to my first kidney transplant, I went through something in the way of suffering that has come to embody a trauma. It is sometimes still hard to believe that it has all happened to me. But kidney failure is by no means the worst that can happen to anyone – in fact, I strangely believe I'm the better for it. Great things have come. Facing something that seems so incomprehensible, I've come out the other side better. Myself, my family and my closest connections are stronger because of it. I say this even despite the fact that I am now back on dialysis, my transplant having failed last year.

The impetus for this book thus emerged from a search to understand how we can find meaning in shocking, incomprehensible, traumatic things, and how that meaning can help us to turn things around, to flourish rather than languish. How do we make meaning from trauma? How does pain shape us? Can the sight of another's trauma inspire those who witness to care? How are we engendered to perceive of some suffering as so traumatic that it warrants a response, while others are left to suffer in silence? The links between emotions and community are central to such questions. But too often in world politics we see these questions left out. With this book I have thus sought to bring them back in. Investigating the intersections between emotions and community is more than just about understanding how trauma can constitute political communities. It is about how we live and interact. It is about how and for whom we really care, and why is it that we do in the ways that we do.

Just as my experiences have pushed me to understand the meaning of trauma, they have also challenged me to understand the meaning of community. This has been a task that has seemed, at least personally, neither straightforward nor easy. Writers such as David Morris and Elaine Scarry intuit much when they stress that chronic pain seems to break down understanding, building up "walls of separation." This book has thus also emerged from my own grappling – from my fears and my hopes – that when in pain, despite our darkest moments, we are never wholly alone.

While this book began as a PhD dissertation, it has in the five years since been almost completely transformed. Many colleagues and scholars have helped me to get it to where it is now. Reviewers from Cambridge University Press provided invaluable insights and queries that pushed me to take the manuscript further than I would have done otherwise. Tim Dunne and Chris Reus-Smit helped to keep my changes for CUP focused. David Campbell, Jenny Edkins and Barbara Sullivan also read an earlier iteration of the book. Their in-depth, encouraging feedback prompted me to rethink aspects of my approach. Many scholars reviewed parts of the book, either as draft chapters or in article form. For their probing comments and questions, I would particularly like to acknowledge Janice Bially Mattern, Katharine Gelber, Susanna Hast, Karin Fierke, Lauren Leigh Hinthorne, Andrew Linklater, Iver Neumann, Kate Manzo, Jonathan Mercer and anonymous reviewers of articles from which select parts of following chapters are based.

A warm thank you must go to the intellectual home from which inklings of this book first sprung: the School of Political Science and International Studies at the University of Queensland (UQ). Ever since my undergraduate days, UQ has provided me with a supportive institutional and scholarly environment. Academic staff – now colleagues – have never ceased to encourage me. I hope that the same kind of intellectual curiosity and rigor that permeates my department bears out in the pages that follow. I owe a special debt to two further scholars who while at UQ have supported and challenged me, taking time to review and discuss my work at length: Prudence Ahrens and Richard Devetak. Cindy O'Hagan also deserves a special mention, as it was she who while at UQ first enticed me away from studying Mandarin into the wider world of international relations. She has remained a constant source of energy, insight and questions for me since. Thank you also to Constance Duncombe, who has been a sheer wonder to work with over the past year and a half. Her invaluable research assistance has kept me lunging toward the finish line. For their collegiality, friendship and ongoing conversations about my work and this book over the past decade, I thank Alex Bellamy, Stephen Bell, Morgan Brigg, Anne Brown, Shannon Brincat, Mark Chou, Sara Davies, Suzanne Grant, Marianne Hanson, Marguerite La Caze, Madeleine-Marie Judd, Sebastian Kaempf, Matt McDonald, Xzarina Nicholson, Andrew Phillips, Heather Rae, Tricia Rooney, Angela Setterlund, Caitlin Sparks, Elizabeth Strakosch, Emily Tannock, Heloise Weber, Martin Weber, Gillian Whitehouse and Erin Wilson. Some of these scholars have since moved on from UQ, but I am honored that they remain colleagues and, in some cases, close friends.

This book has also benefited from many workshops, panels, seminars, email exchanges and conversations with friends and colleagues in the academic community. Many of these connections have been concentrated on emotions and world politics, and have provided a rich source of insight, inspiration and debate. One such workshop, which preceded a special forum section on "Emotions and World Politics," co-edited with Roland Bleiker, brought together scholars who helped me to crystallize the contribution of this book. For these and other scholarly discussions that have been key to my thinking about emotions and associated aspects of world politics, my sincere thanks go to Linda Åhäll, Ken Booth, Frank Costigliola, Neta Crawford, Tuomas Forsberg, Thomas Gregory, Lene Hansen, Marcus Holmes, Lily Ling, Simon Koschut, Katrina Lee-Koo, Renée Jeffery, Swati Parashar, Laura Shepherd, Oliver Richmond, Brent Sasley, Jacqui True and Wes Widmaier.

Various grants and fellowships made it possible for me to continue to focus on researching and writing this book, even when times of ill health have taken over. An Australian Research Council Discovery Grant (DP110100546) on "how images shape responses to humanitarian crises" undertaken together with Roland Bleiker and David Campbell allowed me to remain in academia. Last year, I was awarded a UQ Postdoctoral Fellowship for Women. Before this, I spent part of 2010 as a Postdoctoral Fellow at the European University Institute (EUI). I am especially grateful to the late Peter Mair and everyone at the Department of Social and Political Science at EUI who were so welcoming during my stay. At earlier stages of my research I also enjoyed two visiting fellowships at the Australian National University. Thank you to the Canberra Branch of the Australian Federation of University Women and the UQ Graduate School for making these fellowships possible.

As an Associate Investigator in the Australian Research Council Centre of Excellence in the History of Emotions, I have also been fortunate to forge connections and glean insight from emotional historians that I might not have otherwise. Thank you to all at the Centre who have made my AI status and funding possible. For their intellectual and institutional support, special thanks go to Merridee Bailey, Ann Brooks, Lucy Burnett, Jane Davidson, Peter Holbrook, Barbara Keys, David Lemmings, Andrew Lynch, Katrina Tap, Tanya Tuffrey, Stephanie Trigg and Charles Zika.

Cambridge University Press has been a particularly supportive publisher during the sometimes winding process of completing this book. Thank you to series editors Chris Reus-Smit, Nick Wheeler and Evelyn Goh for supporting the book from the very beginning. Thank you also to the Political and Social Sciences publisher, John Haslam, as well as the Politics, Sociology and Psychology editor, Carrie Parkinson, who have patiently guided me through the various publishing processes. I would also especially like to thank all at Cambridge University Press for their understanding during times when my deteriorating health further delayed the manuscript's delivery.

Parts of this book draw on from material previously published elsewhere. Chapter 4 has been adapted from "Trauma and the Politics of Emotions: Constituting Identity, Security and Community After the Bali Bombing," *International Relations*, 24.1 (2010), 65–86, copyright © Sage. Chapter 5 expands on "A Global Politics of Pity? The Emotional Construction of Solidarity after the 2004 Asian Tsunami," *International Political Sociology*, 8.1 (2014), 1–19, copyright © Wiley. I thank the publishers for permission to reproduce passages.

Finally, the people I owe the most thanks to are also the hardest to know how to begin to thank. It is impossible to articulate the role Roland Bleiker has played in supporting me through the production of this book. As my colleague, collaborator and first reader, he has helped me to find my scholarly voice and communicate my passion with both order and care. As my confidant and partner, he is somehow – remarkably – always right beside me. His everyday optimism and out-of-the-box thinking are a constant source of wonder. Together, we look beyond life's traumas. I cannot imagine this book – and indeed, life – without him.

My final thank you is for my family: my parents, Roslyn and Brian Hutchison, and my brothers, Fergus and Darren. They have for long been my support crew, helping to celebrate the good times and beside me when things seem to go bad. Since I was little they have watched and wondered as I retreated with books. While encouraging me with questions, they also know when to pull me out and keep me grounded. Without them, I would not be where I am today. They have always helped me to do what I do and be who I am. This is why, in appreciation and with much love, I dedicate this book to them.

Introduction

Few phenomena in world politics are as central yet as under-explored as are trauma and emotions. Trauma is a defining human experience embedded in global political relations. Wars are fought and the ensuing emotional, traumatic memories help to constitute and divide societies and nations for centuries. Other forms of violence, such as terrorism, cause insufferable pain and trauma for victims, families and communities. Yet, political violence is not the only cause of trauma in the global arena. Trauma can also stem from more incremental physical suffering, such as poverty, famine and disease, that causes long-term psychological damage. Such damage occurs at the individual level, but when trauma is widespread the damage is more far-reaching: it stretches into the social landscape through which communities live out their lives and shape their politics.

No matter what the cause, whether instigated by political violence or natural catastrophe, experiences of widespread or publicly visible trauma influence not only how individuals and communities interact and define themselves, but also how ensuing political outlooks and policies are formed. No clearer is this illustrated than through the terrorist attacks in New York and Washington on September 11, 2001. The ensuing trauma deeply affected how people – and governments – perceive of issues of security and national identity. Moreover, the attacks mobilized a substantial coalition of states around the shared goal of eliminating fundamentalist terrorism. But trauma can also be politically constitutive – and enabling – in other more humanitarian ways. Witnessing natural catastrophe, even if from the far-off safety of one's home, can help to configure communities dedicated to alleviating others' suffering. Consider the transnational solidarity that emerged in the aftermath of the 2010 earthquake in Haiti or the December 2004 tsunami in Southeast Asia. No doubt the unprecedented and very substantial international aid community emerged at least in part as a consequence of the highly visible and intensely emotional nature of the massive suffering depicted.

The central focus – and objective – of this book lies in examining how traumatic events can constitute forms of community in world politics. Some excellent studies have begun to conceptualize the role trauma plays in politics and international relations.[1] However, very few systematically examine the processes through which seemingly individual and inimitable experiences of suffering can attain wider collective political influence. Added to this is that this body of literature is characterized by a certain tension. Many inquiries, particularly those emerging from studies of the Holocaust, consider trauma to be isolating.[2] With a few notable exceptions, these studies tend to emphasize the solitude and deep sense of anxiety that accompany traumatic encounters. They stress that the difficulties involved with representing trauma obviate the possibility of understanding it in a social and thus collective manner.

Even though trauma may be experienced individually, as a rupture of the social fabric upon which individuals rely, traumatic events can also help to form the social attachments needed to constitute community. Significant here is an understanding of trauma that goes beyond that of a lone or direct victim suffering post-traumatic stress disorder (PTSD). Trauma is in this conception understood as in part a construct, produced through social discourses that widely prevail and resonate after catastrophe.[3] A growing number of scholars draw from this understanding and now speak of the phenomenon of "cultural trauma."[4] They refer to events or historic periods so extreme that they

[1] Prominent contributions include Jenny Edkins, *Trauma and the Memory of Politics* (Cambridge: Cambridge University Press, 2003); K. M. Fierke, *Critical Approaches to International Security* (Cambridge: Polity, 2007), pp. 123–143; James Brassett and Nick Vaughan-Williams (eds.), "Governing Traumatic Events," *Alternatives: Global, Local, Political*, 37.3 (2012), 183–281.

[2] For example, Cathy Caruth, *Unclaimed Experience: Trauma, Narrative, History* (Baltimore: Johns Hopkins University Press, 1996). Insightful works that examine the history and theory of trauma and trauma studies include Didier Fassin and Richard Rechtman, *The Empire of Trauma: An Inquiry into the Condition of Victimhood*, trans. Rachel Gomme (Princeton: Princeton University Press, 2009); Ruth Leys, *Trauma: A Genealogy* (Chicago: University of Chicago Press, 2000).

[3] Brassett and Vaughan-Williams, "Governing Traumatic Events," 183–187, at 183–184; Fierke, *Critical Approaches to International Security*, p. 123.

[4] Jeffrey C. Alexander, *Trauma: A Social Theory* (Cambridge: Polity, 2012), pp. 6–30; Jeffrey C. Alexander, Ron Eyerman, Bernard Gieson, Neil J. Smelser

shatter identities and debase a wider sense of public meaning or cohesion. There is also a push to restore or reconfigure collective identity in the wake of such fragmentation. Atrocity and its memory can in this way become, as sociologist Piotr Stompka argues, at least partially constitutive of the "main values, roles and central expectations" that bind community.[5]

Trauma thus involves a fundamental paradox, and this paradox has a dual nature: trauma isolates individuals, yet it can also seep out, affecting those who surround and bear witness and, in doing so, shape political communities.

One of the distinguishing features of my inquiry is that it explicitly addresses the disjuncture between the two very different conceptualizations of trauma. I focus on understanding how seemingly individual traumatic encounters can acquire larger societal and political importance. I do so by underlining the key role that processes of representation play in making traumatic events collectively meaningful, including to those who do not experience trauma directly, but only bear witness, from a distance. By giving voice to or visually depicting what are unique and somewhat incommunicable experiences of shock and pain, representational practices craft understandings of trauma that have social meaning and significance. In particular circumstances, such practices and the shared meanings that are produced resonate with shared, culturally ascribed notions of mutual bereavement, loss and solidarity. A community bound by shared understandings and a common purpose of working through trauma may ensue.

The primary contribution – and argument – of the book emerges from the observation that emotions are a crucial, though largely underappreciated element of the process through which traumatic events construct political communities.[6] To be sure, I argue that in particular circumstances traumatic events and histories proliferate collective forms of meaning and feeling that distinguish a community as

and Piotr Stompka, *Cultural Trauma and Collective Identity* (Berkeley: University of California Press, 2004); Ron Eyerman, *Cultural Trauma: Slavery and the Formation of African American Identity* (Cambridge: Cambridge University Press, 2001); Piotr Stompka, "Cultural Trauma: The Other Face of Social Change," *European Journal of Social Theory*, 3.4 (2000), 449–466.

[5] Stompka, "Cultural Trauma," 457.

[6] One excellent exception is the classic text, Judith Lewis Herman, *Trauma and Recovery: From Domestic Abuse to Political Terror* (London: Pandora, 1992); see esp. pp. 175–195.

an "affective community." With this concept, I mean that the respective community is welded together, at least temporarily, by shared emotional understandings of tragedy. What a community makes of traumatic occurrences – that is, the social and political significance of trauma – is thus linked to, and contingent upon, the emotional resonance of the events at issue. This may seem a commonsensical proposition. Horrific and unexpected events shatter expectations and defy established meanings in part because their impact is of an inherently emotional nature. The emotions felt in response to trauma long haunt victims and witnesses through memory as well. Representations as well as wider discourses of trauma are also intimately emotional: they tend to draw attention to the harrowing nature of traumatic events: they signify shock, vulnerability and confusion. However, while the emotional dimensions of pivotal traumatic events are obvious, the political roles they play are yet to be systematically examined in relation to how communities endure and recover.

My inquiry shows that much can be learned from taking emotions seriously. Yet, to do so it is important that scholars cease to consider emotions in opposition to reason and rationality. I instead underline the pervasive nature of emotions and suggest that emotions play a particularly important political role during times of crisis and trauma. For far too long social science research has sidelined emotions. They were largely seen as feelings that are either purely personal or too ephemeral to be systematically examined for their political relevance. This is why I offer a systematic and comprehensive engagement. In doing so, I draw on a rapidly growing body of literature that examines the role of emotions in world politics.[7] I see emotions as inseparable

[7] In the past decade research on emotions in world politics has undergone a radical transformation. Several articles, journal special issues and forum sections, as well as a growing number of edited collections and monographs turn to emotions for political insights. They do so from a range of theoretical perspectives and emotional purviews. Among the most referenced include Janice Bially Mattern, "A Practice Theory of Emotion for International Relations," in Emanuel Adler (ed.), *International Practices* (Cambridge: Cambridge University Press, 2011); Roland Bleiker and Emma Hutchison (eds.), "Forum Section on 'Emotions and World Politics'," *International Theory*, 6.3 (2014); Neta Crawford, "The Passion of World Politics: Propositions on Emotions and Emotional Relationships," *International Security*, 24.4 (2000), 116–136; Khaled Fattah and K. M. Fierke, "A Clash of Emotions: The Politics of Humiliation and Political Violence in the Middle East," *European Journal of International Relations*, 15.1 (2009), 63–97; K. M. Fierke, *Political Self-Sacrifice: Agency, Body and Emotion in International Relations*

components of our personal and social life – and therefore as a pervasive part of political life. Emotions matter in a range of circumstances. They can shape, in often unseen and inaudible ways, the motives and behaviors of states and they underpin phenomena such as terrorism, international security and cooperation. Emotions also influence normative issues, such as humanitarian intervention, international justice and reconciliation. In short, emotions are intrinsic to all social and political action. They lie at the core of how communities, including nation-states, are organized and function – hence making possible the particular "affective communities" that I uncover and examine. But a widely perceived traumatic event is a time when private emotions are arguably the most publicly pronounced.[8] This is why studying the politics of emotions in the context of an acute catastrophe is particularly revealing.

I engage the issues at stake in both a conceptual and empirical manner. After establishing a framework to appreciate the links between trauma, emotions and political community, I present three empirical case studies. The first two involve situations of "immediate" or sporadic catastrophe that precipitated both widespread trauma and powerful forms of community: the October 2002 Bali bombing and the December 2004 Southeast Asian tsunami. I examine media representations of these two very different but equally pivotal traumatic events. At issue with the Bali bombing was the transnational constitution of

(Cambridge: Cambridge University Press, 2012); Renée Jeffery, *Reason and Emotion in International Ethics* (Cambridge: Cambridge University Press, 2014); Jonathan Mercer, "Emotional Beliefs," *International Organization*, 64.1 (2010), 1–31; Jonathan Mercer, "Approaching Emotion in International Politics," paper presented at the annual meeting of the International Studies Association, San Diego, California, April 25, 1996; Dominique Moïsi, *The Geopolitics of Emotions: How Cultures of Fear, Humiliation, and Hope are Reshaping Our World* (New York: Doubleday, 2009); Dominique Moïsi, "The Clash of Emotions," *Foreign Affairs*, 86.1 (2007), 8–12; Roger Petersen, *Understanding Ethnic Violence: Fear, Hatred and Resentment in Twentieth-Century Eastern Europe* (Cambridge: Cambridge University Press, 2002); Andrew A. G. Ross, *Mixed Emotions: Beyond Fear and Hatred in International Conflict* (Chicago: Chicago University Press, 2014); Andrew A. G. Ross, "Coming in from the Cold: Emotions and Constructivism," *European Journal of International Relations*, 12.2 (2006), 197–222; Brent E. Sasley, "Theorizing States' Emotions," *International Studies Review*, 13.3 (2011), 453–476.

[8] Crawford, "The Passion of World Politics," 130; Ross, "Coming in from the Cold," 211–214; Maja Zehfuss, *Wounds of Memory: The Politics of War in Germany* (Cambridge: Cambridge University Press, 2007), pp. 240–242.

an insular and parochial sense of Australian nationalism and corresponding form of political community. The tsunami catastrophe, in contrast, demonstrated how representations of a traumatic event can produce the shared meanings and sense of common purpose required to mobilize political community beyond the nation-state.

I then move on to a third empirical engagement. Here, I examine two more long-term cases: China and South Africa. Scrutinizing China's history of colonial trauma and ensuing humiliation and, in turn, South Africa's struggle over the traumas of apartheid, I show how representations can help to cultivate the social space conducive to acknowledging and working through the painful emotions that often cohere communities in destructive and politically antagonistic ways. Thus together with constituting emotional communal linkages, I show that traumatic events and histories can also provide an opportunity to transform the nature of such linkages.

The rest of this introduction now maps out my journey in more detail. I first offer a preliminary understanding of trauma's dual, paradoxical nature, tracing its significance within the broader study and practice of world politics. I then highlight why emotions play such a crucial – and so far underappreciated – role in the respective political processes. Here I engage with some of the recent burgeoning literature on emotions and world politics. My purpose, however, is not to offer a comprehensive survey of the respective field of study. Rather, my main aim is to advance debate by offering detailed empirical case studies and by bringing into conversation contributions from a range of different disciplines, including psychology, anthropology, sociology, political geography, feminist theory, philosophy, neuroscience, political science and international relations.

The paradox of trauma: the breaking and remaking of community

Scholars are paying more and more attention to the sociopolitical dimensions of trauma. Where the term "trauma" was once restricted to use in the mental health field, it is now also understood to be a social phenomena, as an open wound that can at once affect both individuals and a wider collective. This growing and somewhat "elastic" usage of the concept has resulted in a rapid expansion of work on trauma.[9] Trauma studies now extend across diverse and somewhat disparate bodies of literature. Uniting them is a challenge, as there are many competing claims concerning trauma's precise nature and impact. But, at the same time, some commonalities can be identified. One such commonality is that trauma tends to be conceptualized as a solitary, isolating experience.[10] Trauma is thought to be an encounter with something so terrifying that it plunges those who experience it into a world of uncertainty and fear. The comfort of normal habits and expectations falls away with trauma. Commonly held assumptions and meanings that have, over the course of our lives, come to define us are stripped away. No longer can we envisage life as a smooth trajectory from here to there. Therefore those who survive traumatic experiences may well have preserved their physical lives, but the meaning ascribed to being becomes altered, often in revelatory and irreconcilable ways.

The unexpected and confronting nature of trauma is also said to belie one's ability to comprehend it. Or so psychoanalytical studies of trauma suggest. Scholars note that feelings of disbelief and terror ensue, disorientating victims and witnesses to such an extent that they are unable to reconcile their experiences with practices and memories they are accustomed to. Cathy Caruth suggests that an event is known as traumatic if it "cannot be placed within the schemes of prior knowledge."[11] Maurice Blanchot goes further still, suggesting that trauma is what "escapes the very possibility of experience."[12] Some scholars have even contended that in contrast to pain – which is said to be an everyday occurrence that is "lived" through – trauma is understood to "inhibit living."[13] As such, traumatic experiences are not processed or

[9] Murray Schwartz, "Locating Trauma: A Commentary on Ruth Leys's *Trauma: A Genealogy*," *American Imago*, 59.3 (2002), 367–384, at 367.

[10] To highlight the isolating features of trauma is, however, not to say that a traumatic experience is purely individual. Every individual is always already shaped by affective dynamics that surround and situate her or him. In this sense, as isolating as trauma feels, an individual's reaction to trauma is always already social and collective.

[11] Cathy Caruth, "Recapturing the Past: Introduction," in Cathy Caruth (ed.), *Trauma: Explorations in Memory* (Baltimore: Johns Hopkins University Press, 1995), p. 153.

[12] Maurice Blanchot, *The Writing of Disaster*, trans. Ann Smock (Lincoln and London: University of Nebraska Press, 1995), p. 7.

[13] Liz Philipose, "The Politics of Pain and the End of Empire," *International Feminist Journal of Politics*, 9.1 (2007), 60–81, at 62.

"known" in the same ways as are other experiences. Trauma shatters the confidence and sense of security that individuals need in order to walk effortlessly through each day. A human vulnerability is revealed, and those who suffer it are left isolated and puzzled, unable to answer important questions or even express the emotions they feel.

As a result, traumatic encounters prompt individuals to feel cut off from the life and world that surround them. Trauma isolates individuals. This may be distinguished by the corresponding feeling of being detached from – or "betrayed" by[14] – the very community that helps to situate and define one's identity. Bonds between one's self and a wider community are broken; the social context in which one ordinarily locates one's self feels ruptured, in a way that at the time may seem beyond repair. The damage to one's sense of security and community may therefore be severe.

Literatures largely agree that the isolation and emotional disorientation of trauma are compounded by the challenge of how to communicate its impact. Scholarly as well as survivor accounts suggest that following traumatic experiences, individuals find it immensely difficult, if not impossible, to communicate the meaning of their experiences.[15] Shocked, pained, and in disbelief, words seem suddenly incapable of representing the physical and emotional sensations experienced. One can say that it felt horrible, that the shock and pain were completely numbing, but the prevailing reaction of people to trauma is that the sense of loss and grief is so great that it cannot be adequately expressed through language. Some commentators even go as far as to suggest that, without words, traumatic experiences take on a shadowy, strangely "unreal" quality, one that traumatized individuals forever fail to comprehend.[16] Unable to adequately express trauma, one's social and linguistic world becomes "frozen pictures of the past,"[17] as traumatic memories continue to structure being and what motivates interactions with others.

[14] Jenny Edkins, "Forget Trauma? Responses to September 11," *International Relations*, 16.2 (2002), 243–256, at 245.

[15] See, for instance, Dori Laub, "Truth and Testimony: The Process and the Struggle," in Cathy Caruth (ed.), *Trauma: Explorations in Memory* (Baltimore: Johns Hopkins University Press, 1995), p. 63.

[16] Caruth, *Unclaimed Experience*, pp. 99–108.

[17] K. M. Fierke, "Whereof We Can Speak, Thereof We Must Not Be Silent: Trauma, Political Solipsism and War," *Review of International Studies*, 30.4 (2004), 471–491, at 482.

However – and paradoxically – trauma can also help to constitute community. This process may be an organic one, emanating from survivors and witnesses searching for acceptance and to re-establish the social connections that have been shattered. It can also be a process that is deeply political, either in its effects or in its motivation.

Publicly witnessed traumatic events are an occasion when a type of "collective trauma" is most likely. Such events tend to precipitate a range of processes that involve the repeated re-mediatization of the accompanying disbelief, shock and horror. In Western literatures, September 11 has become the most commonly referred to occurrence. Ann Kaplan captures the prevailing sentiment well when she relays that after the attacks "[e]veryone was in shock: people did not laugh out loud in the streets or in the Square; voiced were muted. People's expressions were sombre. I felt a connection to strangers that I had never felt before."[18] Sara Ahmed argues that in such circumstances a collective sense of shock and of being injured can inspire communal "attachments."[19] Central in this regard is a social environment that recognizes, accepts and responds to the sight of another's pain. According to Ahmed, in such environments "the wound is a sign of identity"; extreme experiences become part of the intimate bonds and feelings that give people a sense that they are tied – or that they belong – together.[20]

Abetting this process are the stages of recovery that victims and witnesses pass through. When confronted with intense feelings of dislocation, individuals tend to seek the consolation and understanding of others. Traumatized individuals, as Judith Lewis Herman contends, must seek to socially reintegrate and have the truth of their experiences acknowledged.[21] Other literatures suggest that however "inexpressible" trauma may ultimately be, the need to speak of it surmounts the difficulties associated with doing so. This process may play out in a number of ways. Often victims and witnesses attempt to express – or give "voice" to – their experiences. They look to a community that will acknowledge, understand and respect the immensity of what they have

[18] E. Ann Kaplan, *Trauma Culture: The Politics of Terror and Loss in the Media and in Literature* (New Brunswick: Rutgers University Press, 2005), p. 9.

[19] Sara Ahmed, *The Cultural Politics of Emotion* (Edinburgh: Edinburgh University Press, 2004), pp. 12, 16, 28.

[20] Ahmed, *The Cultural Politics of Emotion*, p. 32.

[21] Herman, *Trauma and Recovery*, pp. 175–181.

endured. By sharing trauma through trying to communicate and represent it, personal feelings of vulnerability and helplessness interweave with social context. Individual trauma is in this way enacted – or "performed"[22] – in a manner that is at once both social and political, for, as the work of Jenny Edkins and K. M. Fierke explains, traumatized individuals are reliant upon socioculturally obtained patterns of language in order to share and make sense of their experiences.[23] Feelings of discomfort – of shock, incomprehension and pain – are sewn into the social fabric in a way that connects us to some and simultaneously distinguishes us from others who are considered unable to identify with our experiences.

The practice of making trauma communally meaningful is often also overtly political. Scholars have underlined that traumatic events can become pivotal in perpetuating the type of inside/outside communal dichotomies that have long constituted international relations.[24] Key here is that traumatic events can become sites that either affirm or deny particular political and communal boundaries. The ensuing negotiations are in many ways a struggle over meaning: a search to make sense of the events that have transpired. It is not surprising that divisive political battles emerge, for when words seek to replace the meaningless of trauma a whole range of interests and power plays are

[22] Throughout this book I borrow from Judith Butler's notion of performativity, which suggests that how we speak and physically carry out (i.e. "perform") particular actions constitutes reality (and identities) by appealing to or transgressing established power relations. Adapting this to trauma is to imply that how individuals speak of and enact traumatic experiences and memories through behaviors is inevitably bound by accepted social codes and discourses for doing so. Many of Butler's works could be cited here. One helpful essay is, for instance, Judith Butler, "Performative Acts and Gender Constitution: An Essay in Phenomenology and Feminist Theory," *Theatre Journal*, 40.4 (1988), 519–531, esp. 527–528. A recent collection that interrogates performativity in world politics is Jenny Edkins and Adrian Kear (eds.), *International Politics and Performance: Critical Aesthetics and Creative Practice* (Milton Park and New York: Routledge, 2013). Cynthia Weber has also drawn from Butler's notion of performativity to theorize the linkages between subjectivity and the sovereign state. See Cynthia Weber, "Performative States," *Millennium: Journal of International Studies*, 27.1 (1998), 77–95.

[23] Edkins, *Trauma and the Memory of Politics*, p. 7; Fierke, "Whereof We Can Speak, Thereof We Must Not Be Silent," 473–482.

[24] R. B. J. Walker, *Inside/Outside: International Relations as Political Theory* (Cambridge: Cambridge University Press, 1993).

at stake.[25] A common reaction, almost a reflex, is the desire to restore a sense of order and normality. The work of Edkins focuses heavily on this conundrum. For her, the "openness" left after trauma is key to understanding why in the restoration process the primary political concern is to somehow regain control.[26]

In these very different responses to trauma we can clearly see trauma's dual paradox at play: it is precisely because trauma seems to suspend reality, imposing a moment of uncertainty and reflection, that individuals and political figures seek to regain control and strengthen community ties.

These residual links between trauma and community can last for years or decades, which is why the issue of historical trauma and memory is of central concern.[27] Scholars often note that prevailing state-based reactions to trauma lead to commemorative practices that affirm existing forms of political sovereignty – most notably, contemporary statehood. Relevant here is that individuals, and in turn societies, come to remember and mourn past traumatic events in ways that are intimately connected to discourses that reinstate modes of political power and social control. The most common and critiqued example involves the customary manner of memorializing the traumas of war, and, in particular, soldiers' deaths.[28] Through such practices, the remnants of war linger, shaping social and political landscapes often for generations to come. Consider the legacy of the Holocaust, two world wars in the

[25] See James Brassett, "Cosmopolitan Sentiments after 9/11? Trauma and the Politics of Vulnerability," *Journal of Critical Globalisation Studies*, 2 (2010), 12–29, at 19–20; Edkins, "Forget Trauma?"; Fierke, *Critical Approaches to International Security*, pp. 132–137; Ross, "Coming in from the Cold," 212–213.

[26] Jenny Edkins, "Ground Zero: Reflections on Trauma, In/distinction and Response," *Journal for Cultural Research*, 8.3 (2004), 247–270, at 253.

[27] Two insightful collections on the politics of traumatic memory are Duncan S. A. Bell (ed.), *Memory, Trauma and World Politics* (New York: Palgrave, 2006); and Erica Resends and Dovile Budryte (eds.), *Memory and Trauma in International Relations: Theories, Cases and Debates* (London and New York: Routledge, 2014).

[28] See Christopher Warinski, "'Post-Heroic Warfare' and Ghosts – The Social Control of Dead American Soldiers in Iraq," *International Political Sociology*, 2.2 (2008), 113–127; Matt McDonald, "'Lest We Forget': The Politics of Memory and Australian Military Intervention," *International Political Sociology*, 4.3 (2010), 287–302; Maja Zehfuss, "Hierarchies of Grief and the Possibility of War: Remembering UK Fatalities in Iraq," *Millennium: Journal of International Studies*, 38.2 (2009), 419–440.

space of half a century, Hiroshima, Nagasaki, China and the events of the "Century of National Humiliation," the Cold War, Vietnam, the break-up of Yugoslavia, the terrorist attacks of September 11 and the recent "War on Terror," and the traumatic legacies that the group Islamic State (ISIS) perceive to lie at the heart of their violent jihadism. Historical events and legacies such as these – no doubt catastrophic and traumatic for millions of people – not only directly influence the conditions through which international relations are formally conducted, but also generate psychological and emotional states that continue to divide the world and shape how contemporary global political relations play out. And, of course, this is only to mention a few of the most extreme and geopolitically destabilizing events in world politics.

The crucial but underappreciated role of emotions

Some links between trauma and community have thus been fairly well explored and understood. But I suggest that a crucial dimension of the ensuing processes has so far not received adequate attention: the political role of emotions.

Experiencing and witnessing trauma is inherently emotional. Dominant discourses of trauma tend to be highly emotive as well. Individual and collective responses to trauma therefore cannot help but be influenced by emotions, and often so in indelible and deeply political ways. Thus in terms of understandings of the linkages between trauma and political community a major challenge remains: to uncover more precisely how trauma intrudes into public awareness and, in turn, plays an important though often silenced and seemingly subliminal role in configuring world politics.

The emotional nature of trauma poses significant challenges to understanding its political impact. Yes, it is commonsensical to assume that emotions are crucial to both individual and collective reckoning with trauma. And, yes, emotions help to shape and give value to the shared understandings and meanings upon which post-trauma forms of community fundamentally rely. But how exactly is this process taking place? And how are we to conceptualize and assess it? The tension between, on the one hand, trauma's solitude and incomprehension, and, on the other, its ability to shape forms of political agency and community in world politics leads to many questions concerning the processes through which something seemingly private and isolating can also help to shape a wider collective – which by nature is both public and political. For instance, if trauma is ultimately ineffable how can it so powerfully construct and maintain community – national, cultural, ethnic, familial or otherwise? How can trauma occupy a space beyond representation, while at the same time solicit a range of social and political discourses that inspire individuals to evaluate themselves in relation to others? If trauma induces a crisis of representation how, then, can and does one make sense of it?

The challenge of understanding the links between trauma, emotions and community is in part linked to certain assumptions in the study of political science and international relations. In the social science-driven discipline of politics, emotions have for long been seen in opposition to reason: as involuntary and irrational feelings.[29] Such seemingly "confused perceptions" were thus seen as having little or no social and political significance.[30] Social science has come a long way since then, but the opposition between reason and emotion is so deeply entrenched in Western philosophy that there remain significant residues today. Dating as far back as Plato, the dominant view has been that "emotions need to be 'tamed', 'harnessed', or 'driven out' by the steady (male) hand of reason."[31] Once perceived to encapsulate women's "dangerous desires"[32] and "seductresses,"[33] emotions were thought to be feelings or bodily sensations that overtook us, distorting thought and the ability to make rational or moral judgment. "[P]assionate politics makes for dangerous politics," or so goes the mantra of traditional liberal ideology.[34] This historical legacy of approaching emotions as

29 See Jon Elster, *Alchemies of the Mind: Rationality and the Emotions* (Cambridge: Cambridge University Press, 1999).

30 See Jeff Goodwin, James M. Jasper and Francesca Polletta, "Introduction: Why Emotions Matter," in Jeff Goodwin, James M. Jasper and Francesca Polletta (eds.), *Passionate Politics: Emotions and Social Movements* (Chicago: University of Chicago Press, 2001), pp. 1–26.

31 Simon J. Williams and Gillian Bendelow, "Introduction: Emotions in Social Life," in Gillian Bendelow and Simon J. Williams (eds.), *Emotions in Social Life: Critical Themes and Contemporary Issues* (London and New York: Routledge, 1998), p. xv.

32 Williams and Bendelow, "Introduction," p. xv.

33 Martha C. Nussbaum, "Emotions and Women's Capabilities," in Martha C. Nussbaum and Jonathon Glover (eds.), *Women, Culture and Development* (New York: Oxford University Press, 1995), pp. 360–395, at p. 370.

34 Cheryl Hall, *The Trouble with Passion: Political Theory Beyond the Reign of Reason* (New York: Routledge, 2005), p. 126.

unlearned, involuntary, "irrational" forms of excitement has led to their neglect. Traditionally deemed significant only to the realm of the personal, emotions have seldom been considered to be at the forefront of the political.

Recent studies have gone a considerable way in rectifying the treatment of emotions in international relations. Studies of emotion have become a vibrant subfield, with a number of contributions prominent in their re-evaluations of the nature and place of human affect. So convincing are these accounts that few would now challenge the idea that emotions play a role in world politics. But even though prominent scholars meanwhile recognize – and increasingly theorize – the political significance of emotions, there are still only a handful of studies that systematically analyze how emotions matter in concrete political settings.[35]

The challenge of forwarding comprehensive empirical investigations into emotions is often attributed to the methodological dilemmas that are involved. Quantifying emotions is extremely difficult. Labeling and measuring them, even in qualitative terms, is also both a delicate process and one fraught, as Renée Jeffery articulates, with questions concerning how exactly experimental findings are to relate to the "…'real world' of international politics" – in other words, it begs "the problem of 'external validity'."[36] This is one of the reasons why many previous studies that underline the central role emotions play in politics end in lamenting about how to analyze the precise political roles they play. Neta Crawford, who authored one of the field's first and most celebrated essays, notes that emotions are "deeply internal," making it very difficult to isolate or distinguish what a "genuine" emotion may indeed be.[37] Jonathon Mercer, also a long-standing proponent of the

[35] See note 7 for recent notable international relations-based contributions. For further studies that examine emotions in specific political contexts, see Lucile Eznack, "Crises as Signals of Strength: The Significance of Affect in Close Allies' Relationships," *Security Studies*, 20.2 (2011), 238–265; Fattah and Fierke, "A Clash of Emotions"; Jack Holland and Ty Solomon, "Affect Is What States Make of It: Articulating Everyday Experiences of 9/11," *Critical Studies on Security*, 2.3 (2014), 262–277; Oded Löwenheim and Gadi Heimann, "Revenge in International Politics," *Security Studies*, 17.4 (2008), 685–724; Paul Saurette, "You Dissin Me? Humiliation and Post 9/11 Global Politics," *Review of International Studies*, 32.3 (2006), 495–522.

[36] Renée Jeffery, "The Promise and Perils of the Neuroscientific Approach to Emotions," *International Theory*, 6.3 (2014), 584–589, at 586.

[37] Crawford, "The Passion of World Politics," 118.

study of emotion in international relations, worries that "emotion is hard to define, hard to operationalize, hard to measure, and hard to isolate from other factors."[38] Even scholars who have for long drawn upon more interdisciplinary methods in their international relations analyses ponder the difficulties of examining emotions. Maja Zehfuss locates the difficulties of studying emotion in the observation that "we seem unsure how to deal with it, even how to analyse it, and therefore it seems safer to exclude it from the proper business of [understanding] war and politics."[39] Paul Saurette puts it more succinctly, contending that to most scholars emotions seem "impossibly fuzzy."[40] Robert Jervis, who played a key role in examining the role of perception and misperception in international politics, perfectly sums up prevailing attitudes by declaring that he would love to extend his research into the relationship between cognition and emotion, but that "at this point the challenge is simply too great."[41] For an international relations scholar working with prevailing methodological frameworks, an investigation into emotions would thus seem to result in research that is speculative or tenuous at best.

Methodological difficulties involved with studying emotions are further complicated by an additional important distinction: between emotion and affect. While the differences and linkages between the two are being increasingly theorized, many politics and international relations scholars use these two terms loosely, as umbrella terms to denote a range of different phenomena. They are each also often used interchangeably. Meanwhile, the differences between emotion and affect are highly contested. Countless theorists have attempted to discern the distinctions between each. A number of theoretically rich debates now surround these two phenomena.[42] It is neither possible, nor my primary task, to review these literatures and their respective claims in full. It is useful, however, to appreciate the key distinctions at hand and how I bring these into focus throughout my inquiry.

38 Mercer, "Approaching Emotion in International Politics," 1.
39 Zehfuss, *Wounds of Memory*, p. 240.
40 Saurette, "You Dissin Me?" 504.
41 Thierry Balzacq and Robert Jervis, "Logics of Mind and the International System," *Review of International Studies*, 30.4 (2004), 559–582, at 565.
42 See, for example, Ruth Leys, "The Turn to Affect: A Critique," *Critical Inquiry*, 37.3 (2011), 434–472.

The central distinction I draw is relatively straightforward: where emotions are typically seen as the conscious manifestation of bodily feelings, affect encompasses a more complete range of nonconscious, noncognitive "inner states"[43] and sensory experiences, including mood, disposition and attachment. Within social science-based inquiries, this separation is of particular significance. The links between emotion and cognition are perceived to lend emotion open to external scrutiny. The nature of affect, in contrast, prompts questions regarding whether it can be similarly analytically scrutinized. Because affect "*unleashes* emotion from cognition,"[44] consisting of corporeal reactions and intensities that defy or at least in part escape deliberate reflection, affect is perceived to be a visceral force that influences political thinking in a diffuse yet analytically inaccessible way.

While recognizing the important phenomenological (as well as experiential) distinctions between emotion and affect, my study approaches the respective phenomena a little differently. My investigation employs both terms, in a manner roughly commensurate with the above differences, yet at the same time sees emotion and affect as inextricably linked. Even if affective states are subconscious bodily enactments, they frame and guide more conscious, cognitive emotional evaluations. Affect is part of the emergent "mind–body" system that gives rise to specific emotions.[45] The influence of affective forces is therefore pervasive, even while examining the politics of emotions. The very collectives in which emotions can manifest are bound by more ubiquitous affective resonances – hence my conception of "affective communities." Still, an appreciation of the linkages between emotion and affect does not necessarily address the challenges involved with studying either phenomenon. For some scholars, it complicates them, further muddling the ability of politics scholars to truly appreciate the emotional dynamics that underlie political practices.

The challenge of understanding the political dynamics of trauma is then akin to the challenge of how to conceptualize the political nature

43 Janice Bially Mattern, "On Being Convinced: An Emotional Epistemology of International Relations," *International Theory*, 6.3 (2014), 589–594, 593.
44 Mattern, "On Being Convinced," 594. Emphasis in original.
45 James A. Coan, "Emergent Ghosts of the Emotion Machine," *Emotion Review*, 2.3 (2010), 274–285, at 278–280; Rom Harré, "Emotions as Cognitive-Affective-Somatic Hybrids," *Emotion Review*, 1.4 (2009), 294–301, at 295.

and roles of emotions, and to an extent, the affective forces that give rise to emotions. Much of trauma's social and political impact is situated in the public expression of what has traditionally been considered "private" emotion, yet as this brief review demonstrates, the emotional dimensions of political trauma have yet to be systematically probed.

Some scholars have, in fact, started to suggest methodological ways forward. Crawford argues that to create a "comprehensive theory of emotion in world politics" we need to be able to "devise valid measures of emotions."[46] Ned Lebow too hopes to arrive at a new paradigm or even a "full-blown theory" that assesses the numerous emotional dimensions of international relations.[47] Jonathan Mercer suggests scholars can search for emotions on each of the three levels of analysis: in the actions of individuals, nation-states and within the international system.[48] More recently, Mercer expanded on this proposition by advocating a focus on "emotional beliefs"; by suggesting that scholars need to analyze how feelings "influence what one believes, and what one does."[49] Other approaches, such as those of Andrew Ross and Paul Saurette, argue for a certain degree of "experimental complexity."[50] Ross, for instance, advocates interpretative methods, such as an examination of historical narratives, popular culture, and other discursive symbols as methods to empirically analyze emotions.[51] Some recent politics and international relations-based emotions contributions have pursued and furthered this interpretative turn.[52] My own approach also aims in this direction, but takes a somewhat different route.

[46] Crawford, "The Passion of World Politics," 155.

[47] Richard Ned Lebow, "Fear, Interest and Honour: Outlines of a Theory of International Relations," *International Affairs*, 82.3 (2006), 431–448, at 439.

[48] Mercer, "Approaching Emotion in International Politics," 11.

[49] Mercer, "Emotional Beliefs," 2.

[50] Saurette, "You Dissin Me?" 504; see also Ross, "Coming in from the Cold'.

[51] Ross, *Mixed Emotions*, pp. 60–61; Ross, "Coming in from the Cold," 210.

[52] For instance, Todd Hall, "We Will Not Swallow This Bitter Fruit: Theorizing a Diplomacy of Anger," *Security Studies*, 20 (2011), 521–555; Matthew Coen Leep, "The Affective Production of Others: United States Policy Towards Israeli–Palestinian Conflict," *Cooperation and Conflict*, 45.3 (2010), 331–352; Holland and Solomon, "Affect Is What States Make of It'; Ty Solomon, "'I wasn't angry because I couldn't believe it was happening': Affect and Discourse in Responses to September 11," *Review of International Studies*, 38.4 (2012), 907–928; Donileen R. Loseke, "Examining Emotion as Discourse: Emotion Codes and Presidential Speeches Justifying War," *The Sociological Quarterly*, 50 (2009), 497–524.

Studying emotions through representations

I suggest that a compelling place to begin to examine emotions is through representations, through the words and images in which emotions are expressed and in turn imbued with social meaning.[53] Representations are, of course, not the only locations to study emotions, but they are particularly crucial in an analysis of trauma and community. In pursuing this line of inquiry I build upon a range of previous studies.[54] I see at least three reasons for this choice.

First, representations are as close as one can get to conceiving of emotions. This is because the internal, ephemeral nature of emotions precludes the possibility of understanding them through anything other than their instrumental display. Consider, for instance, the difficulty of explaining one's feelings to another. One person can never truly know how another person feels. They can only assume to know, provided those feelings have been outwardly expressed – represented, that is – in a language or communication system able to be understood by them. In this way, as both constitutive, discursive approaches to emotion and studies of representation imply, representations inevitably stand for or embody particular contextually bound forms of feeling.

Second, emotions can be seen as wider social and cultural phenomena that are shaped by processes of representation and interpretation. Key here is that not simply do practices of representing reality give

[53] In doing so I draw upon previous co- and single-authored work that theorizes and positions representations as a place to empirically examine the politics of emotions. See Emma Hutchison and Roland Bleiker, "Theorizing Emotions in World Politics," *International Theory*, 6.3 (2014), 491–514; Emma Hutchison, "A Global Politics of Pity? Disaster Imagery and the Emotional Construction of Solidarity after the 2004 Asian Tsunami," *International Political Sociology*, 9.1 (2014), 1–19; Roland Bleiker and Emma Hutchison, "Fear No More: Emotions and World Politics," *Review of International Studies*, 34.S1 (2008), 115–135. I am grateful to Roland Bleiker for both constant conversations that led to the further development of these points, and for enabling me to draw upon our collaborative work.

[54] One of the most influential for my inquiry has been Catherine A. Lutz, *Unnatural Emotions: Everyday Sentiments on a Micronesian Atoll and Their Challenge to Western Theory* (Cambridge: Cambridge University Press, 1988); and in disciplinary international relations: Ross, "Coming in From the Cold"; Löwenheim and Heimann, "Revenge in International Politics," 706–707; Fierke, *Political Self-Sacrifice*; K. M. Fierke, "The Liberation of Kosovo: Emotion and the Ritual Reenactment of War," *Focaal: European Journal of Anthropology*, 39 (2002), 93–113, at 95–99.

meaning to the world around us, but crucially that in doing so representations inevitably "say something" emotionally.[55] They evoke feelings and affects, which in turn help to shape how one perceives of and belongs in the world. Emotions can be seen as inherently sociocultural phenomena, embedded in language, habit and historically constituted patterns of knowledge through which individuals and collectives make the world meaningful. It is through representations, therefore, that emotions can be embodied, enacted, transmitted and interpreted in ways in that elicit particular sociocultural meanings, values and beliefs.[56]

Third, the links between representations of emotions and the constitution of sociopolitical meaning gets to the heart of a key concern of international relations: the issue of power. Emotions – the ways we feel and why we do so in the circumstances we do – are inevitably shaped by dominant political discourses and the entrenched interests that are associated with them.[57] But the emotional rupture created by trauma does, at the same time, open up spaces for alternative political conceptions. The struggle over representations is key to this process for it goes to the heart of how emotional meanings are imbued with wider collective, political significance.

In short, representational practices are central to – and an ideal starting place for – examining the collective politics of emotion. Representational practices provide a pathway through which emotions acquire (and, indeed, always already possess) a collective dimension and, in turn, shape social and political agency, behaviors and policies. Focusing on how representations both symbolize and

[55] Stuart Hall, "Introduction," in Stuart Hall (ed.), *Representations: Cultural Representations and Signifying Practices* (London: Sage and The Open University, 1997), pp. 1, 5.

[56] Nico H. Frijda, Antony S. R. Manstead and Sacha Bem, "The Influence of Emotions on Beliefs," in Nico H. Frijda, Antony S. R. Manstead and Sacha Bem (eds.), *Emotions and Beliefs: How Feelings Influence Thoughts* (Cambridge: Cambridge University Press, 2000), pp. 1–9; Mercer, "Emotional Beliefs," 2.

[57] Lila Abu-Lughod and Catherine A. Lutz, "Introduction: Emotion, Discourse and the Politics of Everyday Life," in Catherine A. Lutz and Lila Abu-Lughod (eds.), *Language and the Politics of Emotion* (Cambridge: Cambridge University Press, 1990), pp. 1–23, at p. 14; Maruška Svašek, "Introduction: Emotions in Anthropology," in Kay Milton and Maruška Svašek (eds.), *Mixed Emotions: Anthropological Studies in Feeling* (Oxford and New York: Berg, 2005), p. 9.

communicate emotions therefore paves a way around many of the methodological difficulties that have inhibited further politics- and international relations-based research into emotions. Representations provide a starting point for turning to methods that enable empirical investigations into how emotions help to constitute and make the social world meaningful in ways that make possible particular political configurations and behaviors.

Emotions and world politics

My inquiry is thus located within, profits from, and seeks to contribute to, the burgeoning literature on emotions and world politics. My engagement with this body of literature is primarily indirect: (1) I show how a range of different literatures – from psychology to anthropology, sociology and feminist theory – offer unique insights into the political and transnational role of emotions; (2) I provide a detailed empirical investigation of the issues at stake. But I would like to at least briefly situate my inquiry in the context of these increasingly important debates in international relations scholarship. Doing so will inevitably be a sketchy and incomplete endeavor. I merely identify a few pointers and outline how they either relate to or provide stepping stones for my own study on the links between trauma, emotion and political community.

While emotions have for long been a central part of world politics, the scholarly study of them tended to attribute them a "taken-for-granted status": they were present in an assumed or implicit sense.[58] Consider the established theories upon which the study of international relations has been founded. From the classical thought of Hobbes and Morgenthau to the postwar structuralism of Kenneth Waltz, political realism has been based on the presence of influential emotions, most notably anxiety and fear. Amity and trust, by contrast, have played a key role in how liberals conceptualized a more cooperative international order. But few if any of these studies systematically focused on and examined how emotions actually operate and whether the assumed roles played by particular emotions are accurate or indeed the only way emotions work. Instead, emotions were largely seen as external phenomena to which rational decision makers respond.

[58] Crawford, "The Passion of World Politics," 120–123, 116.

There are notable exceptions, of course. Feminist international relations scholarship has long refused to accept the dichotomy between mind and body and between reason and emotion.[59] There is also a long tradition of examining the psychological dimensions of foreign policy. Contributors here question the assumption that political decisions are taken on the basis of "classical rationality." Instead, they stress that leaders have often no choice but to draw upon ideas and insights that may involve "the emotional rather than the calculating part of the brain."[60] In addition to this, decision makers are shaped by deeply seated emotional predispositions, such as those that were acquired in the early, formative stages of their life.[61]

These and numerous other studies have made important contributions to our understanding of emotions in world politics. But the legacy of rationalism continues to shape many of these approaches, particularly those in political psychology that focus on deterrence. Emotions are studied in detail but they tend to be perceived as interferences with, or deviations from, rationality. Hence, emotions are not seen as complex biocultural and sociopolitical forces but merely as sources of misperceptions and misjudgments.[62]

Recent theorizing of emotion in world politics has begun to address this gap in understanding. Jonathan Mercer and Neta Crawford were pioneers, arguing early on for a "richer view of rationality" that includes both cognition and emotion. Doing so, they contended, would enhance understandings of political decision making as well as behavioral processes.[63] Crawford then drew on classic, psychological-cognitive and cultural constructionist theories to outline how "preexisting emotions"

[59] For feminist theories that place emotion at the center of ways of knowing, see, for instance, Alison M. Jaggar, "Love and Knowledge: Emotion in Feminist Epistemology," in Susan R. Bordo and Alison M. Jaggar (eds.), *Gender/Body/Knowledge: Feminist Reconstructions of Being and Knowing* (New Brunswick, NJ: Rutgers University Press, 1989), pp. 145–171. I engage more directly with feminist international relations sources throughout both my conceptual and empirical inquiry.

[60] Christopher Hill, *The Changing Politics of Foreign Policy* (Basingstoke: Palgrave Macmillan, 2003) p. 116.

[61] A. L. George and J. L. George, *Presidential Personality and Performance* (Boulder, CO: Westview, 1998).

[62] For instance, Robert Jervis, *Perception and Misperception in International Politics* (Princeton, NJ: Princeton University Press, 1976).

[63] Mercer, "Approaching Emotion in International Politics," 10; see also Crawford, "The Passion of World Politics," 117–118.

shape political perceptions and behaviors.[64] She has since extended her theorizing to argue that political institutions can become "path dependent" upon particular emotional predispositions: emotions can, in essence, become institutionalized and routinized in world politics.[65] Mercer, by contrast, advocated a focus on "emotional beliefs," suggesting that feelings influence not just what one believes and does, but also how political identity functions.[66]

Researchers have gleaned much from Mercer and Crawford's early attempts to underline the importance and capacity to include emotion in international relations theorizing and practices.[67] While there is considerable debate and disagreement concerning how to best theorize emotions and isolate the political roles they play, some broad trends in the literature can be identified.

One of the most prominent of such trends is the push to investigate how emotions emerge at the collective level, and how in doing so emotions help to shape not only political identity and community but also ensuing political actions, behaviors and policies.[68] Constructivist and poststructuralist approaches play a particularly important role in these endeavors. Their focus lies predominantly on theorizing how emotions constitute group identities and, with this, ensuing political practices and policies. Key attention is given to the emotional dimensions of the state and state identity. Emotions take on an explicitly collective dimension

[64] Crawford, "The Passion of World Politics," 119.

[65] Neta C. Crawford, "Institutionalizing Passion in World Politics: Fear and Empathy," *International Theory*, 6.3 (2014), 535–557; Neta C. Crawford, "Emotions and International Security: *Cave! Hic Libido*," *Critical Studies on Security*, 1.1 (2013), 121–123.

[66] Mercer, "Emotional Beliefs," 10; Jonathan Mercer, "Feeling Like a State: Social Emotion and Identity," *International Theory*, 6.3 (2014), 515–535.

[67] A number of studies after Mercer and Crawford drew upon arguments that stressed the need to fundamentally rethink dichotomies of emotion in contrast to reason and rationality. See, for instance, Richard Ned Lebow, "Reason, Emotion and Cooperation," *International Politics*, 42 (2005), 283–313; Rose McDermott, "The Feeling of Rationality: The Meaning of Neuroscientific Advances for Political Science," *Perspectives of Politics*, 2.4 (2004), 691–706. Prominent scholars, such as Robert Jervis, also lamented their neglect of emotion as a key source of political insight. See Balzacq and Jervis, "Logics of Mind and International System," 564–565.

[68] Contributions in Roland Bleiker and my Forum section on "Emotions and World Politics" tackle the challenge of theorizing collective emotions directly, from a range of diverse theoretical perspectives. See Bleiker and Hutchison (eds.), "Emotions and World Politics."

here or, as Brent Sasley put it, the idea is to explore how states can themselves "experience and act on emotions" and how, in turn, this emotionality abets political understanding.[69]

Other studies seek to understand how particular emotions take on political significance in concrete circumstances. These studies generally do so to demonstrate how particular political actions and policies are dependent upon emotional forms of meaning and agency. A prominent example here is the examination of how emotions associated with humiliation and dishonor – such as shame – can influence the formation of belligerent political policy and political violence.[70] Other studies look at how memories of political violence produce emotional conditions instrumental to the constitution of modern statehood.[71] Emotions associated with trust, friendship and honor are said to be key to the dynamics of interstate diplomacy, alliances and treaties.[72] There are also inquiries into the emotional foundations of humanitarian intervention,[73]

[69] Sasley, "Theorizing States' Emotions," 452.

[70] For example, Fierke, *Political Self-Sacrifice*; Fattah and Fierke, "A Clash of Emotions," 76–81; Victoria Fontan, "Polarization Between Occupier and Occupied in Post-Saddam Iraq: Colonial Humiliation and the Formation of Political Violence," *Terrorism and Political Violence*, 18.2 (2006), 217–238; Evelin Lindner, *Making Enemies: Humiliation and International Conflict* (Westport: Praeger Security International, 2006); Saurette, "You Dissin Me?"; Gearóid Ó. Tuathail, "'Just Out Looking for a Fight': American Affect and the Invasion of Iraq," *Antipode*, 35.5 (2003), 856–870; David Wright-Neville and Debra Smith, "Political Rage: Terrorism and the Politics of Emotion," *Global Change, Peace and Security*, 21.1 (2009), 85–98.

[71] William A. Callahan, "Trauma and Community: The Visual Politics of Chinese Nationalism and Sino-Japanese Relations," *Theory and Event*, 10.4 (2007); Edkins, *Trauma and the Memory of Politics*; Fierke, "Whereof We Can Speak, Thereof We Must Not Be Silent'; Zehfuss, *Wounds of Memory*.

[72] For example, Lucile Eznack, "The Mood Was Grave: Affective Dispositions and States' Anger-Related Behaviour," *Contemporary Security Policy*, 34.3 (2013), 552–580; Eznack, "Crises as Signals of Strength'; Sarah Ellen Graham, "Emotion and Public Diplomacy: Dispositions in International Communication, Dialogue and Persuasion," *International Studies Review*, 16.4 (2014), 522–539; Lebow, "Fear, Interest and Honor"; Brian C. Rathbun, *Trust in International Cooperation: International Security Institutions, Domestic Politics and American Multilateralism* (Cambridge: Cambridge University Press, 2012); Brent E. Sasley, "Affective Attachments and Foreign Policy: Israel and the 1993 Oslo Accords," *European Journal of International Relations*, 16.4 (2010), 687–709; and Nicholas J. Wheeler, "Beyond Waltz's Nuclear World: More Trust May Be Better," *International Relations*, 23.3 (2009), 428–445.

[73] Vanessa Pupavac, "Pathologizing Populations and Colonizing Minds: International Psychosocial Programs in Kosovo," *Alternatives: Local, Global,*

development[74] as well as broader conceptions of international ethics[75] and international political economy.[76] Finally, there are recent studies that return to what is probably the most theorized of all emotions: fear.[77]

Even though there are a range of important contributions to the study of emotions in international relations, major challenges still exist. For one, there are major disagreements when it comes to conceptual frameworks that are most suitable for the study of emotions. For instance, Andrew Ross and Janice Bially Mattern are concerned that a focus on the tangible aspects of emotion may neglect the nonmaterial complexities that comprise the full sensory and affective bodily experience.[78] I engage some of these and other debates in the pages that follow. I do so while establishing and empirically applying a conceptual framework that assesses the sociopolitical and collective dimension of emotions in particular. I believe that this endeavor is crucial if scholars and policymakers are to gain a more complete understanding of the links between trauma, emotions and world politics.

Structure of the book

The book is divided into three parts. The function of these three parts is to separate the conceptual and empirical sections of my inquiry.

Political, 27 (2002), 489–511; and Vanessa Pupavac, "War on the Couch: The Emotionality of the New International Security Paradigm," *European Journal of Social Theory*, 7.2 (2004), 149–170.

[74] Sarah Wright, "Emotional Geographies of Development," *Third World Quarterly*, 33.6 (2012), 1113–1127.

[75] Renée Jeffery, *Reason and Emotion in International Ethics* (Cambridge: Cambridge University Press, 2014); Renee Jeffery, "Reason, Emotion and the Problem of World Poverty: Moral Sentiment Theory and International Ethics," *International Theory*, 3.1 (2011), 143–178; Andrew Linklater, *The Problem of Harm in World Politics: Theoretical Investigations* (Cambridge: Cambridge University Press, 2011), esp. Chapter 5, "Historical Sociology and World Politics: Structures, Norms and Emotions."

[76] Earl Gammon, "Affect and the Rise of the Self-Regulatory Market," *Millennium: Journal of International Studies*, 37.2 (2008), 251–278; Wesley W. Widmaier, "Emotions Before Paradigms: Elite Anxiety and Populist Resentment from the Asian to Subprime Crises," *Millennium: Journal of International Studies*, 39.1 (2010), 127–144.

[77] Ken Booth and Nicholas J. Wheeler, *The Security Dilemma: Fear, Cooperation, and Trust in World Politics* (Basingstoke: Palgrave, 2007).

[78] Ross, "Coming in from the Cold"; Mattern, "A Practice Theory of Emotion for International Relations," 67–69.

Part I – which comprises Chapters 1–3 – establishes a conceptual framework to examine the relationship between trauma, emotion and political community. I explore the nature of trauma and specifically examine how traumatic events can come to inspire the collective meaning and agency needed to consolidate or constitute political identity and community. Key here are practices of representing traumatic events, and how ensuing discourses implicate and resonate with (and hence can both discipline and transform) socioculturally embedded forms of feeling. To establish my conceptual framework I draw on a broad range of cross-disciplinary sources that include contributions from anthropology, sociology, critical and cultural studies, history, feminist and political theory, international relations, philosophy, psychology and neuroscience.

Part II – Chapters 4–6 – then empirically implements my conceptual framework. I analyze how representational practices helped to evoke solidarity and a sense of community in three very different yet equally pivotal traumatic circumstances: the perceivably "national" trauma associated with an act of terrorism (Chapter 4); an unforeseen natural catastrophe of devastating global proportions (Chapter 5); and, finally, historical traumas that often constitute communities following prolonged and unresolved periods of violence, suffering, inequity and injustice (Chapter 6). In all of the cases, I focus on prevailing representations of each event and analyze how the emotional meanings they produce are implicated in generating the respective communal solidarity that emerged after. In doing so, the final historical step of my empirical inquiry additionally – and crucially – probes the politically transformative possibilities that can be opened by representing trauma.

I first focus on the Bali bombing of October 12, 2002 (Chapter 4). At issue in the case of the Bali bombing was the transnational constitution (or re-constitution) of an insular and parochial sense of Australian nationalism and corresponding form of political community – that is, an archetypal "Australian" identity and community. The "Bali bombing" is the generic name given to the first terrorist attack in Kuta on the island of Bali, Indonesia. During the night of October 12, 2002, two bombs exploded outside of the popular expatriate-only Sari Bar. The bombing resulted in the deaths of 202 people, 88 of whom were Australian. Australia thus quickly became one country in which the impact of the Bali bombing was sharply felt. Indeed, as the extent of the atrocity unfolded – if one were to use the media as a gauge – it also seemed that so too did any differences that had ever kept the very diverse Australian community apart. The nation was said to be at one with victims. A sense of trauma was invoked as damaging Australia as a collective whole.

Here it can be seen that the trauma generated a conservative rather than transformative effect. Immediate responses are illustrative. In the days after, politicians and media appealed to well-known cultural tropes and icons in an expression of communal outrage, attempted healing and redemption. The public was presumed to be – and portrayed as – bearing witness together, in shock, grief, loss and in anger, but always in complicit agreement with the prevailing portrayal of both Australian national identity and the appropriate Australian national communal response.

A different dynamic was at play following the 2004 Southeast Asian tsunami (Chapter 5). It was a truly global natural catastrophe: fourteen countries were directly affected; people of more than fifty-one nationalities were killed. However, just as incredible as the destruction was the outpouring of transnational solidarity that emerged swiftly after.

We see here a case of distant trauma where a subsequent transnational sense of community can be realized in the form of a collective responsibility; in the willingness to help others face the challenges of both emotional and practical, day-to-day survival. Needless to say, the type of community in this case is more fleeting and different than if it were embedded in stable institutions, such as states. But numerous scholars before me have stressed that a sense of community can be seen to emerge through the giving of aid in order to alleviate hardship and ensuing trauma.[79] This conceptualization pivots on the notion that traumatic events can bring individuals together in a community bound by some form of sympathetic, possibly empathetic, understanding of human suffering. This is not to say, however, that the ensuing political process was neutral or unproblematic. I identify and discuss a strong

[79] For examples of studies that conceptualize international political community in this way, see David Campbell, "The Deterritorialization of Responsibility: Levinas, Derrida, and Ethics After the End of Philosophy" and Daniel Warner, "Searching for Responsibility/Community in International Relations," in David Campbell and Michael J. Shapiro (eds.), *Moral Spaces: Rethinking Ethics and World Politics* (Minneapolis: University of Minnesota Press, 1999), pp. 29–56, 1–28, respectively.

colonial theme that runs through prevailing representations of the tsunami catastrophe – a form of an emotional power-play that is widespread in depictions of suffering and revolves around notions of pity and Western privilege. For this reason, I conclude – not without lament – that the ensuing transnational community could not have been the wholly transformative moment that it may have initially appeared to be.

The final empirical inquiry further pursues the transformative potentials that can be opened after trauma. I examine how representations can either function to preclude or make possible necessary processes of emotional grieving and healing. By prompting traumatized individuals and communities to consciously "work through"[80] painful emotions, I show how grief holds the potential to emotionally transform communities haunted by trauma and its memory.

I juxtapose two different cases of working through grief in the wake of protracted, historical trauma: (1) China and the "Century of National Humiliation," and (2) South Africa and the traumas endured under apartheid.

Inquiring into China's relationship to past trauma enables me to scrutinize a communal situation where trauma has been insufficiently worked through. Representations of China's colonial trauma – spanning roughly from 1839 to 1949, and popularly known as the "one hundred years of humiliation" – are overtly political. Crafted precisely to enhance social and political cohesion, predominantly singular representations of this so-called traumatic "Century" proliferate a continuing sense of collective injury that keeps the trauma "alive," and in doing so precludes the successful mourning and working through of historical grievance. Chinese nationalism is thus at least in part constituted around "structures of feeling" that ensue from an ongoing sense of victimization and suffering.[81] Chinese national identity and community are consequently mobilized in opposition to a "negative"

[80] Dominick LaCapra, *Writing History, Writing Trauma* (Baltimore: Johns Hopkins University Press, 2001), pp. 148–149; and in international relations, Kate Schick, "Acting Out and Working Through: Trauma and (In)security," *Review of International Studies*, 37.4 (2011), pp. 1837–1855.

[81] William A. Callahan, *China: The Pessoptimist Nation* (Oxford: Oxford University Press, 2010), pp. 19–28. This term was first used by Raymond Williams and is further discussed in the insightful article, Jennifer Harding and E. Deidre Pibram, "The Power of Feeling: Locating Emotions in Culture," *European Journal of Cultural Studies*, 5.4 (2002), 407–426, at 416–419.

foreign other. Left unresolved, the historical trauma motivates a search for international recognition and status.

South Africa is then positioned toward the other end of the possible spectrum of responses to historical trauma. South Africa, specifically the Truth and Reconciliation Commission (TRC), provides an instance in which a national community acknowledged and represented trauma in a manner that attempted to actively work through the injury and loss. While South Africa is not without continuing challenges, the TRC provided a social and emotional space through which apartheid traumas could be fully recognized and collectively grieved. Victims, perpetrators and the whole community as bystanders were prompted to reflect upon the traumatic history and the roles they played in the shared injury and loss. Moreover, by guiding the truth-telling process through narratives of societal healing and reconciliation, the TRC sought to reframe destructive trauma narratives and make new, shared meanings out of past injustice and pain. The emotional contours of South African community were as such rethought and reshaped. No longer did trauma divide society, but instead it united it.

In the conclusion, I further theorize the linkages between emotions, trauma and community in order to articulate the broader significance of my inquiry for the conception and practice of international relations. I focus on how the notion of "emotional cultures" improves our understanding of the linkages between political identity, power and community in world politics. Of particular significance is an appreciation of how, in some circumstances, seemingly individual (yet inherently social) emotions can enact and reconstitute established forms of community, and thus political power, yet, in other circumstances, emotions can act as social forces capable of transgressing power, in turn fundamentally transforming the social and political order. I then further outline how an appreciation of the constitutive political nature of emotions is significant to a range of political, ethical and normative issues in international relations, from the formation of foreign policy and security strategy to human-rights-based challenges, such as humanitarian intervention, international justice and the politics of reconciliation.

PART I

Conceptual framework

The first part of this book conceptualizes the relationship between trauma, emotion and community in world politics. The inquiry begins by exploring the nature of trauma more generally, and in turn specifically examines how traumatic events can come to inspire the collective agency needed to construct or consolidate forms of political community. Motivating the inquiry is thus a concern for not simply the personal challenges associated with experiencing trauma, but moreover the social and symbolic processes through which ostensibly individual trauma can be constitutive of a wider collective. To examine these linkages, I draw on theories of representation, and an understanding of how representational techniques provide a frame through which trauma can become a phenomenon meaningful to many. Put differently, representations enable trauma to be collectively experienced and enacted – within a wider society or community of others that bear witness, from up close or at a far off distance. As such, the central objective of this part is to conceptualize how ways of telling and thinking about traumatic events can shape shared meanings and, in some circumstances, the social attachments that are intrinsic to political identity and community.

The three chapters in this first part are structured around one central theme: the dual or paradoxical nature of trauma: the idea that trauma can both break and remake communities. Experiences of trauma may feel solitary and emotionally isolating, yet after trauma various processes may help to reestablish social connections and rekindle security and community. Bonds shattered by trauma can in this way be reconstructed.

Trauma literatures help us to appreciate how the fracturing feelings instigated by trauma can have social and political consequences as well (Chapter 1). These literatures are diverse, crossing many disciplines in an effort to understand the complexities involved with experiencing and recovering from acts of violence and atrocity. Notable also is a degree of scholarly disagreement. Consensus is reserved largely for the "pivotal" and deeply personal nature of trauma – that trauma can prompt feelings of fragmentation, disorientation, contingency and shock. An inability to express these feelings is also commonly understood to ensue. But no matter how seemingly "personal" trauma may feel, individuals are always already embedded in social settings that shape their understanding of trauma. Making "sense" of trauma is therefore an activity that is socially, culturally and often politically framed. Drawing out these tensions, I traverse trauma literatures with a particular focus on how the terror and torment associated with seemingly inimitable trauma can – and, indeed, does – influence the configuring of society and politics.

Still, no matter how much scholars profess to conceptualize trauma and its impact, significant tensions remain in our understanding. Chapter 2 of my inquiry shows that the difficulties involved with understanding trauma and its seemingly paradoxical relationship to political community can be at least partially attributed to trauma's intensely emotional nature. Trauma's impact is felt largely through emotion. One reflection of this is the problem of how to adequately communicate the feeling and meaning of trauma. Scholars tend to agree that even though one may speak or write of trauma, words fail to convey the perceptual intensity of how it is experienced, through feelings – whether they are either physical or emotional ones, or a combination thereof.

Even though scholars profess the inadequacy of language, they also highlight that emotional reactions to trauma are intertwined with the processes that reconnect individuals with the social world. I draw out this tension and argue that it is key to understanding the paradoxical relationship between trauma and community. Trauma is experienced (not exclusively, but in many ways) emotionally, and while emotions often feel inherently internal and private, they in fact perform important social functions. It is moreover in part because of trauma's intense, yet never wholly expressible emotions that traumatic occurrences can become crucial sties through which communities grapple to reassert political boundaries and a corresponding sense of power and control. Hence, I suggest that in order to more fully appreciate how trauma can help to constitute communities, research needs to be undertaken into roles that emotions play in furnishing attachments between individuals.

Yet, the problem of how to appreciate the linkages between trauma, emotions and community is further complicated by the methodological difficulties of how one is to study an unquantifiable phenomenon such as emotion. As central as emotions are to trauma – indeed, to every form of action – emotions have only recently become an accepted object of political scrutiny. And even while the social nature of emotions is now more widely acknowledged, the precise processes through which emotions play social and political roles require further investigation in social science-based research. Emotions occupy a space outside the normal linguistic and symbolic tools with which one makes sense of the world. This makes quantifying them very difficult, if not impossible. Labeling and studying emotions in a qualitative manner can be equally perilous. Hence, even once one recognizes their sociality and social significance, questions concerning how to systematically examine a phenomenon as intangible and contingent as emotions remain. From a traditional social scientific perspective, emotions appear as too ephemeral to be evaluated analytically.

What is puzzling about this position is that constitutive and discursive approaches to the anthropology, philosophy, history, sociology and psychology of emotion have long recognized that emotions cannot be separated from social context. These literatures cast off the traditional prejudice of emotions as irrational and highly individualized sentiments. Moreover, rather than considering emotions as biologically grounded, as it was once thought, these literatures contend that emotions are phenomena with a history. They emerge at least in part through sociocultural interactions and thus tend to be most meaningful in specific social and cultural contexts. Expressed in a different way, how we feel emerges from and is constitutive of the social, institutional and discursive processes that bind society together.

Theories of representation, discourse and narrative provide insights that help us to theorize and empirically examine the possible linkages between trauma, emotions and the formation of political communities (Chapter 3). These literatures suggest that whether one can feel for, or identify with, another's trauma has much to do with how it is represented. More specifically, they maintain that if an experience or event is to be meaningful to a wider society or community it must find expression in a language common (or at least able to be understood) to all. Distinct here is that although trauma and its emotions highlight the limits of human expression, communicative practices nonetheless make trauma in some way knowable to many. In doing so, practices of communication and representation eventually smooth over the feelings of discontinuity and fragmentation, prompting trauma to be considered and emotionally enacted in a collectively meaningful (and often politically restorative) way. This process can take place almost automatically, through a need to overcome isolation and locate a community that cushions trauma's pain. It can also be employed, strategically, in order to foster a sense of identity and community that can enhance social and political cohesion.

1 *Trauma and political community*

Trauma is swiftly becoming one of the most compelling psychological and political phenomena today. No longer is it merely consigned to psychological or medical inquiries into survivors of extreme experiences; rather, trauma is now seen as a defining social and cultural condition. Didier Fassin and Richard Rechtman go so far as to claim that trauma "has become the major signifier of our age."[1] In short, the concept of trauma is now often invoked as key to understanding how a wide range of violent or turbulent events can create historical legacies of suffering that live on in the present day, casting a "collective imprint" that shapes societies and their politics.[2]

Of course, this broader conception of trauma was not always commonplace. Since the notion of "trauma" was identified, it has gone through numerous shifts in terms of its usage and diagnosis.[3] First used in the mid-nineteenth century to describe the psychological distress endured by train crash victims and becoming more prevalent in the post-Holocaust world a century later, the notion of trauma has become instrumental to understanding the challenges of surviving and recovering from extreme, usually in some way violent, experiences. Trauma is thus able to be experienced directly, as a blunt physical injury and harm, and it can also be the collective result of the culturally symbolic mediations through which the respective events and

[1] Didier Fassin and Richard Rechtman, *The Empire of Trauma: An Inquiry into the Condition of Victimhood*, trans. Rachel Gomme (Princeton: Princeton University Press, 2009), p. xi.

[2] Fassin and Rechtman, *The Empire of Trauma*, p. xi.

[3] Trauma scholars largely agree that trauma is a historically situated and socially constructed psychological condition. It is not, therefore, an illness that was miraculously "discovered." See Ruth Leys, *Trauma: A Genealogy* (Chicago: University of Chicago Press, 2000), pp. 5–6; Allan Young, *The Harmony of Illusions: Inventing Post-Traumatic Stress Disorder* (Princeton: Princeton University Press, 1997), p. 5.

injuries are represented.[4] This widened, more "everyday" usage reflects a significant shift from the initial psychiatric, mental field: there is now, as Fassin and Rechtman explain, a "new language of the [traumatic] event."[5] Still, consensus regarding trauma – how to distinguish it, determine how it is physically and emotionally experienced, ascertain its psychological impact, and also how to best help traumatized individuals through recovery – continues to be a somewhat contested terrain, even despite debates waged in a range of scholarly literatures.[6] One agreement, however, is that events known as "traumatic" are pivotal, impacting upon those who endure them in a deeply personal and often incommunicable way. The suffering, disorientation and sense of isolation triggered by trauma have never been in doubt.

Even though the concept of trauma is more prevalent than ever in contemporary Western societies, many people still think of trauma as something distant in time and place – a condition limited to victims of abuse, near fatal accidents or to returned servicemen and women who have suffered the scourge of war. But all our lives are structured in some way by violence and ensuing trauma. An omnipresent illustration of this is one's own national community. Since the Treaty of Westphalia and the institutionalization of modern statehood, the nation-state has been considered the custodian of security and survival, the sanctifier of human life.[7] Soldiers fight and die to achieve or maintain this form of community, and for the most part we commemorate their deaths and forget that their trauma belies the very boundaries that it also strengthens.[8] Similarly, consider how international media networks deliver the traumas of distant others into living rooms around the globe, thus shaping the manner in which we perceive of politics. These examples show that although trauma may seem distinctly individual

[4] Jeffrey C. Alexander, *Trauma: A Social Theory* (Cambridge: Polity, 2012), pp. 2–4.

[5] Fassin and Rechtman, *The Empire of Trauma*, p. 6.

[6] For a rich discussion of the various conflicts and tensions in trauma writings, see Murray Schwartz, "Locating Trauma: A Commentary on Ruth Ley's *Trauma: A Genealogy*," *American Imago*, 59.3 (2002), 367–384.

[7] Giorgio Agamben, *Homo Sacer: Sovereign Power and Bare Life*, trans. Daniel Heller-Roazen (Stanford: Stanford University Press, 1998).

[8] See Jenny Edkins, *Trauma and the Memory of Politics* (Cambridge: Cambridge University Press, 2003), esp. pp. 9–16, 95–100, 229–233. Michael Shapiro also examines the constitutive nature of cultures of war in relation to the nation-state. See Michael J. Shapiro, *Violent Cartographies: Mapping Cultures of War* (Minneapolis: University of Minnesota Press, 1997).

and isolating, it is also an inherently social and political phenomenon. It can draw individuals together around shared meanings and common bonds; trauma can help to shape communities.

The purpose of this chapter is to present in more detail the puzzle that is central to my conceptual framework – the seemingly paradoxical, dual nature of trauma – that traumatic events can both break and remake community. On the one hand, trauma is thought to isolate individuals, damaging their sense of security and community. But on the other hand, trauma can also seep out, affecting those who surround and bear witness. Significant in this respect is that traumatic events are experienced in inherently social ways, which can shape shared meanings and common bonds. As such, trauma can – paradoxically – constitute communities.

I argue that an appreciation of this paradoxical, dual nature of trauma is a crucial precondition to understanding its political impact. The chapter is separated into two parts. The first half focuses on the sense of isolation that is often considered characteristic of trauma. Bringing together literatures in social and political theory, feminist theory, sociology, philosophy, psychology, history, cultural studies and literary criticism, I examine how trauma detaches individuals from the social context that has come to constitute their sense of self and belonging, manifesting a crisis of identity and meaning. This conception of trauma is largely the result of the prominence of psychoanalytic studies, and is most synonymous with post-traumatic stress disorder (PTSD) based understandings, which tend to focus on the personal and psychological consequences of traumatic experiences. Attachments and assumptions previously taken as absolute and defining are ruptured. And the comfort and stability of one's normal social reality falls away. Traumatic events therefore not only shatter one's sense of self, but also damage one's sense of security and community. But it is in this way, precisely through collapsing private/public distinctions upon which individuals rely,[9] that traumatic experiences involve not only some form of physical, psychological or emotional wounding, but also inherent social and political dimensions.

The second half of the chapter shows that while trauma isolates, it can also construct or consolidate forms of political community. Central

[9] Eli Zaretsky, "Trauma and Dereification: September 11 and the Problem of Ontological Security," *Constellations*, 9.1 (2002), 98–105, esp. 101.

to this part of the inquiry is an investigation of the mechanisms through which traumatic events can generate shared meanings and common bonds between individuals. Even though intimately personal and arguably in some way incomprehensible, trauma is necessarily experienced and apprehended in accordance with a social context, one which helps to attribute trauma with an accepted meaning. Several mechanisms are important, particularly the processes through which traumatized individuals reconstruct their social world and sense of trust and security. Literatures suggest that the stages of recovery that victims and witnesses pass through are especially significant, and fundamental to understanding the constitution of community after trauma. When faced with an experience that disrupts one's sense of normality, there is often a push – either by victims or from those who surround and bear witness – to make sense of trauma: to give the respective experience meaning precisely because it feels as if it has none. Traumatized individuals often turn to a wider community in an attempt to both better understand and gain recognition for – and attempt to grieve – what they have gone through. They tell of their trauma, seeking acknowledgment within a group or community that is able to understand or identify with their shock and pain. Political and media accounts are equally important: they explicitly situate and often re-enact individual testimony, generating wider narratives that position traumatic events within a social and political context. These processes play a key role in bestowing trauma with both a personal and publicly recognized meaning, which can, in turn, furnish a sense of common purpose and shared identity. I trace these processes, specifically demonstrating how individual experiences of trauma are in fact "performed"[10] in inherently social ways that can come to affect the fabric of whole societies and delineate boundaries of political community.

[10] The now wide, cross-disciplinary usage of the concept of "performativity" is derived from the work of J. L. Austin and Judith Butler. For Butler, performativity essentially means that how individuals carry out – or "perform" – actions imitates and in turn constitutes dominant social conventions of identity and subjectivity. The "performative" nature of social behavior is in this way enmeshed in social power, capable of either reifying or transgressing social norms. With regard to trauma, therefore, how individuals experience, physically enact, express and remember trauma is then a performance through which social identities and subjectivities can be constituted and reconstituted. See my introduction, note 22, for further elaboration on the concept of performativity.

Before I begin, a disclaimer is in order. Surveying such broad margins of literatures inevitably involves particular trade-offs. Many of the theoretical approaches and scholarly contributions I discuss are distinct, and in some cases result in very different ways of conceptualizing the impact of trauma.[11] However, in order to appreciate the social and political processes at issue in my inquiry, it is necessary that I search for commonalities across such differences. Doing so inevitably entails glancing over some of the more disciplinary-based debates and distinctions between particular authors. Yet, at the same time, the strengths of identifying consistencies are considerable: trauma can be perceived of in a fresh light, thus opening up new forms of knowledge that are central to the task of more holistically theorizing the make-up of our social and political world.

The isolation of trauma

This part of the chapter surveys literatures that help us to appreciate the feelings of isolation that are commonly considered characteristic of trauma. The inquiry proceeds in three parts. First, I discuss the concept of trauma and what constitutes an experience distinguished as "traumatic." I then discuss the personal and ostensibly individual impact of trauma, demonstrating how the horrifying and incomprehensible nature of trauma shatters one's sense of self and challenges basic assumptions and meanings. The final section in this part then considers the inherent social and political dimensions and implications of the feelings of isolation that distinguish individual and collective trauma.

[11] To be clear, some conceptualizations are derived more from original medicalized, mental health and PTSD conceptions, which focus predominantly on the psychological dimensions of trauma and how they affect individuals. Others advocate that experiencing and recovering from trauma is never a wholly "private" experience in so far that trauma is inevitably situated and understood within a social setting. In this latter sense, individual trauma is always already social – and, because of how it is made intelligible and meaningful through discourse, political. My inquiry, while not discounting or dismissing that individuals experience trauma as a profound and often unresolvable injury and loss, hinges upon the latter conception, which implies not only the social but also inherently political nature of such injury and loss.

Conceptualizing trauma

Scholars largely agree that trauma is an encounter with an event or series of events so shocking that our understanding of the world and how it works is seriously disrupted. Whether it is experienced immediately or witnessed from a safe distance, trauma is an encounter with something so terrifying that it plunges those who experience it into a world of uncertainty and fear. The comfort and stability of normal habits and expectations fall away with trauma. Commonly held assumptions and meanings that have, over the course of our lives, come to define us are stripped away. One's normal sense of reality seems ruptured, in what at the time may feel irreparably so. Therefore, those who survive traumatic experiences may well have preserved their physical lives, but the meaning ascribed to being becomes altered, often in revelatory and irreconcilable ways.

While all forms of pain involve an acute or more enduring sense of injury – to the body, to the psyche, or to the social environment – what is also thought to distinguish a painful experience or set of experiences as "traumatic" is that they are so horrific and confronting that they belie one's ability to comprehend them. Trauma is experienced with corresponding feelings of disbelief and terror, disorientating victims to such an extent that they are unable to reconcile their experiences with practices and memories that they are accustomed to. It is in this way that Cathy Caruth suggests we consider trauma as "the confrontation with an event that, in its unexpectedness and horror, cannot be placed within the schemes of prior knowledge."[12] Lawrence Langer also explains that the force of trauma is not in the experience of pain alone, but in the particular encounter's "sheer impossibility."[13] The impossibility, that is, of accepting what has happened – the trauma – as one's reality. Elsewhere, Maurice Blanchot implies a conception of trauma as "the disaster, unexperienced. It is what escapes the very possibility of experience – it is the limit of writing."[14] Therefore, while the

[12] Cathy Caruth, "Recapturing the Past: Introduction," in Cathy Caruth (ed.), *Trauma: Explorations in Memory* (Baltimore: Johns Hopkins University Press, 1995), p. 153.

[13] Lawrence L. Langer, *Holocaust Testimonies: The Ruins of Memory* (New Haven and London: Yale University Press, 1991), pp. 39–40.

[14] Maurice Blanchot, *The Writing of Disaster*, trans. Ann Smock (Lincoln and London: University of Nebraska Press, 1995), p. 7.

act of being injured may be intensely painful, it is the failure to comprehend and integrate particular experiences that distinguish them as "traumatic."

Events known as "traumatic" are consequently not processed or apprehended in the same way as others. Psychoanalytic research in particular suggests that, for victims and witnesses, traumatic experiences seem to occupy a surreal space that is incapable of being understood as part of normality. Reality seems broken, and in an important way trauma prevents victims and witnesses from restoring a sense of normality. Caruth goes as far as to claim that trauma may never be able to be "fully known" by victims.[15] Traumatic experiences present individuals with an "impossible real,"[16] something so horrific that it seems more like a terrible dream than one's reality. Victims may draw back into themselves, as if the encounter has reduced their awareness of the world to the space of the painful moments and the bodily surfaces in which it is contained.

For many scholars of trauma, its so-called incomprehensible nature is a puzzling contradiction. While trauma clearly exists within the bounds of everyday reality, it seems to exist independent of reality as well. Victims tend to doubt not only themselves, but also their faith in their surroundings and in others. Jenny Edkins and Judith Lewis Herman are two scholars who suggest that we think of trauma as a form of "betrayal."[17] Significant in this distinction is that traumatic experiences generate an often catastrophic challenge to the trust that individuals have come to have in their community. As survivors of intense psychological trauma have put it: "things are no longer what they seem."[18] Nonetheless, psychologists such as Bessel van der Kolk and Robert Lifton have also recognized that the challenge of trauma is derived from how experiences of it take over, helping to constitute the very reality it seems to also transgress. The almost transcendental

[15] Cathy Caruth, *Unclaimed Experience: Trauma, Narrative, History* (Baltimore: Johns Hopkins University Press, 1996), p. 4; see also Patrick J. Bracken, *Trauma: Culture, Meaning and Philosophy* (London and Philadelphia: Whurr, 2002), pp. 63–81.

[16] Langer, *Holocaust Testimonies*, p. 39.

[17] Jenny Edkins, "Forget Trauma? Responses to September 11," *International Relations*, 16.2 (2002), 243–256, at 245–247; Judith Lewis Herman, *Trauma and Recovery: From Domestic Abuse to Political Terror* (London: Basic Books, 1992), pp. 98, 100, 111.

[18] Herman, *Trauma and Recovery*, p. 53.

quality of trauma pushes victims to constantly try to better understand or in some way know their experiences.[19] As such, an impression or image of trauma – known sometimes as trauma's "reality imprint"[20] – prompts victims to remember and recall their trauma so frequently that it becomes a kind of timeless "truth" (rather than a subjective experience), constituting and reconstituting a vision of themself and their place in the social world.

It is in this way that severe trauma can involve the repeated reliving of the wounding experience. Due to the difficulties comprehending traumatic events when they happen, they return belatedly, creating a gap between the actual experience and the continuing emergence of trauma through memory.[21] Such reemergence – or "rememory," as author Toni Morrison aptly calls it[22] – instills victims with the feeling that they are possessed by a phenomenon they cannot know or understand, or even integrate. Yet, because victims long to understand, to know, and to incorporate their trauma into their sense of normality they may become transfixed on the site of their wounding. Through memory, individuals access the site of their trauma over and over, mostly in an effort to come to terms with it, to "work through"[23] what has happened and how the encounter continues to shape their life.

Because victims continually relive and remember their painful sensations and emotions, trauma thus seems to exist independent of space and time. As Langer's study of Holocaust survivors shows, time collapses or "stops" at the moment of trauma.[24] That trauma forces its way into one's everyday life and mindscape lends trauma victims to believe, as Jeanette Winterson's fictional war-time characters make one aware, that "the future is only possible because of the past." That

[19] Bessel van der Kolk cited in Leys, *Trauma*, pp. 229–265.

[20] Bessel van der Kolk cited in Leys, *Trauma*, p. 7.

[21] See Caruth, *Unclaimed Experience*, pp. 1–9, 58–65; Roberta Culbertson, "Embodied Memory, Transcendence, and Telling: Recounting Trauma, Re-establishing the Self," *New Literary History*, 26.1 (1995), 169–195, esp. 174–176; Judith Greenberg, "The Echo of Trauma and the Trauma of Echo," *American Imago*, 55.3 (1998), 319–347.

[22] Toni Morrison, *Beloved* (New York: Penguin, 1987), p. 36.

[23] Dominick LaCapra, *Writing History, Writing Trauma* (Baltimore: Johns Hopkins University Press, 2001), esp. pp. 22–23.

[24] Langer, *Holocaust Testimonies*; Lawrence L. Langer, "The Alarmed Vision: Social Suffering and Holocaust Atrocity," *Daedalus*, 125.1 (1996), 47–65.

"without the past ... the present is partial."[25] Time seems strangely altered or suspended by trauma. And the past is felt so intensely in the present that trauma becomes distinguished most prominently by its belated return. Victims attempt – consciously or otherwise – to gain access to the traumatic moments, to live and breathe the instance of their pain, and to speak of it in order to forget it and move on.[26]

Significant to the concept of trauma is therefore that it involves an experience with something so horrific and confronting that the notion of normality is shattered. An inability to adequately comprehend or express how this feels is also thought to further compound the challenge of experiencing or witnessing trauma. Trauma thus isolates individuals. It turns worlds upside down, severing individuals from their ordinary moorings and setting them adrift.

Identity and meaning after trauma

The disorientating nature of trauma therefore has a significant impact on one's sense of identity and meaning. Both scholars and survivors concur that the advent of trauma challenges fundamental assumptions about the world, including beliefs and the certainty individuals have in themselves.[27] The faith one has in their ability to be in control collapses with trauma, revealing a world awash with insecurity, hesitation and doubt.

Distinct here is that the meanings and attachments once taken as absolute and constitutive of one's identity are undermined, possibly shattered, with trauma. Judith Butler intimates that in this way traumatic encounters are like a forced confrontation with an irreducible other. Trauma pushes back what were thought to be the knowable aspects of one's self, while simultaneously fusing the self with that of a demanding and diminishing other: the shock and often repeated

[25] Jeanette Winterson, *The Passion* (London: Vintage, 2004), p. 62.

[26] See Linda Alcoff and Laura Gray, "Survivor Discourse: Transgression or Recuperation?" *Signs: Journal of Women in Culture and Society*, 18.2 (1993), 260–290; Culbertson, "Embodied Memory, Transcendence and Telling," 170; Dori Laub, "Truth and Testimony: The Process and the Struggle," in Cathy Caruth (ed.), *Trauma: Explorations in Memory* (Baltimore: Johns Hopkins University Press, 1995), p. 63.

[27] Using her academic training in feminist philosophy, sexual assault survivor Susan Brison provides an insightful account of the challenges of experiencing and recovering from trauma. See Susan J. Brison, *Aftermath: Violence and the Remaking of a Self* (Princeton: Princeton University Press, 2002).

horror of what has happened. One's sense of self – the "I" at the center of trauma – is confronted by an encounter that seems ineffable and without meaning, in turn prompting questions concerning how one's self and community were so defined and assured to begin with.[28]

Some scholars have suggested that the continual confrontation with events that seem to speak only in their impossibility comes to reflect a crisis of meaning.[29] The repetition of trauma through memory is thus seen as not so much an attempt to understand the trauma itself, but more as part of a process of coming to terms with the sense of contingency, or even the meaninglessness, which trauma reveals. Joan Didion, in writing of the trauma of confronting her husband's death, says that the shock was simply "obliterating" – it was "dislocating to both mind and body." Didion further claims that for her the void opened by trauma was "the very opposite of meaning"; it consists of "the relentless succession of moments during which we will confront the experience of meaninglessness itself."[30] Other scholars suggest that rather than being an experience devoid of meaning, the crisis of trauma is precisely that meaning is defined by or embedded within the specific traumatic encounter. So deeply does the trauma seem to constitute one's sense of self that the significance of all previous forms of meaning fall away. For these scholars, existential questions after trauma become focused on the absence of meaning; it is the inimitable, incomprehensible dimensions of trauma that dictate how survivors define and structure their lives.

Other scholarly understandings of trauma suggest we think of this loss of meaning as a form of "dissociation."[31] Dissociation is a rupture or fragmentation of the smooth, narrative flow of one's life – indicating that one's conception of their meaning and the sense of identity are no longer assured and homogenous. Rather, meaning and identity are severely disrupted – or "dissociated," as these scholars put it. Ways

28 Judith Butler, *Precarious Life: The Powers of Mourning and Violence* (London: Verso, 2004), pp. 22–23.

29 Caruth, *Unclaimed Experience*, pp. 1–10, 62–65, 101.

30 Joan Didion, *The Year of Magical Thinking* (London: Fourth Estate, 2005), pp. 188, 189.

31 For instance, Laurence J. Kirmayer, "Landscapes of Memory: Trauma, Narrative, and Dissociation," in Paul Antze and Michael Lambek (eds.), *Tense Past: Cultural Essays in Trauma and Memory* (London: Routledge, 1996), pp. 178–182.

of being and knowing – both individually and collectively – are as a consequence fundamentally altered.

The significance of this kind of "narrative dissociation" becomes clearer when one considers our reliance upon stories – or narratives – to give structure to our everyday. According to literary theorists and philosophers, "narratives" are just that: stories.[32] Ordinarily, one's sense of reality necessarily takes shape through narratives that follow a straight-forward linear progression of time. Moments run forward, each one building upon the previous like links connecting a chain. As Hayden White maintains, "Narrative … is meta-code"; it is the "basis of which … the nature of shared reality can be transmitted."[33] Like a "long sentence," narratives are threaded through (and constituted by) one's language, thought, actions and feelings.[34] Moreover, as if one's life – both its dilemmas and its dreams – was simple and unified, personal and social meaning is found through such narratives. "Every life," Richard Kearney writes, "is in search of a narrative."[35] More boldly, Kearney even goes as far as to contend that coherent narratives "are what make our lives worth living."[36] Narratives give confidence and stability, Kearney continues; stories help to link our life together smoothly. A sequential flow of narratives reflects that the world and its meaning are cohesive, rather than fragmented or "falling apart."[37]

A sense of "life narrative" is important to an individual's purpose and to the development of their identity. If, for instance, such narratives are broken or fragmented, as they commonly are with trauma, one's sense of self and meaning too becomes disjointed – even if such disruption is fleeting. Indeed, trauma is said to reverse the sequence of stories that cohere one's life; it is said to be "clearly disruptive of

[32] See, for instance, Richard Kearney, *On Stories* (London: Routledge, 2002); Paul Ricoeur, "On Narrative Imagination: On Life-Stories," in Richard Kearney (ed.), *Debates in Continental Philosophy: Conversations in Continental Thinkers* (New York: Fordham University Press, 2004), pp. 330–337.

[33] Hayden White, *The Content of the Form: Narrative Discourse and Historical Representation* (Baltimore: Johns Hopkins University Press, 1987), p. 1.

[34] Roland Barthes, *Image, Music, Text*, trans. Stephen Heath (London: Fontana Press, 1977), p. 84.

[35] Kearney, *On Stories*, pp. 4, 129.

[36] Kearney, *On Stories*, p. 3.

[37] White, *The Content of the Form*, p. 21.

settled stories";[38] it is what we refuse or find intensely difficult to make part of our story.[39] This is for many scholars one of the most troubling characteristics of trauma. Sexual abuse survivor Roberta Culbertson comments, "There is no temporal, single self" following trauma. There are only "fragments of one's former self and the untellable feelings of the self constituted by survival."[40] Holocaust survivor Charlotte Delbo has also written about this kind of "splitting" of the self after trauma. Delbo's poetry and memoir tell of how she emerged from the camps a different person, unrecognizable from "the self that was in Auschwitz."[41] At the same time, Delbo perceived a part of herself to remain in the camps even after liberation. "My former life?" she wrote. "Had I a former life? My life afterwards? Was I alive to have an afterwards, to know what afterwards meant?" Delbo continues, revealing how she fails to recognize herself after Auschwitz, how she felt alive yet not alive, and of how her self survived in the present yet at the same time seemed to endure "in a present devoid of reality."[42] A common consequence of this kind of severing or split from reality is a constant questioning of one's identity. Stripped of the substance that previously situated and gave meaning to one's sense of self, traumatized individuals feel alienated.

This is but one way that trauma disturbs the smooth, seemingly homogenous stories we create in order to provide a sense of internal coherence and stability. "Traumatic memory"[43] or "trauma time"[44] is

[38] Jenny Edkins, "Remembering Relationality: Trauma Time and Politics," in Duncan Bell (ed.), *Memory, Trauma and World Politics: Reflections on the Relationship Between the Past and the Present* (London: Palgrave Macmillan, 2006), pp. 99–115, at p. 107.

[39] See also K. M. Fierke, "Whereof We Can Speak, Thereof We Must Not Be Silent: Trauma, Political Solipsism and War," *Review of International Studies*, 30.4 (2004), 471–491, esp. 477.

[40] Culbertson, "Embodied Memory, Transcendence, and Telling," 178. Interestingly, many trauma literatures do not seem to support the idea that one's "normal" self is in fact made of multiple selves to start with. Nonetheless, the question of how one is to remake themself after the dislocation of trauma remains.

[41] Charlotte Delbo, *Days and Memory*, trans. Rosette C. Lamont (Malboro: Malboro Press, 1985), p. 3.

[42] Charlotte Delbo, *Auschwitz and After*, trans. Rosette C. Lamont (New Haven: Yale University Press, 1995), p. 237.

[43] Pierre Janet, a student of Freud, first identified "traumatic memory." See also Allan Young, "Suffering and the Origins of Traumatic Memory," in Arthur Kleinman, Veena Das and Margaret Lock (eds.), *Social Suffering* (Berkeley: University of California Press, 1997), pp. 245–260.

[44] Edkins, *Trauma and the Memory of Politics*, p. xiv.

considered to be another. Memories of particularly harrowing events do not fit with everyday notions of temporality. Further condemning victims to repeat their suffering through memory, the trauma victim is said to be plagued by a "mass of firing images,"[45] images that flicker over and over and over, continually disrupting and randomly breaking through into a trauma victim's every day. Trauma thus alters time, amputating any sense of before or after. As such, trauma defies a linear conception of experience and memory; it hovers outside of one particular moment, seeming to pervade all moments; it confuses the boundaries of normal time. In her study of the politics of trauma and its memory, Edkins connects the "stopping" of time with the challenge of reestablishing meaning after trauma. She maintains that in altering one's conception of time trauma is "something ... that does not fit, that is unexpected. It does not fit the story we already have, and instead demands that a new account of reality be invented, one that will produce a place for what has happened and make it meaningful."[46] This is why victims and witnesses are frequently shifted back to the moment of their trauma in an effort to better understand or somehow conquer and integrate their experiences.

Recovery after trauma is therefore motivated most prominently by the search for some form of unity, or by attempts to restore coherent meaning. Put differently, because linear narratives of time and personhood are suspended, seeming to be broken by trauma, victims and witnesses search for continuity; there is an urgent need to smooth over the disturbance and harrowing feelings brought on by what happened. Some scholars even argue that trauma is in fact a condition most distinguished by the challenge of recovery.[47] In this respect, narratives become important. Individuals use stories – processes of "telling" – in order to search for meaning, and in an attempt to make feelings that accompany traumatic loss (such as anxiety, fear, anger, shame and grief) bearable. They try to recollect and rekindle their sense of self by

[45] Culbertson, "Embodied Memory, Transcendence, and Telling," 178.

[46] Edkins, *Trauma and the Memory of Politics*, p. xiv. See also Culbertson, "Embodied Memory, Transcendence, and Telling," 180–188.

[47] See, for example, Ariel Y. Shalev, "PTSD: A Disorder of Recovery?" in Laurence J. Kirmayer, Robert Lemelson and Mark Barad (eds.), *Understanding Trauma: Integrating Biological, Clinical, and Cultural Perspectives* (New York: Cambridge University Press, 2007), pp. 207–223. Moving away from personal conceptions of trauma, Zaretsky argues that collective trauma is also foremost distinguished by the search to recover trust in a shared social world. See Zaretsky, "Trauma and Dereification," 98–101.

rethinking and somehow communicating the emotions and embodied sensations and affects that trauma solicits. Through stories, that is, individuals strive to discover a pattern to cope with experiences of chaos and confusion; they try to grieve. A common response is to mourn trauma in ways that reinstate previous notions of normality. The respective trauma becomes less harrowing and more normal. It is forced to fit, as neatly as possible, with previous visions of one's personal and social world. In doing so, trauma is ultimately rewritten to fit a more comforting story through which we can live out our lives.

The social and political dimensions of trauma

The effects of the processes I have discussed so far are, however, not confined to the private realm. Trauma possesses inherent social and political dimensions and implications. The most readily apparent of these is that trauma and its memory dislocate victims and witnesses from the social world. Just as trauma interrupts the narratives that give structure and meaning to individuals, trauma also disrupts the social, historically embedded narratives that help define communities and bind them together. Indeed, in many conceptions traumatic encounters are thought to fragment the self to such an extent that individuals can no longer situate themselves in a collective of others. Bonds between individuals and community can thus be broken by trauma.

Through trauma, the very basis of one's phenomenological attachment to the world, and one's apprehension of it, is challenged. The confrontation with an event that speaks to survivors most boldly in its horror and incomprehension makes it difficult for both survivors and witnesses to situate themselves in a normal social context. As Elaine Scarry famously put it, painful experiences "unmake" the world, fracturing the social context that it has taken most of one's life to attain.[48] Sara Ahmed even suggests that in shattering one's social existence painful experiences reduce life to the confines of the body; trauma transgresses and blurs the borders between what is inside and what is outside.[49] Similarly Eli Zaretsky contends that trauma disrupts fundamental ontological structures upon which a secure social order

[48] Elaine Scarry, *The Body in Pain: The Making and the Unmaking of the World* (New York: Oxford University Press, 1985), esp. pp. 29–37, 118.

[49] Sara Ahmed, *The Cultural Politics of Emotion* (Edinburgh: University of Edinburgh Press, 2004), pp. 20–42, esp. pp. 23–28.

depends: the private/public distinction. "[T]error liquidates the structural foundations of private life, and thereby the capacity to reflect, to be comfortable with oneself, to predict danger, and to trust," he tells us.[50] Trauma has in this way been considered an experience that decenters the subject, which in turn de-stabilizes one's sense of social and political reality.

Significant here is that by questioning settled assumptions about who we are and how we exist in the world, trauma reveals social, cultural and political attachments as contingent. It deconstructs everyday personal and social distinctions. If placed in a secure environment people tend to forget their human fragility. We disguise our mortality, our human vulnerability, and take our well being and our satisfaction as givens. And for the most part believe we are secure. Yet traumatic events force us to see our social world and sense of security anew – often in ways that highlight how confidence and security are little more than a fragile, constructed illusion. Thus, by exposing the constructed nature of social and political structures, trauma suggests "how untenable, how insecure, distinctions and assumptions about life really are."[51] Hence, at worst, trauma can mean not simply a loss of confidence in oneself, but moreover a loss of confidence in established social structures and forms of community.

Politically orientated scholars of trauma have in this way contended that extreme events disrupt not only the flow of personal or individual existence, but also the continuity of society and politics. Just as traumatic experiences disorient individuals from established ideas about their self, trauma – especially that which ensues from politically motivated violence – also fails to fit with existing visions of social and political order. Some commentators even suggest that trauma suspends politics. They claim that after trauma "a moment of silence"[52] takes over, which reflects the powerlessness and loss of control that is felt in the face of catastrophic and sudden pain.

Edkins suggests that the concept of "trauma time" is particularly important to understanding the social and political dynamics of

[50] Zaretsky, "Trauma and Dereification," 101.

[51] Jenny Edkins, "Ground Zero: Reflections on Trauma, In/distinction and Response," *Journal for Cultural Research*, 8.3 (2004), 247–270, at 255.

[52] David L. Eng, "The Value of Silence," *Theatre Journal*, 54.1 (2002), 85–94; and see also David B. Morris, "About Suffering: Voice, Genre, and Moral Community," *Daedalus*, 125.1 (1996), 25–45.

trauma. In stopping a sense of time – if only momentarily – trauma also stops or obscures the linearity (and thus cohesion) of forms of political community.[53] Moreover, in doing so trauma provides an "openness"[54] through which fresh perspectives of social and political life can be formed. It is along these lines that scholars also contend that in trauma's incursion into normal social reality, trauma provides a kind of reflective "space" – a space through which individuals and communities can rethink how just and desirable prevailing political structures and patterns indeed are. Trauma is in this sense conceptualized as an event that may be able to prompt a type of self-reflexive "irony" and ambiguity that philosophers such as Richard Rorty suggest is needed to instigate political change.[55] Or, put in the terms of the political theorist William Connolly, experiences of suffering are thought to be capable of facilitating the reflexivity through which boundaries of identity and community can be renegotiated.[56] Trauma can as such be a regenerative political experience capable of shifting and reshaping identities and corresponding conceptions of community.

This line of theorizing about trauma emerges from the notion that traumatic events not only shock and dislocate those who survive or directly witness them. At a time when political events are broadcast instantly through the global media, traumatic events, such as the terrorist attacks of September 11, 2001 (9/11) or large-scale natural catastrophes, have the potential to affect people in all parts of the world. A telling example of the wider social impact of 9/11 is the fact that the attacks prompted thousands upon thousands of people to travel to the site of the World Trade Center.[57] It prompted such shared shock and affinity that it was not enough to hear of what happened, or to witness it over and over on television. The site of trauma had to be seen, to be witnessed and to be felt. With respect to natural catastrophes,

[53] Edkins, *Trauma and the Memory of Politics*, pp. 19, 58–59, 91–96.

[54] Edkins, "Ground Zero," p. 253.

[55] Richard Rorty, *Contingency, Irony, and Solidarity* (Cambridge: Cambridge University Press, 1989). See also Philip Darby, "Security, Spatiality and Social Suffering," *Alternatives: Global, Local, Political*, 31.4 (2006), 453–473, esp. 454–456; and Zaretsky, "Trauma and Dereification," 102.

[56] Connolly refers to this process as the politics and ethics of "becoming." See William E. Connolly, *Why I Am Not a Secularist* (Minneapolis: University of Minnesota Press, 1999), pp. 47–71, esp. pp. 57–62.

[57] Debbie Lisle, "Gazing at Ground Zero: Tourism, Voyeurism and Spectacle," *Journal for Cultural Research*, 8.1 (2004), 3–21, esp. 8.

consider the 2004 Southeast Asian tsunami or the more recent 2010 earthquake in Haiti. The shocking and highly visible media coverage of the catastrophe and ensuing suffering helped in both instances to mobilize two of the largest international humanitarian aid communities that the world has ever seen.

Thus while literatures tend to agree that trauma is an isolating, overwhelming experience, some contend that trauma can precipitate social and political transformation. Cathy Caruth similarly suggests that trauma can be thought of as an "awakening," as an opportunity to develop a more informed understanding of what it means to be human.[58] Presenting larger questions of how "real" one's social reality is, trauma is an encounter that opens us to the inadequacy of human consciousness and the subjectivities we live with every day. In this respect, traumatic events can be seen to "undo" contemporary conceptions of society and politics and provide a space to reflect upon and potentially reconstitute prevailing social and political configurations.

By altering reality and uprooting entrenched social and political patterns, traumatic experiences are thereby thought to expose and suspend relations of power. Indeed, not only does trauma reveal structures of power and authority as imagined, it also renders them, at least temporarily, without meaning. This is why after widespread catastrophe and trauma political elites often struggle to reinstate their social control. The "space" or "emptiness" of trauma is an impossible political terrain to traverse, so they strive to fill the void.[59] Political powers seek to forget or reshape trauma, to disregard or erase the social dislocation that it brings. Of course, in this view trauma is less transformative and instead often fuels insular, conservative visions of identity/community.

Politics scholars have thus demonstrated how the isolation and disturbance of trauma are linked inextricably to trauma's social and political impact.[60] Whether instigated by political violence or natural

[58] Cathy Caruth, "Traumatic Awakenings," in Hent de Vries and Samuel Weber (eds.), *Violence, Identity, and Self-Determination* (Stanford: Stanford University Press, 1997), pp. 208–222, esp. pp. 217–218.

[59] Edkins, *Trauma and the Memory of Politics*, p. 11; Michael Humphrey, *The Politics of Atrocity and Reconciliation: From Terror to Trauma* (London: Routledge, 2002), pp. 11–25; Maja Zehfuss, "Forget September 11," *Third World Quarterly*, 24.3 (2003), 513–528.

[60] See, for instance, Edkins, *Trauma and the Memory of Politics*; Fierke, "Whereof We Can Speak, Thereof We Must Not Be Silent," 490; K. M.

catastrophe, experiences of trauma produce discourses that shape not only how individuals are connected to the world, but also how such connections influence the way one responds to the needs of suffering. Investigations of memory and contemporary statehood show that generally such discourses commemorate trauma in ways that foster the reification of existing forms of political sovereignty. How individuals, and in turn societies, come to remember past traumas and mourn lives lost to events such as war is intimately connected to discourses that reinstate modes of political power and social control. Furthermore, through memory, remnants of such acts endure, often shaping societies for generations. It is in this way that scholars such as James Brassett and Nick Vaughan-Williams argue that trauma discourses have become a "paradigmatic lens through which the dynamics of contemporary international politics are framed, understood, and responded to."[61] Put differently, traumatic events and the social discourses that create wider understandings of them have come to be a normalized feature of world politics: narratives of trauma can be widely understood and integrated into existing conceptions of community, their politics and their ethics. Legacies of the twentieth century are illustrative. Consider the traumas of the Holocaust, the two world wars, Hiroshima, Nagasaki, the Cold War, Vietnam, September 11 and the more recent "War on Terror." Among a great many others, the violence and trauma of such events not only had direct consequences for the nature of world politics, but also today continue to generate psychological and emotional states that influence contemporary global political relations.

Seemingly less extreme examples also point toward the social and political dimensions of trauma. Consider the political and traumatic nature of witnessing instances of distant and sometimes prolonged periods of natural catastrophe. Such occurrences have become everyday phenomena, particularly in the Global North. Scholars even argue that witnessing distant atrocities has become a "spectator sport,"[62] which

Fierke, "Trauma," in her *Critical Approaches to International Security* (Cambridge: Polity, 2007); Humphrey, *The Politics of Atrocity and Reconciliation*; Kate Schick, "Acting Out and Working Through: Trauma and (In)security," *Review of International Studies*, 37.4 (2011), 1837–1855; Zaretsky, "Trauma and Dereification."

[61] James Brassett and Nick Vaughan-Williams, "Governing Traumatic Events," *Alternatives*, 37.3 (2012), 183–187, at 183.

[62] Humphrey, *The Politics of Atrocity and Reconciliation*, p. 102.

objectifies victims and generates narratives of indifference (rather than ones of care).[63] Yet, often it is the foregrounding of trauma that blinds us to the landscape of violence against which it takes place. This is to say that the social and political context of witnessing and perceiving trauma shapes trauma's meaning and significance. In the instance of witnessing distant trauma from afar, an inability or uncertainty of how to respond to the suffering of others often prevails. So much is this the case that it leads to questions concerning how such trauma helps individuals position themselves socially and politically. What I get at here is that distant trauma has come to be largely considered a "normal" (although not to imply acceptable) form of social suffering, and as such it helps to define the identity and subjectivity of the distant individuals witnessing it as much as it does those who are directly affected.[64]

The social and political implications of trauma can then be far-reaching. Most notably, traumatic events can solicit a wider sense of social dislocation, prompting not only victims but also witnesses (both near and far) to reexamine their self and how they are connected to the world around them. Assumptions associated with one's sense of normalcy fall away following trauma, encouraging those affected to rethink, and possibly reshape their attachments with others. Although trauma presents a serious challenge to communal self-understandings, it can also play a crucial role in subsequent political perceptions, affiliations and actions; it can call into question the social and political structures that organize one's sense of community. Conversely, the overwhelming and somewhat incomprehensible nature of trauma can also inspire individuals to seek out (or attempt to restore) a community that is capable of understanding and ameliorating the immanent sense of shock and dislocation.

[63] For instance, Lilie Chouliaraki and Keith Tester examine the political and ethical effects of witnessing distant catastrophe in such a manner. See Lilie Chouliaraki, "Post-Humanitarianism: Humanitarian Communication Beyond a Politics of Pity," *International Journal of Cultural Studies*, 13.2 (2010), 107–126, esp. 108–114; Keith Tester, *Humanitarianism and Modern Culture* (University Park: Pennsylvania State University Press, 2010).

[64] Jeffery Alexander forwards a similar point regarding the constitutive nature of witnessing distant suffering; see his *Trauma*, p. 6.

From individual to collective: performing trauma and constituting community

My engagement with trauma literatures has so far shown trauma to be experienced as a somewhat solitary, lonely encounter; a dive into unknown depths that reveals fragility and fear. Victims and witnesses often feel cut off from the life and world that surrounds them. The immediate and wider social and political communities to which one belongs may feel distant. An inability to adequately express how this feels – either physically or emotionally – may plummet traumatized individuals deeper into what seems their own private abyss. However, processes of recovery – both those of a personal nature and the strategies that draw attention back to an individual's societal context – can construct or restore a sense of cohesion and crucially, community after trauma. It is to these processes that my inquiry now turns.

This half of the chapter is again divided into three parts. The first section examines literatures that help us to initially appreciate how seemingly individual experiences of trauma can translate into phenomena able to be understood by (and made meaningful to) many. Foremost is that, while a personally embodied experience, individuals are necessarily exposed to trauma within social environments that bestow the experience of injury and loss with meaning.[65] Individual and collective trauma and its aftermath are thus social and very much political. Processes of recovery and reconstruction after traumatic events are particularly important in this respect: ways of "telling" and narrating trauma – that is, the various culturally symbolic practices through which trauma is represented[66] – situate traumatic occurrences in relation to a wider social group or community. Following this – and second – I show that a sense of shared or collective identity can be forged or further solidified through this process. Third and finally, I discuss the memory of trauma, demonstrating that modes of communicating

[65] Derek Summerfield, "Addressing Human Response to War and Atrocity: Major Challenges in Research and Practices and the Limitations of Western Psychiatric Models," in Rolf J. Kleber, Charles R. Figley and Berthold P. R. Gersons (eds.), *Beyond Trauma: Cultural and Societal Dynamics* (New York and London: Plenum Press, 1995), p. 19.

[66] Direct testimony, public speeches, the traditional and new media, even dramatized representations such as plays, films, songs and all kinds of storytelling are potential examples.

and understanding trauma can not only abet the construction of a present-day form of political community, but also shape a form of collective vision or memory of trauma that can help to make such community an enduring one. Significant in this respect are the historical legacies that are left by shared trauma, and how trauma is frequently memorialized in ways that bind and strengthen communities through the concurrent preservation of injury and loss and failure to properly grieve.

Situating individual trauma in a communal context

Although trauma is experienced and witnessed in seemingly individual, isolating ways, communities can be produced or sustained as a consequence of it. More specifically, communities can be constituted by shared, inherently social understandings of trauma's meaning and impact. In some circumstances, the collective search for recovery and reckoning with trauma can further bring individuals together after catastrophe as well.

Literatures widely recognize that a communal environment is vital to those who survive extreme, catastrophic events. In particular, the social context and intimacy of a community are important for the success of processes of traumatic healing and recovery. Not only does a supporting community help victims to feel assured of their safety, but also it helps survivors to mourn their loss and in turn to reestablish social bonds and the sense of self and meaning that trauma disrupted.[67] Herman goes further in arguing that "recovery can only take place in the context of relationships."[68] Traumatized individuals, Herman maintains, must ultimately seek to socially reintegrate and have the truth of their experiences acknowledged.[69] Sociologist Kai Erikson too considers a form of "post-trauma community" essential, further suggesting that it is precisely because individuals feel estranged after trauma that they attempt to reconnect with others who recognize and can possibly identify with their experiences. After

[67] Ahmed, *The Cultural Politics of Emotion*, pp. 42–61; Fierke, "Whereof We Can Speak, Thereof We Must Not Be Silent," 473–475, 488–489; Herman, *Trauma and Recovery*, pp. 61–70, 155–156, 196–207.

[68] Herman, *Trauma and Recovery*, p. 133; see also pp. 133–140, 205–207.

[69] Herman, *Trauma and Recovery*, pp. 70–73, 230–231.

trauma, Erikson suggests, victims and witnesses look to a community as a "cushion for [their] pain."[70]

However, there is one key requisite for the construction of such a community: individual experiences of trauma must be both understood by and made meaningful to others. Given the ostensibly individual and solitary conception of trauma – a prevailing legacy of the medicalization of trauma through PTSD – the task of constructing shared meaning would at first glance seem difficult, if not impossible. Yet, not simply can and is trauma made collectively meaningful, but trauma that directly affects only a few frequently leaves indelible marks on forms of collective consciousness. Trauma can fundamentally underpin and secure a group or community's central purpose and meaning.

To view trauma as solely isolating, through a medicalized lens that prioritizes supposedly inimitable psychological aspects of trauma, is thus to obscure the broader social and political context within which trauma inherently takes place.[71] Two overarching, interrelated points are of note. First is that even though trauma seems to shake the foundations of one's social existence, forcing forward a personal world full of insecurity and doubt, trauma both illuminates and is a product of the social and political constitution of one's supposedly personal world. As intimated in my introductory chapter, trauma can be seen as a socially constituted and "performed" encounter, in so far that how trauma is experienced and enacted is shaped by accepted social conventions that determine what constitutes trauma and what trauma means. In this way, traumatic encounters show exactly how the personal and political intersect. And it is therefore through this personal and political "performing" of trauma that the ostensibly isolating nature of trauma can, at the same time, possess and be ascribed wider sociopolitical meaning. Yet still, even so – and second – for trauma to become "collective" it must be transcribed (i.e. mediated through modes of communication) into a language through which it can be shared. Seemingly inimitable encounters with trauma need to

[70] Kai Erikson, *A New Species of Trouble: Explorations in Disaster, Trauma, and Community* (New York: W.W. Norton, 1994), p. 234; Kai Erikson, "Notes on Trauma and Community," in Cathy Caruth (ed.), *Trauma: Explorations in Memory* (Baltimore: Johns Hopkins University Press, 1995), pp. 183–200.

[71] Alison Howell, *Madness in International Relations: Psychology, Security, and the Global Governance of Mental Health* (London and New York: Routledge, 2011), p. 12.

be situated and contextualized in terms of a community that is sympathetic to understanding their significance and impact. It is in this way, as Jeffery Alexander explains, that "[c]ollective traumas are reflections of neither individual suffering nor actual events, but symbolic renderings that reconstruct and imagine them."[72] Communal trauma, that is, is the product of "performative power" which requires "cultural work."[73]

The stages of recovery that trauma victims pass through are significant in this respect. When confronted with feelings of dislocation individuals can seek the consolation and understanding of others. This process may play out in a number of ways. One is through the attempt to give testimony – the assigning of "voice" to one's suffering.[74] Victims and witnesses may search to communicate and somehow share their experiences. Hopes of being understood, accepted and of finding continuity amidst emotional disorientation facilitate such expression, and in turn help to draw people together. Some commentators even suggest that communicating trauma can create a "culture of pain,"[75] or indeed a "trauma culture,"[76] which pulls people together, simultaneously separating them from others who are considered unable to identify with the particular traumatic encounter.

Attempts to communicate and express trauma are considered one mechanism through which individual experiences are situated in a wider communal context. Speaking about trauma (or sharing one's experiences through another mode of communication) has additionally been shown to have a therapeutic function. No matter how much trauma challenges accepted opinions about the limits of language and logic, sharing a traumatic past is considered instrumental to being able to carry on. Psychologists in particular insist that the "telling" of trauma is an important component of the healing process. The communicative act of bearing witness is a difficult yet often necessary step toward reestablishing social relationships and one's place in a community. Victims and witnesses, these scholars determine, must share their experiences in order to reintegrate into society

72 Alexander, *Trauma*, p. 6.
73 Alexander, *Trauma*, pp. 2, 4.
74 See Caruth, *Unclaimed Experience*, pp. 1–9; Morris, "About Suffering," 26–32.
75 David B. Morris, *The Culture of Pain* (Berkeley: University of California Press, 1993).
76 E. Ann Kaplan, *Trauma Culture: The Politics of Terror and Loss in the Media and in Literature* (New Brunswick: Rutgers University Press, 2005).

and to move on.[77] As Dori Laub puts it, victims "tell their stories in order to survive ... unimpeded by ghosts of the past."[78] Susan Brison suggests something similar. She stresses that the possibility of a stable future for traumatized individuals is contingent upon the ability tell and retell "stories about the past";[79] victims need to transform what might seem to be an incomprehensible and voiceless experience into narratives that help to situate and rebuild one's self. Distinct in these literatures is that the "telling" of trauma not simply provides an avenue through which individuals can in some way come to know their trauma. Telling of one's trauma allows individuals to socially enact their experiences, and in doing so restore a meaningful social and communal environment.

Scholarly writings on testimony intersect with these thoughts on the processes of traumatic healing.[80] These studies suggest that trauma is socialized through testimony. The communicative act of telling of trauma is not simply a statement but rather "a speech act" capable of generating public awareness and taking on a life of its own.[81] In this sense, testimony provides a "public space of trauma," a space through which "fragments of personal memory can be assembled, reconstructed, and displayed."[82] At stake here is that giving (public) testimony can help to establish or rebuild connections with a group of understanding, perhaps empathetic, others. K. M. Fierke also explains that it is this "connection" that is crucial to survivors of major trauma. When overwhelmed by the incomprehension of trauma's shock and pain, victims and witnesses need a community of individuals that will respect, understand and acknowledge the legitimacy of their experience, she contends.[83] Individuals who either experience trauma directly or bear witness to it thus need to reestablish social relationships based on a shared understanding or image of trauma's impact and meaning. Sharing trauma through testimony is in this respect crucial.

77 See Herman, *Trauma and Recovery*, pp. 175–181.
78 Laub, "Truth and Testimony," p. 63.
79 Brison, *Aftermath*, p. 104.
80 For examples, see Humphrey, *The Politics of Atrocity and Reconciliation*, pp. 105–108; Nancy K. Miller and Jason Tougaw, "Introduction: Extremities," in Nancy K. Miller and Jason Tougaw (eds.), *Extremities: Trauma, Testimony, and Community* (Urbana: University of Illinois Press, 2002), pp. 1–24.
81 Humphrey, *The Politics of Atrocity and Reconciliation*, p. 116.
82 Kirmayer, "Landscapes of Memory," p. 190.
83 Fierke, "Whereof We Can Speak, Thereof We Must Not Be Silent," 473–482.

But therapeutic or conciliatory practices of individual testimony are not the only way through which a supporting community can take shape around trauma. Trauma can also be politically appropriated in order to strengthen prevailing forms of community. In the disorder and confusion that follow trauma, strategies designed to restore social cohesion and community are often swiftly invoked. Despite feelings of bewilderment and fragmentation, catastrophic and traumatic events can, for instance, be "smoothed over" by processes of commemoration and remembrance.[84] Notable about these practices is that they often reinstate or renew a sense of identity and community that is explicitly political. By representing traumatic occurrences in culturally specific and often highly politicized ways, techniques of representation and narrative diminish social dislocation, translating individual experiences of trauma into a social phenomenon capable of adding to and reconstituting the ties that bind community together.[85] This process can take place almost automatically, without critical thought. It can also be an intensely political process. The aftermath of trauma can be a site in which sovereign powers urgently grapple for political control.

Whether it is through community-orientated processes of healing or through attempts to politicize (and collectivize) a response to trauma, individual experiences of trauma can therefore translate into shared or collective experiences through modes of communication, through telling and retelling stories about trauma. During particularly acute or more widespread instances of crisis, these stories engage not only close friends and family but also a wider community. A horrific or harrowing situation that immediately impacts upon only a few can be portrayed in a way that suggests individual and distant trauma is shared – or that it is at least collectively acknowledged and understood.[86] Catastrophe that directly affects a few can in this way be portrayed as damaging to many, to the individuals and wider society that bear witness, at a distance, rather than feel trauma's impact

[84] Jenny Edkins explores this process following the events of September 11; see Jenny Edkins, "The Rush to Memory and the Rhetoric of War," *Journal of Military History and Sociology*, 31.2 (2003), 231–251.

[85] Michael Humphrey, "From Terror to Trauma: Commissioning Truth for National Reconciliation," *Social Identities*, 6.1 (2000), 7–27, at 10–13.

[86] A helpful theorization of the role social discourses play in this process is Thomas J. Scheff and Suzanne M. Retzinger, *Emotions and Violence: Shame and Rage in Destructive Conflicts* (Lexington, MA: Lexington Books, 1991).

immediately. Whether consciously achieved or not, responses of this kind are often aimed at generating the feelings of shared experience and common purpose needed to underpin identity and community.

Communicating or giving testimony of trauma has in this way been described as a selective, discriminating process. When one speaks of trauma it is contextualized within times, places, images and speech patterns that victims consider most "touching": the things that people identify with and can use to make sense of each other's (and their own) experiences of shock and pain.[87] Alan Radley suggests that by attempting to communicate trauma, "the suffering that is indicated in the wound is given form, recontextualising the scar and giving it new meaning."[88] Put differently, trauma is expressed in ways that enact, as well as enable, the respective events to be ascribed with social meaning.

Significant here is that communicative practices (for example, patterns of speech, photographic and other aesthetic depictions, even facial expression and bodily gesture) employed by individuals, public figures, politicians or the media can only make sense and find meaning within the community through which they have been constructed. Take language, for instance. Words attain relevance and meanings from the social contexts in which they emerge. The social world is thus organized in relation to speech, and how language facilitates different forms of understanding and meaning that are often taken as symbolic of social closure.[89] But when individuals experience trauma, social context and the possibility of such closure are precisely what individuals feel dislocated from. Trauma renders language as well as the social world constituted by one's language as contingent. Speaking of trauma – either by victims or witnesses – is therefore a search to find the expressions considered to be the most appropriate measures of trauma and its pain. This is how trauma attains meaning, socially and collectively, by appropriating social symbols and linguistic patterns that are specific in time and place.[90]

[87] Ahmed, *The Cultural Politics of Emotion*, p. 28.

[88] Alan Radley, "Portrayals of Suffering: On Looking Away, Looking At, and the Comprehension of Illness Experience," *Body & Society*, 8.3 (2002), 1–23, at 10.

[89] Michel Foucault, *The Archaeology of Knowledge*, trans. A. M. Sheridan Smith (London: Routledge, 2002); and see also Michael J. Shapiro, *Language and Political Understanding: The Politics of Discursive Practices* (New Haven: Yale, 1981).

[90] Edkins, *Trauma and the Memory of Politics*, p. 11; Fierke, "Whereof We Can Speak, Thereof We Must Not Be Silent," 477–479, 490. And on

Telling of trauma is thus not solely a task of locating expressions that adequately represent one's feelings. These reflections prompt one to view practices of representation as part of a socioculturally embedded process of making meaning. They give trauma the ability to be in some way understood and expressed – and then as a consequence translated into something that can be meaningful to many. At issue here is that processes of representation mediate the reality of suffering; they are key both to the experiencing of trauma and to the task of replacing the shock and sublime horror of trauma with something meaningful to – and at least partially constitutive of – a community.

It is in this way that scholars and writers describe the language of trauma as a function of power.[91] When one puts trauma into words they speak the language of the "status quo,"[92] the language of the powerful. Indeed, expressions of trauma are part of the process of inclusion and exclusion, of blocking access to those who cannot grasp the symbolic meaning hidden beneath everyday words. Through this example one can see that language belongs to a wider set of representational practices that allow individuals to communicate with a wider community, one that understands the affective sensibilities inherent in modes of traumatic expression.

Thus where trauma may appear to be solitary and privatizing, traumatic experiences expose intimate bonds between selfhood and community, between the personal and the political. Through victims' and witnesses' need to understand and speak of it – as well as through culturally symbolic modes of communicating (or politically appropriating) trauma – wider social understandings and meanings can take shape. Bonds between victims and a wider community that bears witness can form, which suggest that a collective is affected by, or dealing with, the trauma in much the same way as individuals. Trauma can in

semiotics – how socially constituted signs and linguistic codes relate to each other in order to create and exclude particular meanings – see Jacques Derrida, "Structure, Sign and Play in the Discourse of the Human Sciences," in Rick Rylance (ed.), *Debating Texts: A Reader in Twentieth Century Literary Theory and Method* (Milton Keynes: Open University Press, 1987), pp. 123–136.

[91] Alexander, *Trauma*, pp. 2, 15; Edkins, *Trauma and the Memory of Politics*, p. 7; Humphrey, *The Politics of Atrocity and Reconciliation*, pp. 2–8, 108–118; Toni Morrison, "Nobel Lecture," lecture presented December 7, 1993. At http://nobelprize.org/nobel_prizes/literature/laureates/1993/morrison-lecture.html. Accessed October 8, 2006.

[92] Edkins, *Trauma and the Memory of Politics*, p. 8.

this way reflect how individuals are situated in a wider community of recognition.

Trauma and collective identity

The shared understandings and meanings that can form after trauma play a key role in shaping a sense of collective or communal identity. It is commonly argued that group or communal identities require a widely shared understanding of history and its meaning. Shared understandings, in turn, help to generate common purpose and, as some scholars contend, "affective bonds"[93] and "attachments"[94] between individuals. The feeling of belonging with, and being loyal to, this group is thought to then ensue.

Processes of sharing or more widely representing trauma are in this respect instrumental. A sense of collective or shared identity can be created from telling trauma stories. Sharing individual experiences of trauma and the emotions associated with it can create an affinity from which a sense of "we" emerges. A "we," that is, that forms from collective meanings attributed to individual trauma. Collective meaning bestows individuals with feelings of solidarity – of being in pain yet being not alone. Not only does this provide a more comfortable lens to view the world, but also – and crucially – it is an important part of the constitution of community. In this way, trauma is seen to be one mechanism whereby the identity of both individual and community is constituted in relation to others, through difference.[95] In the instance of trauma, commonality of experience and emotion binds people together, defining them in relation to others who are considered incapable of identifying with their pain.

Identities can therefore be constituted, at least in part, through the shared understandings of trauma. However shocking traumatic events may be, however much they prompt us to question who we are and how we exist in the world, however much we will their memory away, traumatic events shape how we interact and therefore define ourselves. Scholarly writing on identity in world politics attenuates these

[93] Duncan Bell, "Introduction: Memory, Trauma and World Politics," in Bell (ed.), *Memory, Trauma and World Politics*, p. 5.

[94] Ahmed, *The Cultural Politics of Emotion*, p. 28.

[95] William E. Connolly, *Identity|Difference: Democratic Negotiations of Political Paradox*, expanded edition (Minneapolis: University of Minnesota Press, 2002).

linkages. According to Michael Shapiro, practices and discourses of violence (and thus trauma) are intricately linked to how the boundaries of the contemporary world have come to be as they are.[96] For Shapiro, the historico-cultural writing of "geo-political imaginaries" (foremost, but not exclusively, the bounded community of the "nation-state") has created not only a world defined by boundaries, but also a world where identity and intercultural violence mutually constitute each other.[97] Other scholars have similarly shown how assumptions of danger come to frame how individuals perceive of different cultural or national identities. They argue that it is precisely by alluding to the dangers beset by the world "outside" that violence and the mere possibility of trauma can align individuals and affirm community limits.[98] These reflections on fear are echoed by international relations scholars who work on the production of "cultures of insecurity."[99]

Also important to how we understand identity after trauma is that extreme experiences are an occasion in which not only individual but also collective identities are most intensely engaged. Distinct here is that traumatic experiences threaten communal identities; trauma damages the cohesion and structure of communities. Yet, it is precisely because trauma presents a challenge to collective identities that shared histories and meanings are often drawn upon in order to resecure them. As Alan Megill argues, collective meanings and memories are "valorized" when a community's identity is threatened;[100] it is during times of acute crisis that people "hark back to the past with amplified intensity."[101] Zaretsky examines these dynamics by juxtaposing

[96] Michael J. Shapiro, "Warring Bodies and Bodies Politic: Tribal Warriors Versus State Soldiers," in Michael J. Shapiro and Hayward R. Alker (eds.), *Challenging Boundaries: Global Flows, Territorial Identities* (Minneapolis: University of Minnesota Press, 1996), pp. 455–480, esp. pp. 458–461.

[97] Shapiro, *Violent Cartographies*, pp. 52–60.

[98] David Campbell, *Writing Security: United States Foreign Policy and the Politics of Identity* (Minneapolis: University of Minnesota Press, 1998), pp. 80–90; Fierke, *Critical Approaches to International Security*, pp. 99–120.

[99] Jutta Weldes, Mark Laffey, Hugh Gusterson and Raymond Duvall (eds.), *Cultures of Insecurity: States, Communities, and the Production of Danger* (Minneapolis: University of Minnesota Press, 1999).

[100] Allan Megill, "History, Memory, Identity," *History of the Human Sciences*, 11.3 (1998), 37–62, at 40–42. See also Barbara A. Misztal, "The Sacralization of Memory," *European Journal of Social Theory*, 7.1 (2004), 67–84.

[101] Bell, "Introduction," p. 6.

processes of "reification" and "dereification" after societal trauma.[102] Dereification refers to the processes of recovery through which individuals rekindle safety and trust and "build a new object world"[103] – one that is the result of collective reflection upon the origins of trauma, the ensuing vulnerability, and in turn, what a more just society might look like. Reification, in contrast, implies "the building up of the ontological structure of normality."[104] Rather than critically reflecting upon trauma and its meaning, trauma is bestowed with a meaning that idealizes and reifies previously existing configurations of trust, safety, authority, power, identity and community – even though such configurations were undermined by the presence of shock, injury and pain. Yet for Zaretsky as well as a range of other scholars, it is precisely because trauma represents vulnerability in the face of the other – that is, because trauma destabilizes collective identity and jeopardizes individuals' faith in political authority – that political discourses that solidify an individual and collective sense of self are invoked.[105]

Recent literature on "cultural trauma" has also sought to better appreciate the relationship between trauma and collective identity. Jeffrey Alexander, Ron Eyerman and Pietr Stompka suggest that a kind of dual process can take place when societies suffer a particularly extreme event or historic period. They show that just as trauma shatters identity and debases a wider sense of public meaning or cohesion, there is often a push to restore or reconfigure collective identity in the wake of such fragmentation.[106] Violence and an ensuing sense of

[102] Zaretsky, "Trauma and Dereification."
[103] Zaretsky, "Trauma and Dereification," 101.
[104] Zaretsky, "Trauma and Dereification," 99.
[105] See also James Brassett and Nick Vaughan-Williams, "Governing Traumatic Events," *Alternatives: Global, Local, Political*, 37.3 (2012), 183–187, at 183–184; Edkins, *Trauma and the Memory of Politics*; Caterina Kinnvall, "Trauma and the Politics of Fear: Europe at the Crossroads," in Nicolas Demertzis (ed.), *Emotions in Politics: The Affect Dimension in Political Tension* (Basingstoke: Palgrave Macmillan, 2013), pp. 143–166, at pp. 151–153.
[106] Alexander, *Trauma*, p. 6; Jeffrey C. Alexander, Ron Eyerman, Bernard Gieson and Neil J. Smelser (eds.), *Cultural Trauma and Collective Identity* (Berkeley: University of California Press, 2004); Ron Eyerman *Cultural Trauma: Slavery and the Formation of African American Identity* (Cambridge: Cambridge University Press, 2001); Ron Eyerman, "The Past in the Present: Culture and the Transmission of Memory," *Acta Sociologica*, 47.2 (2004), 159–169; Piotr Stompka, "Cultural Trauma: The Other Face of Social Change," *European Journal of Social Theory*, 3.4 (2000), 449–466.

trauma can then come to shape the social landscape through which individuals define and redefine the place they occupy in the world. Atrocity and its memory can in this way become, as Stompka argues, at least partially constitutive of the "main values, rules and central expectations" that bind community.[107]

Feminist theorists Sara Ahmed, Lauren Berlant and Wendy Brown also contend that trauma can prompt a distinctive "wound culture."[108] Notable in this regard is that today's heightened visibility of trauma attracts significant public attention to catastrophic and shocking encounters. So much is this the case that a trauma that only immediately affects a few can impact upon the psyche of a collective or entire society. Such has the interest in trauma intensified that traumatic legacies are habitually employed to furnish a wider a sense collective identity. Trauma is in this way perceived to empower a group;[109] trauma becomes a way through which a community can reclaim their need for being.

Trauma and memory

Memory – and especially perceptions of a traumatic past – has been shown to play a pivotal role in shaping collective identities and communities. At issue here is that traumatic events can precipitate a form of social memory. A desire to recollect, remember and memorialize catastrophe transforms what seem to be individualized experiences of trauma into a phenomenon that can be collectively remembered. This form of collective remembrance can take shape through two divergent responses to trauma. Trauma can be remembered and memorialized in ways that preserve the sense of injury and loss, thereby constituting

[107] Stompka, "Cultural Trauma," p. 457.

[108] Ahmed, *The Cultural Politics of Emotion*, pp. 58–60; Lauren Berlant, "The Subject of True Feeling: Pain, Privacy, Politics," in Jodi Dean (ed.), *Cultural Studies and Political Theory* (Ithaca: Cornell University Press, 2000), pp. 42–62, esp. pp. 43–48, 55–58; Wendy Brown, *States of Injury: Power and Freedom in Late Modernity* (Princeton: Princeton University Press, 1995), pp. 52–76.

[109] Meanwhile, I would argue that when trauma is employed in such a manner – which essentially keeps the sense of injury and loss unresolved – a community is not in fact empowered by trauma per se but instead the product of passive, reflex-like forms of agency that prevent the respective community from rethinking existing configurations of political authority and order.

communities around shared pain. Alternatively, processes of grief and mourning can be properly initiated and seen through, which results in communities committed to and constituted more around shared attempts to work through and grieve injury and loss.[110] This is an important disjuncture as it plays a key role in shaping the nature the ensuing community, as well as its politics. In both scenarios, however, it is through practices of collective remembrance – albeit either ritualistic type commemorations or successful mourning – that common bonds and communal attachments can be constituted and affirmed.

After an instance or period of widespread catastrophe, the telling or wider representation of trauma can generate what is known (somewhat contentiously) as "collective memory."[111] Scholars of memory consider "collective memories" to be a shared understanding of the past. Drawing foremost from the work of French sociologist Maurice Halbwachs, these scholars stress that dominant modes of representing and perceiving of past events tend to generate a socially, publicly accepted version of history. One can conceive of collective memory as discursively produced – or, more simply, as constructed. Paul Ricoeur professed that rather than reflecting an accurate or "true" vision of how an historic event unfolded, forms of collective memory are the product of the creative, imaginative ways that stories about the past have been predominantly told.[112] Collective memory has as such been

[110] Butler, *Precarious Life*, pp. 29–30; Fierke, "Whereof We Can Speak, Thereof We Must Not Be Silent," 476; Jay Winter, *Sites of Memory, Sites of Mourning: The Great War in European Cultural History* (Cambridge: Cambridge University Press, 1995), pp. 5, 29.

[111] Collective memory studies are meanwhile now vast. See, for instance, Noa Gedi and Yigal Elam, "Collective Memory – What Is It?" *History and Memory*, 8 (1996), 30–50; Jeffrey K. Olick, "Collective Memory: The Two Cultures," *Sociological Theory*, 19.3 (1999), 333–348; Eviatar Zerubavel, *Time Maps: Collective Memory and the Shape of the Past* (Chicago, IL: University of Chicago Press, 2003). For insightful and constructive critique of "collective memory" literatures, see Susan Crane, "Writing the Individual Back into Collective Memory," *American Historical Review*, 102 (1997), 1372–1385; and Wulf Kansteiner, "Finding Meaning in Memory: A Methodological Critique of Collective Memory Studies," *History and Theory*, 41 (2002), 179–197.

[112] Paul Ricoeur, "The Creativity of Language," in Richard Kearney (ed.), *Dialogues With Contemporary Continental Thinkers: The Philosophical Heritage: Paul Ricoeur, Emmanuel Levinas, Herbert Marcuse, Stanislas Breton, Jacques Derrida* (Manchester: Manchester University Press, 1984), p. 18.

considered a social phenomenon.[113] For some, it is a cultural phenomenon as well.[114] And it is perceived to have an important social and political function. Scholars contend that a shared form of remembering plays a key role in shaping perceptions and then ensuing affiliations and attachments. Memories can in this way help to furnish and maintain a wider sense of social or communal identity, and as such may help to stabilize a society.[115] Halbwachs, who is particularly distinguished for his contribution to the study of social memory, even considers collective memory as that which ensures a certain cohesion within communities.[116] More recently, Jeffrey Prager notes that "[t]oday the past has achieved a kind of iconic, even sacred status. We have become a society of 'memory groups' where one's claim to group membership typically goes unchallenged because of a common past."[117] Shared or so-called collective memories thus not only help to shape one's social and cultural landscape, but also in so doing play an important role in determining the dynamics of individual and communal identity formation.

Because of its nature trauma produces memories that are difficult to forget. This is the case not only for immediate victims, but also for those who bear witness, at a safe distance or belatedly, through the media. Traumatic memories also persist because of their tendency to spread through a society, to be passed down not only between people but also across generations. Again, ways of communicating or expressing the particular impact or historic perceptions of trauma are key. Processes of giving testimony – either by direct victims, witnesses or through the media – shape how past grievances are considered and in turn remembered and commemorated through history. Often, individual

113 See James Fentress and Chris Wickham (eds.), *Social Memory* (London: Blackwell, 1992).

114 Mieke Bal, Jonathon Crewe and Leo Spitzer (eds.), *Acts of Memory: Cultural Recall in the Present* (Hanover: University Press of New England, 1999); Maria Sturken, *Tangled Memories: The Vietnam War, The Aids Epidemic and the Politics of Remembering* (Berkeley: University of California Press, 1997).

115 Duncan S. A. Bell, "Mythscapes: Memory, Mythology and National Identity," *British Journal of Sociology*, 54.1 (2003), 63–81; John Gillis, "Memory and Identity: The History of a Relationship," in John Gillis (ed.), *Commemorations: The Politics of National Identity* (Princeton: Princeton University Press, 1994); Megill, "History, Memory, Identity," 38–40.

116 Maurice Halbwachs, *On Collective Memory*, trans. Lewis A. Coser (Chicago, IL: University of Chicago Press, 1992 [1925]).

117 Jeffrey Prager, *Presenting the Past: Psychoanalysis and the Sociology of Misremembering* (Cambridge, MA: Harvard University Press, 1998), p. 1.

testimony combines with or translates into popular social modes of representing and perceiving of trauma. As Michael Humphrey suggests, experiences and memories of trauma are conveyed through a "cultural repertoire of stories,"[118] stories that not only etch individual trauma into a social landscape but also – and crucially – construct a wider public impression of the particular traumatic period in history.

Other scholars have furthered our understanding of the significance of traumatic memory by showing how collective memories of it are constructed through dominant modes of storytelling, through representing trauma in a way that helps it to fit with prevailing modes of social and political power.[119] For these scholars, what is important is how stories about trauma are circulated. As indicated by studies of representation and narrative, stories about trauma are shaped by conventions of language, time, place and, crucially, of how one perceives the incident to have taken place. Often, such stories carry instructions for how they should be integrated into the existing narratives that structure social and political life – that is, narratives that lend continuity to the social and political sphere. As *New York Times* op-ed commentator Serge Schmemann once declared, "memories depend less on history than on how a people wants to see itself at any given moment."[120] They are selected and narrated; memories – especially those of trauma – take shape within (and as a result of) already existing power relations between the narrator and the narrated. Important in this respect, as Caterina Kinnvall explains, "is how these past grievances or glories are constantly reproduced in contestations of power in which other stores or vents are pushed aside, marginalized or ignored."[121] Traumatic memory can thus be a politically discerning

[118] Humphrey, *The Politics of Atrocity and Reconciliation*, p. 112.

[119] See Bell, "Mythscapes"; W. James Booth, "Communities of Memory: On Identity, Memory, and Debt," *American Political Science Review*, 93 (1999), 249–263; Paul Connerton, *How Societies Remember* (Cambridge: Cambridge University Press, 1989); Edkins, *Trauma and the Politics of Memory*; Edkins, "The Rush to Memory and the Rhetoric of War"; Andreas Huyssen, *Present Pasts: Urban Palimpsests and the Politics of Memory* (Stanford: Stanford University Press, 2003); Misztal, "The Sacralization of Memory"; and Victor Roudometof, "Beyond Commemoration: The Politics of Collective Memory," *Journal of Political and Military Sociology*, 31.2 (2003), 161–170.

[120] Serge Schmemann, "The Anniversary of World War II is an Invitation to Continue Fighting," *The New York Times*, March 22, 2005.

[121] Kinnvall, "Trauma and the Politics of Fear," p. 154.

process. Dominant stories of trauma are a resource through which collective perceptions and memories are generated. These in turn influence not only individual ways of being and knowing, but also how individuals feel and perceive of their attachments with others.

Social conceptions of memory can thus act as subtle yet powerful mechanisms for constructing or sustaining feelings of communal solidarity.[122] In particular, memories can be called upon to legitimize communal identities. Several scholars have argued that through memory trauma is habitually "acted out" in ways that influence feelings of identity and belonging.[123] A case in point is that of Israeli identity and how experiences of the Holocaust have been woven into it. Not only did the genocide of the Jews give legitimacy to the Israeli state, but also it is commonly argued that it instilled a legacy of humiliation and anxiety – a legacy that has been instrumental in mobilizing Israeli aggression toward the Palestinians.[124] Images of Holocaust trauma continue to poignantly shape and define Jewish identity today. Testimonial work in divided or contested societies has also shown that survivors of gross historical injustices are often not simply still preoccupied with their suffering, but moreover that their suffering remains a source for political contestation. For instance, Bina D'Costa's research into the systematic rape of Bengali women links their trauma with the continuing search for a distinct identity and political autonomy in Bangladesh.[125] Reporters in the Balkan Wars too noted that stories of recent atrocity were steeped in memories of historical injustices perpetrated in World War II, as well as long before.[126] At issue here is that the psychological

[122] See Michael Lambek and Paul Antze, "Introduction: Forecasting Memory," in Antze and Lambek (eds.), *Tense Past*, pp. xi–xxxviii; and Megill, "History, Memory, Identity," 38–40.

[123] K. M. Fierke, "Bewitched by the Past: Social Memory, Trauma and International Relations," in Duncan Bell (ed.) *Memory, Trauma and World Politics* (Basingstoke: Palgrave Macmillan, 2006), pp. 116–134, at p. 125; Kate Schick, "Acting Out and Working Through: Trauma and (In)security," *Review of International Studies*, 37.4 (2011), 1837–1855 at 1842–1847.

[124] Peter Novick, *The Holocaust and Collective Memory* (London: Bloomsbury, 1999); Avi Shlaim, *The Iron War: Israel and the Arab World* (London: Penguin).

[125] Bina D. D'Costa, "The Gendered Construction of Nationalism: From Partition to Creation," unpublished PhD thesis, The Australian National University (2003).

[126] Steven M. Weine, *Lives and Memories of Ethnic Cleansing in Bosnia-Herzegovina* (New Brunswick: Rutgers University Press, 1991),

effects and memories of trauma linger long after physical dangers disappear. Indeed, trauma's memory can create a legacy of injustice that continues to constitute and divide societies for generations.

Studies of commemoration also help us to appreciate the role memory can play in constituting communities after trauma. Processes of commemoration are thought to provide a communal space that pays tribute to the suffering of victims and allows them to mourn their loss. Processes of commemoration memorialize trauma, and ensure that communities remember and pay tribute to past trauma. Some scholars suggest that commemoration is essentially about making difficult periods of history – the memory of trauma and violence – easier to bear. Tzvetan Todorov goes so far as to argue that commemorative practices tend to "reflect the image that a society ... wishes to give itself." Put differently, "commemoration is to adapt the past to the needs of the present."[127] Commemoration celebrates the ways things are – often reinstating and maintaining existing forms of community – rather than what might have changed as a result of trauma. Dominant discourses of trauma are used to fulfill or fuel motives to restore a sense of social and political order.

A number of scholars have also sought to understand the relationship between practices of commemoration and nationalism.[128] These scholars demonstrate that the interplay between private mourning and public commemoration tends to give way to national renewal and a strengthened state. Irrespective of whether it was a war won or lost, states write suffering into preexisting narratives of sovereign control and security. Casualties of war are mourned, yet often in such a way that the disquieting paradox of their death is forgotten. Rather than remembering the lesson trauma reveals – the contingency and fragility of self and state – suffering inscribes the same boundaries it belies.

p. 161; Vamik K. Volkan, "Transgenerational Transmissions and Chosen Traumas: An Aspect of Large Group Identity," *Group Analysis*, 34.1 (2001), 79–97, at 89–95.

127 Tzvetan Todorov, *Hope and Memory: Lessons from the Twentieth Century*, trans. David Bellos (Princeton: Princeton University Press, 2003), p. 133.

128 For examples see Richard McNally, *Remembering Trauma* (Cambridge, MA.: Harvard University Press, 2003); Larry Ray, "Mourning, Melancholia and Violence," in Duncan Bell (ed.), *Memory, Trauma and World Politics* (Basingstoke: Palgrave Macmillan, 2006), pp. 135–156; Winter, *Sites of Memory, Sites of Mourning*; and Nancy Wood, *Vectors of Memory: Legacies of Trauma in Postwar Europe* (Oxford: Berg, 1999).

Prevailing ways of remembering trauma can therefore work to smooth over the ruptures and discontinuities that might have occurred in a society's history. Put differently, practices of commemoration and remembrance frame (or narrate) trauma in a way that helps to dissolve feelings of contingency and isolation. We forget that the nation-state, the presumed guarantor of security, sanctions the very suffering that its boundaries are supposed to prevent. We forget that states send individuals to war, to fight and die. And we take "the experience of the soldier faced with sudden and massive death around him ... as a central and recurring image of trauma" throughout history and forget that war is not an inescapable feature of human existence.[129] We forget that trauma shatters our image of how the world was. Particular ways of remembering trauma are mobilized in the public domain in order to restore continuity and community. Established narratives of the nation-state are used to shape our response to trauma, the intimate emotions that are associated with trauma and its memory. Wendy Brown and Barbara Misztal have shown that it is through the memorialization of trauma that that personal injury and wounding can reinforce forms of collective identity and community.[130] Trauma and the memory of being injured can be appropriated through prevailing patterns of discourse and language that dictate what and how we remember. Individual trauma can be transformed into a "history" of shared experience. Forms of social memory ensue, in turn consolidating or constructing the collective identity that is needed to support the nation-state.

It is in this way that past trauma often remains unresolved within affected communities. Through collective memory, trauma is in essence kept "alive"; a sense of past injury and loss is co-opted (consciously or otherwise) in the present, and coheres communal meaning and identity. Vamik Volkan refers to this dynamic as "chosen trauma," meaning that a group's present identity is indelibly marked by the previous generation's trauma.[131] He contends that chosen trauma arises from the inability or failure of the group to mourn the trauma properly. The

[129] Caruth, *Unclaimed Experience*, p. 11.
[130] Brown, *States of Injury*, pp. 73–76; Misztal, "The Sacralization of Memory," 67–84.
[131] Vamik Volkan, *Bloodlines: From Ethnic Pride to Ethnic Terrorism* (Boulder, CO: Westview Press, 1997), pp. 36–49.

trauma is kept "fresh," causing continued feelings of loss, victimization and insecurity.

The legacy of trauma can thus be a powerful influence in present-day communal and political configurations. Trauma frequently produces a form of memory that is often used as a political resource for shaping the future. Through memory – through a shared understanding and remembrance of difficult points in the past – trauma can shape and define forms of political community.

Summary

This chapter has constituted the first step of my inquiry into the nature of trauma. It has argued that a crucial component of understanding the political dimensions of trauma is to recognize its paradoxical, dual nature. Yet I have also observed that perceivably solitary experiences of trauma can, at the same time, help to construct links between individuals. Key here is the inherent social and political nature of trauma: that trauma is inevitably experienced and can be passed on through the social context in which it occurs and is made meaningful. Through processes of telling and retelling, trauma can translate into a phenomenon that helps to constitute identities and cohere forms of political community. This investigation is of direct relevance to my more specific aim of examining the role emotions play in constructing communities after trauma. But in order to appreciate how the emotions and affects associated with trauma shape political perceptions and affiliations it has been necessary to first understand the communal connections that traumatic events can help to construct.

The first part of the chapter highlighted the dislocating and isolating dimensions of trauma. I have shown that trauma is largely considered an encounter so confronting that it defies comprehension and manifests an unparalleled sense of dread and fear. Whether it is experienced directly or witnessed at a distance, trauma unsettles commonly held assumptions about one's life and its meaning. Traumatic events prompt individuals to question their ability to control their own fate. In this way, trauma damages social relationships and fractures established forms of community. Feelings of detachment and isolation are considered common after major trauma.

The second half of the chapter addressed the seeming paradox that can ensue after experiences of trauma: as solitary as trauma may feel, traumatic events can also constitute forms of political community.

After trauma, feelings of uncertainty and isolation are often met with a push to restore or configure an empathetic or at least understanding community. Ways of communicating and more widely representing trauma become key. Telling of or otherwise expressing experiences of trauma provides a mechanism through which victims and witnesses can together reenact the traumatic experience. This takes place through the collective search to work through the trauma, and in doing so to reestablish and reconnect with a meaningful social and communal environment. As isolating as trauma may feel, therefore, trauma can also furnish a common bond between victims and a wider community that either bears witness immediately or belatedly, through testimony.

Significant here is that through communication individual experiences of trauma can be made meaningful to – and at least partially constitutive of – a wider community. This process can take place on an intimate scale. Or, following a far-reaching, widely publicized catastrophe, trauma can unite a much larger group of people as well. Indeed, I have shown that trauma can seep out, affecting entire societies and prompting a collective response that can be politically instrumental. Post-trauma communities can take shape after trauma almost automatically, through the need of victims and witnesses for consolation and understanding. Studies have shown that trauma can be employed through politics and the media in order to manipulate identity and reinstate forms of political community and sovereignty as well. However, both instances rely upon translating an essentially incomprehensible experience into comprehensible, meaningful stories. Such stories ground trauma in language or forms of expression that are common to a particular community. Trauma thereby attains a socially recognizable – and sometimes communally constitutive – meaning. For, indeed, it is the meaning trauma attains – rather than the "actual" experience itself – that helps to constitute forms of collective identity and political community.

2 *Theorizing political emotions*

The previous chapter presented the puzzle that is key to developing my conceptual framework. It demonstrated how trauma – as seemingly isolating as it is – can abet the construction or consolidation of forms of political community. The present chapter represents the second stage of my conceptual framework. It further probes the processes involved with constituting community after trauma through an examination of trauma's emotional dimensions, an aspect that remains relatively underappreciated by studies that seek to conceptualize the social and political significance of pivotal traumatic events.

Events known as "traumatic" leave a profound emotional legacy. They generate a complex range of painful emotions, which stem from the shock, disbelief, fear, terror, anger and even guilt, shame and humiliation that can be associated with extreme violence and catastrophe. So overwhelming are the emotions felt that victims and witnesses struggle to find speech that can match the feelings that are instilled. Yet, at the same time, emotional reactions to trauma are intertwined with both the processes of recovery and political restorations through which traumatized individuals reconnect with the social world. Victims and witnesses try to give "voice" to emotions and still more ephemeral affects when they speak of what they have endured. Political and media-based accounts of traumatic events similarly attempt, often through dramatic words and images, to capture the mass shock, terror and confusion. A wider social mode of thinking and feeling about trauma can consequently ensue. Communities may take shape or be reconstituted.

The task of this chapter, then, is to conceptualize how exactly emotions are involved in constituting communities after trauma. I argue that the key to this endeavor lies in theorizing how emotions are not private but social and thus collective phenomena. The crucial link that unites these two realms lies in an appreciation of the processes through which emotions both attain and shape shared social meanings, which are in turn fundamental to post-trauma forms of community. While I explore the complex and interwoven range of mechanisms that point to the social nature of emotion, I highlight one process that is central to the politics of, and linkages between, trauma and ensuing communities – the public expression of seemingly private emotions.

To attenuate these connections and further establish my respective conceptual framework, this chapter draws on a range of different bodies of literature that are not usually brought into dialogue with each other. For the most part these lie beyond the study of world politics, although an "affective" or "emotional turn" is increasingly entering disciplinary international relations as well. The literatures I survey lie predominantly in fields including anthropology, sociology, philosophy, feminist theory, cultural studies, history and political theory – all of which are also progressively incorporating neuroscientific developments made to theorizing affect and emotion into their own conceptualizations.

The chapter is structured as follows: the first section presents a case for why a consideration of emotions is central to understanding the intersection between personal and political encounters with trauma. It begins by discussing a problem that is intimately related trauma's emotional impact: the so-called inexpressibility that is often considered characteristic of trauma. I draw on literature that helps us to appreciate the difficulties associated with communicating the meaning of, and feelings associated with, traumatic experiences. I then focus more explicitly on the intensely emotional nature of trauma, discussing how the problems associated with expressing trauma are akin to the challenge of reckoning with, and giving voice to, emotion. In doing so, I highlight that an appreciation of the intensely emotional, inexpressible dimensions of trauma is central to trauma's political significance. It is because traumatic events challenge comprehension and defy emotional expression that they can become crucial sites of unconscious or conscious political appropriation. Emotions are thus, as such, one aspect through which traumatic events are "governed."[1]

This centrality of emotions gives cause to examine them more closely. The second half of the chapter therefore turns specifically to the task of theorizing the social and political nature of emotions. It argues that

[1] James Brassett and Nick Vaughan-Williams, "Governing Traumatic Events," *Alternatives: Global, Local, Political*, 37.3 (2012), 183–187.

we need to consider emotions as an important and pervasive – as well as both constituted and constitutive – component of society and politics. Following growing interdisciplinary research on human emotion, I demonstrate that purportedly "personal" elements of our lives are not innate psychobiological phenomena that arrive preformed in individuals. Neither are emotions individual phenomena that can be excavated when feelings seem to "get in the way." Instead, I show that emotions have a history and also, importantly, a future: they are derived, at least in part, from our inherently social and political existence. Emotions are an emergent component of the interwoven (or "hybrid") cognitive, affective and sensory mind–body "system" that allows individuals to navigate the social world and give it meaning.[2] They connect human beings to each other, attribute value and shade the lens through which we each view the world. Emotions are in this way endemic within the configurations of identity and belonging through which we constitute visions of our self and of others; they help to distinguish (and discipline) how and to whom individuals are attached. Emotions are, as such, a necessary, and, what is more, inextricable, part of all political thought and behavior. To underline this point, I end the chapter by further investigating the relationship between emotions and the communal bonds that can form or be reconstituted after widespread or publicly visible traumatic occurrences. I discuss how ties binding communities are not merely politically utilitarian or instrumental but infused with collective forms of meaning and feeling that can distinguish communities as "affective communities."

The challenge of expressing trauma

Literatures that examine the relationship between trauma and language suggest that when one's world is displaced or severely disrupted, as it is with trauma, individuals suffer a corresponding loss of words.[3] Words suddenly seem incapable of representing the physical

[2] See James A. Coan, "Emergent Ghosts of the Emotion Machine," *Emotion Review*, 2.3 (2010), 274–285; Rom Harré, "Emotions as Cognitive-Affective-Somatic Hybrids," *Emotion Review*, 1.4 (2009), 294–301; Renée Jeffery, "Reason, Emotion and the Problem of World Poverty: Moral Sentiment Theory and International Ethics," *International Theory*, 3.1 (2011), 143–178, at 144.

[3] For example, Cathy Caruth, *Unclaimed Experience: Trauma, Narrative, and History* (Baltimore: Johns Hopkins University Press, 1996), esp.

and emotional sensations that fill one's moments; speech seems unable to convey what trauma feels like and how it is experienced. One may speak and write of trauma yet words fail to adequately convey the perceptual intensity of feelings, either physical or emotional ones. According to Jenny Edkins, when we describe trauma "[t]here is always, inevitably, something that is missed out, something that cannot be symbolised."[4] Hence, even though victims and witnesses may speak or write of trauma, it is often thought to lack an appropriate language: "there is no [normal] language for it."[5]

The concept of "voice" clarifies the challenges of understanding trauma.[6] Lawrence Langer's study of Holocaust testimony suggests that survivors of major trauma can only speak of their experiences with "a form of verbal distance."[7] We can say "it felt like I died," that the shock and pain was "numbing," that it "ground into us, like a vice," or that to witness catastrophic events unfold felt like a "freak show." Yet, words fail to truly describe the shock and profound sense of confusion. It is as if the loss and grief associated with trauma is so great, while the language permitting us to express this, so small. At issue, therefore, is that trauma makes individuals acutely aware of the inadequacy of everyday language. Some even contend that trauma is by nature "voiceless," meaning that when individuals encounter extreme pain one's voice is simultaneously silenced.[8]

The voiceless dimensions of trauma can be linked to the experience of pain and the problem of pain's expression. Physical pain is, of course, not the only aspect of trauma, but it crystallizes the dilemmas involved. The influential work of Elaine Scarry shows why this is the case. She reveals how pain is inextricably involved in the "making"

pp. 1–9, 91–92; Roberta Culbertson, "Embodied Memory, Transcendence, and Telling: Recounting Trauma, Re-establishing the Self," *New Literary History*, 26.1 (1995), 169–195, esp. 173, 176, 178–180; Martha Minow, "Surviving Victim Talk," *UCLA Law Review*, 40 (1993), 1411–1445.

4 Jenny Edkins, *Trauma and the Memory of Politics* (Cambridge: Cambridge University Press, 2003), pp. 11–12.

5 Edkins, *Trauma and the Memory of Politics*, p. 7.

6 Caruth, *Unclaimed Experience*, pp. 1–10.

7 Lawrence L. Langer, "The Alarmed Vision: Social Suffering and Holocaust Atrocity," *Daedalus*, 125.1 (1996), 47–65, at 58.

8 Dori Laub, "September 11, 2001 – An Event Without a Voice," in Judith Greenberg (ed.), *Trauma at Home: After 9/11* (Lincoln and London: University of Nebraska, 2003), pp. 204–215; David B. Morris, "About Suffering: Voice, Genre, and Moral Community," *Daedalus*, 125.1 (1996), 25–45, at 27.

and "unmaking" of almost every cultural creation. Scarry traces this phenomenon to the relationship between pain and what she sees as the absence of a language able to adequately express it.[9] According to Scarry, "pain does not simply resist language but actively destroys it."[10] Pain "resists objectification in language," pushing us into the "deeper obscurity" of a "pre-language of cries and groans."[11] It resists embodiment through language because "the incontestable reality of the body – the body in pain ... makes all further statements and interpretations seem ludicrous and inappropriate."[12] As such, pain is thought to deprive individuals of one of the most precious of all human endowments: the ability to speak.

The vocabularies available for describing pain – either through medical language that codifies pain or the metaphors that create an illusion of likeness – seem equally inadequate in the face of prevailing feelings. Resorting to metaphorical descriptions, we may say that pain is "burning," "knifelike," "pinching," "pressing," "searing" or "throbbing," yet our words cannot encapsulate or authentically communicate the intensity of our feelings. Some scholars go further in arguing that the voice individuals eventually find for pain enables them not to better understand pain and how it has affected their world, but rather to move away from pain and to forget the uncertainty that it has prompted.[13]

These reflections on pain mirror the thoughts of many trauma scholars. Some even suggest that the challenge of expressing trauma is best reflected by a common response to it: silence. Several scholars note that by resisting language, trauma is at least initially overtaken by shocked and "unspeakable" seconds of silence. In the immediate

[9] Elaine Scarry, *The Body in Pain: The Making and Unmaking of the World* (New York: Oxford University Press, 1985).

[10] Scarry, *The Body in Pain*, p. 4.

[11] Scarry, *The Body in Pain*, pp. 5–6, 20.

[12] Scarry, *The Body in Pain*, pp. 60, 62.

[13] See Marni Jackson, *Pain: The Science and Culture of Why We Hurt* (London: Bloomsbury, 2003), pp. 1–10; David B. Morris, *The Culture of Pain* (Berkeley: University of California Press, 1993); Scarry, *The Body in Pain*, pp. 45–50, 66–72. In international relations, Alison Howell examines how the prevailing medicalization of trauma renders it susceptible to "medical and technical intervention" and in doing so obscures the politics that lies at the heart of such trauma in the first place. See Howell's excellent *Madness in International Relations: Psychology, Security, and the Global Governance of Mental Health* (London and New York: Routledge, 2011), p. 12.

aftermath of the September 11, 2001 attacks on the World Trade Center, for instance, David Eng observed that "hundreds, then thousands, of home-made posters of missing persons" were juxtaposed with an entire city, "utterly silent," muted by shock and the profundity of public expressions of loss and confusion.[14] Similarly, Edkins comments that "[o]ne of the most striking images ... was that of people in the sidewalks of New York, their hands clasped over the mouths, transfixed in horror as they watched the impossible turning into the real in front of their eyes."[15] "Those watching the collapse," she continues, were "speechless" before what was the unfathomable imagery flashing endlessly in front of their eyes.

Recognizing the difficulties involved with expressing pain raises questions concerning precisely how it is then that physically and emotionally painful events, such as trauma, can become a shared, social phenomenon. At first glance, the problem of pain's expression appears to close off painful experiences to others. Moreover, not only does the difficulty of adequately expressing pain seem to remove the hope that others can understand, but also it is indicative of the psychologically and emotionally puzzling aspects of pain: that painful experiences may be in some way beyond even our own knowing. Crucially, then, the silence of trauma would seem to be a sign that traumatic experiences are incomprehensible and unique; trauma is a phenomenon unable to be – yet necessarily – shared through words alone.

Trauma is an emotional experience that language can capture only partly. So how, then, can and do we make sense of it? What is "in" the moments of silence surrounding trauma? Is there something other than or beyond language, an "other of language," which words can only ever partially represent?[16] Words attain meanings from the social contexts in which they have been constituted. Yet, it is an understanding of social context that trauma seems to dislocate individuals from. Traumatic events exist outside the framework of normal social reality,

[14] David L. Eng, "The Value of Silence," *Theatre Journal*, 54.1 (2002), 85–94, at 85–86.

[15] Jenny Edkins, "Forget Trauma? Responses to September 11," *International Relations*, 16.2 (2002), 243–256, at 243–244.

[16] Or so suggests Julia Kristeva. Kristeva locates "other of language" in the psychic life of the human soul. See Julia Kristeva, *Desire in Language: A Semiotic Approach to Literature and Art* (New York: Columbia University Press, 1980) and "New Maladies of the Soul," in *The Portable Kristeva* (New York: Columbia University Press, 1997).

which means that when individuals endure trauma they are without the symbolic or linguistic tools ordinarily used to locate and share meaning. Language cannot measure the shattering of self that occurs with trauma, because traumatic encounters seem to have destroyed the very understanding that socially acquired patterns of language have themselves constituted.

The problem of expressing trauma alludes to the challenge of how one is to investigate the subsequent building of communal bonds. If traumatic events truly resist representation, it could be claimed that trauma is not only incomprehensible but also a phenomena unable to be shared. Therefore, if individuals can never truly adequately describe their own emotionally and physically felt pain, how is it that one's identity and community can be so powerfully shaped by another's encounter with catastrophe? And what does the challenge of representing the emotional impact of traumatic events say about trauma as a social experience?

Political trauma, political emotions

The problem of how to adequately express trauma can be at least partially attributed to the emotional nature of experiencing an event as harrowing and confronting as trauma. Traumatic experiences prompt an inevitably emotional response, commonly manifesting feelings of shock and of detachment from previously assured social bonds and structures.

Trauma is experienced not only physically but also psychologically, through emotions. Trauma is a sensory experience, associated with either actual tissue damage or with the feeling that such damage has either physically or metaphorically taken place. As feminist scholar Liz Philipose puts it, trauma is "an experience of a world unmade and undone."[17] Still more revealing, David Morgan contends that trauma is illuminated by "emotion and memory, by the anticipation of continuing distress, by anxiety, anger and resentment, by ominous fears and future hopes."[18] Indeed, trauma scholars suggest that the sense of loss that generally accompanies trauma has such a profound and visceral

[17] Liz Philipose, "The Politics of Pain and the End of Empire," *International Feminist Journal of Politics*, 9.1 (2007), 60–81, at 62.

[18] David Morgan, "Pain: The Unrelieved Condition of Modernity," *European Journal of Social Theory*, 5.3 (2002), 307–322, at 314.

effect that individuals cannot always comprehend what they have experienced or when it might end. Trauma can in this light be seen as a form of "psychic pain,"[19] an emotional pain touching intimate parts of one's self and being, a form of pain that is unrecognizable through the words searched for in order to express it.

The challenges of representing trauma are interwoven with the difficulties of linguistically expressing emotion. When speaking or writing of trauma, what victims and witnesses try to give "voice" to is how they feel, their emotions. When it is said that victims and witnesses are struggling to speak of their trauma, what is meant is that they are struggling to translate what has happened from a "missed" (yet all-consuming) experience to one that "fits," psychologically and emotionally.[20] Literary inquiries have even suggested that this is why some poets, such as Paul Celan, have attempted to "stretch" language. Poetics searches to strip everyday words and expressions of their familiar usage and meanings in order to create a medium through which trauma can speak.[21] Other scholars suggest that such efforts will still be to no avail. Holocaust scholar Dori Laub contends that telling stories of survival or of witnessing is inevitably constrained by the impossibility of ever adequately representing trauma. "No amount of telling," Laub maintains, "seems to do justice to inner compulsion ... There are never enough words or the right words, there is never enough time or the right time, and never enough listening to articulate the story that cannot be fully captured in thought, memory, and speech."[22] Neither written nor spoken words can sufficiently encapsulate the emotions that accompany trauma.

Although individuals and collectives who experience trauma do speak of it after, they ultimately speak of what can only be spoken incompletely: their emotions. In her memoir and study of children of Holocaust survivors, Ruth Wajnryb goes so far as to contend that the emotions associated with Jewish trauma seem to forever speak louder

[19] Jackson, *Pain*, p. 21.

[20] Caruth, *Unclaimed Experience*, pp. 60–63.

[21] See, for instance, Roland Bleiker, "'Give it the Shade?': Paul Celan and the Politics of Apolitical Poetry," *Political Studies*, 47.4 (1999), 661–676; Gail Jones, "Surviving a Bootprint," *The Australian Literary Review*, May 2, 2007, 24–25.

[22] Dori Laub, "Truth and Testimony: The Process and the Struggle," in Cathy Caruth (ed.), *Trauma: Exploration in Memory* (Baltimore: Johns Hopkins University Press, 1995), pp. 61–75, at p. 63.

than any concrete thoughts or words. For her, "[e]motion rather than language is etched in [my] memory." One respondent in her study even said, "I don't remember the words [of my parents' telling]. But I do remember the emotions."[23] Sexual assault survivors Susan Brison and Roberta Culbertson suggest that the struggle for words after trauma is synonymous with the hope that speech can free the parts of them that remain trapped by pain.[24] Yet, as words form, shaping emotions from the outside-in, giving social meaning to what is individually felt pain, survivors often say they then struggle to free what becomes trapped by language: the emotional dimensions of one's self that have been marked, inimitably, by their experiences.

It is here – in the intense difficulty yet paradoxical compulsion to recount trauma and articulate its emotions – that the emotional politics of trauma emerge. As victims and witnesses search to locate a language for what they have been through, they reach out to those around them, and, importantly, to the customary yet inevitably incomplete social practices (languages, bodily gestures, etc.) through which painful experiences are routinely understood. The emotional aftermath of trauma is in this way channeled – via recognized social codes, symbols and discourses – in ways through which similarly extreme events have been understood. Words used to express trauma are a crucial aspect. Through words, the emotions associated with trauma become (insufficiently) encoded within the culturally situated linguistic structures and metaphors that are believed to best give voice to the wounds victims and witnesses feel inside. Traumatic events are in this way emotionally enacted in ways that are inherently social and political. The languages used to describe trauma (and its emotions) become constitutive of it as an individual and also social experience.

For these reasons, the grieving processes that follow trauma are one prominent place where the social and political nature of traumatic emotions play out. Indeed, emotional processes of grief and mourning are central to reckoning with trauma.[25] Grief is part of the process

[23] Ruth Wajnryb, *The Silence: How Tragedy Shapes Talk* (Crows Nest, NSW: Allen and Unwin, 2001), p. 37.

[24] Susan J. Brison, *Aftermath: Violence and the Remaking of the Self* (Princeton: Princeton University Press, 2002), pp. 15–16, 26–35, 49–59; and Culbertson, "Embodied Memory, Transcendence, and Telling," 178–179.

[25] Brison, *Aftermath*, pp. 20–21, 73–77; Judith Lewis Herman, *Trauma and Recovery: From Domestic Abuse to Political Terror* (London: Basic Books,

whereby traumatized individuals mourn their injury and loss, and work through what has happened in a way that allows the respective experience to be integrated into their normal social life. But while frequently conceptualized as a personal, therapeutic process, there are distinctive elements that draw further attention to its social and political nature. In particular, studies of grief point to the idea that to grieve and mourn is to rekindle meaning, to orientate perceptions of trauma and loss in a way that enables one's normal life and social world to make sense again.[26] What individuals seek when they grieve is comfort and stability. It is a process of finding new meaning – or of transforming meaning – and establishing a world where the significance of one's pain and loss is accepted. Although others may never truly understand or feel pain and loss in the same way, the process of grieving establishes a public context where the private nature of trauma is ascribed social meaning and value.

Recognizing that post-trauma processes such as testimony and grief involve the public interplay with seemingly personal emotions is important as it points directly to the political nature of how we reckon with trauma. Emotions are bound up in the process of socializing oneself in the aftermath of what seems to be solitary, privatizing pain. They are key to both how trauma is experienced firsthand and to connecting individuals with the social world after. Emotions are, in this sense, part of how trauma is at once personally and socially "performed." Emotions inform the meanings ascribed to trauma and enable them to be socially understood and in turn individually (and collectively) enacted. This is how, in times of crisis, feelings can be the "glue" binding people together in the face of what may feel like isolating and seemingly inexpressible loss and pain. Even though only incompletely expressed, traumatic emotions prompt individuals to interpret and make trauma collectively meaningful.

But while central to trauma, the political roles emotions can play after collective traumatic, catastrophic events are yet to be fully appreciated. Much of trauma's social and political significance is situated in

1992), pp. 175–195; Graham Little, *The Public Emotions: From Mourning to Hope* (Sydney: Australian Broadcasting Commission, 1999), esp. pp. 81–94.

26 Robert A. Neimeyer, Holly G. Prigerson and Betty Davis, "Mourning and Meaning," *American Behavioral Scientist*, 46.2 (2002), 235–251, at 238–240; Clive Seale, *Constructing Death: The Sociology of Dying and Bereavement* (Cambridge: Cambridge University Press, 1998), p. 55.

the public expression of what is still frequently considered "private" emotion. Systematic explorations of emotions – and of precisely how emotions play a role constituting combined individual and collective ways of understanding trauma – are therefore needed. It is only by appreciating the social nature of human emotion that we can more fully understand how traumatic events can constitute or strengthen communal attachments.

In my ambition to establish a framework that can theoretically and empirically assess the linkages involved, I now draw upon a range of different literatures that have been largely developed in isolation from each other. But all of them have one ambition in common: to move away from the traditional prejudices that have long characterized Western approaches to conceptualizing emotion, namely that emotions are individualized sentiments that exist in opposition to reason. Studies from anthropology, sociology, psychology, philosophy, literary criticism and feminist theory have for long scrutinized such traditional understandings, and in doing so have problematized dichotomies such as mind/body, reason/passion. Examining a range of these rich and varied sources, the next section forwards a multidisciplinary approach to emotions, which is designed to enable us to conceive more precisely of their political nature and potentials. This is a broad and important theoretical task in and of itself. However, doing so is also necessary in so far that it further highlights precisely how it is that emotions lie at the center of research into trauma and community: investigating the political nature of emotion helps us to appreciate how traumatic events can pull people together, constituting communities and their politics in the face of the apparent isolation of suffering and pain.

The politics of emotion

To begin the task of theorizing the political nature of emotion, I turn to both historic and contemporary ideas about the sociality of emotion. Key here is to highlight the socioculturally constituted and discursive production of emotions: emotions are not inherently internal biological mechanisms that arrive preformed in individuals but are instead historically constituted and constitutive social, cultural and political phenomena. As the pioneering works of cultural anthropologists such as Michelle Rosaldo and Catherine Lutz tell us, "emotional meaning is fundamentally structured by particular cultural systems and particular social and material environments."[27] The ways we feel both attribute and are attributed meaning within a contextually bound "relational world."[28] Once we gain an understanding of the processes of socialization that attribute emotions with meaning (and can therefore also transform such meaning) a further crucial factor becomes central: the links between emotions and power. Conceiving of emotions as phenomena shaped at least in part by social and political circumstance means that emotions can be seen as forces enacted upon by prevailing forms of power: how we feel is part of how we present, constitute, legitimize and enact political views, values, attachments and even policies.[29] Power in this sense is not something possessed materially, but a type of power that is capable of creating and legitimizing meanings, identities and the linkages that bind them. It is the type of power that is imbued within the social processes that constitute "how actors are differently enabled and constrained to determine their fates."[30] Because emotions are constituted and enacted through these same social processes, power is, as I show, central to the constitution of emotional subjectivity.

To better appreciate the politics and sociality of emotion, I first review broader conceptions of emotionality and the intersections between emotions, society and politics. As the section progresses, I focus more closely on deepening understandings of how emotions – seemingly personal elements of individual lives – entail inherently social and political dimensions, which, I suggest, once fully appreciated allow us

[27] Catherine A. Lutz, *Unnatural Emotions: Everyday Sentiments on a Micronesian Atoll and Their Challenge to Western Theory* (Chicago: University of Chicago Press, 1988), p. 5. Also see Michelle Z. Rosaldo, *Knowledge and Passion: Ilongot Notions of Self and Social Life* (Cambridge: Cambridge University Press, 1980), esp. pp. 35–36, 54.

[28] K. M. Fierke, *Political Self-Sacrifice: Agency, Body and Emotion in International Relations* (Cambridge: Cambridge University Press, 2012), p. 92.

[29] Lila Abu-Lughod and Catherine A. Lutz, "Introduction: Emotion, Discourse, and the Politics of Everyday Life," in Catherine A. Lutz and Lila Abu-Lughod (eds.), *Language and the Politics of Emotion* (Cambridge: Cambridge University Press, 1990), pp. 13–14; Lutz, *Unnatural Emotions*, pp. 5–6; Maruška Svašek, "Introduction: Emotions in Anthropology," in Kay Milton and Maruška Svašek (eds.), *Mixed Emotions: Anthropological Studies in Feeling* (Oxford: Berg, 2005), pp. 8–10.

[30] Michael Barnett and Raymond Duvall, "Power in International Politics," *International Organization*, 59.1 (2005), 39–75, at 41.

to make sense of how emotions are implicated in the constitution of post-trauma communities in world politics.

Emotions in social research

Emotions are inescapable elements of being human. They exert an enormous influence in our lives. Conceiving of them broadly, emotions can be understood as highly complex and subjective dispositional inclinations characterized by a changed state of psychological, bodily and cognitive awareness. Such emotional "awareness" is essential to human being as it aids individuals to perceive, judge and make sense of the world by distinguishing memories and values with forms of feeling. Emotions enable individuals to navigate situations according to what they perceive really matters. They are, as Jon Elster writes, "the stuff of life": "... emotions matter because if we did not have them nothing else would matter."[31] Without them, we would literally function like robots, waiting to be programmed, and, even then, only mechanically and unfeelingly carrying out our actions.

But despite the pivotal place emotions occupy in human life, "emotions" have been intensely difficult to define.[32] They have been the intrigue of researchers for centuries. Much of the debate has emerged from differing conceptions of what emotions are and from where they emerge. Discussed in particular are the origin of emotions, how many emotions in effect exist, how bodily feelings and sensory affects "fit with" (precede or precipitate) emotions, and the relationship between emotion and cognition.[33] In the nineteenth century, for instance, William James famously defined emotion in terms of physical

[31] Jon Elster, *Alchemies of the Mind: Rationality and the Emotions* (Cambridge: Cambridge University Press, 1999), 403.

[32] See the Special Section, Carroll E. Izard, Maria Gendon, Anthony Landreth, Geoffrey White, Sherri C. Widen, James A. Russell, Anna Wierzbicka, and Peter Zachar, "On Defining Emotions," *Emotion Review*, 2.4 (2010), 363–385.

[33] For a snapshot into some of these debates, see, for example, Joseph E. Le Doux, "Emotion: Clues From the Brain," *Annual Review of Psychology*, 4 (1995), 209–235; Gerard L Clore. and Jeffrey R. Huntsinger, "How the Object of Affect Guides Its Impact," *Emotion Review*, 1.1 (2009), 39–54; Gerard R. Clore and Andrew Ortony, "Cognition in Emotion? Always, Sometimes, Or Never?" in Richard D. Lane and Lynn Nadel (eds.), *Cognitive Neuroscience of Emotion* (New York: Oxford University Press, 2000), pp. 24–61; Elizabeth A. Phelps, "Emotion and Cognition: Insights from Studies of the Human Amygdala," *Annual Review of Psychology*, 57 (2006), 27–53, at 46; Norbert Schwarz, "Emotion, Cognition and Decision Making," *Cognition and Emotion*, 14.4 (2000), 433–440.

stimulation.[34] Neo-Jamesians such as Antonio Damasio continue to distinguish between bodily arousal and the mental interpretation of such bodily feeling in the brain.[35] Cognitivist accounts, in contrast, problematize the body as the core of emotional experience and instead see emotions as mental events that enable evaluations and judgments.[36] Recent neuroscientific developments, however, now enable a way through the conflicts in these two accounts. Neuroscience is proving that emotions are in fact "neurosocial": emotions are increasingly seen to emerge circumstantially from an interwoven, indistinguishable mix of bodily, psychological and cognitive perceptual processes, all of which are, moreover, conditioned by socialization.[37]

Through the differing conceptions of what emotions are and how they function, there is one thing, however, that emotions theorists have never doubted: emotions are pervasive and endemic within our information (thought) processing. Emotions are not an optional extra that individuals can delve into to enrich daily experiences. They are an "obligate" part of the humanly "reasoning system."[38] Emotions both shape and are inevitable perceptual responses to external events and stimuli.

In the last two decades more and more social science-based scholars have turned to emotions in order to more fully understand social and political life. So prominent is the burgeoning emotions field that it has become commonplace to speak of an emotional or affective "turn."[39]

[34] William James, "What Is an Emotion?" *Mind*, 9 (1884), 188–205; William James, "The Physical Basis of Emotion," *Psychological Review*, 1.5 (1894), 516–529.

[35] Antonio Damasio, *The Feeling of What Happens: Body and Emotion in the Making of Meaning* (London: Vintage, 2000); Antonio Damasio, *Descartes' Error: Emotion, Reason and the Human Brain* (London: Vintage, 2006 [1994]).

[36] In philosophy, see Martha Nussbaum, *Upheavals of Thought: The Intelligence of Emotions* (Cambridge: Cambridge University Press, 2001); and Robert C. Solomon, *Not Passion's Slave: Emotions and Choice* (Oxford: Oxford University Press, 2003). In psychology, see Nico H. Frijda, *The Emotions* (Cambridge: Cambridge University Press, 1986).

[37] For example, Jaak Panksepp, *Affective Neuroscience: The Foundations of Human and Animal Emotions* (Oxford: Oxford University Press, 1998); Jesse J. Prinz, *Gut Reactions: A Perceptual Theory of Emotion* (Oxford: Oxford University Press, 2004).

[38] Damasio, *Descartes' Error*, preface.

[39] For instance, Patricia Ticineto Clough (ed.), with Jean Halley, *The Affective Turn: Theorizing the Social* (Durham: Duke University Press, 2007); Forum

A key premise underlying political-based inquiries draws upon the evaluative nature of emotions.[40] Emotions are perceived to play a role in society and politics precisely because it is at least in part through emotions that individuals interpret past experiences and evaluate current ones.[41] To put it differently, emotions are seen as part of the perceptive processes that allow individuals and collectives to make sense of political issues and phenomena around them. They are like "an unseen lens that colours all our thoughts, actions, perceptions, and judgments."[42] Emotions permeate all aspects of society and politics.

Historically, however, the social and political significance of emotions has been far from assured. Emotions were seldom a celebrated component of political analysis. Long considered sporadic, unpredictable and individually felt phenomena, emotions have been traditionally considered too fleeting, too ephemeral, and too capricious to be a positive political influence. A dominant view in social science has been that emotions are best kept private. This line of thinking emerged from strands of Western political philosophy that sought to decouple emotion and rationality.[43] Political liberalism, too, subordinated emotions both because of its separation of public and private and its refusal to incorporate the sacred into its institutions. Emotions were thought not be forms of contemplation, thinking, reason and judgment. And, indeed, in everyday speech as much as historically in political analysis, emotions are often seen as the very opposite of reason: "Don't get emotional," people commonly say, "be reasonable."[44] Justice is seen as having to be free of passion because it is that very passion that impels

section on "The Emotional Turn," *Millennium: Journal of International Studies*, 39.1 (2010), 89–144.

40 Historically, the cognitivist tradition has been particularly influential as it has been instrumental in changing perceptions of emotions as something less than cognitively formed rationality. Increasingly, however, scholars are questioning the intersection between mind and body in the formation of emotions, hence the burgeoning interest in what is seen as nonconscious yet also pervasive bodily affect.

41 George E. Marcus, "Emotions in Politics," *Annual Review of Political Science*, 3 (2000), 221–250, at 221.

42 Goodwin, Jasper and Polletta, "Introduction: Why Emotions Matter," p. 10.

43 See Elster, *Alchemies of the Mind*, pp. 287–298, 386–387; Solomon, *Not Passion's Slave*, pp. 33–41.

44 Jonathon Mercer, "Approaching Emotion in International Politics," paper presented at the International Studies Association Conference, San Diego, CA, April 25, 1996, p. 3.

people to perform supposedly "irrational" acts of violence and harm. Barry Hoffmaster shows how the very use of contemporary metaphor reflects a moral reticence toward emotion: guilt "infects" us, fear "paralyses" us, shame "sweeps over" us, we are "struck" by jealousy and "blinded" by both love and hate.[45] It is not surprising, then, that social scientists have generally portrayed humans (as well as individual and collective decision making) as rational, technical and instrumental, characteristics that are oddly assumed to preclude emotion.

In recent years this restrictive understanding of the relationship between reason and emotion has been significantly challenged. Emotions are now seen to matter. Scholars increasingly explore the roles emotions play in social life, including in politics and ethics.[46] Feminist theorists have played a particularly pioneering role. They have for long stressed the need for social science to enrich the scope of behavioral and sociological understanding. Part of this engagement is a refusal to accept a strict separation between mind and body, reason and emotion.[47] Other bodies of literature have since paralleled or followed this trend.[48] As a consequence, emotions are no longer demonized and reason is no longer seen as unemotional, nor is political choice considered free of feeling.

Add to the growing cross-disciplinary literature on emotion is also an increasingly nuanced conception of what emotions are and how they function. In particular, numerous scholars have shifted their focus from examining "emotions" per se to debate the significance of, as well

[45] Barry Hoffmaster, "Fear of Feeling," *The Hastings Center Report*, 33 (2003), 45.

[46] The work of philosopher Martha Nussbaum has been at the forefront in illuminating the public, political and ethical components of emotions. See in particular her *Upheavals of Thought*. A recent compelling contribution in international ethics is Renée Jeffery, *Reason and Emotion in International Ethics* (Cambridge: Cambridge University Press, 2014).

[47] See, for instance, Susan R. Bordo, *Unbearable Weight: Feminism, Western Culture, and the Body* (Berkeley: University of California Press, 1994); Alison M. Jaggar, "Love and Knowledge: Emotion in Feminist Epistemology," in Susan R. Bordo and Alison M. Jaggar (eds.), *Gender/Body/Knowledge: Feminist Reconstructions of Being and Knowing* (New Brunswick, NJ: Rutgers University Press, 1989), pp. 145–171.

[48] Debates on emotion and affect are now waged extensively in a range of disciplines, such as within anthropology, sociology, political geography, cultural studies, history and psychology. I continue by surveying some of the most prominent of these contributions and trends.

as the linkages and phenomenological distinctions between, emotion, affect and feeling. In some disciplines, disputes regarding the respective phenomena are meanwhile so established that they each constitute distinct fields of inquiry.[49] Emerging literatures employ other terms too, including "the passions"[50] – classically drawn from philosophy – intuition, and even "alief."[51] Distinguishing between these phenomena is important, however; at the outset I underline a point that is essential and common across the field: emotions inevitably help to shape ways of seeing, perceiving and understanding, and can as such anchor the behaviors and attitudes from which political affiliations and decisions emerge. Emotions draw connections between thoughts, actions, the past and the present.[52] They are a part of how political attitudes and beliefs are constituted.[53]

Over the past decade research on emotions in politics and international relations has undergone a similar transformation.[54] Scholars

[49] As is the case, for instance, in "emotional geography" versus "affective geography." See, for example, Deborah Thein, "After or Beyond Feeling? A Consideration of Affect and Emotion in Geography," *Area*, 37.4 (2005), 450–456; Nigel Thrift, "Intensities of Feeling: Towards a Spatial Politics of Affect," *Geogrfiska Annaler: Series B*, 86.1 (2004), 57–78.

[50] Neta C. Crawford, "Institutionalizing Passion in World Politics: Fear and Empathy,"*International Theory*, 6.3 (2014), 535–557; Neta C. Crawford, "The Passion of World Politics: Propositions of Emotion and Emotional Relationships," *International Security*, 24.4 (2000), 116–157. On the historical creation and shift from the passions to the emotions, see Thomas Dixon, *From Passions to Emotions: The Creation of a Secular Psychological Category* (Cambridge: Cambridge University Press, 2003).

[51] Marcus Holmes, "Believing This and Alieving That: Theorizing Affect and Intuitions in International Politics," *International Studies Quarterly*, 59.4 (2015), 706–720.

[52] Kay Milton, "Afterword," in Milton and Svašek (eds.), *Mixed Emotions*, p. 216.

[53] Nico H. Frijda, Antony S. R. Manstead and Sacha Bem, "The Influence of Emotions on Beliefs," in Nico H. Frijda, Antony S. R. Manstead and Sacha Bem (eds.), *Emotions and Beliefs: How Feelings Influence Thoughts* (Cambridge: Cambridge University Press, 2000), pp. 1–9; and Marcus, "Emotions in Politics" 225–227. Jonathan Mercer goes further in arguing that some emotions can constitute beliefs when a "belief's meaning changes without emotion." For instance, as he puts it, "Emotion is not just an addition to a belief about trust, nationalism, or justice: it is essential to those beliefs." See Jonathan Mercer, "Emotional Beliefs," *International Organization*, 64.1 (2010), 1–31, at 6, 7.

[54] Here, and in passages that follow, I draw upon a recent essay coauthored with Roland Bleiker. See Emma Hutchison and Roland Bleiker, "Theorizing Emotions in World Politics," *International Theory*, 6.3 (2014), 491–514.

from a range of theoretical perspectives now look to emotion to enhance global political understanding.[55] But while many important contributions have been made there is still considerable debate and disagreement concerning exactly how to conceptualize – and then systematically analyze – the political roles of emotions. Much of this discord emerges from the perceived challenges involved with theorizing and also methodologically accounting for the public, collective and political dimension of emotions. Even while recognized as politically important, at both the individual and collective level emotions retain their place as one of the least measurable aspects of human experience, at least in an analytical sense. Systematic investigations of a phenomenon as ephemeral and as shifting as emotions are thus perceived to pose significant analytical challenges, making credible research appear speculative or tenuous at best. Even poststructuralist toolkits that have vastly expanded the scope of politics research methods – in terms of

[55] There are now numerous journal articles as well a growing number of journal forum sections and monographs that either theorize emotion as part of their analysis or, in some cases, locate emotions as the central object of political analysis. In disciplinary international relations alone, some of the most prominent contributions include: Linda Åhäll and Thomas A. Gregory (eds.), "Intervention on 'Security, Emotions, Affect,'" *Critical Studies on Security*, 1.1 (2013), 117–141; Roland Bleiker and Emma Hutchison (eds.), "Forum on 'Emotions in World Politics,'" *International Theory*, 6.3 (2014), 491–594; Roland Bleiker and Emma Hutchison, "Fear No More: Emotions and World Politics," *Review of International Studies*, 34.S1 (2008), 115–135; Crawford, "The Passion of World Politics"; Khaled Fattah and K. M. Fierke, "A Clash of Emotions: The Politics of Humiliation and Political Violence in the Middle East," *European Journal of International Relations*, 15.1 (2009), 67–93; Fierke, *Political Self-Sacrifice*; Todd H. Hall, "We Will Not Swallow This Bitter Fruit: Theorizing a Diplomacy of Anger," *Security Studies*, 20.4 (2011), 521–555; Simon Koschut, "Emotional (Security) Communities: The Significance of Emotion Norms in Inter-Allied Conflict Management," *Review of International Studies*, 40.3 (2014), 533–558; Richard Ned Lebow, "Reason, Emotion and Cooperation," *International Politics*, 42 (2005), 283–313; Janice Bially Mattern, "A Practice Theory of Emotion for International Relations," in Emanuel Adler (ed.), *International Practices* (Cambridge: Cambridge University Press, 2011); Mercer, "Emotional Beliefs"; Andrew A. G. Ross, *Mixed Emotions: Beyond Fear and Hate in International Conflict* (Chicago: Chicago University Press, 2014); Andrew A. G. Ross, "Coming in from the Cold: Constructivism and Emotions," *European Journal of International Relations*, 12.2 (2006), 197–222; Brent Sasley, "Theorizing States' Emotions," *International Studies Review*, 13.3 (2011), 453–476; Ty Solomon, "The Affective Underpinnings of Soft Power," *European Journal of International Relations*, 20.3 (2014), 720–741.

narratives, social symbols, discourses and frames – have provided relatively little explicit guidance that helps us to grapple with the social and political dimensions of feelings.[56] Emotions may be a pervasive element of human life, but precisely how they play a part in constituting everyday social attachments and can set in motion a range of political interactions and movements is an area that traditional social science appears to be without tools to systemically examine. Methodological barriers have persisted.

Conceptualizing collective, political emotions

There are, however, many scholarly traditions and academic disciplines that scholars can look to for insight into how to best conceptualize and methodologically evaluate the collective, political roles of emotion. Inquiries in anthropology, philosophy, sociology, historical and cultural studies, and feminist theory are among some of the most promising places to start. These studies largely take an interdisciplinary approach to theorizing the exact character of emotions as well as the place they retain in society and politics. The most compelling inquiries additionally tend to combine these two objectives. They focus on the sociocultural, discursive production of emotion, and thereby situate the processes through which emotions are at once individual yet also inherently public, social, collective and political at their core.

Constitutive or social constructivist approaches to understanding emotions have been among some of the earliest to take the role of emotions in society seriously. They provide a starting place to think about how personal intimacies such as emotions intersect with the wider social or public sphere. Ranging predominantly from disciplines such as sociology, philosophy and history, this approach focuses on the sociocultural construction of emotions and suggests that ways of

[56] However, for examples of contributions in this direction, see Jack Holland and Ty Solomon, "Affect is What States Make of It: Articulating Everyday Experiences of 9/11," *Critical Studies on Security* 2.3 (2014), 262–277; Matthew Coen Leep, "The Affective Production of Others: United States Policy Towards the Israeli–Palestinian Conflict," *Cooperation and Conflict*, 45.3 (2010), 331–352; Oded Löwenheim and Gadi Heimann, "Revenge in International Politics," *Security Studies*, 17.4 (2008), 685–724; Matthew Norton, "Narrative Structure and Emotional Mobilization in Humanitarian Representations: The Case of the Congo Reform Movement," *Journal of Human Rights*, 10.3 (2011), 311–338.

feeling cannot be separated from social context.[57] Put differently, emotions are formed (at least in part) from the society in which they are made. They are constituted by people and objects that fill the world around each of us and, more specifically, by the existential and social attachments that are formed in relation to them.

Constitutive perspectives thus clearly reject the traditional Cartesian division between self and society. Human beings, such an approach maintains, are "social selves"[58] and emotions are an inescapable component of our inherently social development. Not biologically grounded, as it was once thought, emotions are phenomena shaped by sociocultural interaction. The ways we feel emerge from and are constitutive of the social and institutional structures and processes that bind society together. This suggests an understanding of emotions as derived from a social context rather than from internal states alone. Yes, particular experiences evoke particular emotions, which seem to be "inside" of oneself. But these emotions are not presocial psychological states already formed in individuals, waiting to be activated.[59] Rather, emotional responses are shaped through patterns of communication, language and social interaction, and, more broadly, through socialization into particular historically grounded ways of being.[60] In this way, as Ian Burkitt suggests, "[f]eelings

57 See, for example, Jack M. Barbalet (ed.) *Emotions and Sociology* (Oxford: Blackwell, 2002); J. M. Barbalet, *Emotion, Social Theory and Social Structure: A Macrosociological Approach* (Cambridge: Cambridge University Press, 2001); Gillian Bendelow and Simon J. Williams (eds.), *Emotions and Social Life: Critical Themes and Contemporary Issues* (London: Routledge, 1998); Rom Harré (ed.), *The Social Construction of Emotions* (Oxford: Blackwell, 1986); Deborah Lupton, *The Emotional Self: A Sociocultural Exploration* (London: Sage, 1998); Thomas J. Scheff, *Microsociology: Discourse, Emotion and Social Structure* (Chicago: Chicago University Press, 1990).

58 Ian Burkitt, *Social Selves: Theories of the Social Formation of Personality* (London: Sage, 1991).

59 The idea that emotions are already always present in individuals, and waiting to be activated in response to particular stimuli, is a position forwarded by "latent" variable models of emotional processing. See Coan, "The Emergent Ghosts of the Emotion Machine," 276–278; James A. Coan, "What We Talk About When We Talk About Emotion," *Emotion Review*, 2.3 (2010), 292–293.

60 See Arlie Russell Hochschild, "Emotion Work, Feeling Rules and Social Structure," *American Journal of Sociology*, 85.3 (1979), 551–575; Nussbaum, *Upheavals of Thought*, pp. 107–109, 175–181; William M. Reddy, *The Navigation of Feeling: A Framework for the History of Emotions* (Cambridge: Cambridge University Press, 2001); Barbara H. Rosenwein, "Worrying About Emotions in History," *The American Historical Review*, 107.3 (2002), 821–845; Peter N. Stearns and Carol Z. Stearns, "Emotionology: Clarifying

say more about the type of social relations in which we live ... than anything about our essential nature as human beings."[61] They emerge from a person's instantaneous evaluation of circumstance, and at the same time reflect historically grounded ways of understanding and being in the world. A kind of cyclical or contingent relationship is implied here, in so far that as social relations or circumstances change so too may emotions, even as slow and gradual a process as such transformation may be. Indeed, emotions, like thoughts, customs and norms, can be said to undergo historical change precisely because they are subject to, and constituted through, the forces of society and culture. It can be understood therefore, as Sara Ahmed appreciates, that "emotions are not 'in' either the individual or the social, but produce the very surfaces and boundaries that allow the individual and the social to be delineated."[62] Through a socially constitutive lens, emotions are situated not only at the core of oneself, but also, and crucially, in the social context within which the self is embedded.

How particular emotions are produced therefore emanates from social expectations as much as from individual personalities. Indeed, one's cognitive assessment of circumstances is partially contingent upon on how emotions and thought processes come to constitute and reinforce each other through historical conditioning. In this way, constitutive approaches highlight not only the pervasive nature of emotions, but also that supposedly "personal" elements of human lives are shaped by and acted upon within our inherently social and political existence.

A constitutive understanding of emotions therefore rejects the traditional dichotomy of rational/irrational and dismisses the connotations that this duality ordinarily imposes on the social significance of emotion.[63] Historically, the strength of the duality between rationality and emotions lay in conventional views that separated processes of emotion and cognition.[64] And even though it has not been until recently that neuroscience has shown emotion and cognition to be

the History of Emotions and Emotional Standards," *American Historical Review*, 90.4 (1985), 813–836.

61 Burkitt, *Social Selves*, p. 2, and see also pp. 200–203.

62 Ahmed, *The Cultural Politics of Emotion*, p. 10.

63 See also Martha C. Nussbaum, "Rational Emotions," in *Poetic Justice: The Literary Imagination and Public Life* (Boston: Beacon, 1995), pp. 53–78.

64 Jeffery, *Reason and Emotion in International Ethics*, pp. 160–161.

interwoven, constitutive approaches long stressed the need to consider the emotional as intrinsic within what social and political analysts have called "rational" decision making or action. Rationality always includes emotion, just as thinking always includes feeling. Hence, the very idea of rationality as unemotional is a chimera. Like other aspects of culture, emotions can be seen as a pervasive element of human being and of social life. Because our thought processes are trained and inescapably informed through ways of feeling, emotions must be seen to accompany so-called rational actions as much as "irrational" or "nonrational" ones.

Discursive approaches highlight different aspects of the same processes. Anthropologists such as Lila Abu-Lughod, Catherine Lutz and Michelle Rosaldo argued early on that emotional meanings are structured by social systems and cultural life.[65] Such an approach emphasizes the key role of language and other forms of communication as sites through which emotions are constituted, embodied and experienced.[66] Identities and the feelings that constitute and bind one's sense of self are constructed through culturally specific patterns of interaction. Emotions are seen to function as discursive practices in so far that emotions are experienced (and embodied) in ways that are productive and constitutive of the social environments in which they emerge. The result is, then, "a less monolithic concept of emotion,"[67] a conception of emotions as denaturalized, cultural phenomena that shift and change through space and time.

Perceiving of emotions as both constituted through and in part constitutive of discourse, discursive approaches moreover focus on how emotions reflect and constitute power relations.[68] Drawing

[65] For an early review of contributions from anthropology, see Catherine Lutz and Geoffrey M. White, "The Anthropology of Emotions," *Annual Review of Anthropology*, 15 (1986), 405–436.

[66] For example, Lutz and Abu-Lughod (eds.), *Language and the Politics of Emotion*; Milton and Svašek (eds.), *Mixed Emotions*.

[67] Abu-Lughod and Lutz, "Introduction," p. 2.

[68] See note 29 in this chapter, as well as, Catherine A. Lutz, "Engendered Emotion: Gender, Power, and the Rhetoric of Emotional Control in American Discourse," in Rom Harré and W. Gerrod Parrot (eds.), *The Emotions: Social, Cultural and Biological Dimensions* (London: Sage, 1996); Jennifer Harding and E. Deidre Pribram, "The Power of Feeling: Locating Emotions in Culture," *European Journal of Cultural Studies*, 5.4 (2002), 407–426, at 413–415; Jonathan G. Heaney, "Emotions and Power: Reconciling Conceptual Twins," *Journal of Political Power*, 4.2 (2011), 259–277.

from Foucault, Abu-Lughod and Lutz suggest that since emotions are socially and culturally embedded, and since power is an inevitable part of the social processes that confound all cultural interactions, power relations are integral to emotions. It is power – and forms of domination and resistance – that informs acceptable modes of emotionality. Power shapes what can or should be said when it comes to the nature of individuals' feelings. Significant here is that what people feel, or indeed what they think they should feel emotionally, is generated over time through social, cultural and political encounters. Conversely, how people then "manage" their emotions in their everyday life is in turn thought to reflect an array of cultural norms, public values, perceived commitments and acceptable practices.[69] Others too demonstrate how culturally specific discourses of emotion and various social practices are mutually (and thus discursively) constituted.[70] Some scholars have even argued that how we each express our emotions – our "emotional liberty"[71] – is regulated through a kind of "emotional regime." Such a regime – sometimes strict, sometimes more relaxed – ultimately sets up accepted ways of feeling and emotionally responding to particular occurrences.[72]

A distinctly different take on the politics of emotions is offered by scholars who continue to view emotions more exclusively as forms of cognition. Recent work in philosophy and ethics suggests that emotions can act as an indicator of wider public or social value. Martha Nussbaum and Robert Solomon are two proponents of this view. They suggest that emotions can be seen to tell us things. "Emotions are not irrational pushes and pulls," Nussbaum argues. "They are ways of viewing the world. They reside at the core of one's being, the part of it

[69] Hochschild's work on "feeling rules," which in her conception govern both the intensity and display of emotions, remains the classic text examining the contextually bound development and management of emotions. See Arlie Russell Hochschild, *The Managed Heart: The Commercialization of Human Feeling* (Berkeley: University of California Press, 1983). A helpful overview can also be found in Jonathan H. Turner and Jan E. Stets, *The Sociology of Emotions* (Cambridge: Cambridge University Press, 2005), pp. 36–42.

[70] For example, Milton and Svašek (eds.), *Mixed Emotions*; Scheff, *Microsociology*; Thomas J. Scheff and Suzanne M. Retzinger, *Emotions and Violence: Shame and Rage in Destructive Conflicts* (Lanham: Lexington Press, 1991).

[71] William M. Reddy, "Emotional Liberty: Politics and History in the Anthropology of Emotions," *Cultural Anthropology*, 14.2 (1999), 256–288.

[72] Reddy, *The Navigation of Feeling*, p. 129; Reddy, "Emotional Liberty," p. 271–275.

with which one makes sense of the world."[73] Therefore for Nussbaum and Solomon the strength of emotions lies in that they are, at minimum, perceptions. An emotion is a perceptive activity reflective of a "kind of knowing"; emotions are a "piece of understanding."[74] Understood in this way, emotions are again recognized not as sources of softness or as indicative of an incontrovertible irrationality, but are instead seen to be intelligent and discriminating features of selfhood and of one's social world. Key here is that emotions either involve, or indeed simply are, judgments. Emotions are always about something, or are directed at something for specific reasons. Anger implies that something thought to be bad or wrong has happened, fear can be attributed to the feeling that something untoward may happen, and similarly, joy and happiness imply something good. Emotions are elements of appraisal. They are formed through interaction and involvement (or a lack of) with the social world, and are at least partly emblematic of the way individuals and collectives apprehend or perceive the world.

The processes involved with emotional cognition are, however, not undisputed. Nor are approaches that appreciate the constitutive and discursive production of emotions. Some scholars fear that such positions fate us with a persistent, intractable relativism. Stressing the nonessentialist characteristics of emotions erases the very subjective nature that opens emotions up to historical change.[75] Others worry that extant approaches tend to exaggerate the uniformity of emotion within different societies and cultures. They stress, in turn, that the centrality of the body and embodiment must not be forgotten.[76]

[73] Martha C. Nussbaum, "Emotions and Women's Capabilities," in Jonathon Glover and Martha C. Nussbaum (eds.), *Women, Culture, and Development* (New York: Oxford University Press, 1995), pp. 360–395, p. 374.

[74] Martha C. Nussbaum, *Loves Knowledge: Essays on Philosophy and Literature* (New York: Oxford University Press, 1990), p. 45. For the work of Robert C. Solomon, see his *Not Passion's Slave*; *The Joy of Philosophy: Thinking Thin Versus the Passionate Life* (Oxford: Oxford University Press, 2003); *The Passions: Emotions and the Meaning of Life*, 2nd edition (Indianapolis: Hackett, 1993).

[75] William M. Reddy, "Against Constructionism: The Historical Ethnography of Emotions," *Current Anthropology*, 38.3 (1997), 327–351, at 327–330.

[76] Examples within disciplines such as anthropology and sociology include: Ian Burkitt, "Social Relationships and Emotions," *Sociology*, 31.1 (1997), 37–55, esp. 42–48; Margaret Lock, "Cultivating the Body: Anthropology and Epistemologies of Bodily Practice and Knowledge," *Annual Review of Anthropology*, 22 (1993), 133–155; Margot L. Lyon, "Missing Emotion: The Limitations of Cultural Constructivism in the Study of Emotion," *Cultural*

For, indeed, emotions cannot be understood without theorizing how emotions are intrinsically linked to bodies. Early anthropology work has again been at the forefront in conceptualizing the significance of the body. They stress that emotions are "*embodied* thoughts."[77] In this view, emotions emerge from feelings that are felt somatically, within the physical body; emotions are seen to arise from a synthesis of bodily experiences, even though, that is, the meanings attached to the respective emotions are culturally determined. Yet, it is because of the former that individual, bodily experiences are afforded precedence when it comes to appreciating the processes that generate forms of feeling, emotion and affect. The body, in other words, is where emotions begin. International relations and political psychology scholar Rose McDermott puts this position simply. For her, a focus on physicality is essential, for "emotion must necessarily be grounded in somatic experience in the physical body or it would not exist at all."[78] However, many scholars who focus on embodiment still argue the body and bodily experiences cannot be divorced from wider social processes. "Feelings are not substances to be discovered in our blood but social practices organized by stories we both enact and tell," Rosaldo reminds us.[79] Emotions are the physical embodiment of wider social discourses, and as such reflect how individuals and collectives engage with and enact the social and political world.[80] It is in this way, as Margot Lyon contends, that "[e]motion thus has a complex mediating role: it is implicate in social and bodily relations and, as product of structured social relations, it is therefore foundational in the creation of society."[81]

Anthropology, 10.2 (1995), 244–263; Margot L. Lyon, "The Material Body, Social Processes and Emotion: 'Techniques of the Body' Revisited," *Body & Society*, 3.1 (1997), 83–101; Simon J. Williams and Gillian A. Bendelow, "The 'Emotional' Body," *Body & Society*, 2 (1996), 125–139.

77 Michelle Rosaldo,"Toward an Anthropology of Self and Feeling," in Richard A. Shweder and Robert A. LeVine (eds.), *Culture Theory: Essays on Mind, Self, and Emotion* (Cambridge: Cambridge University Press, 1984), p. 143. Emphasis in original.

78 Rose McDermott, "The Body Doesn't Lie: A Somatic Approach to the Study of Emotion in World Politics," *International Theory*, 6.3 (2014), 557–562, at 560.

79 Rosaldo, "Toward an Anthropology of Self and Feeling," p. 143.

80 Abu-Lughod and Lutz, "Introduction," p. 13; Hochschild, "Emotion Work, Feeling Rules, and Social Structure," 561–566.

81 Margot L. Lyon, "Emotion and Embodiment," in Alexander Laban Hinton (ed.), *Biocultural Approaches to Emotion* (Cambridge: Cambridge University Press, 1999), pp. 182–212, at pp. 182–183.

This is why it is imperative that political theorizations position emotions within the human body while, at the same time, recognize that emotions are far from innate or "natural." What people feel physiologically as emotions in the product of social and cultural encounters and of how individuals have been socialized into managing their emotions through and within such encounters.

A further emerging body of literature is helpful in theorizing a way around an implicit prioritization of either the body or the mind: the turn to emotions as practices. This literature conceives of emotions as practices that are performed within *both* the mind and the body.[82] To be clear, the term "practices" is, in this sense, essentially an abbreviated way of saying "how we do things," or, "how we do the things we do" – the gestures, habits, rituals and everyday pastimes that fill our days and provide purpose and meaning. "Emotional practices," then, refers to how the very act of being human and doing the various things we do necessarily imply expressive (affective) states through which individuals find such meaning. Practice theorists therefore concur with earlier emotions work that has argued emotions are an inextricable part of cognition. However, they, like some work in anthropology, go further to suggest that cognition exists not just in the mind but also in the body. Cognition is itself always "embodied," and "grounded," meaning that bodily manifestations are tied to the mind, and vice versa.[83] Monique Scheer explains this when she writes that "[t]he socially and environmentally contextualized body thinks along with the brain."[84] From this point of view, it is, moreover, through such practices that individuals as subjects (and agents) are constituted; individuals are a product of the emotional practices they strive for and enact everyday.

Once again, this is not to claim that bodies possess innate emotions. It actually means the opposite. For practice theorists, emotions are seen to be socially and culturally situated bodily performances. Emotions are physical enactments of culturally predisposed forms of feeling. In international relations, Janice Bially Mattern has forwarded a compelling argument for conceiving of emotions as practices. She

[82] Bially Mattern, "A Practice Theory of Emotion for International Relations," p. 76.

[83] Monique Scheer, "Are Emotions a Kind of Practice?" *History and Theory*, 51 (2012), 193–220; Lawrence W. Barsalou, "Grounded Cognition," *Annual Review of Psychology*, 59 (2008), 617–645.

[84] Scheer, "Are Emotions a Kind of Practice?" 197.

argues that emotions are capabilities – practices – that bodies acquire through the contextually bound (and analytically indistinguishable) interplay of biological and social forces.[85] Drawing on Bially Mattern, K. M. Fierke likewise purports such a conception of emotions, suggesting that scholars understand "emotions as competent, socially meaningful bodily performances that generate human being or human doing."[86] Consequently for both Bially Mattern and Fierke, the way that politics is emotionally performed through practices offers inroads to potentially analyze the significance of emotions in particular circumstances.

The relationship between emotion and the body are additionally often highlighted in order to draw attention to the significance and differences between emotion and affect. Whereas emotions are often seen to be the conscious manifestation of bodily feelings, affective dynamics are often perceived to lie outside of representation.[87] To speak of affect is thus to perceive of a wide range of nonreflective and subconscious sensations enacted through a range of bodily changes and practices, such as mood, intuition, temperament and disposition.[88] Affective dynamics are, then, viewed as much broader phenomena that exist both before and beyond consciousness. Considering these differences it is not surprising that debates on emotion versus affect are lengthy, traversing many scholarly

[85] Bially Mattern, "A Practice Theory of Emotion for International Relations," p. 66, 76.

[86] Fierke, *Political Self-Sacrifice*, p. 93.

[87] Lisa Blackman and Couze Venn (eds.), Special Issue on "Affect," *Body & Society*, p. 16.7 (2010); Brian Massumi, *Parables for the Virtual: Movement, Affect, Sensation* (Durham, NC: Duke University Press, 2002); Eve Kosofsky Sedgwick, *Touching Feeling: Affect, Pedagogy, Performativity* (Durham: Duke University Press, 2003); Thrift, "Intensities of Feeling"; Nigel Thrift, *Non-Representational Theory: Space, Politics, Affect* (London: Routledge, 2008).

[88] International relations scholarship that theorizes these phenomena as affective states includes: Lucile Eznack, "The Mood Was Grave: Affective Dispositions and States' Anger-Related Behaviour," *Contemporary Security Policy*, 34.3 (2013), 552–580; Holmes, "Believing This and Alieving That"; Ross, "Coming in from the Cold"; Brent E. Sasley, "Affective Attachments and Foreign Policy: Israel and the 1993 Oslo Accords," *European Journal of International Relations*, 16.4 (2010), 687–709. Janice Bially Mattern also argues a shift from emotion to affect may better capture the combined nonconscious bodily and also more conscious, cognitive aspects of emotional experience in her piece "On Being Convinced: An Emotional Epistemology of International Relations," *International Theory*, 6.3 (2014), 589–594.

disciplines, and are deeply contested.[89] There is no space to detail the full scope of these exchanges here. Nonetheless I would like to stress that for me the distinctions are not so clear-cut. I see affect and emotions as intrinsically linked, for even if affective states are subconscious bodily factors, they frame and influence our more conscious emotional evaluations. Ross alludes to this kind of mediating role of affect by explicating that even though "nonconscious and corporeal … [a]n affect is not the property of an individual but the capacity of a body that brings it into some specific social relation."[90] Hence, it does not matter whether affect lies within or beyond representation. Affect still provides the conceptual linkage to understand how a range of socially conditioned, psychosomatic predispositions produce or mediate emotions.

There are, then, extensive debates about how to theorize the political nature of emotions. There are numerous disagreements that I have not been able to discuss completely, including further differences in how emotions, feelings, passion and affect are conceptualized and theorized. Many of the issues at stake have also been advanced by the now burgeoning field of neuroscience. But we can nevertheless identify a number of common traits that are essential for establishing a political conception of emotions and how emotions matter in world politics. Three stand out.

First, and as the growing emotions field persistently stresses, scholars must do away with traditional dichotomies that cast emotion in opposition to reason. "Reason" is not a passionless, calculating skill that one can tap into; individuals cannot "switch off" their emotions. Rather, emotions are endemic within what we traditionally call rationality. As neuroscientific developments increasingly tell us, emotions are a natural and moreover inevitable part of the cognitive processes from which so-called traditional "rationality" is based.[91] Rose McDermott sums up this position neatly by stressing that "[e]motions

[89] For an insightful discussion and critical appreciation of the seeming scholarly shift toward affect over emotion, see Ruth Leys, "The Turn to Affect: A Critique," *Critical Inquiry*, 37.4 (2011), 434–472.

[90] Ross, "Coming in from the Cold," 199, 213.

[91] More specifically, neuroscientific contributions stress the interwoven nature of cognition and emotion, and how cognition and emotion are together the product of a range of neurological, psychological, bodily and cultural perceptions. See note 37 in this chapter, as well as an overview by Jeffery, *Reason and Emotion in International Ethics*, pp. 16–19, 157–167; and Mercer, "Emotional Beliefs," 4–6.

are intertwined with cognition in a way that requires the processes to be analyzed interdependently; emotion is, inescapably, an essential component of rationality."[92] Admittedly, in politics and international relations the erroneous nature of this duality has been stated and in many circles acknowledged. However, this recognition remains largely theoretical. When it comes to the everyday practice of world politics and also to more instrumentalist international relations theory, rational actor paradigms prevail.

Second is the recognition that emotions are not individual accomplishments but are instead deeply social and cultural phenomena. Emotions are formed and structured within particular social and cultural environments. They are discursively constituted, embodied and performed in relation to culturally specific traditions and practices, such as language, habits, rituals and memories. This means that not only are emotions conceived, at least in part, within a predominant sociocultural environment, but also that individuals gain an understanding of what it means to feel in particular ways from within the same social and cultural surroundings. Simply put, one's emotionality is dependent upon a culturally grounded set of meanings to both inspire feelings and to in turn provide a basis for their interpretation. Shared forms of emotional expression and meaning are therefore necessary for individuals to make sense of the world in the context of a wider community.

Third, and to take the previous point a step further, is the idea that emotions *can* and *do* therefore tell us things: emotions provide information about how individuals conceive of themselves and the values and communities to which they feel attached.[93] Because prevailing cultural principles, standards of behavior and power relations structure how individuals emotionally experience the world around them, scholars can, in other words, look to emotions and to the discourses that shape emotions for clues about how people are socially and

[92] Rose McDermott, "The Feeling of Rationality: The Meaning of Neuroscientific Advances for Political Science," *Perspectives on Politics*, 2.4 (2004), 691–706, at 699.

[93] A similar proposition is forwarded by more cognitively orientated emotions scholars, as I discussed earlier. However, I do not mean to imply a cognitive perspective here. I mean more simply that as a result of the sociality of emotion – the unique ways that emotions are constituted and reconstituted – particular insights can be gleaned.

communally situated. Crucially too, I suggest that such a position also provides the tools necessary to examine how such situatedness – and the communal attachments that result – shifts and changes through space and time. The ways people feel in response to particular happenings in the social world, whether in their immediate space or at a distance, can be conduits of social, political – and communal – change.

My own task now consists of using these key insights into the politics of emotion and linking them up to theorizing the relationship between trauma, emotions and community. This, in turn, requires asking a number of questions. Understanding emotions as socially situated capacities that individuals acquire, could emotion and still more unconscious affects play a role in framing the conceptions of identity and belonging that are intrinsic to communities? What is it about the public display of private emotions that prompts people to pull together? What role do emotions play in generating ties that bind (or divide) communities? Finally, specific to my inquiry, how might these social emotional processes play out after widespread or widely perceived trauma?

Political communities as affective communities

This final section now draws upon and extends theorizations of the social, political and collective nature of emotion. I do so in order to begin to conceptualize how emotions are implicated within the shared meanings, purpose and identity that are integral components of political communities. More specifically, I examine how communal ties are forged through emotional discourses that frame how individuals perceive of the world and, as such, enable them to situate and enact their place within it. Emotions as well as nonconscious bodily affects are part of shared "structures of feeling"[94] – affective logics – that help to inform how, where and with whom individuals belong.

An appreciation of the social nature of emotion is invaluable to the task of theorizing the linkages between emotions and forms of political community. The sociocultural and historical basis of emotion tells us that the ways we each feel are best understood within the same

[94] Mabel Berezin, "Secure States: Towards a Political Sociology of Emotion," in Jack Barbalet (ed.), *Emotions and Sociology* (Oxford: Blackwell, 2002), pp. 33–52, at p. 39; Harding and Pribram, "The Power of Feeling," 416.

environments in which such feelings have been socialized and constituted. Emotions, and, more specifically, shared forms of emotional expression, meaning and value, distinguish social groups, and make the world intelligible in culturally attuned and thus collective ways. Understanding emotions as at least in part structured through social and cultural environments therefore opens up political inquiries into how emotions can both make possible or preclude connections between individuals. If emotions are structured within particular social environments then emotions must, by virtue of their extent relativity, also help to bind together those who are located within the same environment.

Like this, emotions can be seen as important components of the bonds that tie people together. Elster again even goes as far as to claim that "[e]motions are the most important bond or glue that links us to others."[95] Through their embodiment and by in turn framing forms of personal (and social) understanding, emotions are part of the perceptive tools that individuals employ to make sense of, and position themselves within, the world around them. Sara Ahmed is a prominent proponent of this position. She has examined how emotions are socialized and embodied in particular cultural contexts, and how in turn it is through the personal embodiment of social emotions that individuals are attached.[96] "[W]hat attaches us, what *connects us* to this place or that place, to this other or that other is (also) what we find most touching; it is what makes us feel," claims Ahmed.[97] To put it simply, emotions help individuals to make sense of their self and how they are situated in relation to others. They help to distinguish the relational ties that constitute an individual's identity and feeling of belonging.

A range of studies, from numerous scholarly disciplines, have begun to theorize the emotional underpinnings of communities in this manner. Some consider the links between emotions and forms of community as bound by sets of "emotion norms," which shape the "expression and value" of particular emotions and thereby the behaviors and connections through which emotions are enacted.[98] Such

[95] Jon Elster, *Alchemies of the Mind*, p. 403.

[96] Sara Ahmed, *The Cultural Politics of Emotion* (Edinburgh: Edinburgh University Press, 2003); Sara Ahmed, "Affective Economies," *Social Text*, 22.2 (2004), 117–139.

[97] Ahmed, *The Cultural Politics of Emotion*, p. 28. Emphasis in original.

[98] Barbara H. Rosenwein, *Emotional Communities in the Middle Ages* (Ithaca: Cornell University Press, 2006), p. 2.

norms are, moreover, perceived to provide the "affective glue" that helps to pull together and "stabilize social order" within communities.[99] Work on emotion norms can also be likened to what sociologist Arlie Russell Hochschild famously called "feeling rules."[100] Feeling rules can be seen as the rules (and historically situated customs and rituals) through which the meaning and display of particular emotions are culturally engendered and regulated. Feeling rules dictate how individuals should emotionally engage in everyday actions and, as such, "reflect where we stand on the social landscape."[101] A number of sociologists and historians in particular have since expanded on Hochschild's findings to discuss, as intimated earlier, the evolution of contextually bound emotional "liberties" and "regimes."[102] Other recent theorizations suggest that individuals and communities are bound by an emotional "habitus."[103] Drawn from Pierre Bourdieu, the concept of an emotional habitus emphasizes the way individuals' emotions are the product of internally embodied, socially and historically situated (and thus adaptive) interactions that preference and discipline individual and collective feelings. Given the focus on emotion as the corporeal embodiment of historically situated sentiments, an emotional habitus is, by its advocates, seen to more adequately capture both the conscious and nonconscious processes through which communal feelings are constituted, and can, as such, also be reconstituted.[104]

Recent studies in political theory further underline how "the passions" play a role in configuring forms of political community.[105] In

[99] Koschut, "Emotional (Security) Communities," 538.

[100] Arlie Russell Hochschild, "Emotion Work, Feeling Rules and Social Structure," *American Journal of Sociology*, 85.3 (1979), 551–575; Arlie Russell Hochschild, *The Managed Heart: The Commercialization of Human Feeling* (Berkeley: University of California Press, 1983).

[101] Hochschild, *The Managed Heart*, p. 57.

[102] Reddy, *The Navigation of Feeling*, p. 129; Reddy, "Emotional Liberty," 271–275.

[103] Scheer, "Are Emotions a Kind of Practice?" 193, 200–202.

[104] Jonathan Heaney, "Emotions and Nationalism: A Reappraisal," in Nicolas Demertzis (ed.), *Emotions in Politics: The Affect Dimension in Political Tension* (Basingstoke: Palgrave Macmillan, 2013), pp. 243–263, at p. 256.

[105] For example, William E. Connolly, *Neuropolitics: Thinking, Culture, Speed* (Minneapolis: University of Minnesota Press, 2002); Cheryl Hall, *The Trouble with Passion: Political Theory Beyond the Reign of Reason* (New York: Routledge, 2005).

a historical analysis of political thinkers such as Plato, Jean-Jacques Rousseau, John Rawls and also various contemporary feminist theorists, Cheryl Hall argues that "[a] community of any kind, however close or loose-knit, requires some threshold of emotional commitment amongst the people who constitute its members."[106] Dismissing what she sees as the traditional liberal dogma of "passionate politics makes for dangerous politics."[107] Hall goes further in arguing that more inclusive forms of community may depend, at least in part, upon acknowledging how and why individuals feel for particular sets of values or cultural ideals in the ways that they do.[108] In a similar manner Andrew Ross advocates the value of examining existing "affective connections" or "affective energies."[109] Examining such connections, he argues, may help to illuminate how political identities are reproduced and how people become intensely committed to them.

The nation-state, together with ethnic forms of nationalism that seek to subvert the sovereign state, has been considered a form of community whose foundations are embedded at least in part in emotions, although the affective underpinnings of statehood are frequently erased through the long-held perception of the legitimate, sovereign state as an inherently rational – and hence an unemotional – actor.[110] In his landmark text *Imagined Communities*, Benedict Anderson remarked on the emotional underpinnings of the nation-state. To understand nations properly, he writes, "we need to consider carefully how they have come into historical being, in what ways their meanings have changed over time and why, today, they command such a profound *emotional* legitimacy."[111] While it may not have been Anderson's

[106] Hall, *The Trouble with Passion*, p. 124
[107] Hall, *The Trouble with Passion*, p. 126.
[108] Hall, *The Trouble with Passion*, pp. 4–7, 131–133.
[109] Ross, *Mixed Emotions*, pp. 35–37, 121; Ross, "Coming in from the Cold," 212–213.
[110] Heaney, "Emotions and Nationalism," p. 247. Heaney points out a tension that has existed in conceptualizing emotions, nationhood and nationalism. He argues that within nationalism literatures, ethnic forms of nationalism have been generally conceived as emotionally motivated in ways that are "normatively 'bad,' irrational, exclusionary," while civic forms of nationalism are "normatively 'good,' and associated with a chosen, inclusionary, and above all, *rational* citizenship." See also Roger D. Petersen, *Understanding Ethnic Violence: Fear, Hatred and Resentment in Twentieth Century Europe* (Cambridge: Cambridge University Press, 2002).
[111] *Imagined Communities: Reflections on the Origins and Spread of Nationalism* (London: Verso, 1991), p. 4. Emphasis added.

meaning directly, significant here is the need to apprehend the processes through which a (national) group becomes a frame through which individuals emotionally enact their meaning and sense of belonging. Added to this is how, as a consequence, the nation-state acts as a hub or locus through which personal and political emotions intersect. After all, is it not commonsensical that conceptions of belonging and security – both fundamental to the state – are derived of what makes individuals *feel* comfortable and secure? The nation-state is intended to diminish fear and create a feeling of a warm, safe "inside"[112] that is free of "harm."[113] It is in this way, through such assurances of citizenship, solidarity and security, that emotions are inextricably embedded in the ideational and institutional structures that support the idea of the territorially bounded nation-state.

Nation-states can in this way be considered "emotional spaces," or, as I suggest, as a type of "affective community." Their boundaries as well as the sense of belonging such boundaries can invoke are constituted through, as well in part constitutive of, "structures" or "logics of feeling." Such structures or logics of feeling can be described as the culturally constituted, emotionally felt impulses, patterns and rituals that socially and collectively position individuals. They are "… the *felt* sense of the quality of life at a particular place and time."[114] Significant in this respect is that such structures or logics of feeling condition and enable the lived experience (particularly affective experience) of individuals within particular collective contexts. They organize and legitimize appropriate and inappropriate emotional responses and behaviors, and thus constitute and affectively position in a relational manner. Jonathan Heaney similarly argues that the nation-state is bound by an "emotional habitus," which in the case of nationhood is best conceived of as the processes through which an individual's being becomes enmeshed in nation-focused social structures, thereby constituting an individual's feeling, thinking and actions. "[N]ationhood is something one feels and one does," Heaney argues.[115] Mabel Berezin also argues for a conception of the nation as a "community of

112 R. B. J. Walker, *Inside/Outside: International Relations as Political Theory* (Cambridge: Cambridge University Press, 1993).
113 Andrew Linklater, *The Problem of Harm in World Politics: Theoretical Investigations* (Cambridge: Cambridge University Press, 2011).
114 Raymond Williams cited in Harding and Pribram, "The Power of Feeling," p. 416. Emphasis added.
115 Heaney, "Emotions and Nationalism," p. 257.

feeling" – a group bound by "emotional energy," which can be used to rally together a polity.[116] These conceptions hinge on the idea that the nation-state as a community is constituted and bound by socially embedded feeling structures that attribute emotional meaning and values. At the same time, this is not to imply a deterministic conception of how emotions and communities intersect. There is inevitably a complex multiplicity of such structures of feeling operating in a person's life at the one time. The constituted nature of such structures also necessarily suggests the indeterminacy of emotion, and that emotions (and the structures of feeling they either reproduce or resist) are social and political forces malleable to change.

During times of trauma the emotional configurations that underpin of communities – state based or otherwise – are particularly pronounced. Traumatic events can invoke collective emotional energies in support of existing political communities, such as the nation-state, thereby reproducing the existing social order.[117] They can also resist and transform the status quo. The emotional receptivity of witnesses to suffering and trauma is in this respect illustrative. Witnessing trauma, from near or afar, directly or indirectly, can tap into and appeal to emotions, and in doing so can help to create the conditions through which such witnesses feel compelled to somehow respond. Put differently, emotions can help to reconstitute shared meanings and moral purpose in the face of human hardship, thereby reconfiguring forms of community.

To appreciate the dual processes at play, I return to an understanding of how emotions are constituted and appealed to through contextually bound social and cultural discourses. Even though the embodied experience of emotion may be individual, the significance and meaning of our emotions are formed in conversation with the social world. "Emotion," Fierke writes, is "like any experience … [it] belongs to the social world."[118] The nature of emotions is based on a system of learned rules and social symbols, which gives meaning and value to the ways people feel. The invocation and appeal of particular emotions is

[116] Berezin, "Secure States," pp. 39–40.

[117] Ian Burkitt, "Powerful Emotions: Power, Government and Opposition in the "War on Terror"" *Sociology*, 39.4 (2005), 679–695.

[118] K. M. Fierke, "Whereof We Can Speak, Thereof We Must Not Be Silent: Trauma, Political Solipsism and War," *Review of International Studies*, f30.4 (2004), 471–491, at 480.

therefore bound by context, and by the prevailing linguistic and cultural practices that are able to appeal to culturally constituted forms of feeling. Here, it can be seen that expressions of our inner self and our experiences are heavily dependent on a common language, one that can communicate a sense of shared emotional understanding. By making use of the social symbols that best convey emotional meaning, linguistic and other communicative customs enable emotions to be understood by others. When emotions are expressed (regardless of how inadequately this may be), it is done in relation to others, in a language common to or understandable by them. To then evaluate or appraise another person's emotions, individuals draw on cultural knowledge that allows them to best understand what the other may be feeling. Language becomes not merely a mode of communication, but also the mechanism through which emotional meaning is conveyed. In this way, experiences that accentuate most vividly the inadequacy of language, such as trauma, are in fact reliant on language or other forms of communication for meaning.

Communicative practices thus situate trauma within collectives that apprehend – and feel in some way for – the shock, injury and loss of trauma. By providing an emotional object of identification, expressing trauma can prompt individuals to situate and work through feelings in conjunction with a wider community, one that possesses shared forms of traumatic meaning and emotional understanding. Therefore, even though emotions associated with trauma feel individual, and isolating, trauma is in fact experienced and emotionally enacted in inherently social ways; it is through emotions that trauma can be collectively anchored. Equally, expressing the impact of trauma can also help to distinguish whom one fails to feel connected with. While representing trauma may affectively appeal in ways that attach or bind people together, it can affectively appeal in ways that separate and divide. In this scenario, emotions that are implied in the act of witnessing take on a different meaning, one that even if comprised in part of shock and sympathy fails to evoke a sense of affinity and shared purpose intrinsic to community. In both instances, however, the emotions and meanings ascribed to trauma play a powerful mediating role. Emotions collectively situate and position individuals within respective communities.

Shared structures or logics of feeling thus enable ostensibly inexpressible trauma to be collectively felt, understood and enacted. Of course, such feeling structures or logics are not isolated to times of crisis and trauma. Every day world politics is replete with such structures of feeling. A product of time and social conditioning, such structures silently underpin forms of identity and community, and help to produce the conditions through which international behaviors take shape. But key traumatic events are a time when such feeling structures – and the communities they support or can rebuild – are especially illuminated. Modes of traumatic expression can invoke forms of shared meaning and feeling that resonate with, and can become constitutive of, communities. The emotions that traumatic events invoke can therefore work through communities in this way, through the modes of representation that shape not only trauma's expression but also the meanings, values and priorities that such expressions are understood to convey.

Summary

This chapter has constituted the second step in my conceptual framework for appreciating the links between trauma, emotion and political community. It has sought to both question and further explore how we understand the social and political impact of trauma by presenting a case for why emotions are critical to understanding the constitution of post-trauma communities. The focus has therefore rested with the dual task of conceptualizing (1) the emotional dimensions of trauma, and (2) the political dimensions of emotions.

I have shown that emotions are not private but inherently social phenomena. Emotions have a history and a future. In times of trauma, the public expression of ostensibly "private" emotion plays a particularly pivotal political role: despite feelings of inexpressibility, expressions of trauma tap into – and can both mobilize and transform – discourses that *emotionally* distinguish how individuals are communally situated. Such discourses are of course not an exceptional occurrence, limited to times of crisis: emotions are enacted through our everyday lives; with every action we carry out they distinguish how and for whom we feel.

The chapter began by highlighting a problem at that is intimately connected to trauma's emotional nature: that traumatic events seem strangely to defy or resist forms of representation. Trauma leaves those who endure it feeling lost, confused, and without the linguistic or symbolic tools through which their experiences can be authentically described. So much is this the case that it has even been suggested that silence may be the most adequate expression of major trauma. However, despite the problems of expressing trauma, victims and witnesses eventually find a voice, regardless of how inadequate. And it is in this way – no matter how inauthentic or insufficiently trauma may have been described – that the emotional, seemingly "inexpressible" dimensions of trauma are guided and ascribed a wider social, collective meaning.

But while emotions are central to experiencing and understanding trauma, their influence in constituting communities after publicly visible, widely perceived traumatic events are yet to be fully appreciated.

The main argument and contribution of this chapter has thus revolved around the need to rectify this shortcoming. To do so, I surveyed a range of emotions literatures. I have drawn upon them to conceptualize emotions as not simply a pervasive element of human life, but, importantly, a socially constituted and constitutive component as well. Distinct here is that these literatures encourage one to examine how emotions develop through continually evolving social relations. In this way, a study into the political roles of emotions would be distinguished by questions that explore precisely how emotions "work" – that is, how emotions function to evoke and enact particular individual and collective responses, decisions and behaviors. Yet, recognizing that emotions are a part of the discursive fabric that binds individuals (and communities) together also suggests that rather than searching for specific emotions and attempting to understand how they function we can examine how emotional discourses may be mobilized in ways that generate a collective vision of trauma.

Also important in this respect is an understanding of the role power plays in mediating the types of emotions and emotional discourses that are summoned after trauma. By this I mean not simply the more explicit "powers-that-be" after trauma, such as political elites that are key to shaping the immediate aftermath of widely perceived trauma, but also how the very notion of trauma and recovery in its aftermath is implicated in a much lengthier social history that shapes how people experience catastrophic events and feel in response to them. A telling passage from Lutz helps us to appreciate the enormity of the intersections between power and the sociality of emotions. She contends that to "talk about emotions is simultaneously to talk about society – about power and politics ... about normality and deviance."[119] How prevailing forms of power have disciplined and legitimized particular emotions in particular circumstances is integral to social and political configurations, which are especially pronounced after catastrophe: Emotions, then, "are the very means by which the power game is played."[120]

Finally, the chapter turned to literatures that help us to appreciate how emotional responses to trauma are reflective of wider social as well as collective or communal sentiments. I showed how emotions and emotional discourses are embedded within the social structures through which individuals live their lives and belong to particular communities. In particular circumstances, communities can thus be conceived of as a group of people bound by roughly shared emotional understandings of the world writ large, thereby distinguishing them as what I term an "affective community."

At issue here is that emotional dispositions underpin the attachments individuals make with the social world, and, in turn, how such attachments come to define a sense of collective identity and community. During times of trauma, these emotional dynamics are particularly pronounced. They can help to delineate and draw boundaries around experiences of suffering and pain, bringing individuals who can understand and empathize together. But trauma may also be reflective of an experience that can reconfigure forms of "fellow feeling." The advent of suffering – whether one's own or the witnessed experiences of others – may be able to solicit forms of emotional receptivity that help to break down and reconstitute boundaries of identity and political community.

[119] Lutz, *Unnatural Emotions*, p. 6.
[120] Jonathan G. Heaney, "Emotions and Power: A Bifocal Prescription to Cure Theoretical Myopia," *Journal of Political Power*, 6.3 (2013), 355–362, at 358.

3 *Representing trauma and collectivizing emotions*

The previous two chapters explored the personal as well as the social nature of trauma, showing that trauma is an intensely emotional experience that can paradoxically fragment and help to constitute communities. My inquiry sought to further our political understanding of trauma, specifically probing how exactly this dual process takes place. To do so, I turned to the emotional dimensions of trauma. As a psychological and affective, sensory encounter, trauma is experienced in the intensity of its emotional impact and in the absence of words able to sufficiently express it. However, trauma is at the same time an inherently social phenomenon, capable of affecting not simply those who endure it directly, but also those who are either forced or strangely compelled to bear witness to it, from both near and far-off distances.

The present chapter constitutes the third and final step in establishing my framework for appreciating the links between trauma, emotion and political community. The chapter argues – and demonstrates – that processes of representation are key to the wider social, political and emotional significance of traumatic events. Even while inevitably incomplete in their expression of trauma, representations allow traumatic occurrences to be known beyond immediate experiences: they play a key role in translating ostensibly individual experiences into a phenomenon able to be understood by many. Representations are as such mediums through which trauma can attain and proliferate wider social meanings – meanings that can be politically influential and help to constitute communities in various national and transnational contexts.

The chapter is divided into four sections. The first section comprises a conceptual examination of representation and narrative theory. It explores how practices of representation and narrative give shape and meaning to social realities. Here, I show that ways of seeing and understanding representations of reality are intimately connected to how individuals are socially situated. Second, I show that even though trauma belies the words used to express it, modes of representation still manage to transcribe trauma into a "language" through which trauma can be collectively understood and enacted. Representations do this by shaping not only trauma's expression (and thus its subsequent ability to be communicated and known within a particular context) but also the social meanings such expressions convey. In other words, representations locate trauma within particular historically embedded ways of understanding; they frame, provide a lens to interpret, and constitute "trauma" by appealing to established discourses concerning what it means to experience extreme events. Trauma is in this way understood and made meaningful in the context of a wider community.

The third section then examines more closely the politics of representing trauma. I demonstrate that post-trauma solidarity and community can seem to take place almost "automatically," as a result of the always implicit social dimensions of experiencing and recovering from trauma – and through individuals' need to overcome isolation and locate a community that cushions trauma's pain. Traumatic events and histories can also be unconsciously or strategically manipulated through politics and the media in order to foster a sense of community that enhances social and political cohesion. I further suggest that the process of representing trauma can help to constitute new, possibly more inclusive political communities. This is a somewhat underappreciated view, yet one that I argue warrants further attention, particularly in international relations where trauma is not only an everyday but also – as a result of global media networks – a potentially deeply politically constitutive experience capable of transcending national boundaries. Fourth and finally, I return full circle, so to speak, and underline that there is a compelling need to systematically examine the role emotions play in bestowing trauma's various representations with shared meaning and political value. I do so by further scrutinizing the social and discursive basis of emotion, and by underlining that individuals make sense and meaning of trauma representations at least partially through historically embedded forms of feeling. The links between representations and emotions are in this way a key site of identity, community, politics and power.

Representation, narrative and discourse

No longer is it contentious to suggest that social reality is constructed, and thus contingent. Countless scholars – from not merely politics and international relations but a broad range of social science and even natural science backgrounds and perspectives – study the way in which the social world is mediated and constituted through practices of representation.[1] From this perspective, objects and events cannot be construed outside of the modes of expression that animate them. How the world is perceived and ultimately understood is inseparable from the processes of presentation and apprehension through which it appears.

As active and persuasive as recent studies of representation have been in politics and international relations, the centrality of representations has, however, remained largely confined to poststructuralist and social constructivist theorizing of the international.[2] Even if more traditional approaches accept the basic tenet that reality is constituted through representations, the full significance of this fact does not seem to be taken seriously: an understanding of the links between representations and the sociopolitical realities that representations construct has not managed to infiltrate and entirely expand orthodox ways of conceiving of world politics. One reflection of this is that in many global political situations "realpolitik" continues to predominate, even though a realist spirit of power politics was itself long ago proved to be a social construction.[3] This is why I now go back to explore the inherent, constitutive role of representations in more detail. I draw from a diverse range of literatures to do so, yet I also stress that there

[1] For instance, Jerome Bruner, "The Narrative Construction of Reality," *Critical Inquiry*, 18.1 (1991), 1–21; Stuart Hall (ed.) *Representations: Cultural Representations and Signifying Practices* (London: Sage and the Open University, 1997); Michael J. Shapiro, *The Politics of Representation: Writing Practices in Biography, Photography, and Policy Analysis* (Wisconsin: University of Wisconsin Press, 1989); Bas C. van Fraassen, *Scientific Representation: Paradoxes of Perspective* (Oxford: Oxford University Press, 2008); Hayden White, *The Content of the Form: Narrative Discourse and Historical Representation* (Baltimore: Johns Hopkins University Press, 1987).

[2] In politics and international relations, the most influential texts for my present inquiry have been Roland Bleiker, *Aesthetics and World Politics* (New York: Palgrave, 2009); David Campbell, *Writing Security: United States Foreign Policy and the Politics of Identity*, 2nd ed. (Minneapolis: University of Minnesota Press, 1998); Roxanne Lynn Doty, *Imperial Encounters: The Politics of Representation in North–South Relations* (Minneapolis: University of Minnesota Press, 1996); Lene Hansen, *Security as Practice: Discourse Analysis and the Bosnian War* (London and New York: Routledge, 2006).

[3] Alexander Wendt, "Anarchy is What States Make of It: The Social Construction of Power Politics," *International Organization*, 46.2 (1992), 391–425.

are significant ambiguities and conceptual differences in the various literatures. Articulating all positions is beyond the scope of this one chapter. In what follows, I thus outline, first, the significance of the relationship between representation, narrative, discourse and social reality, and, second, why in turn an understanding of representation is crucial to appreciating the linkages between trauma and political community.

When literary theory, history and cultural studies literatures discuss "representations of reality," what they are referring to are essentially images, reproductions of people, objects and events as they appear and come to constitute the reality before each of us. Practices of representation – whether they are linguistic, bodily, or aesthetic forms of expression and description – are the mediums through which the world comes to be known and understood. According to art critic John Berger, representations are "an attempt to explain how, either metaphorically or literally, you see things."[4] Here, a connection between seeing, telling and knowing is implicit. Ways of seeing and interpreting representations of reality are affected by beliefs, by the things thought to be known, and how that knowledge shapes one's perspective.[5] Similarly, for something to be known, literatures suggest that it must be susceptible to some form of description. It must be free to be captured through the representational reflexes most familiar to our everyday – language.[6]

Even though representations of reality appear to be "real," they are interpretations rather than fact. Representations do not mimic reality, but are instead more like a painting with shifting shades of gray. The part of the picture that is in shadow depends upon where one stands in order to see. Simply put, how reality is represented is never just about the object, event or person under observation. Representations of reality are inevitably concerned with the relation between subject and object; practices of representation concern the relationship between who is seeing and who or what is being seen.[7] An object or

[4] John Berger, *Ways of Seeing* (London: Penguin, 1972), 9.
[5] Berger, *Ways of Seeing*, p. 8.
[6] See Elaine Scarry, *Resisting Representation* (New York: Oxford University Press, 1994), 3–41.
[7] Shapiro, *The Politics of Representation*, p. xi; Roland Bleiker, "The Aesthetic Turn in International Political Theory," *Millennium: Journal of International Studies*, 30.3 (2001), 503–539, at 511–514.

event cannot, in other words, be represented through mediums that are value-free. Ways of representing reality reflect how one is situated in relation to an other – whether that other be an object, person or even an event or type of encounter. Bound up in the values of the perceiver, practices of representation cannot portray the world as it is, for both the world and strategies of perception do not exist as pure objective fact.[8] Representations are thus interpretations, inevitably subjective abstractions about the nature of reality. Indeed, representational genres can in one sense be considered to be stories, spun in a particular way and in particular light, rather than the "factual" depictions of reality that they are often unknowingly taken to be.

Considering representational practices in this way highlights the contextually bound nature of not only modes of representation, but also the ways of seeing that shape how representations are understood. Processes of socialization engender responses toward particular concepts, ideologies, emotional schema and behavioral stimuli. Or, said differently, various cultural, linguistic, psychological and historically embedded perceptual codes and processes constitute one's experience of the world. These processes have enabling and disabling effects on how individuals understand and find meaning in the world, in turn prompting representations of reality to be interpreted through a particularistic lens. It is in this way – through the genres used to represent reality and the techniques of abstraction that allow us to interpret the world around us – that objects and events gain the meanings that they do. Hayden White explains that the various ways reality is represented are part of a cultural "meta-code." They are "messages" through which "the nature of a shared reality can be transmitted."[9] Lene Hansen likewise explains that representations situate reality by providing a "particular interpretative optic."[10] Representational practices provide and situate particular political issues and problems within a particular frame, or lens, which is central to how the respective phenomena come to be understood. As Hansen continues, political policies are in this way "dependent upon representations of the threat, country, security

[8] See Jonathon Crary, *Suspensions of Perception: Attention, Spectacle, and Modern Culture* (Cambridge, MA: MIT Press, 1999), esp. pp. 19–20; Stuart Hall, "Introduction," in Hall (ed.) *Representations*, pp. 1–13; Shapiro, *The Politics of Representation*, pp. xi-xii, 7–13.

[9] White, *The Content of the Form*, p. 1.

[10] Hansen, *Security as Practice*, p. 6.

problem, or crisis they seek to address."[11] By appealing to socioculturally and historically embedded "orders of meaning,"[12] practices of representation provide mechanisms (of signification) through which reality can not only be described, but also distributed and made meaningful in a wider (or indeed, more limited) social or communal context.

For meaning to be shared, therefore, there must be some common standard or basis of perception, a shared social structure that unites individuals in the ability to interpret linguistic or otherwise-expressed meanings. Here, literature highlights the significance of language.[13] According to early analyses of discourse and semiotics, the social world is carved up (and identities constituted) by the ways we speak. Words and their various connotations divide the world, creating social groupings (and identities) that are bound by the understandability of speech. This is not to suggest that verbal language is the only medium of communication. Critiques of this "linguistic turn" underline that individuals communicate through an array of nonverbal mechanisms just as much as they do speech.[14] Gesture and visual stimulation are all equally regarded as powerful mediums of expression and representation.[15] Yet, significant here is that even nonlinguistic, aesthetic forms of representation remain reliant upon language for wider social signification and meaning. Even while modes of representation are of a visual or visceral nature, language remains an instrumental component of how individuals "make sense" of aesthetic sources and what they perceive to be their meaning.

Recognizing the power and potential of language is, moreover, fundamental to understanding what John Tagg has called "the burden

[11] Hansen, *Security as Practice*, p. 6.

[12] Roland Barthes, "Introduction to the Structural Analysis of Narratives," in *Image, Music, Text* (London: Harper Collins, 1977), pp. 79–124.

[13] Michael J. Shapiro (ed.), *Language and Politics* (New York: New York University Press, 1984); Michael J. Shapiro, *Language and Political Understanding: The Politics of Discursive Practices* (New Haven: Yale University Press, 1981. Explicitly on the linguistic constitution of identity, see Anne Norton, *Reflections on Political Identity* (Baltimore: Johns Hopkins University Press, 1988).

[14] See Donald Brook, "On Non-Verbal Representation," *British Journal of Aesthetics*, 37.3 (1997), 232–245.

[15] See, for instance, Giorgio Agamben, *Means Without Ends*, trans. Vincenzo Binetti and Cesare Casarino (Minneapolis: University of Minnesota Press, 2000), pp. 48–62; W. J. T. Mitchell, *Picture Theory: Essays on Verbal and Visual Representation* (Chicago: University of Chicago Press, 1994).

of representation."[16] Because all representations are ultimately mediated through linguistic means, modes of representation gain meanings that are bound by one's ability to understand that language. Power is, in this way, what is centrally at issue in practices of representation.[17] Because practices of representation are value-laden and socially and discursively produced, they reflect the relations of power from which such values and forms of communication have been derived.[18] They emerge from and appeal to particular contexts; they both shape and are shaped by communicative processes specific in space and time.

The concept of "narrative" is equally important to scholars of representation. "Narratives" can be commonly understood to be stories. When applied to real or even imagined events, narratives shape experiences so that they unfold as if occurring in a smooth continuous sequence or chain, like a story. Not necessarily fiction and yet also not indisputable fact, narratives construct a kind of life-flow, bestowing a pattern upon life and the happenings within it. They provide life with a beginning, a middle and an end, and in doing so they construct a vision of life as continuous, as a harmonious search for personal and social meaning irrespective of any discontinuity or disruption.[19] Narratives can therefore help individuals to cope with confusion and chaos. Like practices of representation, narratives are not a simple reflection of events themselves. They are a construction, a linguistic and symbolic artifice, involving the creative and perceptive activity of the storyteller. In this way, narratives constitute an important and often invisible form of thought. Employed often unconsciously, David Olson comments that "[n]arrative is a natural, unreflective, uncritical form of discourse."[20] For Olson, narratives are socially significant in that how

16 John Tagg, *The Burden of Representation: Essays in Photographies and Histories* (Basingstoke: Palgrave Macmillan, 1988).

17 For an analysis of the nature of power in society and how it pervades discourse – the actions and language that constitutes the everyday, see Michel Foucault, *Archaeology of Knowledge*, trans. A. M. Sheridan Smith (London: Routledge, 2002); Frederic Jameson, *The Political Unconscious: Narrative as Socially Symbolic Act* (Ithaca: Cornell University Press, 1981).

18 Shapiro, *The Politics of Representation*, pp. 7–13; Tagg, *The Burden of Representation*, pp. 21–22.

19 See Roland Barthes, "Introduction to the Structural Analysis of Narratives," in *Image, Music, Text* (London: Fontana, 1977), pp. 79–82, 85–91; Richard Kearney, *On Stories* (London: Routledge, 2001), pp. 3–7, 129–131.

20 David R. Olson, "Thinking About Narrative," in Bruce K. Britton and A. D. Pelligrini (eds.), *Narrative Thought and Narrative Language* (Hillsdale, NJ: Lawrence Erlbaum, 1990), pp. 99–112, at p. 99.

individuals envisage their own "life narrative" – their own story – can affect how they conceptualize both their self and their relationships with others.

In a broad analysis of political history, art, psychotherapy and literature, Richard Kearney suggests that we are each compelled by a search for narrative. According to Kearney, a so-called narrative mission,[21] prompting us to unravel and articulate even the darkest moments in our lives, characterizes human existence.[22] So much is this the case that, for Kearney, an "unnarrated life" seems simply "not worth living."[23] Implicit in our search for narrative is the desire for coherence and continuity – the desire to iron out any ill-suited unsubtleties that contradict how individuals have come to define their sense of self. In this sense, narratives can be understood as continually revised stories about the nature and meaning of both individual and social (and by extension, communal) existence.[24] A sense of narrative invites individuals to define their self and to view the world in ways that allow their own story to continue smoothly. John Lahr quips, "[w]e all need stories, but the story we need most is the continually revised one that we tell about ourselves."[25] If something does not "fit" with how we consider our identity or purpose, it can be omitted, or perceived in a way that it does. Put differently, when it comes to constructing and reconstructing a sense of narrative, reality can simply be "bent into shape" – "narrativized" – through the practices employed to represent it.[26]

Finally, to fully conceptualize the significance of both representations and narratives in framing (and constituting) political realities it is also important that we distinguish the role of discourse. While it is important to conceive of representational practices as distinct from

[21] I borrow the term "narrative mission" from John Lahr, "Down and Out: Twenty-Seven Characters in Search of a Play," *The New Yorker*, May 31, 2004, p. 92.

[22] Kearney, *On Stories*, pp. 3–4, 125–129; and see also Richard Kearney, "Narrative and the Ethics of Remembrance," in Richard Kearney and Mark Dooley (eds.), *Questioning Ethics: Contemporary Debates in Philosophy* (London: Routledge, 1999), pp. 18–32.

[23] Kearney, *On Stories*, p. 14.

[24] Kearney, *On Stories*, p. 129. Another author who explicitly credits story telling with providing both individuals and collectives with a sense of identity and meaning is William L. Randall, *The Stories We Are: An Essay on Self-Creation* (Toronto: University of Toronto Press, 1995).

[25] Lahr, "Down and Out," p. 91.

[26] Scarry, *Resisting Representation*, p. 3.

discourse, representations are an intrinsic element of the signification processes that constitute a discourse. Likewise, prominent social discourses are key indicators of how representations of reality are to be interpreted.

An understanding of discourse helps us to apprehend how the meanings attributed to representations are created and prioritized. Discourse is used, very broadly, to designate (either accepted or transgressive) ways of thinking about a particular issue or phenomena or about one's social world writ large; discourses encompass the codes, conventions and habits of language (spoken or otherwise) that mediate one's experience of the social world and bestow it with culturally and historically located meaning. To elaborate, I draw from Jennifer Milliken's classic article on the study of discourse in international politics. Milliken understands discourse as "structures of signification which construct social realities ... discourses make intelligible some ways of being in, and acting toward, the world, and of operationalizing a particular 'regime of truth' while excluding other possible modes of identity and action."[27] Roxanne Lynn Doty similarly suggests that "discourse delineates the terms of intelligibility whereby a particular 'reality' can be known and acted upon." While "inherently open-ended and incomplete ... discourse enables one to make sense of things."[28] Discourses often function silently, or implicitly; the beliefs and values they hold and communicate are not always overtly asserted. Indeed, discourses that possess most power draw some of their influence from their presupposed, "hidden" nature.[29] As Foucault put it, discourse is about "the said as much as the unsaid."[30] Examples would include, for

[27] Jennifer Milliken, "The Study of Discourse in International Relations: A Critique of Research and Methods," *European Journal of International Relations*, 5.2 (1999), 225–254, at 229.

[28] Roxanne Lynn Doty, *Imperial Encounters: The Politics of North–South Relations* (Minneapolis: University of Minnesota Press, 1996), p. 6. To be clear, discourses are "inherently incomplete" in so far that they can be reconstituted – legitimized and de-legitimized – over space and time in accordance with prevailing sociocultural norms and expectations.

[29] To analyze discourse is then "to make explicit what normally gets taken for granted." See Deborah Cameron, *Working with Spoken Discourse* (London: Sage, 2001), p. 7; see also Lilie Chouliaraki and Norman Fairclough, *Discourse in Late Modernity: Rethinking Critical Discourse Analysis* (Edinburgh: Edinburgh University Press, 1999).

[30] Michel Foucault, "The Confession of the Flesh," in Colin Gordon (ed.), *1972–1977*, trans. Colin Gordon, Leo Marshall, John Mephan and Kate Soper (New York: Pantheon, 1980), p. 194.

instance, discourses on gender and sexuality, and nationalism. Even when unspoken and inexplicitly articulated, the normative conventions associated with, for instance, what it means to be either a "man" or "woman," or "Chinese" or "Australian" are in particular contexts very clear.

A scholarly examination or analysis of discourse is concerned with uncovering the either implicit or explicit social symbols and codes that signify and constitute – thereby enabling and disabling – meaning in particular circumstances. Therefore, when referring to "discourse" through the guise of a text or an analysis of a text, policy, image or even gesture or action (let us say, for example, X), what is most important are the social practices, norms, customs, ways of thinking and perceiving that inextricably confine how X is interpreted. This is to say that prevailing discourses produce the "truth" and "knowledge" about representations of X, which signify and feed back to an audience the respective (contextually bound) content or meaning.[31] Significant here is that discourses "work to define and enable, and also to silence and to exclude ... [by] endorsing a certain common sense ... [and by] making other modes of categorizing and judging meaningless, impracticable, inadequate or otherwise disqualified."[32] It is in this way that discourse – as much as the representations and narratives through which reality is understood – is a key part of the constitution of social and political realities.

Certain critical questions for politics – and in particular for our understanding of political identity – emerge from conceptualizing the constitutive role of representation, narrative and discourse. Most potently, in the words of Doty, "[t]hinking in terms of representational practices highlights the arbitrary, constructed, and political nature ... through which we have come to 'know' the world and its inhabitants."[33] Continuing, she argues that to examine representations is thereby to scrutinize how "we have come to 'know' the world and its inhabitants" and how this knowledge has in turn "enabled and justified certain practices and policies."[34] How an actor views itself, then,

[31] See Milliken, "The Study of Discourse in International Relations," 228–230, 232.
[32] Milliken, "The Study of Discourse in International Relations," 229.
[33] Doty, *Imperial Encounters*, p. 3.
[34] Doty, *Imperial Encounters*, p. 3.

is not based on a pre-given sense of self and interests, but is deeply linked to its narratively constructed self. Practices of representation frame how individuals understand reality and situate themselves in relation to others, and are thus inherently connected to the formation and renegotiation of identity. In a comprehensive analysis of narrative and politics, Maureen Whitebrook also understands group or collective identity as a narrative construct. According to Whitebrook, "identity requires the telling of stories both by and about the self."[35] The sense of belonging that is necessary for the configuration of community can also be understood as bound by such stories, or, more generally speaking, by the representational practices that constitute an individual's subjectivity and how an individual's subjectivity inevitably situates them in a particular social and collective context.

These insights are particularly significant to the task of understanding the social impact of trauma. Like all events, trauma presents itself in the social sphere not through an authentic mechanism of description, but through the representational practices considered best able to express it. Such practices are inevitably subjective and constituted through the social and cultural discourses and narrative structures in which they have been derived. Recognizing this is key to understanding the social and political significance of trauma. Even though in one sense victims and witnesses feel as if they live alone with their suffering, representational practices allow trauma and associated emotions to be in some way conceived of and worked through in a social and communal context. Indeed, the practices used to represent individual trauma enable particular understandings of trauma to resonate and constitute a "trauma story," which is much more than a collective account of the individual encounters that make it up. Stories that individuals tell themselves and each other about trauma are in this respect "performative"; they are socially constituted and also constitutive, in that they can change the way that individuals perceive of themselves and their relationships with others. Recognizing the political power and potential of representations and narratives is, therefore, key to understanding how traumatic events can pave the way for the restoration or reconstruction of social cohesion and community.

[35] Maureen Whitebrook, *Identity, Narrative, and Politics* (London: Routledge, 2001), p. 22.

Representing trauma, no matter how inadequately

To comprehend how traumatic experiences and the emotions that accompany them can help to constitute communities, it is therefore necessary to examine how processes of representation and interpretation shape the wider social meanings that traumatic events and histories can acquire. I need to examine how an experience as emotional and sensory as trauma translates into language (as well as other forms of expression), which in turn makes possible the shared understandings that bind community.

At first glance, however, the centrality of representation sits uneasily with the communicative crisis that trauma scholars identify. For these scholars, much of trauma's impact is felt in the challenge of its representation.[36] While all objects and events are understood and ascribed meaning through processes of representation, literature suggests that trauma at least initially resists it. Jenny Edkins comments that "[c]ommunicating trauma is very difficult ... [trauma] is something that cannot be conveyed in speech."[37] Elsewhere, Ulrich Baer likens the problem of trauma's representation to an "enigma."[38] Encoded more in sensations and images than in verbal narrative, trauma evades the parameters of everyday expression, and in doing so highlights the limits of the representational codes and processes upon which human existence relies for understanding and meaning. Trauma's "enigma" can in this way be seen as the challenge of placing traumatic experiences within a coherent psychological, textual and sociohistorical context.

This "crisis of representation" that accompanies trauma is telling, for the inability to psychologically and linguistically process traumatic experiences results not simply in a loss of faith in oneself, but also

[36] See, for instance, Cathy Caruth, *Unclaimed Experience: Trauma, Narrative, and History* (Baltimore: Johns Hopkins University Press, 1996); Jenny Edkins, *Trauma and the Memory of Politics* (Cambridge: Cambridge University Press, 2003); Leigh Gilmore, *The Limits of Autobiography: Trauma and Testimony* (Ithaca: Cornell University Press, 2001); Dominick LaCapra, *Writing History, Writing Trauma* (Baltimore: Johns Hopkins Press, 2000); Nancy K. Miller and Jason Tougaw (eds.), *Extremities: Trauma, Testimony, and Community* (Illinois: University of Illinois Press, 2002).

[37] Edkins, *Trauma and the Memory of Politics*, p. 41.

[38] Ulrich Baer, *Spectral Evidence: The Photography of Trauma* (Cambridge, MA: The MIT Press, 2002), p. 8.

in a detachment from the various communities that victims and witnesses had previously thought themselves situated. Meaning seems to fall away following trauma; trauma becomes an experience distinguished foremost by its abjection.[39] Psychological research that has examined the everyday life and survival of trauma victims and witnesses demonstrates the significance of trauma's representational inadequacy. Studies of Holocaust survivors and their children, returned Vietnam veterans, victims of political persecution, torture, rape and sexual abuse suggest that speaking about or otherwise representing traumatic experiences is central to regaining a sense of familiar social context and narrative flow of life.[40] Yet, how can those who experience trauma reinstate the so-called narrative flow of their lives, whilst that very flow is fragmented by an experience that haunts, seeming to exist outside of or beyond representational and narrative control? If modes of representation provide the link between trauma and the possibility of moving on, how do victims and witnesses express an experience that is so strangely resistant to representation? And is there something politically significant about the apparent "space" or "gap" between the (affective) experiencing of trauma and the practices used to represent it?

Despite the linguistic challenge and emotional difficulty of recounting trauma, those who endure or bear witness to traumatic events often feel the need to provide testimonial accounts of what they have witnessed or suffered.[41] Sarah Kofman writes that even though words

[39] Julia Kristeva, *Powers of Horror: An Essay in Abjection*, trans. Leon S. Roudiez (New York: Columbia University Press, 1982); Michael Humphrey, "Horror, Abjection and Terror," in *The Politics of Atrocity and Reconciliation: From Terror to Trauma* (London: Routledge, 2002), pp. 11–25.

[40] See, respectively, J. E. Dimsdale (ed.), *Survivors, Victims, and Perpetrators: Essays on the Nazi Holocaust* (Washington, DC: Hemisphere, 1980); Lawrence L. Langer, *Holocaust Testimonies: The Ruins of Memory* (New Haven and London: Yale University Press, 1991); Barry Heard, *Well Done, Those Men: Memoirs of a Vietnam Veteran* (Carlton: Scribe Books, 2005); John Conroy, *Unspeakable Acts, Ordinary People: The Dynamics of Torture* (Berkeley: University of California Press, 2000); Judith Lewis Herman, *Trauma and Recovery: From Domestic Abuse to Political Terror* (London: Basic Books, 1992).

[41] See, for instance, Susan J Brison, *Aftermath: Violence and the Remaking of a Self* (Princeton: University of Princeton Press, 2002), pp. 86–104; Herman, *Trauma and Recovery*, pp. 175–181; Humphrey, *The Politics of Atrocity and Reconciliation*, pp. 105–108; Langer, *Holocaust Testimonies*; Dori Laub,

feel inadequate, victims and witnesses live with the feeling that there is a "duty to speak" of and somehow transmit the debilitating nature of their trauma.[42] Dori Laub goes as far as to claim that trauma survivors "tell their stories in order to survive."[43] So desperately do they seek confirmation for what they have experienced that they continue to search for ways of sufficiently communicating the impact of their trauma.

Speaking of trauma – regardless of how inadequately, unsuccessfully or incompletely – is thus one medium through which victims and witnesses attempt to represent trauma. Language essentially translates the incomprehensible and ostensibly antisocial nature of trauma into comprehensible patterns of speech. Perhaps in some sense speech can be thought of as a constant, as the residue of a reality that has been torn apart by the shock, horror and dislocation of trauma. The logic behind a victim's or witness's search for language becomes clearer when speech is considered in this way. The communicative act of expressing and belatedly bearing witness (and thus reexperiencing) mediates and transforms trauma and traumatic memory into a more "normal" encounter, one that can be incorporated into the narratives that frame one's everyday reality. Put differently, when transcribed into speech, trauma can be more readily integrated into the survivor's sense of self and view of the world.[44] Therefore, narrating trauma – telling a story about trauma and linguistically encoding one's emotions – re-associates victims with the social world and enables them to reconstruct a sense of normality.

Because of this, finding a language for traumatic experiences is generally understood as therapeutic.[45] Words provide a way of transforming what feels like a meaningless experience into something meaningful, and additionally provides a mechanism through which trauma can be understood by others. Akin to Judith Butler, Susan Brison suggests

"Truth and Testimony: The Process and the Struggle," in Cathy Caruth (ed.), *Trauma: Explorations in Memory* (Baltimore: Johns Hopkins University Press, 1995), pp. 61–75.

42 Sarah Kofman, *Smothered Words*, trans. Madaleine Dobie (Illinois: Northwestern University Press, 1998), p. 36.

43 Laub, "Truth and Testimony," p. 63.

44 Herman, *Trauma and Recovery*, pp. 44–45.

45 See, for example, Herman, *Trauma and Recovery*, pp. 133–140; Mihnea Moldoveanu and Nitin Nohria, *Master Passions: Emotion, Narrative, and the Development of Culture* (Cambridge, MA: The MIT Press, 2002), p. 38.

that in this sense speech is "performative."[46] Saying something about trauma does something to it, she argues. Not only does it provide a path through which victims and witnesses can (in some way) know their trauma, but also it locates survivors within a community. It is in this way that trauma literatures suggest that testimony and language more generally provides the first step toward sharing one's experiences.[47] This is to say that by appealing to a linguistic community that shares both one's vocabulary and the sensibilities implicit in the ways one speaks, language provides a way of reestablishing a victim's or witness's connection to the social world.[48] Speech is, in other words, one step toward locating a wider collective that is sympathetic to understanding the nature and impact of trauma. Recognizing the significance of speech, we see that trauma is tied to modes of representation not only in order to obtain social meaning, but also so that victims and witnesses can work through their trauma and piece themselves back together in a sympathetic social or communal context.

But speech is not the only medium through which trauma can be represented. Nonverbal modes of representation provide a way of working through and understanding the disorientation of trauma as well. Some scholars even question whether nonverbal, aesthetic mediums of representation are more adept at depicting – and then in turn communicating – trauma's emotional impact.[49] At issue for these

[46] Brison, *Aftermath*, p. x.

[47] See Edkins, *Trauma and the Memory of Politics*, pp. 8, 11, 41; K. M. Fierke, "Whereof We Can Speak, Thereof We Must Not Be Silent: Trauma, Political Solipsism and War," *Review of International Studies*, 30.4 (2004), 471–491, esp. 472, 477–480.

[48] Roland Barthes does not write specifically on the linguistic translation of trauma. However, the understanding of language and its socially embedded meaning employed here is taken from his Saussurian-based work on linguistic signs and semiotics. See Barthes, *Elements of Semiology*, trans. Annette Lavers and Colin Smith (New York: Farrar, Straus and Giroux/Hill and Wang, 1967, esp. pp. 21–26.

[49] Literature often turns to alternative, aesthetic modes of representation, such as photography, visual art and sculpture, poetry and literature, and creative movement and dance for more adequate expression of trauma and political violence. See, for example, Baer, *Spectral Evidence*, esp. pp. 8–14; Laura Di Prete, "Don DeLillo's *The Body Artist*: Performing the Body, Narrating Trauma," *Contemporary Literature*, 46.3 (2005), pp. 483–510, esp. at 483–484, 491–492; J. Brooks Bouson, *Quiet as It's Kept: Shame, Trauma and Race in the Novels of Toni Morrison* (Albany: State University of New York Press, 2000); Amelia Jones, *Body Art/Performing the Subject*

scholars is that aesthetic sources are capable of transforming or even displacing language and, in so doing, finding a way through which trauma can "speak." This is why some scholars argue that to appreciate the impact of trauma we must elevate the importance of gesture, and, more broadly, aesthetics. Distinct within these literatures is that aesthetic sources – such as visual and dramatic arts, poetry and fiction – can help victims and witnesses to come to terms with trauma, perhaps more than conventional modes of giving testimony. As Laura Di Prete explains, such mediums might be better equipped to "capture the truth of an experience lived primarily within the skin."[50] Aesthetic sources may therefore hold greater possibilities of finding a voice emotionally attuned to expressing the wounds of trauma.

Representing trauma through photographs is therefore a way of capturing the impact of trauma without first mediating it through words. Indeed, it is for this reason – for their lack of words – that literatures often consider photographs and visual culture more generally to be a particularly potent medium for the expression of trauma.[51] Scholars such as Marianne Hirsch, Ann Kaplan and Nancy Miller have researched the relationship between photography and the period of recovery that followed the September 11 attacks on the World Trade Center.[52] Their studies examine the concept of "photographic testimony," and broadly conclude that the psychic and peculiarly visual nature[53] of trauma makes photographs particularly well suited to

(Minneapolis: University of Minnesota Press, 1998); Laura Di Prete, "*Foreign Bodies": Trauma, Corporeality, and Textuality in Contemporary American Culture* (New York: Routledge, 2006).

[50] Di Prete, "Don DeLillo's *The Body Artist*," 484.

[51] See, in particular, Baer, *Spectral Evidence*; W. J. T. Mitchell, "The Unspeakable and the Unimaginable: Word and Image in a Time of Terror," *ELH: Journal of English Literary History*, 72 (2005), 291–308; Jay Prosser, *Light in the Dark Room: Photography and Loss* (Minneapolis: University of Minnesota Press, 2005).

[52] Marianne Hirsch, "I Took Pictures: September 2001 and Beyond," in Judith Greenberg (ed.), *Trauma at Home: After 9/11* (Lincoln and London: University of Nebraska, 2003), pp. 69–88; E. Ann Kaplan, "A Camera and A Catastrophe: Reflections on the Trauma and the Twin Towers," in Greenberg (ed.), *Trauma at Home*, pp. 95–106; E. Ann Kaplan, *Trauma Culture: The Politics of Loss in Media and Literature* (New Brunswick: Rutgers University Press, 2005), pp. 136–148; Nancy K. Miller, "'Portraits of Grief': Telling Details and Testimony of Trauma," *differences: A Journal of Feminist Cultural Studies*, 14.3 (2003), 112–135.

[53] See Kaplan, "A Camera and a Catastrophe."

communicating the wounds and memories left by extreme experiences. Miller even goes so far as to argue that photographic portrayals of loss safeguard against the "watering down" of trauma through words.[54] This argument is reinforced by how several key international newspapers chose to represent and mourn the lives that were lost when the Twin Towers fell: they measured the tragedy not through words but through pictures. A prominent example is that of the *New York Times*, which ran individual portraits (rather than stories) of those who were missing or presumed dead. These "portraits of grief" consisted of the victims' faces, unaccompanied by description.[55] Recent studies of the atrocities perpetrated by the Khmer Rouge in Cambodia also point to the potential of photographs to provide testimony.[56] Notwithstanding the deceptions, multiple meanings and even possible "untruths" that photographs can convey, these studies largely suggest that portraits of the victims provide an account of the innocence and injustice of their deaths, and as such incite a responsibility of witnesses to act. Elsewhere, in his study of the influence of trauma photographs on foreign policy, David Perlmutter suggests that "iconic" images can arrest the emotions and senses not only of those who directly experience violence and ensuing trauma, but also of those who watch and bear witness – even if such witnessing takes place from the comfort of home.[57] Perlmutter's research reflects a growing trend in social and political research. Increasingly, interdisciplinary political science and international relations studies are recognizing the representational significance (and influence) of photographs of either distant or forgotten instances of trauma.[58]

[54] See Miller, "Portraits of Grief," 122–123.

[55] See Miller, "Portraits of Grief," 123–131.

[56] Jenny Edkins, "Exposed Singularity," *Journal for Cultural Research*, 9.4 (2005), 359–386, esp. 375–378; Rachel Hughes, "The Abject Artefacts of Memory: Photographs from Cambodia's Genocide," *Media, Culture & Society*, 25.1 (2003), 23–44.

[57] David D. Perlmutter, *Photojournalism and Foreign Policy: Icons of Outrage in International Crises* (Westport, CT: Praeger, 1998).

[58] Examples include David Campbell, "Horrific Blindness: Images of Death in Contemporary Media," *Journal for Cultural Research*, 8.1 (2004), 55–74; David Campbell, "Geopolitics and Visuality: Sighting the Darfur Conflict," *Political Geography*, 26 (2007), 357–382; David Campbell, "Atrocity, Memory, Photography: Imaging the Concentration Camps of Bosnia," Parts I and II, *Journal of Human Rights*, 1.1/2 (2002), 1–33, 143–172; Cori Dauber, "Image as Argument: The Impact of Mogadishu on U.S. Military Intervention," *Armed*

Artistic representations are also thought to play an important role in the working through of trauma. The most ubiquitous of these mediums are the monuments erected to represent and commemorate trauma – most often that of national tragedy and war. Many literatures focus on their therapeutic and conciliatory dimensions. Sites of commemoration and remembrance, such as memorials, museums and national holidays, provide a social, public (and ultimately communal) context in which survivors and witnesses are urged to remember a history of trauma and pain.[59] They help to shape the physical and social landscape in arguably much the same way that the psychological and emotional pain of trauma has shaped the landscape of victims' minds. By encouraging a spirit of commemoration and of paying tribute to trauma, monuments tend to direct individuals to consider trauma in a particular way – often a communally reinforcing one. Scholars reveal that the reason for this is that meaning becomes attached to the physical structure or commemorative site, which is no different from processes involved in linguistically representing trauma. When given a meaning that enables "life to go on" – either through words or, as suggested here, through architectural structures – trauma is made to be a seemingly "normal" component of the landscapes and historical narratives that give structure to one's everyday.

Scholars have also reflected upon the significance of representing trauma through personal art.[60] One of the most discussed examples is

Forces and Society, 27.2 (2001), 205–229; Edkins, "Exposed Singularity"; John Hariman and John Louis Lucaites, "Public Identity and Collective Memory in U.S. Iconic Photography: The Image of the Accidental Napalm," *Critical Studies in Media Communication*, 20.1 (2003), 35–66; Miller, "Portraits of Grief"; Frank Möller, "Rwanda Revisualized: Genocide, Photography, and the Era of the Witness," *Alternatives: Global, Local, Political*, 35 (2010), 113–136; Simon Philpott, "A Controversy of Faces: Images from Bali to Abu Ghraib," *Journal for Cultural Research*, 9.3 (2005), 227–244; and finally: the Special Issue titled "Securitization, Militarization and Visual Culture in the Worlds of Post-9/11," in *Security Dialogue*, 38.2 (2007).

59 See, for instance, Edkins, *Trauma and the Memory of Politics*, pp. 153–154, 190; Nuala C. Johnson, "Cast in Stone: Monuments, Geography and Nationalism," *Environment and Planning D: Society and Space*, 13 (1995), 51–65; James M. Mayo, "War Memorials as Political Landscape," *Geographical Review*, 78.1 (1988), 62–75; Maria Sturken, "The Wall, the Screen and the Image: The Vietnam Veterans' Memorial," *Representations*, 35 (1991), 118–142.

60 See, for instance, Jill Bennett, *Empathic Vision: Affect, Trauma and Contemporary Art* (Stanford, CA: Stanford University Press, 2005).

that of the Holocaust. Survivors and their children as well as indirect witnesses have used various forms of art in an attempt to depict and come to terms with the atrocity and its memory.[61] Matthew Biro discusses the work of artists Joseph Beuys and Anselm Kiefer, who used sculpture and painting in order to problematize the prevailing postwar West German perspective of the Holocaust.[62] Biro suggests that the works of Beuys and Kiefer capture the brutality of the Holocaust so powerfully that they inspire a kind of "reflexivity" in those who view them. They prompt people to engage with the suffering of the Jews and in so doing provoke both a personal and political awareness of what took place.

Thus while trauma's shock and grief first appear to be isolating and privatizing, literatures show that practices of representation provide a mechanism through which so-called inexpressible experiences of trauma can be expressed and in some way shared. Modes of representation provide a way for trauma to be spoken of, written about, or pictorialized through images. Importantly, they allow trauma to be translated into something able to be known and made collectively meaningful. Some strategies of representation are thought to socialize trauma, in an important way "normalizing" an encounter that seems far from normal. Key here is that rather than producing new forms of personal and social meaning, representations frequently shape traumatic events in ways that make them "fit" with existing personal and social narratives. Feelings of isolation and emotional distress can consequently be "smoothed over" by practices of representation and the narratives that are subsequently generated. Put differently, processes of representation give trauma the ability to be narrated, to be ascribed

[61] For academic texts that discuss some of these attempts, see Aaron Haas, *In the Shadow of the Holocaust: The Second Generation* (Ithaca: Cornell University Press, 1990); Marianne Hirsch, "Surviving Images: Holocaust Photographs and the Work of Postmemory," *The Yale Journal of Criticism*, 14.1 (2001), 5–37; Amy Hungerford, *The Holocaust of Texts: Genocide, Literature and Personification* (Chicago: University of Chicago Press, 2003); Sue Vice, "Yellowing Snapshots: Photography and Memory in Holocaust Literature," *Journal for Cultural Research*, 8.3 (2004), 293–315; Barbie Zelizer, *Remembering to Forget: Holocaust Memory Through the Camera's Lens* (Chicago: University of Chicago Press, 1998).

[62] Matthew Biro, "Representation and Event: Anselm Kiefer, Joseph Beuys, and the Memory of the Holocaust," *The Yale Journal of Criticism*, 16.1 (2003), 113–146, esp. at. 116–117.

meanings that can underpin shared understandings and can mobilize a sense of common purpose. It is therefore in this way – through the genres used to "voice" trauma and the culturally embedded, affective perceptual processes that allow it to be interpreted – that trauma can become a collective event or experience that helps to "fix" meaning and identity. This type of "naturalization of meaning"[63] may be part of a process of reinscribing existing configurations of identity and community. Or, given that representation, narrative and the discourses that bind them are inevitably incomplete and evolving, it can possess the possibility for transformation and help to form the foundations of new ones.

The politics of representing trauma

The previous two sections have theorized the processes through which individual, unique experiences of trauma can be shared and made collectively meaningful. The focus of this section rests with the political nature and consequences of doing so. Drawing on politically orientated studies of both trauma and representation, I show that representing trauma is an intensely political endeavor. Of course, representations can be overtly political in motivation or intention. But as intimated earlier, what I also mean to imply is that the "real" location of the politics of trauma is situated in the very space between the experience of trauma and the practices used to represent it. It is within this space that the central paradox I identify lies: experiencing trauma may feel isolating, yet modes of expressing and representing trauma highlight trauma's sociality. It is therefore precisely in *how* trauma (and associated emotions) are shared and "collectivized" after that reflects the politics at stake. The "how" question is important because, to again follow Doty, it examines the meanings that are "produced and attached" to the respective "traumatic" occurrence, and how in turn these meanings "create certain possibilities and preclude others."[64] While this type of "gap" or space should not be something to be feared,[65] it calls for a particular attentiveness to the politics of practices of representation: the meanings they produce hold both potentials and

[63] Doty, *Imperial Encounters*, p. 7.
[64] Doty, *Imperial Encounters*, p. 4.
[65] Bleiker, "The Aesthetic Turn in International Political Theory," 512–513.

limits for how one conceives of boundaries of identity and community in both national and transnational political contexts.

Representational and narrative practices associated with trauma have significant social and political possibilities. By involving not only those who endure trauma directly but also those who bear witness, practices of representation can translate individual, distant experiences of trauma into influential social and political phenomena. This is because representational practices and narratives of trauma shape how individuals perceive extreme events, and how they interact and connect with others as a consequence. Importantly, practices of representing trauma are part of a process of ascribing trauma with social meaning – meanings that narrate (i.e. tell a particular story about) trauma and in so doing can diminish feelings of isolation and disruption. They can tap into sensibilities and prompt trauma to be considered in a collectively meaningful (and often politically influential) way. Communities bound by shared emotional understandings and discourses can ensue. Given the increasingly transnational dimensions of media representations today, this process can play out in not only the national but also the international and transnational arena.

Even though some scholars argue that trauma is an encounter through which community can be reconfigured, most agree that traumatic events tend to reinstate existing forms of political community. They highlight that dominant representations of trauma (by politicians, policy makers, journalists and scholars) present the particular event's shock and horror in ways that are designed to restore faith and allegiance in the prevailing social and political authority.[66] In this way, representational practices are thought to be key to reinstating the communal bonds that trauma previously deconstructed. This process of communal renewal can take place almost automatically, through a need for a social environment conducive to working through the discomfort and terror of trauma. It can also be an intensely political moment, an occasion where political powers purposefully grapple to reinstate meaning and control. Herein lies the central paradox of trauma that I identify: because trauma isolates it also reconstructs. Just as trauma seems

[66] See Edkins, *Trauma and the Memory of Politics*, pp. 229–231; K. M. Fierke, *Critical Approaches to International Security* (Cambridge: Polity, 2007), pp. 123–143; Kate Schick, "Acting Out and Working Through: Trauma and (In)security," *Review of International Studies*, 37.4 (2011), 1837–1855.

to detach individuals and damage the fabric of communities, representational practices can be employed – strategically or unconsciously – to restore the social and political cohesion that trauma has disrupted.

The period following traumatic events is consequently not only intensely emotional, but also of great political significance. Work by Richard Devetak, Jenny Edkins, K. M. Fierke and Kate Schick has drawn attention to the political dimensions of the aftermath of trauma. Their research suggests that political elites often "rush" to reinstate their narratives of control after catastrophe.[67] It is precisely because trauma shatters a sense of belonging and uproots entrenched political patterns that politicians and the media (again, either consciously or otherwise) focus on restoring community and concomitant notions of authority.

Distinct here is that by recognizing that traumatic experiences can never truly "fit" existing configurations of power (and thus politics), political elites often represent and frame trauma in ways that force it to fit with established narratives of politics and community. Here, too, the political responses to 9/11 are illustrative. Washington's foreign policy became immediately centered around the terrorist attacks. Couched in a rhetoric of "good" versus "evil," the United States' (US) reaction sought to reestablish the sense of order[68] and certitude that had existed during the Cold War: an inside/outside world in which, according to the words of former US President George W. Bush, "you are either with us or against us."[69] So the process of memorializing the trauma, through commemorative and arguably belligerent representations, gave way to not simply a more unified American national community but also a culture through which wars of retaliation were made possible.[70] Across the Pacific, a similar situation soon took hold in

[67] Richard Devetak, "After the Event: Don DeLillo's *White Noise* and September 11 Narratives," *Review of International Studies*, 35 (2009), 795–815, at 805–811; Jenny Edkins, "The Rush to Memory and the Rhetoric of War," *Journal of Political and Military Sociology*, 31.2 (2003), 231–251, at 235–238. See also Edkins, *Trauma and the Memory of Politics*, pp. 229–231; Fierke, *Critical Approaches to International Security*, esp. pp. 123–143; K. M. Fierke, "Bewitched by the Past: Social Memory, Trauma and International Relations," in Duncan Bell (ed.), *Memory, Trauma and World Politics* (Basingstoke: Palgrave Macmillan, 2006), pp. 116–134; Schick, "Acting Out and Working Through."

[68] See David Campbell, "Time is Broken: The Return of the Past in the Response to September 11," *Theory & Event*, 5.2 (2002).

[69] "You are either with us or against us," *CNN*, November 6, 2001.

[70] See Gearóid Ó Tuathail, "'Just Out Looking for a Fight': American Affect and the Invasion of Iraq," *Antipode*, 35.5 (2003), 856–870; David Simpson,

Australia. When a terrorist attack in a well-known expatriate nightclub in Bali, Indonesia, killed more than 200 people (almost 100 of whom were Australian), the then Australian Prime Minister John Howard was quick to resecure the national community that the attacks had fractured.[71] Reviews of domestic security and counterterrorism legislation were immediately ordered and the Defence Department even went so far as to call their white paper "Fortress Australia."

These examples indicate that the social dislocation brought by trauma can lead to an urgent, overtly political narration of the respective event as well as subsequent commemorative legacies. The "powers that be" seek to smother the social and political disorientation that trauma brings. This is particularly the case during times of perceived "national trauma"[72] – when a catastrophe (such as the Bali bombing) that directly affects only a few is thought to be (and represented as) an attack on a much larger, distinctly national community. In such circumstances, moments of grief and remembrance are often represented as an occasion where an entire nation is seemingly brought together in an expression of outrage and loss.

Significant in this respect is that representations of trauma can enable – yet paradoxically also limit – the boundaries of political community. Representations can reinstate power structures traditional to the nation-state, which while seemingly strengthening a national community simultaneously silences alternative discourses through which new configurations of community can be generated. In this way, it may be useful to consider the various ways of representing trauma as modes of "cultural governance."[73] According to Michael Shapiro, forms of cultural governance involve the consistent support for communicative and representational strategies that constitute and legitimize existing configurations of political sovereignty. In this view, representational strategies that are thought to consolidate a sense of collective identity and community after trauma are actively pursued, while, in contrast, modes

9/11: A Culture of Commemoration (Chicago: University of Chicago Press, 2006).

71 See Matt McDonald, "Constructing Insecurity: Australian Security Discourse and Policy Post-2001," *International Relations*, 19.3 (2005), 297–320.

72 Jill Bennett, "The Limits of Empathy and the Global Politics of Belonging," in Greenberg (ed.), *Trauma At Home*, pp. 132–138, at p. 133.

73 Michael J. Shapiro, *Methods and Nations: Cultural Governance and the Indigenous Subject* (New York: Routledge, 2004).

of expression that challenge or diminish social cohesion and political sovereignty are restricted. This may involve contextualizing (representing) trauma in terms concomitant with rebuilding national allegiance. Such stories smooth over trauma's disturbance, and help to constitute and reconstitute the ways that individuals are connected to each other. Thus, through modes of representation, trauma can be shaped in ways that serve the political interests of those who have the power to represent it. Trauma can be appropriated in order to legitimize particular political positions or policy prescriptions.

This situation – when traumatic events come to restore prevailing forms of political community – has been observed not simply during times of politically motivated trauma and violence. Scholars comment that natural catastrophe and incremental forms of suffering can foreclose the boundaries of communities as well.[74] Consider how Western viewers readily bear witness to various atrocities and suffering, yet only infrequently do anything substantial to help. Scholars have long critiqued the way the Western world seems to ambivalently play "spectator" to suffering in the developing world. Ann Kaplan argues that emotions associated with witnessing suffering may be "empty," because rarely does another's suffering solicit indignation, responsibility and action.[75] In a similar manner, Arthur and Joan Kleinman claim that the widespread – yet utterly ineffectual – representation of distant trauma can only be considered with dismay.[76] International relations scholars have additionally cautioned against such "sentimentality," arguing that in reality emotions such as pity tend to generalize (rather than sensitize) onlookers to cultural difference, in turn perpetuating the selectivity toward those needing to be "saved."[77] To varying degrees these thoughts are also shared by scholars who write of "compassion fatigue" or an "exhaustion of

[74] For example, Philip Darby, "Security, Spatiality and Social Suffering," *Alternatives: Global, Local, Political*, 31 (2006), 453–473; Arthur Kleinman, Veena Das and Margaret Lock (eds.), *Social Suffering* (Delhi: Oxford University Press, 1998); Martin Shaw, *Civil Society and Media in Global Crises: Representing Distant Violence* (London: Pinter, 1996).

[75] Kaplan, *Trauma Culture*, pp. 93–94.

[76] Arthur Kleinman and Joan Kleinman, "The Appeal of Experience; The Dismay of Images: Cultural Appropriations of Suffering in Our Times," *Daedalus*, 125.1 (1996), 1–25.

[77] See, for instance, Patricia A. Owens, "Xenophilia, Gender, and Sentimental Humanitarianism," *Alternatives: Global, Local, Political*, 29.3 (2004), 285–305.

empathy."[78] So common is this kind of indifference to others' trauma that when sudden natural disasters occur individuals and governments sometimes do not know how to respond. Is it that we are constituted not only by "our own" trauma but also by witnessing the trauma of others? Could the sight of distant trauma help to constitute boundaries of witnessing communities as well?

International relations scholars have studied the political implications of representational strategies more generally. These scholars draw attention to how dominant practices of representing the social world – for example, people, places, nationalities and cultures – frame individuals' perceptions and in so doing produce forms of knowledge that shape global political relations.[79] Some in turn show – and often lament – that processes of communication prioritize particular traumas and crises over others, which may be believed to be more worthy of attention. Yet, it is not simply the prioritizing of particular incidents that is important. Key for these scholars is that some crises are portrayed with a corresponding sense of "danger."[80] They show that it is precisely by alluding to the danger of the world outside that processes of communication – representation – can bestow events with meanings that close off forms of community and political sovereignty.

Reflections on the construction of danger also link with literatures that examine the securitization of identity. Scholars have demonstrated that it is in this way – through processes of representation and interpretation – that disingenuous, often antagonistic perceptions of particular identities or cultural groups are cultivated. From these, a legacy of violence may consequently ensue, in turn perpetuating the very opinions

[78] See Stanley Cohen, *States of Denial: Knowing About Atrocities and Suffering* (Cambridge: Polity, 1993); Susan D. Moeller, *Compassion Fatigue: How the Media Sells Disease, Famine, War and Death* (New York: Routledge, 1999); Keith Tester, *Compassion, Morality and the Media* (Milton Keynes: Open University Press, 2001).

[79] See, for instance, Bleiker, *Aesthetics and World Politics*; Campbell, *Writing Security*; François Debrix and Cynthia Weber (eds.), *Rituals of Mediation: International Politics and Social Meaning* (Minneapolis: University of Minnesota Press, 2003); Doty, *Imperial Encounters*; Janice Bially Mattern, *Ordering International Politics: Identity, Crisis, and Representational Force* (New York: Routledge, 2005); Hansen, *Security as Practice*.

[80] Campbell, *Writing Security*, pp. 1–13; K. M. Fierke, *Critical Approaches to International Security* (Cambridge: Polity, 2007), pp. 80–90, 100–119; Michael Williams, "Words, Images, Enemies: Securitization and International Politics," *International Studies Quarterly*, 47 (2003), 511–531.

that fueled the conflict in the first place.[81] David Campbell and K. M. Fierke have specifically examined this process in the context of the violence in the Balkans.[82] Analyzing dominant representations – or as Fierke puts it, "pictures"[83] – of the conflict, they contend that not only was the violence mobilized through belligerent perceptions of self and other, but also that similar dichotomies limited the international community's ability to respond. Also relevant here is research that has linked the configuring of world politics with the various communicative and sociolinguistic exchanges through which international relations take place.[84]

One can thus see that the representational, narrative and discursive practices associated with trauma have immense social and political significance. They hold the possibility of constructing forms of identity and community. Yet traumatic events can do still more than this. They can also mark the beginning of a new political era. Intended here is the idea that representing human suffering holds possibilities for transforming identities and renegotiating political affiliations, potentially so as to form communities of responsibility beyond the nation-state. Put differently, if forms of community are constituted through representations, then it follows that to alter how we represent the social world may also be to alter and rebuild the foundations of community – to reshape how and to whom we feel attached. William Connolly and Philip Darby are two scholars who advocate that we consider suffering as a point through which such critical engagements with others can take place.[85] They argue that recognizing the commonality of pain

[81] For example, Michael J. Shapiro, *Violent Cartographies: Mapping Cultures of War* (Minneapolis: University of Minneapolis Press, 1997).

[82] David Campbell, *National Deconstruction: Violence, Identity, and Justice in Bosnia* (Minneapolis: University of Minnesota Press, 1998); David Campbell, "MetaBosnia: Narratives of the Bosnian War," *Review of International Studies*, 24 (1998), 261–281; K. M. Fierke, "The Liberation of Kosovo: Emotion and the Ritual Reenactment of War," *Focaal: European Journal of Anthropology*, 39 (2002), 93–113.

[83] Fierke, "The Liberation of Kosovo," 93, 95–99.

[84] Janice Bially Mattern, "Why 'Soft Power' Isn't So Soft: Representational Force and the Sociolinguistic Construction of Attraction in World Politics," *Millennium: Journal of International Studies*, 33.3 (2005), 583–612; K. M. Fierke, "Links across the Abyss: Language and Logic in International Relations," *International Studies Quarterly*, 46 (2002), 331–354; Thomas Risse, "'Let's Argue!' Communicative Action in World Politics," *International Organization*, 54.1 (2000), 1–39.

[85] William E. Connolly, "Suffering, Justice, and the Politics of Becoming," in David Campbell and Michael J. Shapiro (eds.), *Moral Spaces: Rethinking*

may prompt individuals to transform their perceptions of others in ways that include them in their sphere of solidarity and support.

Feminist and interpretative scholars also write – with hope – of the possibility of shifting or "contingent" identities.[86] They argue that if one recognizes how the social world is constituted, through representations, it may then be possible to reimagine (and thus reconstitute) it in more inclusive ways – in ways that afford suffering minorities a space to voice their interests and desires. One may also see that each individual is constituted by a vast array of alternative or shifting identities, rather than an identity that is fixed and unchanging. These scholars further argue that political inclusion can be achieved through representational practices that help to "disturb" entrenched perceptions of identity.[87] These insights may be practically relevant during times of crisis and trauma. This is to say that we may be able to consider representing trauma as a process through which identities can be disrupted in order to transform understandings of community. Central here is the possibility of harnessing the contingent and shifting nature of identity (and concomitant notions of responsibility) in order to respond to the needs of suffering. Questions of how to represent trauma are also key. Some strategies of representing trauma disrupt prevailing social attachments and hold possibilities for creating new ones. Others close off the boundaries of one's self, generating meanings that limit the boundaries of community.

There are rare occasions when representations of trauma and catastrophe created understandings that resulted in the constitution of a uniquely transnational form of community. Consider the Southeast Asian tsunami disaster of December 2004. When the giant wave struck the shores of more than fourteen countries on Boxing Day an unprecedented outpouring of international aid and support was set off. Several scholars have suggested that the inundation of critically

Ethics and World Politics (Minneapolis: University of Minnesota Press, 1999), pp. 125–153; Darby, "Security, Spatiality and Social Suffering," 453–473.

86 For example, Judith Butler, *Giving an Account of Oneself: A Critique of Ethical Violence* (Fordham University Press, 2005); Kathy Ferguson, *The Man Question: Visions of Subjectivity in Feminist Theory* (Berkeley, CA: University of California Press, 1993).

87 A recent article by Christine Sylvester suggests that artistic representations may hold potential to transform configurations of community and responsibility. See her "The Art of War/The War Question in (Feminist) IR," *Millennium: Journal of International Studies*, 33.3 (2005), 855–878.

emotional visual representations of the catastrophe were in this respect crucial. Lilie Chouliaraki and Virginie Mamadouh, for instance, contend that the twenty-four-hour global media coverage played a key role in mobilizing the transnational collective response.[88] Benedict Korf has also analyzed the micropolitics of aid giving in response to the tsunami, suggesting that the representational responses of humanitarian aid organizations had (more than ever before) opened private donors to "practicing generosity as a global symbolic act of solidarity."[89] A recent article by Brent Steele also suggests that linguistic representations of the tsunami were instrumental in persuading foreign governments to give as generously as they ultimately did.[90]

Key to these very different political situations is how traumatic events are represented. Rather than an arbitrary or even impartial system of depicting trauma's "truth," representations of trauma both communicate and are filtered through the particular cultural, aesthetic and affective sensibilities of those who view or listen to them. Trauma gets its shape, its public meaning, from the way it is represented and the messages that such representations are perceived to convey. Representational practices thus shape how individuals perceive of trauma, and create perceptions that help to bestow trauma with meaning. And it is the meanings that trauma attains that can help to either open up or close off how individuals perceive of their attachments to others. Identity and community can be constructed and also manipulated in this way. Trauma that directly affects a few can – through techniques of representation and narrative – be portrayed as damaging to many, to the individuals and wider society that bear witness, at a distance, rather than feel trauma's impact immediately. Practices of speaking, writing and imaging trauma can be consciously crafted in order to foster particular perceptions and furnish the social attachments and feelings of solidarity that are needed to consolidate forms of political community. However, representing trauma can also

88 Lilie Chouliaraki, *The Spectatorship of Suffering* (London: Sage, 2006), p. 1; Virginie Mamadouh, "After Van Gogh: The Geopolitics of the Tsunami Relief Effort in the Netherlands," *Geopolitics*, 13.2 (2008), 205–231.

89 Benedikt Korf, "Antinomies of Generosity: Moral Geographies and Post-Tsunami Aid in Southeast Asia," *Geoforum*, 38 (2007), 366–378, at 370.

90 Brent Steele, "Making Words Matter: The Asian Tsunami, Darfur, and 'Reflexive Discourse' in International Politics," *International Studies Quarterly*, 51 (2007), 901–925.

be a politically enabling – and possibly politically transformative – act. Representations of trauma can disturb entrenched perceptions of identity and community, and in so doing can mobilize the agency needed to question prevailing forms of power and configure new forms of political community.

Representing trauma and the power of emotions

The preceding three sections examined the role that practices of representation and narrative play in constructing or consolidating community after trauma. They showed that the representational practices used to express trauma provide frames to help individuals to "make sense" of extreme, catastrophic events, and that they do so by situating individuals within a social and communal context. Practices of representation make trauma socially meaningful, and, in so doing, allow trauma to be incorporated into both the personal and political narratives that give structure and meaning to communities.

This section extends our understanding of this process. It does so in one crucial way: through an examination of the relationship between representation, discourse and emotion. I show that emotions and seemingly more ephemeral affects are an inextricable part of making meaning; the ways we feel are a constituted and constitutive part of the interpretive processes that allow individuals to make sense of practices of representation. To this end, I return to and further explore the key theme introduced in the previous chapter: the argument that in order to more fully understand how practices of representing trauma can help to constitute forms of community we need to examine how emotions are implicated in bestowing trauma's various representations with meaning and value.

Recognizing that emotions are social phenomena constituted through discourse renders the linkages between emotions and representations of critical importance. This is because discourses – the everyday codes and norms of signification that attribute meaning, value and, as such, "define the (im)possible, the (im)probable, the natural, the normal"[91] – do not take shape in a vacuum. Discourses are constituted and reconstituted through an array of culturally and historically located languages, customs and social practices: in other

[91] Clarissa Rile Hayward, *De-Facing Power* (Cambridge: Cambridge University Press, 2000), p. 35.

words, through *representations*, those that are relied upon as much as those that are excluded. So, to be clear, since emotions and discourse are inherently linked, as are discourse and practices of representation, then so too are emotions and representations. Representations serve as the primary vehicle for expressing emotions. They are like a metaphorical black box filled with a specific emotional history, symbolism and meaning.[92] How you make sense of (or, indeed, whether you can at all) what is inside that box then of course depends upon one's own vantage point, one's own emotional history. One of the most renowned early theorists of representation, Stuart Hall, explains how the words, images and various other gestures and symbols we use to portray the world essentially "stand for or represent our concepts, ideas and feelings."[93] For instance, "[t]he expression on my face 'says something' about who I am (identity) and what group I feel I belong to (attachment)," he continues. Expressions can in this way "be 'read' and understood by other people, even if I didn't intend deliberately to communicate anything formal."[94] To put this simply, through the words of William Reddy, "[e]motions are the real world-anchor of signs."[95] Emotions help to signal and locate meaning. Thus, just as "thinking and feeling are themselves 'systems of representation,'" contingent upon context,[96] representations also embody, dictate and gain salience within particular contextually bound forms of feeling.[97]

[92] This is not to argue, however, that elements of affective experience do not lie outside of representations. While I suggest representations act to symbolize and communicate emotions, I also agree that there is inevitably something "missed" or outside of representations. Nigel Thrift and Brian Massumi are two scholars who argue for the nonrepresentational qualities of affect. See Nigel Thrift, *Non-Representational Theory: Space, Politics, Affect* (Milton Park: Routledge, 2008); Brian Massumi, *Parables for the Virtual: Movement, Affect, Sensation* (Durham: Duke University Press, 2002). In international relations Janice Bially Mattern provides a compelling argument against simplifying the affective dimensions of emotions, which she suggests much political work inadvertently does in an attempt to render emotions susceptible to systematic political scrutiny. See Janice Bially Mattern, "A Practice Theory of Emotions for International Relations," in Emanuel Adler (ed.), *International Practices* (Cambridge: Cambridge University Press, 2011).

[93] Stuart Hall, "Introduction," in Hall (ed.) *Representation*, p. 1.

[94] Hall, "Introduction," p. 2.

[95] William M. Reddy, "Against Constructivism: The Historical Ethnography of Emotions," *Current Anthropology*, 38.3 (1997), 327–351, at 331.

[96] Hall, "Introduction," p. 4.

[97] See also Martha C. Nussbaum, *Upheavals of Thought: The Intelligence of Emotions* (Cambridge: Cambridge University Press, 2001), pp. 151–169;

Understanding that emotions and representations are inherently linked buttresses earlier ideas concerning the intrinsically social nature of emotions. As I surveyed, emotions are constituted in relation to culturally specific traditions, such as language, habits, customs and memories – all of which pivot on the practices through which they are represented and communicated. Emotions are also inherent within the sociocultural and historically constituted patterns of "knowledge" through which individuals and collectives make the social and political world meaningful – thus again underlining the key role of the representations through which we each come to "know" the world.

Representations are therefore central to examining the individual and collective politics of emotions. They form crucial links not simply between personal/public and individual/collective emotions, but also to how we understand the discursive processes through which emotions take shape. Practices of representation give meaning to the world around us. The expressions one uses also "say something" about one's identity, emotions and to whom one feels they belong. As I just intimated, Hall goes further in arguing that not simply is the social world given meaning through representations, but that "thinking and feeling are themselves 'systems of representation,' in which our concepts, images and emotions 'stand for' or represent ... things which are or may be 'out there' in the world."[98] It is through representations, therefore, that emotions can be embodied, transmitted and interpreted; representations allow our feelings to be attributed with particular sociocultural meanings, values and even beliefs.[99] To put it differently, it is through representations that affect and emotions are socially embedded and can thus "function as the 'force' of bonding that connects subjects to their identities."[100]

Representations thus gain power in part through how they affectively resonate in particular circumstances among receiving audiences.

William M. Reddy, *The Navigation of Feeling: A Framework for the History of Emotions* (Cambridge: Cambridge University Press, 2001), p. 47.

98 Hall, "The Work of Representation," p. 5.

99 See Nico H. Frijda, Antony S. R. Manstead and Sacha Bem, "The Influence of Emotions on Beliefs," in Nico H. Frijda, Antony S. R. Manstead and Sacha Bem (eds.), *Emotions and Beliefs: How Feelings Influence Thoughts* (Cambridge: Cambridge University Press, 2000), pp. 1–9; and in international relations scholarship, see Jonathon Mercer, "Emotional Beliefs," *International Organization*, 64.1 (2010), 1–31, at 2.

100 Ty Solomon, "The Affective Underpinnings of Soft Power," *European Journal of International Relations*, 20.3 (2014), 720–741, at 731.

As some scholars put it, ways of representing and narrating the social world can have a particular kind of emotional "pull," or perhaps more adeptly, a "circulation,"[101] "stickiness"[102] or "grip."[103] This means that representations of particular events, issues, people and so on find (are attributed) value and significance in a particular context at least in part through the emotions that are evoked. How or whether representations get "stuck" is then "a function of the connection to past social experience and norms."[104] Ty Solomon articulates the affective dynamics at stake eloquently. He does so by adding to extant work on the "attractiveness" of soft power in international relations,[105] showing how affect plays a central role in constituting the identities and actions that undergird notions of soft power. Policies and political narratives that prevail, he contends, are dependent upon the extent to which they can affectively resonate with audiences – hence the idea of "affective attraction."[106] Fierke makes a related yet slightly different point. She illustrates the salience or emotional "stickiness" of representations through an examination of the image of the dying body in acts of political self-sacrifice. Examining the emotional and bodily dynamics of suicide terrorism and civil disobedience, she shows how dying or injured bodies evoke certain emotions and how these emotions in turn become political by reaching and relating to various audiences. She highlights that this contextually bound circulation of emotion is in turn important to shaping collective agency and identities.

Yet, it is important we conceive of this emotional resonance (of representations) as not simply a process through which power is "gained" but moreover as the product of forms of power that ordinarily remain concealed as well. Put differently, the emotional receptivity of an

[101] Sara Ahmed, *The Cultural Politics of Emotion* (Edinburgh: Edinburgh University Press, 2004), 11; Andrew A. G. Ross, *Mixed Emotions: Beyond Fear and Hatred in International Conflict* (Chicago: Chicago University Press, 2014), pp. 1, 10, 21–38, 36; K. M. Fierke, *Political Self-Sacrifice: Agency, Body and Emotion in International Relations* (Cambridge: Cambridge University Press, 2012), 90–95.

[102] Fierke, *Political Self-Sacrifice*, p. 79.

[103] Solomon, "The Affective Underpinnings of Soft Power," 727.

[104] Fierke, *Political Self-Sacrifice*, pp. 79–80.

[105] Most prominent here is Janice Bially Mattern, "Why 'Soft Power' Isn't So Soft: Representational Force and the Sociolinguistic Construction of Attraction in World Politics," *Millennium: Journal of International Studies*, 33.3 (2005), 583–612.

[106] Solomon, "The Affective Underpinnings of Soft Power," esp. 727–732.

audience to specific representations depends upon how emotions have been constituted, through discourses and social structures and norms that are themselves governed by historical and contemporary power relations.

Implicated, once again, is thus a different notion of power than is customary in the study of world politics. As introduced in the previous chapter, power in this conception is structural and "productive"; it lies within the social structures that shape and confine identities and their capacities. Moving beyond traditional realist, materialist understandings of power in world politics, Michael Barnett and Robert Duvall explain that "[p]ower is the production, in and through social relations, of effects that shape the capacities of actors to determine their fate."[107] To be "productive" means that power functions through "the social processes and the systems of knowledge through which meaning is produced, fixed, lived, experienced and transformed."[108] Power is thus implicated in the very possibility of meaning, and in which meanings are legitimate and prioritized, in turn enabling an actor with the autonomy "to make or to receive any change, or to resist it."[109] From this purview, Barnett and Duvall conclude that any "[a]nalysis of power in international relations, then, must include a consideration of how social structures and processes generate differential social capacities for actors to define and pursue their interests and ideals."[110]

Of significance here is that emotions are inherently imbued within the representational and interpretative practices that are both constituted by and also come to constitute the very social structures through which power is enacted. Emotionality – the ways we seem to feel almost automatically in response to particular representations – is part of the signification (and interpretative) processes through which social meanings are formed. The capacity of particular issues, events, people and so on to emotionally resonate is consequently a productive function of power.

Representations can politically resonate by appealing to discourses (and associated emotional meanings) that are already established,

[107] Michael Barnett and Raymond Duvall, "Power in International Politics," *International Organization*, 59.1 (2005), 39–75, at 39.

[108] Barnett and Duvall, "Power in International Politics," 55. See also Fierke, *Political Self-Sacrifice*, pp. 67–69.

[109] Steven Luke, "Power and the Battle for Hearts and Minds," *Millennium: Journal of International Studies*, 33.3 (2005), 477–493, at 478.

[110] Barnett and Duvall, "Power in International Politics," 42.

therein perpetuating hegemonic or dominant ways of understanding the respective phenomena.[111] In a recent essay, Jack Holland and Ty Solomon employ the concepts of "naming" and "affective investment" to better understand the links between affect, emotions and political resonance. While adopting the perspective that "affect is ... somehow beyond or before discourse,"[112] they contend that it is precisely through articulating affect as emotion – that is, the process of naming emotion in response to the particular circumstances – that political standpoints and policies can be made possible. They specifically examine the construction of "crisis" after 9/11, suggesting that while processes of socialization conditioned the ways American people affectively responded to the terrorist attacks (predominantly with shock, incomprehension and fear) it was only through the incorporation of these affective experiences within official constructions of the event and its aftermath that they became politically salient and, ultimately, instrumental in legitimizing the war in response. It is furthermore only through this emotional disciplining (or construction) of events that audiences come to enable particular foreign policy possibilities: foreign policy choices, they contend, are partially dependent upon the "ability to affectively invest" audiences within the prescribed course of action.[113] Here, Holland and Solomon's concept of "naming" equates very much with the concept of representation, and of the potential "power" held by the presentation of political events. For them, it is precisely therein this "naming" – or representation – of intangible affect through language that the politics (and power) of emotions take place. In this instance, too, it can be seen that representations gained credence by resonating with hegemonic discourses (of security and of terrorism as "incomprehensible" attack on US "way of life"[114])

[111] Examples of other work in international relations that have begun to examine the links between affect, emotions, discourse and representations include: Jack Holland and Ty Solomon, "Affect is What States Make of It: Articulating Everyday Experiences of 9/11," *Critical Studies on Security*, 2.3 (2014), 262–277; Andrew A. G. Ross, "Coming in from the Cold: Constructivism and Emotions," *European Journal of International Relations*, 12.2 (2006), 197–222; Paul Saurette, "You Dissin Me? Humiliation and Post 9/11 Global Politics," *Review of International Studies*, 32 (2006), 495–522; Williams, "Words, Images, Enemies," 522.

[112] Holland and Solomon, "Affect is What States Make of It," 264.

[113] Holland and Solomon, "Affect is What States Make of It," 273.

[114] Holland and Solomon, "Affect is What States Make of It," 267–271.

and the emotional meanings they evoke. Prevailing links between emotions and power were as such reinforced.[115]

Power has in this way been said to be "dangerous" in terms of human emotionality, in so far that it "stifles the experimental nature of emotional expression."[116] Prevailing power disciplines emotional liberties and freedoms, and, as a consequence, people rely on "emotional conventions [which] allow for only a few overlearned habits." Rather than enabling and enriching, emotions constrain us, and as historian Barbara Rosenwein concludes, we can consequently "suffer."[117] But this is not always so. A number of prominent instances also show that emotions can be important sources of societal change: from the more recent Arab Spring uprisings that swept the Middle East, global reactions to devastating natural disasters such as in Haiti in 2010 and Southeast Asia in 2004, political responses to the rise of global terrorism, and even within the domestic realm such as was the case following the public's reaction to the death of Princess Diana in the UK.[118] In all of these situations, collective emotions ostensibly informed the conditions through which social and political relations and even behaviors were mobilized and transformed. Rosenwein captures these paradoxical, performative elements of emotions by revealing that even while emotions can be "stifled" they can also be "engines of conversion."[119] "[N]o emotion is pure and unchanging," she argues.[120] Emotions and emotional norms shift and change in response to particular social, political, economic, religious and other pressures. What is central, however, is exactly how such pressures are captured and communicated to audiences; representations are fundamental, in other words, to whether links between power and emotions are reinforced or indeed transgressed.

115 See also Ian Burkitt, "Powerful Emotions: Power, Government and Opposition in the 'War on Terror,'" *Sociology*, 39.4 (2005), 679–695, at 682–683.

116 Barbara H. Rosenwein, *Emotional Communities in the Early Middle Ages* (Ithaca: Cornell University Press, 2006), p. 18.

117 Rosenwein, *Emotional Communities in the Early Middle Ages*, p. 18–19. Here, Rosenwein also draws from the work of Reddy; see his "Emotional Liberties."

118 Jennifer Harding and E. Deidre Pribram, "The Power of Feeling: Locating Emotions in Culture," *European Journal of Cultural Studies*, 5.4 (2002), 407–426.

119 Rosenwein, *Emotional Communities in the Early Middle Ages*, p. 19.

120 Rosenwein, *Emotional Communities in the Early Middle Ages*, p. 19. See also pp. 197–202.

Representations are therefore politically significant also because of the immanent potentials they possess: representations can transform social, collective contexts and political prerogatives by tapping into previously marginalized or dissident forms of feeling. In this sense, emotions (evoked in response to a particular phenomenon) can help challenge prevailing sets of power relations and reposition subjects and attachments. Representations and the emotions they implicate can, simply put, mobilize transformative understandings and meanings, which can be key to new forms of political agency. Andrew Ross forwards a compelling theorization of emotions as "a creative source of collective agency."[121] Examining conflict and its aftermath, he both forwards a more nuanced understanding of how emotions are transmitted and circulated before and after violence, while at the same time showing that social transmissions of affect provide "an opportunity for change: new [political] movements may succeed while established ones fail, distant memories can revive a cultural symbol in decline; or an institution may resonate with popular expectations in ways its architects never anticipated."[122] Alternative, transformative political and communal configurations may consequently ensue from collective emotional mobilizations.

Key to both of these possibilities, however – that is, whether emotions circulate in ways that reinforce prevailing power and agency or transform it – are modes of representation. Emotions are constituted by, while at least also partially constitutive of, the forms of meaning that ensue from representing social realities. They are a pervasive yet often neglected part of the historical discourses and social structures that situate representations and make them contextually meaningful.[123] At the same time, forms of feelings can reshape how individuals and collectives interpret and perceive of the social world. Emotions can transform the meanings of the very representations they also simultaneously emerge from; hence making "emotions themselves the causes of their own transformation."[124]

[121] Ross, *Mixed Emotions*, p. 9.
[122] Ross, *Mixed Emotions*, pp. 45–46.
[123] J. M. Barbalet, *Emotion, Social Theory and Social Structure: A Macrosociological Approach* (Cambridge: Cambridge University Press, 2001).
[124] Rosenwein, *Emotional Communities in the Early Middle Ages*, p. 197.

Representing trauma is in this respect no different. Emotions are inherent within the various ways trauma is represented. A range of affective reactions – feelings, sensitivities and emotions – can be stimulated and mobilized in response to the needs of suffering. These emotions shape not only the meanings attributed to trauma, but also the social forces and agency that can cohere community after. Important here is that representations of trauma both convey and solicit particular socially embedded emotions, shared structures of feeling that can, due to their social and historical nature, in turn help to generate the sense of shared purpose and understanding needed to constitute identity and inscribe boundaries of comfort and belonging. The emotions and sensibilities that are implicated in the various ways trauma is represented can in this way play a pivotal role in constituting communities.

The influence of trauma's emotions becomes clearer when we consider the cultural (and collectivizing) dynamics of its representation. Immediately following catastrophe, a wider community or society is often depicted as feeling the disorientating effects that others, who experience the events more directly, consequently suffer. By portraying the terror of trauma in this way – as something that touches not simply direct victims but also those witnessing at "home" – representational practices prompt trauma to be considered in a way that appeals emotionally to many. Claudia Aradau comments that it is in this way that witnesses may be "emotionally affected and experience solidarity with victims."[125] Carefully mediated by mass or collective representation, "popular imagination"[126] can thus translate individual and often distant trauma into emotional discourses that shape and define a community. Affects – feelings, sensibility, mood and emotions – sink into how one represents the seemingly abstract and unspeakable, and how one transcribes the incomprehension of trauma into comprehensible patterns of words and pictures. A kind of social connection and moral relationship between victim and witness is summoned in this way.[127]

125 Claudia Aradau, "The Perverse Politics of Four-Letter Words: Risk and Pity in the Securitisation of Human Trafficking," *Millennium: Journal of International Studies*, 33.2 (2004), 251–277, at 255.

126 Ross, "Coming in from the Cold," 213.

127 Lilie Chouliaraki, "The Aestheticization of Suffering on Television," *Visual Communication*, 5.3 (2006), 261–285, at 264; John Silk, "Caring at a Distance: (Im)partiality, Moral Motivation and the Ethics of Representation," *Ethics, Place and Environment*, 3.3 (2000), 303–309.

Feelings of sympathy and also solidarity can emerge between witness and victim, and processes of mourning can in turn solidify communal connections.[128] Although forms of collective identity and community can be constituted and reconstituted by communicating trauma, it is often found that existing communities are reinforced or strengthened by spatial and linguistic constraints that are inextricably linked to practices of representation.[129]

One way to consider this process is to think of emotions as phenomena that can be "pulled upon" or "framed"[130] by both by one's own experiences and by events that one is exposed to in the social realm. Illustrative here is the process of bearing witness to distant trauma. Witnessing trauma through the mediations of photographers, journalists and politicians prompts one's emotions to be "steered" – "pulled" this or that way depending on what is seen. Individuals may be presented with images of death and heroic survival, of families and friends in mourning, and the expedience of political responses. Such mediations may not go so far as to specifically tell individuals what to think and how to feel, yet by invoking culturally specific modes of representing trauma and its pain they provide a mechanism through which individual and distant experiences can affectively appeal to a wider society, or – as nationalism scholars have long suggested – to some kind of "imagined" community of feeling.[131] Fierke specifically examined this process, arguing that it is because images of dying bodies prompt a search for meaning that they in turn become "a symbol for social objects and worlds."[132] Put differently, through processes of representation and interpretation, injured bodies are imbued with emotional meaning, meaning that then circulates "outwards towards a nascent community, that … is restored and expands through its

[128] See J. R. Martin, "Mourning: How We Get Aligned," *Discourse & Society*, 15.2–3 (2004), 321–344.

[129] See Ahmed, *The Cultural Politics of Emotion*, pp. 21–39; Edkins, *Trauma and the Memory of Politics*, pp. 229–233; Fierke, "Whereof We Can Speak, Thereof We Must Not Be Silent," 472, 477–481.

[130] Kimberly Gross and Lisa D'Ambrosio, "Framing Emotional Response," *Political Psychology*, 25.1 (2004), 1–29.

[131] Benedict Anderson, *Imagined Communities: Reflections on the Origin and Spread of Nationalism* (London: Verso, 1991); see also Thomas J. Scheff, *Bloody Revenge: Emotions, Nationalism and War* (Boulder: Westview, 1994).

[132] Fierke, *Political Self-Sacrifice*, p. 22.

identification."[133] The emotional meanings attributed to dying or injured bodies "becomes 'stuck to' the nascent community," thereby constituting or reconstituting the body politic.[134]

Representations of trauma are in this way fundamental to the emotionally embedded discourses that can be mobilized after catastrophe. To return to the work of Lila Abu-Lughod and Catherine Lutz, emotional discourses are those that "seem to have some affective content or effect."[135] I would go further than this, to suggest that all discourses possess emotional underpinnings and effects, even if they do so implicitly or in unobvious ways. Abu-Lughod and Lutz do, however, extrapolate to further theorize that emotional discourses can be considered to be forms of social and thus collective action, in so far that discourses are inevitably interpreted through a culturally sensitive (affective) lens, which in turn shapes how discourses are perceived and the social and political consequences they produce. Representing trauma can in this view be seen to inspire discourses that have the function of enabling individuals to emotionally situate themselves within (or indeed apart from) a community that is feeling similarly traumatized or aggrieved by the idea of suffering fellow community members.

Representation is thus the process through which seemingly individual emotions associated with trauma acquire a social, collective dimension and can, in turn, help to shape political processes. Although witnesses can never truly understand the emotions of someone directly affected by tragedy, processes of representation – communication – establish a public context where the private and possibly inimitable nature of trauma can be ascribed wider social, emotional meaning and significance.[136] It is therefore through practices of representation that the emotional dimensions of trauma can be transcribed into influential political, and communally constitutive discourses.

Theorizing the relationship between trauma and representation in this way helps to make clear how catastrophe can help to underwrite

133 Fierke, *Political Self-Sacrifice*, p. 28.
134 Fierke, *Political Self-Sacrifice*, p. 79.
135 Lila Abu-Lughod and Catherine A. Lutz, "Introduction: Emotion, Discourse and the Politics of Everyday Life," in Catherine A. Lutz and Lila Abu-Lughod (eds.), *Language and the Politics of Emotion* (Cambridge: Cambridge University Press, 1990), pp. 1–23, at p. 10.
136 Ahmed, *The Cultural Politics of Emotion*, pp. 20–39, 92–100.

the emotional dynamics of political communities. Important here is an understanding of how emotions can help to shape the representational and interpretative processes through which trauma gains social meaning and, in some cases, the kind of social and political significance needed to constitute boundaries of identity and community. In turn, by conceptualizing how representational processes may intersect with or align individuals, emotionally, we may be able to more fully comprehend how trauma can constitute communities, as well as the commemorative legacies that often glorify traumatic loss, generating animosity and divisive political relations.

Summary

This chapter has constituted the final step of the conceptual part of my inquiry into the relationship between trauma, emotions and constitution of political community. It has argued that practices of representation play a critical role in transcribing trauma and its associated emotions into a phenomenon able to be shared and made collectively meaningful.

The chapter began by discussing literatures concerning the theory of representation and narrative. In doing so, I demonstrated that the process of representation is fundamental to how we perceive of social and political realities. Objects, people and events attain meaning only through the representational and interpretative strategies that we bring to them. I also showed that for meaning to be shared there must be a common (or accepted) history and social structure that enables individuals to make sense of representations in similar ways.

I then drew out why an understanding of representation and narrative is crucial to conceptualizing the constitution of community after trauma. I demonstrated that although trauma is commonly conceptualized as an isolating and somewhat incommunicable experience, representational practices help to "make sense" of trauma. Practices of representation and narrative make trauma knowable; they shape trauma's expression and also the meanings such expressions convey. Whether through mediums such as speech or writing, visual arts, photography or even creative movement and dance, representations translate what may seem to be an isolating, indescribably emotional experience into something able to be understood by many. As such, trauma can attain meanings that are instrumental in diminishing feelings of uncertainty and isolation, and can generate shared understandings and common bonds. It is in this way – through practices used to represent trauma, and interpretative processes that come to construct narratives around it – that individuals experience and can emotionally enact trauma in ways that help to constitute political communities.

My inquiry then turned to the political dimensions of representing trauma. In particular, I highlighted that representations of trauma can both limit and transform how we think about our attachments to others. Put differently, representations of trauma can both consolidate existing forms of community and mobilize individuals in ways that generate new ones. Most scholars stress the former process. But some also emphasize that representations of trauma hold immanent possibilities for change. This latter scenario taps into emotions and sentiments that disrupt how individuals consider their attachments to others. Representations of trauma then generate emotions and meanings that are capable of creating a new sense identity and community.

The final section of this chapter brought the conceptual part of my research into trauma full circle by more closely showing how emotions are central to a more holistic appreciation of the relationship between the representation of trauma and the constitution of political community. Most important here is recognizing how emotions inevitably help to shape and give value to the representational and interpretative practices from which (post-trauma) forms of community are produced. Forms of feeling distinguish representations of trauma by attributing value and signaling meaning. This attribution of meaning and value is, as I showed, inevitably laden with power. Yet, it can also hold immanent potential in so far that emotions can either work to reinforce the status quo or they can disrupt how individuals and collectives consider their attachments and responsibilities. Existing forms of community may be replicated, or forms of feeling can inspire the collective agency needed to transform or fundamentally rebuild the foundations of community.

PART II

The emotional constitution of political community

The first part of this book established a framework to appreciate how the emotional dimensions of traumatic events can help to constitute forms of community in world politics. I explored the nature of trauma, theorizing the processes through which ostensibly individual experiences of trauma can become that of a collective. My inquiry showed that even though trauma may be a solitary, lonely encounter – experienced through an inability to psychologically process or adequately communicate its horror – practices of representation can nonetheless translate trauma into something able to be known and made meaningful to many. Understanding the relationship between trauma and community in this way prompts questions concerning the social and political influence of trauma's intensely emotional nature. Indeed, as I have argued, the connection between trauma and various associated emotions is crucial to considering the often collectivizing role of representing key traumatic events.

The second part of the book now implements my conceptual framework: it supplements the macro, theoretical analysis with three concrete, micro-level empirical inquiries. The first two cases examine the communal linkages that can be emotionally forged in the wake of different types of "immediate" catastrophe, whereas the final empirical inquiry turns to the longer-term emotional and political dynamics inured by historical trauma. I examine how past injury and loss can edge into present-day communities and their politics, both constituting a sense of shared identity and attachment and also, importantly, potentially transforming them.

Chapters 4 and 5 investigate the October 12, 2002 Bali bombing and the December 26, 2004 Southeast Asian tsunami, respectively. The first event was a terrorist attack and the second a natural catastrophe. But both were major traumas that had a significant impact, shattering the smooth functioning of social life and generating political responses that were transnational in nature.

While of a similarly considerable social impact, these two cases are symptomatic of two different political and communal dynamics that can emerge after trauma. The Bali bombing shows how traumatic events can invoke a conservative or insular type of communal response: a strengthening of the nation-state and its corresponding value system. The Southeast Asian tsunami, by contrast, presents trauma in a different light: it shows that representations of tragedy and suffering can transgress sovereign boundaries and create a transnational sense of solidarity and community, fleeting as it may well be.

I examine how the intensely emotional nature of media representations was critical to the respective communal dynamics following each event. Audiences world-wide were immediately inundated with painful stories and distressing images, shaping how people near and far away perceived, engaged with and felt for each event and the ensuing suffering. Dominant representations of the trauma – which I examine through front-page images and texts in leading newspapers – produced the shared meanings necessary to constitute the forms of political community that emerged in response.

I show how textual and visual sources facilitate links between individuals and a wider collective – a group of people brought together by a shared concern and impetus to help those affected by the catastrophe. Hence, I focus most closely on the types of social meanings the representations mobilize and also tap into, and how, in turn, these meanings enable particular shared and political understandings of the each catastrophe. Central here is the emotional content of the words and images and how the emotional nature of both the bombing's and the tsunami's media coverage produced meanings that can be linked to various wider socioculturally embedded emotional dispositions – emotions that can, because of their social nature, work hand-in-hand with collective forms of identity, agency and community.

These two cases demonstrate that emotions can orientate and attach communities in different, albeit intersecting ways. But they also illustrate a prevailing tendency after "collective" trauma: the reflex-like push to narrate what has happened in order to find meaning in an experience that has so shattered the very essence of prior meaning. Ensuing representations therefore constituted community – both Australian national community and the incredible transnational solidarity – primarily through dominant, established discourses of suffering, which, by nature of their affective constitution, also intimate the ways those who experience and witness such suffering should feel. The national community configured after the Bali bombing is highly typical: when acting as a protector of its people, the nation-state has long been a custodian of "secure" feeling. Similarly, the transnational community after the tsunami, as progressive as it also was, was at least in part constituted through patterns of feeling for distant others that limit the same community they help to mobilize.

In this light, my third empirical inquiry – Chapter 6 – examines the possibility and conditions through which trauma can be politically transformative. To do so, I explore how trauma can be represented and in turn perceived of in a manner that promotes grieving and healing. A turn to grief recognizes the inherent need for individuals and communities to confront intensely difficult traumatic emotions and memories in order to be free of, rather than trapped by, past pain.

I offer two historical illustrations that demonstrate the challenges and potentials of socially and politically grieving collective trauma: China and South Africa. China and the so-perceived "Century of National Humiliation" present a situation of a community that has thus far failed to work through historical trauma properly. Toward the other end of the spectrum, South Africa illustrates the political opportunities that are opened by taking time to work through and grieve. In both instances, I continue to underscore the power and potentials of representing trauma, and how doing so is a process imbued with, and capable of mobilizing and even transforming, the emotions that underpin and circulate through communities. Ways of remembering and commemorating trauma can either keep it "alive," or they can help traumatized individuals and communities to acknowledge and successfully mourn injury and loss. The latter, I suggest, is critical. Too often the failure to work through and resolve painful, post-trauma emotions leads to destructive communal patterns and even further violence.

Through all the cases I examine, however, I state at the outset that I am making no claims about the actual impact of the representations I study. Doing so would require a completely different methodology and analysis: surveys, for instance, or psychological experiments or ethnographic inquiries. Expressed in other words, I do not pretend to establish a causal link between representations of catastrophe, emotional reactions and the emergence of a sense of community. But I do deliver a crucial prerequisite for understanding such linkages. I offer detailed insights into the "how" of representation: the processes involved in representing and sharing the respective trauma. I show how trauma is, through representations, emotionally performed in ways that are inherently social. This social, emotional enactment of trauma is then key to the wider meanings that align with, tap into or even help to construct from scratch a sense of civic solidarity and, ultimately, political community. The emotional insights I provide can hence be thought of as a part of the social processes that make particular political conditions – and, in the case of my present inquiry, communities – possible. Recognizing that emotions are bound up in how the respective traumatic events were represented and in the political discourses that followed is thus a crucial first step to understanding the constitution of identity and community that emerged. Emotions are inseparable from both the various representational and interpretative process used to communicate and make sense of the trauma. Understood in this way, emotions can be seen as central to how representations of each event elicited particular ideologies and meanings consonant with the respective communal response.

4 *Emotions and national community*

Late on October 12, 2002, the Islamic group Jemaah Islamiyah set off two bombs in Kuta, Bali's popular tourist and nightclub district. The more powerful of the bombs – a car bomb – was detonated outside the Sari Bar, a Westerners'-only nightclub renowned for its jam-jar cocktails, multiple dance floors and thumping music.[1] The ensuing explosions were to cause inconceivable destruction and carnage. There were 202 people killed. A further 240 were injured. Of all nations affected by the attacks, Australia had the largest number of victims, with eighty-eight of its citizens killed.

The impact of the tragedy was thus felt deeply in Australia. Media and political representations confirmed this response. While the immediate national reaction was one of immense "cultural shock,"[2] within hours journalists and politicians wove reports of the dead and missing into a narrative that told of a distinctly Australian national tragedy. Powerful cultural imagery and political polemics were invoked, rallying the Australian community together around the trauma of what was at the time claimed to be "the world's most devastating terrorist outrage since the September 11 attacks."[3]

Media reporting in particular recounted the crisis and trauma in relation to numerous national concerns and hegemonic cultural and historical frames: dominant conceptions of Australian nationalism, patriotism, culture and identity as well as military mythology were

[1] The other bomb exploded at Paddy's Bar, which in contrast to the Sari Bar bombsite, fails to evoke the same symbolic meanings and memorializations. This is both due to the less severe destruction and, importantly, loss of life, and that, due to this, the Paddy's Bar bombsite has since been remade.

[2] Jeff Lewis and Sonya de Masi, "Unholy Wars: Media Representations of the First Bali Bombings and their Aftermath," *Media International Australia, Incorporating Culture and Policy*, 122 (2007), 59–72, at 62.

[3] Former Prime Minister John Howard cited in M. Moore, L. Dodson and D. Gray, "Dozens of Australians Feared Dead. PM Brands Act 'Barbaric,'" *The Age*, October 14, 2002, p. 1.

frequently evoked.[4] Contemporary debates on terrorism and national security provisions were also repeatedly appropriated: dichotomies of good/evil prevailed and citizens were reminded that "terrorism can touch anybody, anytime and in any country."[5] Further to such remarks the international media even suggested that Australia, as a nation, must now "prepare itself for the worst."[6] But as security focused political concerns bourgeoned both in Australia and overseas, so too did the commemorative discourses that so often prevail in times of perceived national tragedy. Calls for remembrance and distinctly national mourning took over the space the violence opened, ascribing meaning to the potential meaninglessness of victims' pain. Front-page articles documented, both through words and images, the distress of survivors – emotions crumbling the composure of their faces, the plight of those left still fighting for their lives, and more generally the blinding destruction that the bombs had reaped. Victims' pain was swiftly referred to as that of a nation.[7] And an ensuing sense of trauma – the shock and the gravity of loss – was invoked as damaging Australia's "collective soul."[8]

That this vivid depiction of the bombing as a unique, and uniquely devastating national tragedy endures in the present day is additionally telling. Each year the bombing is ceremoniously marked and commemorated by the affected families, Australian and Indonesian politicians, the media and the public alike. Wreaths are laid, candles and lanterns are lit, surfer friends and family bring their boards and together head out to the waves, joining hands in a symbol of respect and freedom. Eighty-eight white doves are released in a tribute of honor and peace. The site of the former Sari Bar is earmarked for a reflective peace

[4] Brad West, "Collective Memory and Crisis: The 2002 Bali Bombing, National Heroic Archetypes and the Counter Narrative of Cosmopolitan Nationalism," *Journal of Sociology*, 44.4 (2008), 337–353, at 343–344, 346–349.

[5] Former Prime Minister John Howard quoted in Don Greenlees, "Terror Hits Home," *The Australian*, October 14, 2002, p. 1.

[6] Dominic Hughes, "Australians in shock after Bali attack," *BBC News*, international edition, October 13, 2002. At http://bbc.co.uk/2/hi/asia-pacific/2324261.stm. Accessed January 13, 2014.

[7] Louise Dodson, "The week the PM felt a nation's pain," *The Age*, October 18, 2002, p. 17; Jennifer Hewett, "Amid a nation's pain, a call to stand together," *Sydney Morning Herald*, October 18, 2002, p. 1.

[8] Mark Ragg, "The numbers no-one wants to figure out," *Sydney Morning Herald*, October 17, 2002, p. 5.

park; however, even in its current unceremonious, "destroyed" and bare state, with the bombing memorial sitting on adjacent land, it continues to be a popular tourist spot and, as commentators and scholars argue, a site of Australian "resilience."[9]

Portrayals of the bombing are among many examples that demonstrate the combined emotional and collectivizing potentials of representing trauma. They show how singular events of trauma can be represented in ways that shift them from an individual experience to a collective and transnational one. To be sure, where individual trauma of direct victims is associated with "repression and denial" followed by an eventual struggle to overcome these symptoms and properly mourn the loss, this kind of "collective trauma" is distinguished by the "symbolic construction and framing" of the event.[10] It depends upon shared processes of cultural interpretation. But in this way it can be seen how the representation and collective enactment of the trauma are inextricably linked: representing the bombing was and continues to be a performative act, both reflective and constitutive of the trauma's social, cultural meaning. In short, representations of the bombing enabled Australian viewers to emotionally enact the trauma in collective ways.

This chapter contributes to my inquiry by forwarding my first empirical case study. Specifically, the chapter probes the linkages between emotions and the constitution of solidarity and community discourses in the wake of this devastating terrorist bombing,[11] an event which has become known, eerily, as Australia's "own" September 11.[12]

[9] Charlotte Heath-Kelly, "Securing through the Failure to Secure? The Ambiguity of Resilience at the Bombsite," *Security Dialogue*, 46.1 (2015), 69–85; Ean Higgins, "Father of Bali Bombing Victim Reflects on his Constant Struggle," *The Australian*, October 13, 2013. At www.theaustralian.com.au/in-depth/terror/father-of-bali-bombing-victim-reflects-on-his-constant-struggle/story-fnpdbcmu-1227088093916. Accessed November 10, 2014.

[10] Jeffrey C. Alexander, *Trauma: A Social Theory* (Cambridge: Polity, 2012), p. 3.

[11] Hereafter referred to simply as the Bali bombing. I note also that the October 12, 2002 Bali bombing is distinguished from the October 1, 2005 Bali bombing, in which twenty people were killed.

[12] Michael Christie, "Flags Lowered as Australia Digests Its Own September 11," *Reuters News*, October 15, 2002. At the twelfth anniversary of the bombing in 2014, Prime Minister Tony Abbott reiterated this metaphor, describing the attack as "our September 11," cited in "Twelfth Anniversary of Bali Bombings to be Marked with Quiet Reflection in Kuta, Australia." At www.news.com.au/world/twelfth-anniversary-of-bali-bombings-to-be-marked-with-quiet-reflection-in-kuta-australia/story-fndir2ev-1227087719623. Accessed November 10, 2014.

The chapter focuses in particular on the effect of media representations, paying attention to how editorials and images published in Australia's sole national newspaper, *The Australian*, drew a very particular and concrete link between individual suffering and the nature and fate of the Australian national community. To do so, I use an interpretative method loosely derived from semiotics and discourse analysis in order to undertake a narrative analysis of textual and visual representations of the bombing. Focusing on the role of emotions in particular, I scrutinize how – through words and images – the trauma was represented in a manner that made it meaningful as a distinctly collective trauma, to not only Australians who experienced it directly but also those who witnessed it, at a distance. Key in this respect is how representations of the bombing attained meaning and resonated in an Australian national context through the sociohistorically embedded emotions they implied, in terms of both the sufferers being depicted and in the Australian audience as distant witnesses.

The chapter argues that representations of the bombing were central to producing meanings constitutive of a particular (and at the time) widely accepted sense of Australian national identity and community. The manner in which media representations repeatedly drew upon a particular perceived national and cultural imaginary as well as particular social and political agenda is most significant: portrayals of the bombing encouraged the wider Australian public to make sense of the trauma in relation to numerous preestablished (historically embedded) culturally bound emotional meanings. At first, these prioritized the unimaginable nature of the attack – the shock and the loss – yet quickly they focused on the anger, outrage and, eventually, shared solace. In this way, I argue that not only were media representations key to how the wider national collective was prompted to make emotional meaning of the trauma, but also, moreover, that at the time such emotional meanings prioritized an insular and seemingly homogenous – as well as xenophobic – form of Australian identity and nationalism. Alternative or marginalized forms of political community (either within or beyond the bounded community of the nation-state) were closed off. In this sense, the bombing became a "national trauma,"[13] even though it was in fact transnational in

[13] Ron Eyerman, *Cultural Trauma: Slavery and the Formation of African American Identity* (Cambridge: Cambridge University Press, 2001), p. 3.

nature: the crisis attained accepted cultural and in this case national meaning through the processes of mass-mediation and popular representation. Emotions, I show, were necessarily embedded within these meanings and within the type of national identity and community that was implicated in response.

Before turning to the media context and then to the analysis itself, a brief disclaimer is, however, first in order. In examining representations of the bombing I stress that I am not trying to provide a comprehensive account of the event and its political implications. It is beyond the scope of my inquiry to ascertain exactly how cohesive such a community was; no doubt there were fissures of dissent, emergent or discordant forms of community that mainstream media accounts are unable to trace. Neither am I making absolutist claims about the kinds of emotions the bombing solicited, nor that multiple interpretations of the event and its various mediations are not possible. My aim, rather, is more modest: to illustrate how representational practices fostered a particular dominant narrative about the catastrophe, and how in turn the wider communal linkages forged – either rhetorically or actually – by such representations are reliant upon mobilizing discourses that are not only socially, culturally and historically based, but also inherently emotional.

Narrating a national trauma across a transnational space: examining media representations of the 2002 Bali bombing

The Bali bombing was a shocking event for Australians both in Kuta and back home. This is even though in reality the attack was a transnational experience: it occurred in a foreign sovereign space, with casualties of more than twenty different nationalities. Yet very quickly Australian media outlets presented the attack as a distinctly Australian national trauma. At the time such an attack – with so many Australian causalities – was unprecedented. Never before had Australians – either at home or overseas – been the direct targets of terrorism.

To understand the trauma of the bombing, one needs to look not only at the unpredictable and devastating nature of the attack itself, but also at the significance of Bali within the broader Australian imaginary. While beyond Australia's sovereign shores, Bali has come to symbolize the laid-back, fun, frivolous lifestyle so much loved by the majority of Australians. For much of the year, the beach and party scene of Bali attracts scores of Australian travelers, honeymooners, surfers and end-of-season sports club celebrations. It is a place where young Australians in particular go to have a good time. So popular has Bali become that some even go as far as to consider it a figurative and geographic "land-bridge," connecting Australia to the rest of the world and in turn to a growing sense of regional belonging.[14] The bombing, and its many young casualties, was thus especially shocking as it was perceived not only to tear at this bond but also to injure the fun-loving, seemingly innocent "way of life" of Australians more generally. And with respect to Bali itself, as Jeff Lewis and Sonya de Masi explain: "it was unimaginable that Australia's playground was paradise no longer."[15]

It was therefore not surprising that news of the bombing dominated the Australian media for weeks. Print news reporting commenced on Monday, October 14, 2002, and was, from the very beginning, explicitly emotional. Both images and stories brought forth the injury and terror of victims. They also sought to communicate the brutality of the bombing's perpetrators. Headlines and the language of stories discussed individual damage as deeply wounding Australia, as a nation. Visual aids were no less candid. Purgatory-like realities presented themselves through front-page images, and as the suffering of so many Australians was made visual, captions gave testimony of compatriots wanting to flee for "home." As such, representations of the bombing may be linked with concomitant notions of compassion and solidarity. They negotiated emotions, explicitly representing the event in ways that called upon a sense of collective fear, anger, grief and solace. In so doing, individual emotions of witnesses were linked, implicitly, with those of both survivors and the political figures that were said to be working desperately toward an official response. The solidarity of an Australian national community was swiftly summoned. Indeed, using the media as a gauge, it certainly seemed that the emotions associated with the shock, outrage and grief were collective ones. A sense of shared meaning, purpose and identity was articulated in what became an "us"/"them" type of rhetoric. Outwardly reflective of this were both the publicly respected calls

[14] Jeff Lewis, "Paradise Defiled: The Bali Bombings and the Terror of National Identity," *European Journal of Cultural Studies*, 9.2 (2006), 223–242, at 224.

[15] Lewis and Masi, "Unholy Wars," 64.

for collective remembrance and commemoration, and the discourses of retributive justice that subsequently emerged.

Underpinning these various representations and subsequent discourses that surrounded the tragedy was, I argue, the interweaving of individual and collective emotion. Or, put differently, representations and ensuing discourses produced meanings that can be distinguished by the widely accepted, and socially formed, emotions they imply. How the media and other representational outlets captured the crisis not only told a story about what happened, but also made one feel. This was accomplished in a way that sought to align individual emotions with the wider emotionally charged social discourses that ultimately narrated and gave meaning to the catastrophe. Individual emotions of witnesses were thus not exactly individual per se, but rather they were socially mobilized and performed. Narratives of national loss, public commemoration and political security helped to guide apparently individualized emotional responses. They sought, either purposefully or naively, to smooth over feelings of discontinuity – the shock and terror – and unite individuals in a spirit of shared experience and bereavement. This was achieved as much through the journalistic and testimonial accounts of the trauma as it was through the images that appeared adjacent to them.

Paradise lost as "Terror Hits Home": the emotional resonance and collectivizing potentials of textual interpretations of trauma

The Australian media established a common frame of reference for the narration of the bombing from early on. This framing promoted understandings consonant with the ensuing trauma being nation-wide in character. Media frames sought to achieve this in both a very explicit, overtly political and also implicit manner. The most explicit way was through the persistent representation of the bombing as an attack not simply against Australians in Bali but against Australians and Australian culture more generally. The innocence of every young, sun- and fun-loving Australian was portrayed as lost, forever. Linkages were quickly drawn between the heroism of victims and the famous Anzacs (Australian and New Zealand Army Corp).[16] In Australian

[16] West, "Collective Memory and Crisis," 346–347.

military history and mythology the latter are perceived to have bravely and defiantly lost their lives young in a foreign country, and are once a year ritually commemorated. Rigorous inquests into appropriate foreign and security policy in a post-September 11 world were initiated. A number of cultural tropes were also frequently invoked, thereby implicitly directing Australians "back home" to consider the bombing alongside further national, emotive messages. The bombing was repeatedly referenced as an attack to the Australian way of life: not only in terms of the Australian beach- and fun-loving culture but also to broader cultural ideals of freedom, democracy and liberty. Prominent political commentator Greg Sheridan, for instance, claimed there was "no doubt" Australia was "specifically targeted ... because it is a democratic, affluent, Western society."[17] Finally, media reporting also extended to remembrance practices, which were already beginning one week after.[18] Beach ceremonies took place and the media passed on the then Prime Minister John Howard's wish for everyone to wear the national flower – wattle – on the official day of mourning.

This is a very broad sketch of the prevailing media portrayals. I now look closely at one specific textual representation. I undertake an interpretative, narrative style analysis of a prominent and representative news editorial that draws heavily on the dominant media frames discussed above. In doing so, I demonstrate how key textual interpretations are implicated in the process of constructing meanings that promoted collective understandings of, reckoning with and feeling about the tragedy.

Published in *The Australian*, one week after the bombing, the (anonymous) editorial was titled "Australians united share the sorrow of Bali."[19] The editorial is an evocative yet also surprisingly prescriptive meditation on the tragedy of the bombing and how wider Australians should respond. It is both influential through its prominent outlet and representative of wider editorial comments and reporting on the Bali bombing, which is why I chose to analyze it in detail here. The editorial sums up much of what was said through the media, by survivors, journalists and politicians alike. From the very beginning

[17] For example, Greg Sheridan, "A Threat We Ignore at Our Peril," *The Australian*, October 14, 2002, p. 11.
[18] Luke McIlveen, "Day of Mourning on Sunday," *The Australian*, October 15, 2002, p. 2.
[19] *The Australian*, October 19, 2002, p. 18.

it illustrates the combined emotional and collectivizing potential of patterns of speech:

It used to be said that no town in Australia lacked its war memorial to young men who had given their lives for the defence of our freedom. Today, as many homes and schools and sports clubs echo to the sobbing of distraught families, friends and lovers of Australians caught in the front line of terror. The front line is everywhere. No longer are we immune. Even though Bali is beyond our shores, it had become almost an extension of our lifestyle. Holidaying at Kuta beach and soaking up the sun, surf and party scene was almost a rite of passage for young Australians.

In a number of ways this passage works to contextualize the trauma for Australians who witnessed from home. It tells of the social and emotional impact of the bombing. Readers are told that broader social institutions (i.e. "homes and schools and sports clubs") mourn the catastrophe alongside victims' families and friends. In another less explicit way, the lives of those lost or directly affected by the bombing are paralleled with those who look on; Bali is represented as not only a place symbolic of Australian lifestyle but also one that most Australians have holidayed in. According to the author, "soaking up the sun, surf and party scene" in Bali is a distinctly – almost ritualistic – Australian activity.

Significant to portrayals such as these are the feelings of sympathy, care as well as affinity and solidarity that are crucial to the collective reckoning with trauma. By representing the bombing in ways that promote common or shared (or at least comprehensible) understandings, as well as the power of stereotypical cultural identification, the passage also diminishes distance. The trauma is pushed into, aligned with, and made relevant to, the lives of Australians more generally. Compounding this are hinted-at notions of collective insecurity and fear. It is claimed that the "front line" at which victims suffered is now "everywhere," and, moreover, that Australians are no longer immune to acts of atrocity. Statements such as this prompt one to question: Should readers fear for their lives as well? If the possibility of terror is pervasive – if it is "everywhere" – where is secure? Likening the trauma of the bombing with that of state-sanctioned war is still another way the editorial contextualizes the catastrophe. Beginning with a comment upon war memorials, and also in using the distinctly war-like term "front line," the editorial traverses the trauma in a way that reinforces the notion of it being a national (if not nationalistic) one. Patriotic language such as this arguably reinforces the idea of the nation as hub of social well-being and political community.

Most of the themes examined in this short passage are reiterated throughout the remainder of the editorial. Continuing, the editorial makes comment that:

> It has not been the general lot of Australian's young people to have to face the scourge of wholesale terrorism, or to be in places where danger remains. By bringing personal accounts, the uttered dying words, and the sentiments of sorrow which might have been suppressed, the journalists and photographers covering this tragedy have empowered us to reach out as a nation. For the outrage was not just against a building but to extract maximum harm to people whose only fault was having a relaxed and happy time.

This passage makes further reference to how the bombing impacts Australia, both as a community of mourning and as an "empowered" nation. An emphasis is placed both on a sense of collective outrage and what the author considers the previously diminished danger young Australians have (until now) been privileged with. Assumptions about the victims are also presented here. Faulting them only with the desire to relax and be happy harps back to a kind of lifestyle that is considered distinctly and traditionally "Australian." The most nationalist and explicitly emotive passage in the editorial does, however, come later.

> If it is true that death defines us, many of us have suddenly had to realise our mortality. We will ponder this during tomorrow's national day of mourning. Even though our participation in many wars has already conditioned us, this new type of war brings us face-to-face with a new situation nationally. But as a nation we have every right to respond strongly. Fundamentalist terrorism is a threat to our way of life. The people of Australian need to resist any notion that anything other than a fierce defence of our values is warranted.

Here, one can see most clearly how textual representational practices attempt to shift individual trauma into that of a wider, distinctly national community. Couched within this passage is the possibility of many different emotions, and also, I suggest, an implicit attempt to share or collectivize them. Although these emotions are embedded within the individual reflections of one author, the passage is written with a kind of collective authority – a collective voice even. Death is represented as something that the bombing has prompted many Australians to now consider. It is additionally claimed that one's own death is something to be reflected upon whilst mourning the trauma of others. This pulls the reader – she/he who witnesses – further into the trauma. A sense of authenticity and identification is invoked. It prompts one to imagine, and to perhaps fear, the possibility (and inevitability) of their own pain, and the direction that readers are to do so alongside the trauma of the victims seems key to the possibility of an empathetic emotional response. Key here is that feelings of solidarity are evoked through a perceived likeness. And, as such, the trauma and terror of direct victims is mediated as a public phenomenon evoking feelings and memories that inhabit a wider culture. Emotions of grief and loss are represented as that of a society; private processes of mourning are depicted as a distinctly collective activity, one with which many Australians identify and will indeed take part in. Moreover, one can see the editorial again drawing upon contemporary discourses of terrorism and collective insecurity. Implicit here is not only a sense of collective fear, but also the call for retribution and the defense of wider Australian societal values. What is striking is that although the bombing took place in Bali, Indonesia, the attack is represented as emblematic of a threat to Australia's collective "way of life"; it is perceived to draw a line around Australian – and as some argue, Western – values, thereby creating the perception of Australian cultural exceptionalism and also a further point of perceived likeness with which an Australian audience may identify.[20]

Other reported responses to the bombing also reflect the attempt to connect the event with a much wider sense of collective (distinctly national) trauma and injury. Corresponding emotional responses, such as fear, were evoked as well. Initially, the bombing was presented as shocking not only for direct victims, but also for the "throngs of Australians"[21] who either holidayed in Bali or watched dumbstruck at home. Through the weeks that followed, private mourning was presented, quickly becoming that of the Australian public. A national day of mourning was called and Australians were urged to wear a native blossom – wattle – in tribute and remembrance.[22] As memorial services

[20] See Lewis and de Masi, "Unholy Wars"; Lewis, "Paradise Defiled."
[21] Greenlees, "Terror Hits Home," *The Australian*, October 14, 2002, p. 1.
[22] See Mark Metherell, "Sprig of Wattle for Mourning," *Sydney Morning Herald*, October 18, 2002, p. 2.

took place Australian survivors openly claimed that the Bali bombing had irreparably changed the shape of their nation.[23] Discourses of terrorism and ensuing themes of collective insecurity, fear and panic also seemed to pervade the media more than ever before.[24] Then Prime Minister John Howard also reminded Australia that the "barbarity" of the Sari Bar bombing "can touch anybody, anytime and in any country."[25] Political editor Dennis Shanahan went so far as to comment that "no one is safe anywhere, Australia as a nation and Australians as a people can't hide."[26] Reviews of domestic security and counterterrorism legislation were immediately ordered and the Defence Department even went so far as to label their white paper "Fortress Australia."[27] Fear invoked from the bombing was represented as the product of a potentially wider threat and representations of the bombing evoked a corresponding sense of societal terror. Interestingly – as with the above editorial – coupled with such fear were calls to defend so-called Australian values and way of life.[28]

One can thus see the collectivizing potential of linguistically representing trauma. By both explicitly detailing the injury and terror, and by implying that Australia is the "home" to which survivors simply wish to return, the language employed to depict the bombing can be seen as an attempt to resonate with and guide individuals' emotions toward the comfort and sanctity of a wider (again national) community – ideationally as well as geographically.[29] Many of the expressions employed can also be distinguished as those of "membership

[23] Hewett, "Amid a Nation's Pain, a Call to Stand Together," p. 1.

[24] One reflection of this was that four out of the five most circulated state broadsheets packaged their coverage under themes that drew upon a wider sense of wounding and panic. For an overview of these, see Sally Jackson and Stephen Brook, "Death in Bali – How Australia's Media Reacted when Terror Hit our Doorstep," *The Australian*, October 17, 2002.

[25] Quoted in Greenlees, "Terror Hits Home."

[26] "Deaths will not Sway PM on Iraq Stand," *The Australian*, October 14, 2002, p. 4.

[27] Defence Minister Robert Hill referenced in Dodson, "The Week the PM felt a Nation's Pain," p. 17.

[28] Sheridan, "A Threat We Ignore at Our Peril."

[29] For an account of how representational practices employed by both the media and politicians after the Bali bombing were used to construct public support for government foreign policy, see Matt McDonald, "Constructing Insecurity: Australian Security Discourse and Policy Post-2001," *International Relations*, 19.3 (2005), 297–320.

categorization"[30] or "naming."[31] Terms such as "our way of life" and the "barbarity" of the implied enemies draw "us"/"them" type distinctions, which in this case essentially group victims together within a wider conglomerate of Australian society.

Thus, in sum, textual representations of the trauma can be interpreted to have enacted and enabled – while paradoxically also limiting – the boundaries of political community.[32] The emotions and meanings invoked by ostensibly ordinary patterns of speech and writing were part of this process, helping to reinforce prevailing forms of political sovereignty – and thus community. Evidenced by the above editorial, mainstream representations of the bombing reinstated power structures traditional to the nation-state, which while seeming to strengthen the Australian national community simultaneously silences alternative discourses through which new configurations of community can be generated.

Grievable lives and sublime horror: from images of the unimaginable to those that invoke outrage and solace

Images of the bombing and subsequent acts of mourning reinforced the emotional undertones of the trauma's linguistic representation. Initial images portrayed the devastation and carnage that the bombs had reaped. Consider the front page of *The Australian* on the first day of full media coverage that followed.[33] The newspaper devoted half the page to a photograph of survivors as they staggered from the burning hull of the buildings (Figure 4.1).

The photograph captures two Australian survivors, injured and helping one another. They are alone; no other victims or rescue workers are in sight; struggling forward as if escaping the depths of a truly traumatic situation. Around them the building burns in a tangled mess. What's normally kept inside – the hardware of wires and

[30] See Ivan Leuder, Victoria Marsland and Jiří Nekvapil, "On Membership Categorization: 'Us,' 'Them' and 'Doing Violence' in Political Discourse," *Discourse & Society*, 15.2/3 (2004), 243–266.

[31] Michael V. Bhatia, "Fighting Words: Naming Terrorists, Bandits, Rebels and Other Violent Actors," *Third World Quarterly*, 26.1 (2005), 5–22.

[32] On the role that "representations of danger" play in constructing international relations, see, for instance, David Campbell, *Writing Security: United States Foreign Policy and the Politics of Identity*, 2nd ed. (Minneapolis: University of Minnesota Press, 1998).

[33] *The Australian*, October 14, 2002.

THE AUSTRALIAN

AUSTRALIA'S BEST SCHOOLS PAGE 16

NUMBER 11,836 MONDAY OCTOBER 14 2002 www.theaustralian.com.au $1.20*

CARNAGE ON BALI – 8 AUSTRALIANS DEAD, 60 CRITICAL

TERROR HITS HOME

■ 183 dead in Kuta nightclub bombings

■ Islamic terror groups chief suspects

■ Howard sends in Australian investigators

Metres from death for lifelong friends

MORE REPORTS PAGES 2-7, WORLDWIDE PAGE 11, EDITORIAL PAGE 14, OPINION PAGE 15

HE has now killed eight but police appear to be no closer to catching the Washington sniper – Page 12

AUSTRALIA'S best schools. We begin a groundbreaking series to celebrate excellence in education – Page 16

AFTER an epic seven-hour battle against the elements and old rival Peter Brock, Mark Skaife wins Bathurst – Page 17

SOLOMON Lew has begun his campaign for re-election with an attack on his fellow Coles directors – Page 27

Sport ... Page 17
Weather ... Page 23
Television ... Page 25
Business ... Page 27
Crosswords ... Page 28

Figure 4.1 Front page of *The Australian*, October 14, 2002.

plumbing – lies exposed. Whether consciously done or not, the image creates a vivid visual metaphor, one that sums up the bewilderment and upside-down world of those directly affected by the bombing.

Images such as this one are instrumental to the expression and collectivizing dynamics of the trauma.[34] By graphically presenting the horror and pain of unknown others, the image stops viewers short. It seems to present things as they really are. Distinct here is the feeling of authenticity, of being there and experiencing the horror too. Forcing one to look at the image may not only prompt one to imagine the victims' trauma, but engage emotions generally associated with witnessing: shock, incomprehension, fear and the guilt of looking on. Yet in the sense that it portrays Australian survivors, this image can be seen to bring the catastrophe and its devastation into focus in a culturally identifiable – as well as emotionally directive and collectivizing – way. Viewing the image in conjunction with the headline is in this respect particularly illustrative. Once again: although the bombing occurred on foreign shores, viewers are prompted, through the eye-catching headline and captions, to make sense of the image and the catastrophe as one perpetrated upon their "home." Representing the event in this way therefore employs very simple representational techniques that push the catastrophe into the lives of Australians, making it appear as a trauma to Australians more generally and not just to the individuals who were directly impacted.

Another way to highlight the collectivizing role of images of the bombing is to examine how – over the course of one week – the publicly available images created a particular narrative, or story. First presented was the above image (Figure 4.1), one of arresting intensity and visual power. By representing the un-presentable the image confronts viewers with confusion and many unknowns. As soon as the following day, however, front-page photographs markedly changed. They were full of the meaning that this initial image lacked. Significant here is the contrast of images – the replacing of shock with images that provide solace or grounds for other forms of emotional understanding.

Below are examples of two such front-page images (Figures 4.2 and 4.3). These were again featured within the initial week of media

[34] See Ulrich Baer, *Spectral Evidence: The Photography of Trauma* (Cambridge, MA.: MIT Press, 2002).

THE AUSTRALIAN

NUMBER 11,837 TUESDAY OCTOBER 15 2002 www.theaustralian.com.au $1.20*

TERROR HITS HOME - THE LIST OF VICTIMS, SURVIVORS COME HOME, LOVED ONES GRIEVE

COUNTING THE TOLL

Jakarta blames al-Qa'ida

The lost who will never return

'When we heard the blast, we ran back to the club and I ran into the flames'

'The blast is related to al-Qa'ida with the co-operation of local terrorists'

Inside

Australia has no option but to work jointly with South East Asian countries to detect, disrupt, degrade and destroy the Jemaah Islamiah organization. Its failure to do so will result in further attacks in the neighbourhood of Australia and even inside Australia. The threat is likely to develop, not diminish, with time.

– Rohan Gunaratna, Opinion, Page 15

MORE REPORTS PAGES 2-8, EDITORIAL PAGE 14, OPINION PAGE 15, BUSINESS PAGE 19

Home delivery 1 800 022 552

POLICE are hunting for the gunman who shot and killed South Australia's mental health chief yesterday – Page 9

THE sex abuse case against George Pell has been dismissed but the judge says the complainant is not a liar – Page 9

RODNEY Adler made me do it – Brad Cooper unloads on his old mate in at HIH hearings – Page 9

AUSTRALIA'S Best Schools: six that have shown a dramatic improvement during the past year – Page 13

Sport .... Page 16
Television .... Page 17
Crosswords .... Page 20
Classifieds .... Page 32
Weather .... Page 36

Figure 4.2 Front page of *The Australian*, October 15, 2002.

THE AUSTRALIAN

NUMBER 11,840 FRIDAY OCTOBER 18 2002 www.theaustralian.com.au $1.20

OFFICIAL WARNING: GET OUT OF INDONESIA – FULL STORY, PAGE 2

Noose tightens on Bali suspect

Four mates drink in the Sari Club: moments later three of them are dead

Adam Howard (dead) Josh Iliffe (dead) Gerard Yeo (dead) Patrick Byrne (survived)

Grieving: From left, Adam Condon, Jason Byrne and Trent and Peter Iliffe at the Iliffe family home in Bowral yesterday Picture: Glenn Campbell

Sarah Bryden-Brown

Inside
The official Australian death toll stands at 33 but could rise as high as 122
– Full report, Page 4

Continued – Page 2
Life cut short – Page 4

Howard leads farewell: 'Our spirit is unbroken'

Roger Martin

LIFE CUT SHORT – A CONTINUING MEMORIAL TO THE VICTIMS OF BALI – PAGE 4

1 800 680 640

NORTH Korea admits it has spent years secretly producing material for nuclear weapons – Page 7

"EVERYONE will think it was about money": Matthew Wales pleads guilty to society murders – Page 7

TEN of the Best – schools that achieved distinction in a particular area but still offer a rounded education – Page 13

Sol-lew.com.au – old king Coles takes his boardroom re-election campaign into cyberspace – Page 25

Opinion .... Page 17
Weather .... Page 18
Preview .... Page 19
Sport .... Page 24

Figure 4.3 Front page of *The Australian*, October 18, 2002.

coverage, when the full scale – and death toll – of the attacks were slowly becoming known.

Key to these images is that they visualize to the wider Australian public the exact impact of the bombing: the young, seemingly resilient lives, lost. Specifically, what was seen were the smiling faces of the young Australians who were either missing or pronounced dead. These photographs were generally taken from family albums. Young Australians were purposefully pictured as they were before the bombing: drinking beer with their mates, cradling infant children, and sitting on beaches, soaking in the sun. Accompanying headlines paradoxically both questioned how such a tragedy could happen to so many innocent and fun-loving Australians while at the same time they implied that Australians were targeted precisely because of their distinct national culture.[35] Photographs and headlines such as these again locate the catastrophe and its direct impact within established societal or cultural meanings. In particular, the images play on the mainstream cultural imaginary within Australia: drinking and partying with mates is (now visually) portrayed as an activity in which most Australians would partake – and moreover one they would undertake in a very typical fun-loving manner. Accompanying front-page stories also reported on the heroism of surviving young men who bravely "bulldozed" their way back into the Sari Bar in order to find their friends.[36] Through these images and stories the emotions associated with witnessing are guided as well, suggesting not only immediate shock but also the loss and grief that are commonly associated with trauma.

To the Australian public, the images thus "fill in" many of the unknowns – who was affected by the bombing and how – and in so doing provide points of commonality that help viewers distinguish how and for whom they should feel. Specifically, the focus on Australian survivors – as carefree mates, as heroes – taps into established (and widespread accepted) cultural stories of what it means to belong as an Australian. To invoke Judith Butler's argument, such imagery distinguishes the lives of the Australians that were lost as "grievable."[37] They provide "'frames' that work to differentiate the lives we can

[35] This point is also made by and reiterated in Lewis and de Masi, "Unholy Wars," 68–69.

[36] Sarah Brydon-Brown, "Four Mates Drink in the Sari Bar, Moments Later Three of Them Are Dead," *The Australian*, October 18, 2002, p. 1.

[37] Judith Butler, *Frames of War: When is Life Grievable?* (London: Verso, 2008).

apprehend from those we cannot."[38] Such frames steer viewers toward particular historically conditioned understandings of who belongs with whom; the images are the visual experience of how individuals are always already socially and collectively situated. A sense of solidarity is summoned through a potential range of combined individual and collective emotions, such as shock (at the bombing), grief (at the sense of loss), fear (of the now present vulnerability), outrage and anger (toward the perpetrators).

Front-page images and associated stories also gave warning of an impending "season of terror."[39] These images filled out the visual narrative still further by summoning conventional security discourses that perpetuate the perception of external threat and, by extension, prioritize the nation as the hub of both security and community.

The below image and again un-missable headline on the first weekend edition of *The Australian* following the bombing is a potent example (Figure 4.4).

The focus of this image lies with the prime minister, surrounded by Australian and Indonesian officials. Looming in the background is the scorched, wrecked hull of the blasted building. Together with associated headlines, captions and stories, the image is a powerful one, communicating various messages: the appalling nature of the catastrophe; the perceived cruelty of the bombing; the elevated security risks for both remaining Australians and those watching at "home"; and, finally, the swift and compassionate political response. The lead article in particular focuses on the now grave security concerns. The article reports of the perceived high possibility that "multiple, simultaneous attacks were being planned."[40] The prime minister reiterated this warning, claiming that he felt further attacks against Australians were "very likely." Based on the high level of threats to Australians, the Department of Foreign Affairs and Trade also issued an urgent warning for citizens to return home.[41] Therefore, once again, we see – through front-page images and texts – the invocation of collective

[38] Butler, *Frames of War*, p. 3.

[39] Roy Eccleston, Don Greenlees and Megan Saunders, "World Alert: Season of Terror," *The Weekend Australian*, October 19–20, 2002, p. 1.

[40] "World Alert: Season of Terror," p. 1.

[41] Department of Foreign Affairs and Trade cited in Eccleston, Greenlees and Saunders, "World Alert: Season of Terror."

THE WEEKEND AUSTRALIAN

NUMBER 11,841 OCTOBER 19-20 2002 www.theaustralian.com.au

INQUIRER SPECIAL DAYS OF LIVING DANGEROUSLY

WHY WEREN'T WE WARNED? PAGE 19

INDONESIA: SEEDBED OF TERRORISM PAGE 21

THE NIGHT TERROR HIT HOME PAGE 24-25

THE HUMAN TOLL PAGE 29

PAUL KELLY NOW WE ARE AT WAR PAGE 30

INSIDE: LIFE CUT SHORT - A MEMORIAL TO THE VICTIMS OF BALI

World alert: season of terror

'You see it in Bali, you see it in Kuwait. They plan in multiple theatres of operations'

Howard weeps at 'cruel view of humanity'

Six degrees of tragedy in west

Survivor to stand tall for his sister

INSIDE STORY

A home loan rate you'll be really comfortable with.

4.49% PA

Fixed for 6 months

National

Bankers recommend Zip instant boiling water. "It's faster than an ATM."

Home delivery 1 800 022 552

Figure 4.4 Front page of *The Weekend Australian*, October 19–20, 2002.

insecurity and fear, not only to direct victims but also to the Australian population more generally. All Australians, in Bali and back home, are put under warning.

Furthermore, while the "Season of Terror" article headlined, the photograph soon draws one's gaze downwards, to another front-page article, "Howard Weeps at 'Cruel View of Humanity.'"[42] This article supplements threat and security orientated messages by communicating the appalling "cruelty" of targeting a place that was "a home away from home for generations of young Australians." While standing at what was said to be "Australia's Ground Zero,"[43] the prime minister repeated this message as well. He told firsthand that "[t]o have that birthright assaulted in such a vicious and cruel fashion does anger me greatly."[44] But the portrayal of the prime minister as a political leader possessing great compassion was also invoked: he was said to be "unable to explain the compassion he felt for families"; and that "[w]earing a sprig of wattle in his shirt" (as, we remember from the textual analysis, he encouraged all Australians to do) he "laid a wreath at the scene and bowed in silence."

The image and associated texts clearly reflect the intensely emotional dynamics of both the event and political response. Yet it is the manner in which they do so that is important to contemplating how the image and texts promote forms of collective emotional understanding. Similar to my editorial analysis in the previous section, we see many shared – supposedly typical "Australian" – attributes being invoked. In particular, holidaying and partying in Bali is a part of a set of cultural practices considered to be Australian by "birthright" – indeed, Bali is even said to be a "home away from home" for Australians. We can also interpret the combined visual and textual portrayals as (either conscious or unconscious) attempts to create and/or mobilize particular typical Australian cultural icons. In the image's background the blasted Sari Bar is claimed and becomes "Australia's Ground Zero"

[42] Roger Martin, "Howard Weeps at 'Cruel View of Humanity,'" *The Weekend Australian*, October 19–20, 2002, p. 1.

[43] The full caption for the front-page image on *The Weekend Australian*, October 19, 2002 reads: "Kuta. Standing at Australia's Ground Zero yesterday, tears welling in his eyes, John Howard was lost for words as he surveyed the blackened wreckage where, just six days earlier, more than 100 Australians were murdered by terrorists."

[44] Prime Minister John Howard directly quoted in Martin, "Howard Weeps at 'Cruel View of Humanity.'"

(just as the site of the World Trade Center was in the US), and the national flower – wattle – fixed to the prime minister's lapel, a silent act of remembrance for the entire nation.

The final step in constructing the bombing's visual narrative – and, in doing so, guiding the wider Australian community's response – took shape through the many public photographs of those in private mourning. Consider the image featured on page one of *The Australian* on October 21 (Figure 4.5).

Again occupying almost half the front page, families were shown – heads bowed and weeping – at a church memorial service. This image, and indeed even the accompanying headline ("Grieving for lost innocents"), appears as a normal and perhaps even a-political visual depiction of the reality of mourning. However, it is precisely in its commonality and so-called obviousness[45] that the image gains representative authority and power.[46] It presents perceivably "ordinary" families expressing grief in seemingly ordinary ways. Certainly many – if not all – who saw this picture would be able to recall similar experiences themselves or (empathetically) imagine how this process might be.

Survivors, families and Australians who themselves bore witness through the media's representations were also featured in visibly emotional stages of grief: families greeting their returned loved ones, the hundreds who rallied together at national commemorative services, and the flowing tears and embraces of children as they look unbelievably on. Politicians were also shown expressing their condolences, presenting honors to those who died. Foremost, then Prime Minister John Howard was pictured in front of hundreds of people paying tribute to those who lost their lives.[47]

As temporary and fleeting as these images may seem, they play an important role in constructing a socially symbolic, collective vision of trauma. By harnessing the "rawness" of the event and ensuing processes of grief, the photographs provide a social space conducive to the collective acknowledgment and reckoning with trauma. They resonate emotionally with viewers and can (in often unrecognized and

[45] Laura Shepherd, "Visualising Violence: Legitimacy and Authority in the 'War on Terror,'" *Critical Studies in Terrorism*, 1.2 (2008), 213–226.

[46] For further insight into the relationship between photographic representation and power, see John Tagg, *The Burden of Representation: Essays in Photographies and Histories* (Basingstoke: Palgrave Macmillan, 1988), pp. 21–22.

[47] *Sydney Morning Herald*, October 18, 2002, p. 1.

THE AUSTRALIAN

NUMBER 11,842 MONDAY OCTOBER 21 2002 www.theaustralian.com.au

INSIDE TODAY

RUGBY WORLD CUP TICKET BOOKLET

Grieving for lost innocents

The man who planted the bomb

Home front priority

Local voters deliver Crean a harsh kick in the seat

Broadband Internet

$19.99

10,000MB FREE!

Pay As You Go!

TPG

Call 1300 360 855

Figure 4.5 Front page of *The Australian*, October 21, 2002.

unintentional ways) act to pull people together with what seems to be their power to authentically represent and create meaning. In showing how ordinary Australians work through the immensity of loss and grief, photographs of the bombing implicitly parallel the experiences of victims and their families with those of Australians who were bearing witness through the television and newspapers back home. Visual representations of the bombing may therefore be linked with feelings of sympathy, empathy, compassion and solidarity, feelings that are often seen as instrumental to the social attachments needed to reinforce a sense of national identity and community.[48]

Summary: emotions and the transnational mediation of a national trauma

This chapter has empirically illustrated the combined representational and emotional processes through which traumatic events can be framed in ways that help to constitute or consolidate collective identity and community. Specifically, it has shown how the representing traumatic events can mobilize social and political discourses that communicate and are made meaningful at least in part through the historically and culturally embedded emotions they suggest. In turn, these emotionally laden discourses situate a group of individuals in relation to the trauma by creating shared forms of perceiving and understanding. Simply put, representations of the bombing appealed to and arguably resonated with the Australian people because of the emotions that shared understandings of the bombing implied. Representations and their meanings resonated affectively, and gained collective credence and power in doing so. In such circumstances and through such processes, a collective sense of identity and political community can consequently – even if temporarily – ensue.

At issue in the case I examined is the transnational construction of a national, collective trauma. This means that through processes of popular representation and mass media coverage the individual trauma of direct victims and witnesses was made meaningful through a range of

[48] See Sara Ahmed, *The Cultural Politics of Emotion* (Edinburgh: Edinburgh University Press, 2004), pp. 8, 9–10, 131–133, 156–158, 193–195; Kate Nash, "Cosmopolitan Political Community: Why Does It Feel So Right?" *Constellations: An International Journal of Critical and Democratic Theory*, 10.4 (2003), 506–518.

social and emotional discourses that prioritized the injury and suffering as the result of an act committed against a nation-state. The narratives and images I analyzed here were the ones recognized, explained, reflected upon, understood and ultimately – I assume, though cannot prove conclusively through my type of analysis – also accepted by a majority of the national community. Opposed to physical or even direct psychological (PTSD-based) trauma, national trauma – which scholars additionally align with the phenomenon of "cultural trauma"[49] – is preceded by events of such magnitude that they seem to rupture the social fabric of a nation. A sense of identity and meaning is shattered or suspended by the event. The event may play over and over in the respective social and communal sphere. Paradoxically, though, swiftly after, attempts to reinstate order and control also take place. The event – as traumatic and as difficult to forget or even to comprehend as it may be – is interpreted in ways that fold into the social landscape it ruptures, defining the very community it in fact transgresses. Nowhere is this transgression more apparent than in the case of national trauma.

The chapter has empirically examined the emotional and collectivizing dynamics of trauma by demonstrating how representations of the Bali bombing positioned Australia as a national affective community. Representations of the bombing created a context in which the catastrophe – as transnational as it was in character – was perceived as traumatic for an entire nation. Textual and visual representations in the media played a particularly important role. They invoked a sense of shared feeling, and promoted meanings that drew on emotions such as fear, outrage and solace. They did so by presenting Australians with images of death and of heroic survival, of families and friends in mourning, and the expedience of political responses. Headlines and associated stories captured the public imagination by suggesting Australia, as a nation, was a community united by shock and grief. While such mediations may not go so far as to specifically tell individuals what to think and how to feel, making sense of representations inevitably involves a reliance upon the sociocultural discourses most familiar to us. Representations of the bombing can thus be seen to

[49] For example, Alexander, *Trauma*, pp. 3–4, 6–10; Eyerman, *Cultural Trauma*, p. 2; Piotr Stompka, "Cultural Trauma: The Other Face of Social Change," *European Journal of Social Theory*, 3.4 (2000), 449–466.

have alluded to meanings that linked the trauma with stereotypical ideals of Australian identity and the search to protect a vulnerable and insecure national political community.

My inquiry underlines the central role emotions and emotional meanings play in constructing the shared understandings of trauma that can underpin a community. Not only are our individual, seemingly private responses to trauma emotional, but official responses – and the media's mass representation – are intimately emotional as well. In this case, the trauma of the bombing is made meaningful through emotional norms typical to the nation-state. Even though suggesting vulnerability, insecurity and security failure, representations mediated the trauma through discourses that point to the resecuritization and, ultimately, resilience of Australia as a nation.[50] The emotions of trauma and traumatic loss therein reinforce and reinstate the vision and feelings associated with the "secure state."[51]

The solidarity discourses that prevailed in the aftermath of the Bali bombing therefore worked to both limit social and political instability by both amplifying a sense of national identity bounded by stereotypically "Australian" attributes (such as mateship, resilience, heroism and light-heartedness) and by mobilizing perceptions of threat. Although, no doubt, not without some forms of dissidence, this has the effect of creating an insular form of emotional nationalism, and stabilizing and reconstituting the nation-state as the preferred arrangement for security and, by extension, political community.

[50] Heath-Kelly, "Securing through the Failure to Secure?"
[51] Mabel Berezin, "Secure States: Towards a Political Sociology of Emotion," in Jack Barbalet (ed.), *Emotions and Sociology* (Oxford: Blackwell, 2002), p. 33–52.

5 *Emotions and transnational community*

The previous chapter empirically illustrated my argument about the linkages between trauma, emotion and political community. It did so by examining how representing traumatic events can mobilize a range of emotionally charged social discourses that help to constitute a sense of shared political identity and, ultimately, community. The chapter focused specifically on how these emotionally collectivizing processes can further cement boundaries of the prevailing form of community in world politics: the nation-state.

The present chapter is the second to empirically ground my conceptual inquiry. It does so by examining a very different instance of trauma and a very different form of community that was summoned in response: the substantial transnational solidarity and aid community that emerged after the 2004 Southeast Asian tsunami.

The giant wave that struck the shores of Southeast Asia on December 26, 2004, caused incredible devastation and one of the largest death tolls of all natural catastrophes in contemporary history. At almost 5,000 kilometers from end to end, the tsunami struck the coastlines of fourteen countries.[1] At the time, this enormous reach, together with the incredible devastation, appeared unprecedented: it produced a truly indescribable global trauma. An estimated 275,000 people of more than fifty nationalities lost their lives in it.[2] The livelihoods of millions more were shattered. Yet swiftly after the tsunami an unusual display of transnational solidarity and support was summoned – and, even though temporal, the then largest aid community in history was constituted. The extraordinary level of aid that was given is one

[1] National Geographic, "The Deadliest Tsunami in History?" January 7, 2005. At http://news.nationalgeographic.com/news/2004/12/1227_041226_tsunami.html. Accessed February 1, 2014.

[2] Tsunami Evaluation Coalition, "The Boxing Day Tsunami in Numbers," no date. At www.alnap.org/pool/files/tsunami-stats-facts.pdf. Accessed February 1, 2014.

indication of the strength of the then community. It has even been commented that the power of the tsunami catastrophe "resides in the rare combination of the tragedy of ruination and the pathos of assistance," both of which were in abundance.[3] Tsunami relief efforts raised almost fourteen billion (US) dollars in total, almost half of which were private, nongovernment sponsored donations.[4] This was an unparalleled showing of international support: a true sense of international community emerged, meaning that individuals, governments and aid organizations rallied together to help alleviate human hardship and work through the devastation and ensuing trauma.

Scholars largely agree that the media's immediate and persistent worldwide coverage was a driving factor behind the unparalleled aid response.[5] Within minutes of the catastrophe, media outlets overwhelmed audiences with news of the crisis. Film and photographs inundated the media, initially in the form of amateur footage and shots taken firsthand by escaping tourists. Through this coverage viewers repeatedly bore witness to the shock and terror of the impending wave. Photojournalists were then flown in. The scope of destruction and human loss was brought more clearly into focus: houses were shown emptied of their foundations. Even more robust tourist resorts were reduced to rubble. Fishing boats had been picked up and dumped beside roads. Train tracks were pushed upwards, bent and incomprehensively contorted. Aid workers were pictured covering their mouths and noses, trying to hold off the stench of disease and the dead. Rows of corpses lay laced in mud.

The task of the present chapter is to empirically investigate how these media representations, and the emotions associated with them,

[3] Didier Fassin, *Humanitarian Reason: A Moral History of the Present*, trans. Rachel Gomme (Berkeley: University of California Press, 2012), p. ix.

[4] Jan Egeland, "Foreword," in Michael Barnett and Thomas G. Weiss (eds.), *Humanitarianism Contested: Where Angels Fear to Tread* (Milton Park: Routledge, 2011), p. xx; Tsunami Evaluation Coalition (2012).

[5] For example, Rony Brauman, "Global Media and the Myths of Humanitarian Relief: The Case of the 2004 Tsunami," in Richard Ashby Wilson and Richard D. Brown (eds.), *Humanitarianism and Suffering: The Mobilization of Empathy* (New York: Cambridge University Press, 2009), pp. 108–117; Lilie Chouliaraki, *The Spectatorship of Suffering* (London: Sage, 2006), p. 4; Virginie Mamadouh, "After Van Gogh: The Geopolitics of the Tsunami Relief Effort in the Netherlands," *Geopolitics*, 13.2 (2008), 205–231; Brent Steele, "Making Words Matter: The Asian Tsunami, Darfur, and Reflexive Discourse in International Politics," *International Studies Quarterly*, 51.4 (2007), pp. 901–925.

set the stage for the emergence of the substantial transnational aid community. They did so, I argue, by depicting the trauma as a distressing emotional phenomenon for which distant audiences should feel. The community here is, of course, very different from what is embedded in the formal institutions of a state. But it is nevertheless a community, though one that is temporally limited and bound by a particular catastrophic event and the ensuing trauma.

As in the previous chapter, I employ an interpretative method derived from both semiotics and discourse analysis. This time I focus on text and images featured in the immediate aftermath on the front page of the *New York Times*. I chose this outlet because it is one of the most recognizable newspapers worldwide. This is not to say, however, that the *New York Times* is neutral or representative of all aspects of the international community. It is an American newspaper and inevitably has a bias. But it also is a global leader in print and online news and in this way reflective of trends in how broader Western media tends to portray disasters. It is in this way that I seek to show how media representations were culturally and emotionally symbolic for distant Western audiences, and how, in turn, these representations evoke understandings of both victims' needs and viewers' responsibilities.

I focus on five front-page photographs and the associated texts. The photographs are an indicative sample of the total nineteen tsunami images featured on the *New York Times* front pages. I selected them based on their representativeness, using a technique adapted from content analysis.[6]

I show how dominant tsunami imagery did more than merely denote the devastating consequences of the catastrophe and massive trauma that ensued. The photographs attained deeper symbolic, cultural and importantly emotional value and resonance: they tap into and resonate with Western audiences in ways that perpetuate culturally bounded ethical sentiments – and, importantly, emotional registers – regarding the obligation to help distant strangers in times of dire need.

I argue that the effect of the tsunami representations linked to their colonial framing: they portrayed survivors of the trauma as

[6] See Gillian Rose, *Visual Methodologies: An Introduction to the Interpretation of Visual Materials* (London: Sage, 2001), pp. 54–68; Michael S. Ball and Gregory W. H. Smith, *Analyzing Visual Data* (Newbury Park: Sage 1992), pp. 20–30.

passive and helpless victims in need of Western aid for their survival. These widespread Western representations of crises in the developing world are crucial to understanding the massive aid response that followed: they tap into emotional cultures that tell audiences how to feel in response to the suffering of others; they are suggestive of the need for compassion – and urgent humanitarian action – in the face of a developing world tragedy. That the ensuing transnational community is imbued with a range of power relations is self-evident, and will thus be exposed in more detail in what follows.

Before I commence I would like to stress, once more, that I am not making any claims about the causal impact of a trauma, in this case the tsunami. Nor am I, as with the previous case study of the Bali bombing, making any exclusive claims about the exact emotions associated with the trauma. There is never just one affective dynamic at play. Various affective dispositions and emotions intersect to produce the political conditions and relations at play. Likewise, multiple interpretations of the event and its various mediations are possible. What my analysis does seek to do, however, is identify the most plausible emotional dimensions of the present trauma representations and show how they helped to set the stage for one of the most substantial showings of transnational political community in contemporary history.

Pitiable pictures: how colonial frames prompted Western viewers to make emotional sense of the tsunami disaster

Upon viewing the tsunami photographs one feature sticks out immediately: the images represent the catastrophe in a spectacular, dramatic and intensely emotional manner. Generally, the photographs do so by focusing on close-up pictures of non-Western victims enduring appalling conditions and suffering visible emotional and physical duress. Striking in this respect is that many tourists in the region were also affected – officially 2,218 tourists died as a consequence of the tsunami[7] – yet their visual presence went largely concealed. Non-Western victims are instead the central subjects in every image: they were typically captured at the most personal and vulnerable of moments,

[7] John Cosgrave, *Synthesis Report: Expanded Summary. Joint Evaluation of the International Response to the Indian Ocean Tsunami* (London: Tsunami Evaluation Coalition, 2007), p. 7.

dwarfed by the destruction and passively waiting, rather than actively responding, for the arrival of aid. When Western aid workers did form part of the picture they were, in contrast, active and full of the power and control that local victims lacked. Also common to the photographs was their prominent size and placement: each was large enough to hold and direct a viewer's gaze. Thus, as graphic and imposing depictions of the horror and helplessness of human suffering, the images unsettle: they focus on the obscenity of the trauma, repeatedly bringing forth the vast extent of the destruction and presenting clichéd depictions of the "cultural others" who suffered as a result.

Photographs of the tsunami were arguably particularly powerful: more than a mere written news item, they created a source of emotional identification with victims. Media photographs have for long been considered a historically privileged medium for representing catastrophe.[8] So much is this the case that some scholars stress that "affectively charged images" – such as those of the tsunami – now shape our understanding of political phenomena much more than the actual phenomena themselves.[9] Images can, simply put, become icons, shaping social understandings and even, some scholars suggest, helping to mobilize collective action.[10]

Prominent visual representations created a context in which the tsunami – its devastation and trauma – was perceived as an unprecedented humanitarian catastrophe worthy of a compassionate public response. The images achieved this by repeatedly visualizing the destruction, human suffering and dependence, and death. They are the type of trauma imagery associated with not only humanitarianism, but

[8] Barbie Zelizer, "Death in Wartime: Photographs and the 'Other War' in Afghanistan," *Harvard International Journal of Press/Politics*, 10.3 (2005), 26–55, at 29.

[9] Elizabeth Bronfen, "Reality Check: Image Affects and Cultural Memory," *differences: A Journal of Feminist Cultural Studies*, 17.1 (2005), 20–46, at 28. See also David Campbell and Michael Shapiro, "Guest Editor's Introduction," *Security Dialogue*, Special Issue on "Securitization, Militarization and Visual Culture in the Worlds of Post-9/11", 38.2 (2007), 131–137; W. J. T. Mitchell, *Picture Theory: Essays on Verbal and Visual Representation* (Chicago: Chicago University Press, 1994); Michael C. Williams, "Words, Images, Enemies: Securitization and International Politics," *International Studies Quarterly*, 47.4 (2003), 511–531, esp. 524–528.

[10] Robert Hariman and John Louis Lucaites, *No Caption Needed: Iconic Photographs, Public Culture, and Liberal Democracy* (Chicago: Chicago University Press, 2007).

also discourses of compassion toward the unfortunate or less privileged. The images emotionally evoke how individuals far away should feel sympathetic, possibly compassionate and be driven to solidarity. Or, put differently, the images convey that at minimum the tragedy is worthy of some form of not only compassionate but also humanitarian response. A collective awareness of the tsunami was thus mobilized around the misfortune and victimhood of survivors – their helplessness and misery – and viewers were prompted to translate their compassionate sentiments into action in an effort to alleviate survivors' pain.

A range of studies suggest that such imagery is now so commonplace in Western societies that the compassion they are intended to solicit is "commonsensical."[11] This is how Michael Barnett and Thomas Weiss put it:

> The humanitarian sector lives on the adage of "one picture is worth a thousand words"... The more graphic the image and the more it screams "innocent victim," the more effective it will be in mobilizing compassion, action, and money.[12]

Such photographs are employed for their political effect: They communicate meanings and construct collective feelings about distant disaster. It is in this context – and primarily among Western audiences – that in the face of human tragedy "compassion is seen as a virtue ... it has become a status symbol" reflective of audiences' perceived humanity and, less explicitly, empowerment due to their capacity to help.[13] Scholars such as Lilie Chouliaraki go as far as to claim that emotionally responding to distant trauma now more than ever involves "an element of 'egoistic altruism,' " which "situates the pleasures of the self at the heart of moral action."[14] This may mark an important shift in

[11] Keith Tester, *Humanitarianism and Modern Culture* (University Park: Pennsylvania State University Press, 2010), p. ix. See also Juha Käpylä and Denis Kennedy, "Cruel to Care? Investigating the Governance of Compassion in the Humanitarian Imagery," *International Theory*, 6.2 (2014), 255–292; Natan Sznaider, "The Sociology of Compassion: A Study in the Sociology of Morals," *Cultural Values*, 13.4 (1998), 117–139.

[12] Barnett and Weiss, *Humanitarianism Contested*, p. 119.

[13] Michael Barnett, *The Empire of Humanity: A History of Humanitarianism* (Ithaca: Cornell University Press, 2013), p. 220.

[14] Lilie Chouliaraki, *The Ironic Spectator: Solidarity in the Age of Post-Humanitarianism* (Cambridge: Polity, 2013), p. 4.

the nature of transnational solidarity after catastrophe and trauma. It also nonetheless reflects a more primal point: there exist inextricable, culturally embedded linkages between emotions and the formation of aid communities following distant disaster.

It is in this sense that the visual and verbal representations in the *New York Times*, together with numerous other similar depictions, set the stage for a dramatic international aid effort. And dramatic, swift as well as compassionate the response was. Indeed, so much so that it clearly disproved the so-called compassion fatigue argument: the belief that media representations of distant suffering lead to emotional paralysis and a lack of compassion.[15]

There are, however, tradeoffs to the manner in which media representations presented the tsunami as a developing world trauma that required immediate, global and far-reaching humanitarian action. Developing world survivors become needy victims, devoid of their personhood; they were reduced to a spectacle. They are presented in a stereotypical and humanistic manner reminiscent of colonial perceptions of the developing world.[16] By focusing on the disabling dimensions of non-Western experiences of the disaster, the images support the identification of victims as helpless, devoid of the resources and, significantly, the agency required for an effective response. As such, the images resonate with historically entrenched ideas that have, since the advent of imperialism, been associated with the developing world: that survival and prosperity are contingent upon Western assistance. Ensuing understandings of the humanitarian situation would consequently be based on not merely a conception of victims' needs but moreover on a sense of power and benevolence that emerges from the imperative and ability to help.

I now turn to a specific analysis of photographs and textual commentaries to gain a deeper understanding of how these colonial representations evoked the emotional meanings associated with the need for an immediate and massive humanitarian response that is possible only in the context of a transnational affective community.

[15] Susan D. Moeller, *Compassion Fatigue: How the Media Sell Disease, Famine, War and Death* (London: Routledge, 1999).

[16] See Anne Maxwell, *Colonial Photography and Exhibitions: Representations of the "Native" and the Making of European Identities* (London and New York: Leicester University Press, 1999).

The disempowerment of local actors: the developing world as dark, primitive and powerless

The first prominent genre of photographs – and associated textual commentaries – brings the catastrophe into focus through imagery that disempowers survivors. The images achieve this by focusing on individual faces and truly traumatic situations that convey a sense of tragedy and, crucially, passivity of local victims. The disaster is in this way humanized, yet it is in a manner that ultimately objectifies survivors and renders them vulnerable, devoid of agency, and dependent. Two types of images were instrumental in this respect.

The first involves imagery that displays victims "struck down" or paralyzed by the combined tragedy and helplessness of their situation. Well-known stereotypes and "humanitarian icons" featured heavily in this imagery. These were largely associated with gender (women as passive and vulnerable), age (the child as innocent victim) and culture/ethnicity (the dependence of the developing world).[17] Mothers were pictured tormented and helpless in their grief. Children too were represented with a corresponding fragility and defenselessness. Refugees – internally displaced, non-Western men – stared up into cameras, the needy recipients of foreign aid.[18] Cumulatively, these images and the stereotypes they conjure typecast victims as vulnerable and powerless and in doing so contribute to understandings of victims' needs.

Consider the following image (Figure 5.1).

This image was one of three front-page photographs that sought to represent the growing numbers of deceased. Other photographs showed body bags laid out and mass funeral pyres alight. More than these, though, this image clearly underscores the horror and sadness of the tsunami's human toll: it provides a confronting depiction of the loss of life and corresponding grief. Crucially, it does so through a very classic – as well as stereotypical and readily identifiable – emotional humanitarian symbol: the mother and child.

There is little doubt that the photograph is emotive, an image capable of "moving" viewers. This is due to the explicit emotional content

[17] Homi Bhabha discusses the significance of these stereotypes to colonial discourses in his article "'The Other' Question: Reconsidering the Stereotype in Colonial Discourse," *Screen*, 24.6 (1983), 18–36.

[18] The reference to the internally displaced, surviving men as "refugees" is the *New York Times*', not mine. See the caption to Figure 5.4.

"All the News That's Fit to Print"

The New York Times

Late Edition

VOL. CLIV . . No. 53,077 — NEW YORK, TUESDAY, DECEMBER 28, 2004 — ONE DOLLAR

TOLL IN UNDERSEA EARTHQUAKE PASSES 25,000; A THIRD OF THE DEAD ARE SAID TO BE CHILDREN

FEAR OF DISEASE

Thousands Are Missing — Many Tourists Are Killed

By SETH MYDANS

A mother at a hospital in Nagappattinam in the southern Indian state of Tamil Nadu sat yesterday with the dead, among them her own children. Nearly 3,000 people died in the state.

Supermarket Giants Crush Central American Farmers

By CELIA W. DUGGER

In Drowned Village, Grim Searches, Quick Burials

By AMY WALDMAN

MORE ON THE QUAKE

That Line at the Ferrari Dealer? It's Bonus Season on Wall Street

By JENNY ANDERSON

At Warning Center, Alert for the Quake, None for a Tsunami

INSIDE

Iraqi Party Office Is Bombed

A Victor, and a Challenge

5 Risks, 5 Altered Lives

Election Boycott Urged

NEWS SUMMARY

Figure 5.1 Front page of *The New York Times*, December 28, 2004: "A mother at a hospital in Nagappattinam in the southern Indian state of Tamil Nadu sat yesterday with the dead, among them her own children. Nearly 3,000 people died in the state." Photograph by Gautam Singh/ Associated Press.[19]

[19] Captions are all taken from the original *New York Times* front pages.

of the image as well as what is signaled to distant viewers. The mother pictured is clearly suffering massive distress; with her hands on her and her head turned upwards toward the sky, as if in prayer or seeking higher consolation, one senses that she is bereft. The viewer gets the feeling that she is spent and has no idea what comes next. In this way, the viewer is thus encouraged to feel for the woman in the picture; her emotions seem so raw and pure that one wants to help her immediately. Through the image the viewer also forms an idea of the terror of the tsunami and of the horrific conditions after. In particular, the photograph focuses the viewer's attention on the incredible ordeal and grave suffering of hundreds, if not thousands, of tiny and defenseless children.

Yet, images of mothers and children enduring such distressing conditions also possess further powerful emotional and cultural symbolism, particularly in what is an obvious humanitarian disaster context.[20]

Representing women (together with children) in this manner presents the stereotype of women as distraught and fragile, incapacitated by turmoil and grief. The image dominates the viewer's perspective, limiting viewer understandings of women's experiences of the disaster by revealing just one (particularly disempowering) aspect of their hardship and suffering. In other words, the image – and those that produced similar meanings (see for e.g. Figure 5.2) – provides viewers with a one-dimensional perspective of the plight of women and children. One could say that in a sense a viewer's vision is consequently blurred, whittled down to this singular image and the stereotypically feminine – yet also deeply humanitarian – connotations it conveys.

Studies of the representation of women in social culture help us to understand the important spin-off effects that such gender stereotyping has in terms of shaping how audiences think and feel. Rey Chow, for instance, suggests that one way women are rendered powerless and especially vulnerable is through how they are "consigned to visuality." She assesses the appropriation of female bodies through practices of representation, arguing that not only are representations such as this an act of power (by what Chow sees as a Western masculine mindset) but moreover that they create an "automatom," which brings into play a host of preconceived ideas that distant viewers may have about how

[20] See Kate Manzo, "Imaging Humanitarianism: NGO Identity and the Iconography of Childhood," *Antipode*, 40.4 (2008), 632–657.

"All the News That's Fit to Print"

The New York Times

Late Edition

VOL. CLIV . . No. 53,087 + NEW YORK, FRIDAY, JANUARY 7, 2005 ONE DOLLAR

SOME IRAQ AREAS UNSAFE FOR VOTE, U.S. GENERAL SAYS

NEW OPERATIONS PLANNED

Government Is Extending Its Emergency Rule — Bomb Kills 7 G.I.'s

By DEXTER FILKINS

Rumsfeld Seeks Broad Review Of Iraq Policy

Wide Leeway Offered to a Retired General

By ERIC SCHMITT and THOM SHANKER

GONZALES SPEAKS AGAINST TORTURE DURING HEARING

JUSTICE NOMINEE ON SPOT

Senators Question Legal Policies Used in Fight Against Terrorism

By ERIC LICHTBLAU

Alberto R. Gonzales, top, the nominee for attorney general, was questioned yesterday by the Senate Judiciary Committee, which includes Senators Orrin G. Hatch, bottom from left, Arlen Specter and Patrick J. Leahy.

First Murder Charge in '64 Civil Rights Killings of 3

By ROBERT D. McFADDEN

Man Held in Mississippi Deaths of Volunteers in Voter Drive

Tsunami's Cruelest Toll: Sons and Daughters Lost

By DAVID ROHDE

Thanaranjani, 28, swears she will never let go of her 4-year-old daughter, who nevertheless perished in the tsunami in Soranpattu, Sri Lanka.

C.I.A. Report Finds Its Officials Failed In Pre-9/11 Efforts

By DOUGLAS JEHL

INSIDE

Bush Officially Elected, But Democrats Protest

Mandela's Anti-AIDS Battle

Spy Case Charges Dismissed

Retrial in Drowning Case

Holyfield Still Pursuing Titles

When Town Meets Country

Change Is Afoot in Albany

NEWS SUMMARY

Updated news: nytimes.com

This Weekend: Page D8

Figure 5.2 Front page of *The New York Times*, January 7, 2005: "Thanaranjani, 28, swears she will never let go of her 4-year-old daughter, who nevertheless perished in the tsunami in Soranpattu, Sri Lanka." Photograph by Sriyantha Walpola/*The New York Times*.

the portrayed subject would be expected to think, feel and act.[21] In this case, a simplistic gender cliché is reproduced: women are typecast as emotionally fragile, vulnerable and at the same time helpless and therefore dependent caregivers.

Similarly, the representation of children who have suffered immensely taps into stereotypical sentiments that again promote particular understandings of the image as well as the trauma of the catastrophe more generally. In the first image (Figure 5.1) this stereotype pertains to what Erica Burman has called our modern society's "sentimentalized"[22] vision of childhood: children have come to be seen as inherently innocent, vulnerable and in need of protection. For Burman, this conception of childhood has much to do with how "childhood has come to carry significations of truth, nature, spontaneity, innocence and dependence."[23] Children are seen as pure, as uncorrupted, untainted by the moral tyrannies that occupy modern life. This heavily idealized understanding of childhood is thought to resonate with our collective psyche as it enables us to recollect the past. Indeed, in this way images of children signify the child in each of us – "the child is a child, any child, our child, the child inside ourselves whom we have irrevocably but regretfully left behind."[24] As a glimpse of our past selves, children then also hold the promise of the future. Images of unhappy or suffering children thus sit uneasily in our imagination. Such imagery – predominantly of "big-eyed, wide-eyed, and sad-eyed"[25] children and here of tiny children, their bodies thrashed

[21] Rey Chow, "Postmodern Automatoms," in Judith Butler and Joan W. Scott (eds.), *Feminists Theorize the Political* (New York: Routledge, 1992), pp. 101–117, at p. 105. See also Susan Dente Ross, "Introduction," in Susan Dente Ross and Paul Martin Lester (eds.), *Images that Injure: Pictorial Stereotypes in the Media*, 3rd ed. (Westport: Praeger, 2011).

[22] Elizabeth Burman, "Innocents Abroad: Western Fantasies of Childhood and the Iconography of Emergencies," *Disasters*, 18.3 (1994), 238–254, at 240.

[23] Burman, "Innocents Abroad," 240. See also Laura Suski, "Children, Suffering and the Humanitarian Appeal," in Wilson and Brown (eds.), *Humanitarianism and Suffering* (New York: Cambridge University Press, 2009), pp. 202–222, at p. 206.

[24] Nancy Ellen Batty, "'We are the World, We are the Children': The Semiotics of Seduction in International Children's Relief Efforts," in Roderick McGillis (ed.), *Voices of the Other: Children's Literature and the Postcolonial Context* (New York: Routledge, 2000), pp. 17–38, at p. 24.

[25] Debbie James Smith, "Big-Eyed, Wide-Eyed, Sad-Eyed Children: Constructing the Humanitarian Space in Social Justice Documentaries," *Studies in Documentary Film*, 3.2 (2009), 159–175.

about and bloated – suggests a lost or "stolen childhood."[26] It suggests that the innocence of childhood has been corrupted. With this, our own sentimentalized vision of childhood is too disrupted. Assumptions about child passivity and helplessness are reinforced. As are, in turn, assumptions about the need for distant donors to step in and help.

Much research has been conducted into the linkages between images of mothers and children and the mobilization of humanitarian agency. Scholars have focused on the manner through which images of mothers and children can act as both receptacles of emotion and as signifiers of humanitarian need. They argue that this has much to do with the perception that such images, such as the two above, can "cut across cultural and political difference" and "address the very heart of humanity."[27] So powerful are images of mothers and children perceived to communicate humanitarian tragedy that some argue they have come to be understood as international "symbols of distress," as markers of charity and humanitarianism.[28] For David Campbell, images of mothers and children visualized in such an emotive, maternal manner call to mind the pieta: the Madonna mourning the loss of her child, a universally recognized icon of compassion and grief.[29] Lisa Malkki goes further to explicitly link the well-known icon with a perceived powerlessness and concomitant understanding that those represented need help: that there is an "international expectation of a certain kind of helplessness" associated with images of women and children. Children in particular have become a "conventionalized" mechanism for the representation of tragic humanitarian situations.[30]

The historical and cultural significance of images of childhood in humanitarian aid and development campaigns is also worth briefly noting. Together with these inherent notions of helplessness and childhood need, Laura Suski contends the now "mainstream" use of images of developing world children has in the West come to suggest and increasingly reinforce ideas about the need for foreign intervention. The seeming prevalence of malnourished, diseased and dying children

[26] Burman, "Innocents Abroad," 243.
[27] Lisa H. Malkki, "Speechless Emissaries: Refugees, Humanitarianism, and Dehistoricization," *Cultural Anthropology*, 11.3 (1996), 377–404, at 388.
[28] For example, Manzo, "Imaging Humanitarianism," 649–651.
[29] David Campbell, D. J. Clark and Kate Manzo (eds.), "Imaging Famine." At www.imaging-famine.org. Accessed January 31, 2014.
[30] Malkki, "Speechless Emissaries," 388.

in the developing world signifies that "[W]estern institutions and organizations are better able to provide for the needs of children than are their own parents."[31] While admittedly this image (i.e. Figure 5.1) is of a humanitarian emergency borne of a natural catastrophe (rather than, for instance, of incremental suffering caused from perceived economic or political difficulties), the history of imaging of developing world children plays a part in shaping viewers' understandings: in making sense of the images a viewer draws upon a range of previous experiences, which includes viewing similar images in the past and situating the present images within a range of associated cultural and ethical connotations. In this way, children are positioned and seen as "poor children," as "pitiable," and, to Western audiences, in need of their aid.

In the context of wider efforts to visualize the tsunami and its aftermath, the frequent appropriation of stereotypes surrounding both women and children also have wider implications for perceiving of the disaster as a whole. While Western women and children are also subject to excessively feminine stereotyping, in this context the focus on women and children (and the gender and age stereotypes this implies) serves further to "feminize" local efforts at overcoming the disaster.[32] Symbolic here is that the women come to represent all local tsunami victims, who then too become perceived with a corresponding sense of stricken powerlessness – the very opposite of the resilience required to make it through.

The second style of imagery that contributed toward a sense of victims as disempowered consists of photographs that focused on the arrival of aid as well as rescue efforts. However, rather than portray victims as active participants assisting the distribution of relief supplies and foreign aid, these images presented victims in positions that lacked initiative and agency.

The following photographs are two such images, which employ similar techniques to represent victims' needs (Figures 5.3 and 5.4).

In their visualization of Indonesian refugees, struggling for supplies, these photographs again present powerful and emotive

[31] Suski, "Children, Suffering and the Humanitarian Appeal," p. 205. See also Vanessa Pupavac, "Misanthropy Without Borders: The International Children's Rights Regime," *Disasters*, 25.1 (2001), 95–112.

[32] Sasskia Sassen, "Women's Burden: Counter Geographies of Globalization and the Feminization of Survival," *Nordic Journal of International Law*, 71.2 (2002), 255–274; Burman, "Innocents Abroad," 243.

"All the News That's Fit to Print"

The New York Times

Late Edition

VOL. CLIV . . No. 53,079 NEW YORK, THURSDAY, DECEMBER 30, 2004 ONE DOLLAR

World Leaders Vow Aid as Toll Continues to Climb

BUSH SPEAKS OUT

Promises Long-Range Relief for Disaster as Impatience Grows

Pentagon Said To Offer Cuts In the Billions

Amid Chaos, Sri Lankans Struggle to Survive

It's About Aid, And an Image

A Chance to Move Past The Battle With Terror

Questions Raised on Warnings at Rail Crossings

INSIDE

Rebels Attack Mosul Outpost

Bombing at Saudi Ministry

Bid to Limit Ethics Panel

AARP to Oppose Bush

Jerry Orbach Dies

Figure 5.3 Front page of *The New York Times*, December 30, 2004: "In Cuddalore, 112 miles south of Madras, India, a young girl reached for clothes and food that were being distributed yesterday by charities. Coordinating relief efforts over a dozen nations is proving difficult." Photograph by Arko Datta/Reuters.

"All the News That's Fit to Print"

The New York Times

Final National Edition

VOL. CLIV . . No. 53,082 SUNDAY, JANUARY 2, 2005

U.S. Copters Speed Pace of Aid for Indonesia Refugees

At the airport in Banda Aceh, in one of the worst battered provinces in Sumatra, Indonesia, refugees reached for relief supplies yesterday.

Wall Street's Designs on '05? A Boom in Merger Activity

By ANDREW ROSS SORKIN

Libya Is Enticing U.S. Executives With Its Abundant Oil Reserves

By JAD MOUAWAD

A fuel facility in Mellitah, built by Libya and foreign companies.

From Heart of Indonesia's Disaster, a Cry for Help

By JANE PERLEZ

Nation's President Visits Ruined Town and Calls for 'Global Unity'

Storms Interfere — 5 Million Need Relief

By ROBERT D. McFADDEN

G.I. Families United in Grief, but Split by the War

By MONICA DAVEY

INSIDE

Rebel Tape Shows Killing of 5 in Iraqi Security Force

Texas Prevails in Rose Bowl

Labor's Loss, Business's Gain

Resolutions, Many Ways

MORE ON THE AFTERMATH

Figure 5.4 Front page of *The New York Times*, January 2, 2005: "At the airport in Bandah Aceh, in one of the worst battered provinces in Sumatra, Indonesia, refugees reached for relief supplies yesterday." Photograph by Abdullah Azam/Associate Press.

images. Both photographs show victims pressed together, reaching out seemingly urgently. Once again both photographs also feature children. While the children in these images seem not so young to be completely defenseless, that they are clearly young and shown struggling for daily survival taps, once again, into the "child as victim" stereotype that functions to amplify an understanding of the humanitarian cause.

Prominent in Figure 5.3 is a lone girl, surrounded tightly by adult others. She stretches out silently; she seems to plead with the viewer for help. Featured three days later, this plea then seems to intensify in Figure 5.4: through this image the viewer sees a blur of outstretched arms and anxious faces, communicating a sense of growing desperation. Focusing on the image more carefully one is then gripped by the unpleasant reality of the bodies stretching and faces painfully pressed up to the wire. So desperate are the men and children that they focus intently on the aid workers even despite (or possibly in ignorance of) the presence of the camera. To the viewer, this once again manifests not only a sense of their dire need but also the idea that, due to the misery and desperation of situation, victims are pitiable objects that need help.

Importantly for viewers, in these images victims are also presented as powerless and submissive. They seem totally reliant upon the distribution of foreign aid (rather than, for instance, helping themselves, or even helping Western aid workers to distribute aid among themselves). The victims pictured, as Anne Orford puts it, are "symbols of helplessness": they are passive (and racialized) characters who lack "power, agency and authority."[33] It also seems that while victims are in need the Western relief workers are "saving the day." Of course, this dichotomous relationship (between survivors and aid workers) may have been in some instances the case, in relation to victims' day-to-day survival, but as a prominent front-page image (among many similar to it) it presents a one-sided picture that helps to mobilize the idea that victims could not help themselves. The Western relief workers are in contrast the active agents; their giving hands indicate assurance and control.

[33] Anne Orford, *Reading Humanitarian Intervention: Human Rights and the Use of Force in International Law* (Cambridge: Cambridge University Press, 2003), p. 171.

The passive/active dichotomy[34] in this imagery (exemplified by Figures 5.3 and 5.4) is significant in that it functions to convey both the urgent situation and seeming dependence of survivors whilst simultaneously prompting that the viewer identify with the aid workers – the "giving hands." In this way a type of hegemonic and superior (and masculine) Western mindset is created. Perceptions about the developing world and its passivity and dependence are also reconstituted. Doing so in turn promotes meanings that hinge not simply on the dire humanitarian situation (and needs) of survivors but also the evoked notion that such a severe situation can only be overcome with outside assistance.

Adjacent stories, captions and testimony also communicated the helplessness and needs of victims, thereby reiterating humanitarian meanings for readers. These spoke of the "tragedy" and the "stubborn fights for life."[35] One told of the "powerlessness" of mothers and their children, and of how the world had watched on helplessly as the tsunami took over.[36] Sri Lankan survivor Wasantakumari Sridhar told that "[e]verything we had is gone ... what we need is clothes."[37] Reporter Jane Perlez told in particular of Indonesian survivors and shared their continuing pleas for help.[38] "When the water came I got out of my house and I ran in panic," said Mr. Roosli, an Indonesian street trader. "I have zero left. I lost seven children. What do I need? Everything. Help us, please." Proffering a red plastic cup, he said a cup of rice was all that could be issued each day. Perlez also passed on Indonesian President Susilo Bambang Yudhoyono's plea for "global unity" and continuing aid.[39] Mr. Yudhoyono professed that "assistance was slow in coming ... to areas in tremendous need." He appealed to the world for help. Calls for help were conveyed on previous front pages as well. Readers were told that charities "scrambled" to help midst such "an

34 Interestingly one of the Tsunami Evaluation Coalition's key post-aid and reconstruction reports showed that it was the local population who provided the majority of all immediate life-saving action and emergency support. See Cosgrave, *Synthesis Report*, p. 4.

35 Wayne Arnold, "At the Epicenter, Tales of Death and of Stubborn Fights for Life." *New York Times*, December 29, 2004, p. 1.

36 Amy Walden, "Motherless and Childless, an Indian Villages Toll," *New York Times*, December 31, 2004, p. A.12.

37 Cited in Seth Mydans, "Amid Chaos, Sri Lankan Struggle to Survive," *New York Times*, December 30, 2004, p. 1.

38 Jane Perlez, "From Heart of Indonesia's Disaster, a Cry for Help," *New York Times*, January 2, 2005, p. 1.

39 Perlez, "From Heart of Indonesia's Disaster."

unbelievable amount of devastation."[40] A pervasive theme was that there were many more in need and still much that distant donors could give. "Disaster Aid" phone numbers were listed every day, without fail, for two weeks. A boxed and bolded list of charities accepting donations was also printed each day. Through these, individuals were explicitly encouraged to ring through credit-card contributions.

How these images suggest a type of paralysis or an inability to respond – as well as those that seem to be blatant and mass "pleas for help" – can be seen as instrumental to generating an understanding of victims as disempowered, and consequently reliant upon overseas aid. A social relationship (between victim and viewer) that is based on the colonial gaze is in this way perpetuated.[41] The graphic photographs and distressed faces embody a sense of desperation and communicate a sense of victims' powerlessness that functions to affirm wider and historically constituted aid discourses, which maintain hierarchical relations between the Western and developing worlds.

It is then precisely through such framing that particular emotional dispositions and associated humanitarian meanings begin to emerge. Specifically, this style of disaster imagery – that promotes colonial understandings of developing world others – constructs victims as objects of sympathy and encourages audiences to engage with the disaster through a sympathetic politics akin to what scholars have called a "politics of pity."[42]

A politics of pity suggests that while Western audiences feel grievous and deep sympathy for the suffering imaged before them, they still remain quietly and safely detached.[43] Philosopher Hannah Arendt, who first delineated the politics of pity, suggests that pity is "to be sorry without being touched in the flesh."[44] Pity, in other words, is perceived to maintain a distance between viewer and victim and, in

[40] Eric Lipton, "Even at Charity Used to Aiding, It's a Scramble," *The New York Times*, December 31, 2004, p. 1.

[41] See also Roland Bleiker and Amy Kay, "Representing HIV/AIDS in Africa: Pluralist Photography and Local Empowerment," *International Studies Quarterly*, 51.1 (2007), 139–163, at 144–146.

[42] For example, Lilie Chouliaraki, "Post-Humanitarianism: Humanitarian Communication Beyond a Politics of Pity," *International Journal of Cultural Studies*, 13.2 (2010), 107–126.

[43] Luc Boltanski, *Distant Suffering: Politics, Morality and the Media*, trans. G. Burchell (Cambridge: Cambridge University Press, 1999).

[44] Arendt cited in Tristen Naylor, "Deconstructing Development: The Use of Power and Pity in the International Development Discourse," *International Studies Quarterly*, 55.1 (2011), 177–197, at 184.

doing so, fosters viewers' incapacity or unwillingness to engage in a deeper form of empathetic identification or understanding. Even other emotions arguably associated with the imagery, such as compassion and sympathy, are seen to privilege "the power of the passionate" over that of the victims being responded to.[45] A hierarchy between viewer and victim is created.[46] Here, the overwhelming focus on victims' vulnerability and dependence – notably through the combined prevalence of women and children as well as through racial difference – implicates pity by positioning pleading victims in relation to a sympathetic, empowered viewer. In this case, such a politics is fostered not only upon perceptions of victims' dire needs but the confluence of perceptions of cultural difference and the representation of humanitarian need.[47] Victims become subsumed into a North/South humanitarian discourse that privileges spontaneous and short-lived bursts of public agency toward distant vulnerable others, such as the solidarity that was mobilized in the tsunami's wake.[48]

A "politics of pity" can in a sense be seen as a superficial form of affective politics, even while its achievements in contributing to the alleviation of suffering may be significant. Yet the stereotypical emotional appeal of distant trauma has become one way, albeit a dominant one, through which international humanitarian actions are "sold."[49] And typically concomitant with pity is the general recognition that political intervention to help is warranted.[50] This presents a difficult ethical conundrum: established emotions associated with humanitarian representations and discourses function in some

45 Barnett, *The Empire of Humanity*, p. 223.

46 An insightful critique of how the productive nature of this hierarchy silences structural inequities that are seen to lie at the core of many developing world humanitarian problems is forwarded by Sheila Nair, in her article "Governance, Representation and International Aid," *Third World Quarterly*, 34.4 (2013), 630–652.

47 See Alan Radley and Marie Kennedy, "Picturing Need: Images of Overseas Aid and Interpretations of Cultural Difference," *Culture & Psychology*, 3.4 (1997), 435–460.

48 Antonio Donini, "The Far Side: The Meta Functions of Humanitarianism in a Globalised World," *Disasters*, 34.S2 (2010), 220–237.

49 Denis Kennedy, "Selling the Distant Other: Humanitarianism and Imagery – Ethical Dilemmas of Humanitarian Action," *The Journal of Humanitarian Assistance* (2009). At http://sites.tufts.edu/jha/archives/411. Accessed November 2, 2014.

50 Boltanski, *Distant Suffering*, p. 155.

instances to alleviate distant pain while also recreating cultural difference and distance. But, increasingly, scholars observe and lament such affective political dynamics – and they stress a need to reorient the type of humanitarian relationship that ensues.[51] Chouliaraki, for instance, suggests that "[w]hereas this moral emphasis on pity has enabled, partially but significantly, the alleviation of suffering among large populations in modern times, it has simultaneously established a dominant discourse about public action that relies heavily on the language of grand emotions ... which ... displaces the long-term concern with establishing structures of justice with the urgent concern for doing something for those who suffer."[52] In other words, such emotions may generate short-term solutions (such as international aid) but fail to address the underlying causes for the underdevelopment that may have led to the need for such aid in the first place. Pity or even short-lived compassion thus becomes a habitual routine for Western audiences; emotions "performed" through the images that represent, and through their context suggest how viewers should perceive of, feel for and act toward others' suffering.[53]

Viewers as responsive distant actors: the need for urgent aid and the West as the developing world's "white knight"

The second theme instrumental in invoking the colonial frames that helped viewers make sense of the tsunami disaster involves understanding how the images mobilize distant viewers and task them with action. Importantly, this theme is a direct corollary of the disempowerment of local actors: in the images, the passivity of local survivors is repeatedly juxtaposed with the responsiveness of Western aid workers and, as I suggest, by extension distant Western viewers.

The images achieve this through both literal depictions of very obvious pleas for help and the concomitant, symbolic implication that, like the Western workers, who are "on the ground" actively helping, viewers can too help by being moved to action. In this sense, the images

[51] For instance, Mika Aaltola, *Western Spectacle of Governance and the Emergence of Humanitarian World Politics* (Palgrave, 2009), pp. 164–170; Käpylä and Kennedy, "Cruel to Care?" 281–286.

[52] Chouliaraki, "Post-Humanitarianism," 108.

[53] Chouliaraki, "Post-Humanitarianism," 110; Lilie Chouliaraki, "Mediation as Moral Education," *Media, Culture & Society*, 30.5 (2008), 831–847.

function on a further symbolic level as well: by establishing a passive/active dichotomy – that is, in revealing local victims as passive and powerless and Western aid workers as active and in control – the images further affirm a hierarchical relationship between victims and viewers, with distant viewers in the position of power. The humanitarian meanings mobilized by the images therefore pivot, once again, not simply an understanding of the urgent need for aid but, moreover, the central role the West plays in the provision of such aid. Hence, the images can be seen to further contribute toward colonial discourses by resonating with, and perpetuating ideas concerning, the inherent dependence of developing world victims, and that consequently the West needs to step in and help – to play the "white knight,"[54] to come to the rescue.

A prominent front-page image featured more than one week after the tsunami illustrates how such imagery produced humanitarian meanings that pivot on the capacity and thus power and imperative of the West to help (Figure 5.5).

The image depicts an American medical officer (later identified as Lieutenant Mark Banks) tending to an injured child in Bandah Aceh, Indonesia. The officer carries the child heroically. Her leg appears to be injured and she wears a white mask over her nose and mouth, protecting her from the stench and possible disease. Beside her, the medical officer's face is exposed. He is a white, clean-cut man in an army uniform, its badges and Red Cross proudly on display.

Humanitarian meanings ensuing from the image are, I suggest, once again both partially dependent upon and, at the same time, evoke distinct colonial understandings of the urgency and need with which the West – and by extension viewers – needed to intervene in order to provide aid. Three features of the image are particularly important.

First is the manner through which the image represents the notion of rescue – in particular, the rescue of (non-Western) children. Suggested previously is that depictions of children who need to be saved are important in the construction of humanitarian discourses: children tend to be perceived as innocent and hence more "worthy" recipients

[54] Orford, *Reading Humanitarian Intervention*, p. 165. See also Christopher Bellamy, *Knights in White Armour: The New Art of War and Peace* (London: Vintage, 1997).

"All the News That's Fit to Print"

The New York Times

Late Edition

VOL. CLIV . . No. 53,085 — NEW YORK, WEDNESDAY, JANUARY 5, 2005 — ONE DOLLAR

An American medical officer carried an injured child yesterday after arriving by helicopter at the military airport in Banda Aceh, Indonesia.

Bush's Counsel Sought Ruling About Torture

Memo Likely to Figure in Gonzales Hearings

IRAQI GOVERNOR SLAIN BY GUNMEN; BOMBING KILLS 10

REBEL BID TO DERAIL VOTE

Iraqi President Questions Whether Election Can Be Held on Jan. 30

Pledges Grow, Hurdles Loom In Relief Effort

Fearing a Sea That Once Sustained, Then Killed

INSIDE

Pentagon Sets Policy On Sexual Assault

Israeli Shelling Angers Abbas

Boggs and Sandberg to Hall

Pioneer of Comics Is Dead

A State Revolution Detoured

No Question

After Retreat, G.O.P. Changes House Ethics Rule

U.S. Said to Weigh Sanctions on Syria Over Iraqi Network

Figure 5.5 Front page of *The New York Times*, January 5, 2005: "An American medical officer carried an injured child yesterday after arriving by helicopter at the military airport in Bandah Aceh, Indonesia." Photograph by Tyler Hicks/*The New York Times*.

of aid.[55] Importantly, this image does so by focusing not only on the needs of "helpless children," but also on the competency with which Western aid workers came "to the rescue." An archetypal situation of developing world calamity is thus depicted: a child who needs saving and the foreign aid workers who fearlessly came to their aid. The child is perched meekly in the officer's arms, seemingly innocent and weak. She looks dependent upon the officer. Although her facial expression is unclear, viewers might imagine her fear. In contrast, the American medic appears in control. He tightly clutches the child and leads the way. He seems brave and unafraid, despite having to traverse what we could assume are the perilous conditions in post-tsunami Indonesia. That the child's face is covered with a mask points concretely to this danger. Mask-less, in contrast, the white rescuer hints at the gallant, fearless and potentially even sacrificial nature of his heroism, despite the significant risks.

The second feature concerns the gendered dimensions of the image. This is significant in terms of both the young "girl child" as well as controlling figure in the image, with whom audiences are invited to identify: the white, male medical officer. Burman's work on children provides clues once again. She contends that, to Western audiences, "little girls are the quintessential child victims." In such images "[f]eminity and childish dependency are collapsed to evoke sympathy," in effect reproducing "patriarchal relations, both within and between donor and recipient countries."[56] There are other gender issues that are significant for viewers as well. In images such as this one, identification with masculine characters can lead to what has been called the "masculinization" of the audience position.[57] This is to say that the viewer's subject position is one largely of power and control, freedom of action and the autonomous ability to take charge of the situation in order to make changes for better or worse. The active agency and heroic actions of the medic are key to this subject position, and also promote perceptions of (Western) autonomy. Again the lack of a mask is important. It appeals to a historical sense of the "white man's burden" to aid the poor and destitute, thereby enhancing the power and agency of

[55] See Batty, "We are the World, We are the Children"; Burman, "Innocents Abroad"; Manzo, "Imaging Humanitarianism."

[56] Burman, "Innocents Abroad," 242.

[57] Laura Mulvey, *Visual and Other Pleasures* (London: Macmillan, 1989) cited in Orford, *Reading Humanitarian Intervention*, pp. 165–166.

Western viewers.[58] In the context of this image, such empowerment of the audience position has, once again, the symbolic effect of reinforcing humanitarian understandings that pivot on both the inability of local actors to step up and help themselves and the subsequent perceived need for help from the outside – specifically, from the West.

Third, and finally, is the notion that the image is to some extent a "comforting" and reassuring one. By depicting rescue efforts as they seem to happen, the image evokes the idea that everything possible is being done. How this type of message solicits the idea and continuing need for solidarity is more complex than a simple plea for help. It may, for instance, give viewers confidence that their efforts have not been in vein, that their help has, as such, "made a difference." In this way, the image sanctions the humanitarian assistance that audiences have already provided; it shows Western viewers how their actions can lead to provision of aid and support and in doing so also assures viewers that Western actions matter deeply.

Particularly striking is that all front-page images analyzed in the *New York Times* in fact employ a passive/active dichotomy in the representation of victims as well as the actual and seemingly expected response of the West.[59] Of the images discussed in the previous section, Figures 5.1 and 5.2 imply victims' passivity through a feminized type of paralysis. Figures 5.3 and 5.4 are more blatant. They are explicit in the representation of victims' helplessness and need. Figure 5.3 denotes more than this too. It actively bestows distant viewers (through the symbolism of the "active" Western aid workers) with agency. Here the passive/active dualism echoes perceptions of the relationship between the developing and Western worlds. The developing world is (again) the needy recipient of aid. The audience, in contrast, is the humanitarian provider. The viewer's vantage-point is thus constructed as one of power, and of the corresponding ability and agency to provide aid by way of donations.

The implication that Western viewers should become responsive actors, contributing toward the plight of victims, is thus the second mechanism through which the images perpetuate colonial frames

[58] William Russell Easterly, *White Man's Burden: Why the West's Efforts to Aid the Rest Have Done So Much Ill and So Little Good* (New York: Penguin, 2006).

[59] Remarkably, all nineteen front-page *New York Times* photographs of the tsunami demonstrate this passive/active dualism.

of understanding. The production of meanings that hinge upon the capacity of the West to alleviate what was nondiscriminatory suffering not only presents a worthy humanitarian cause but also correspondingly empowers distant audiences by showing how (their) actions can lead to concrete assistance. Here, again, colonial dynamics of a superior Western – and an inferior developing – world are implicated.

Through these dynamics, emotional dispositions associated with the ensuing humanitarian solidarity are consolidated. The implication that the West – and by extension Western audiences – is (and should be) urgently concerned with addressing the horror and suffering depicted corresponds with the moral emphasis on pity, as well as other compassionate emotions, that has long distinguished Western politics and ethics.[60] So much is this the case that some scholars even contend that Western audiences are more distinguished by a perceived moral obligation to feel emotions such as pity and sympathy than they are by actually acting upon such emotions for the long- or even short-term betterment of the distant others they are supposedly feeling for.[61] In this way, I suggest that feeling (or even the belief that one should feel) such emotions too becomes a kind of Western privilege, a type of "emotional hegemony" that is complicit with the colonial visual framing,[62] both of which work together to form exactly the kind of temporal solidarity that was formed after the Asian tsunami catastrophe.

Summary: from pity and compassion to a transnational aid commitment

This chapter has comprised the second of my empirical engagement with the linkages between the emotional power of representing trauma and the subsequent constitution – and in the present case, dramatic mobilization – of political community.

[60] Hannah Arendt, *On Revolution* (London: Penguin, 1990 [1963]).

[61] Lilie Chouliaraki, "The Theatricality of Humanitarianism: A Critique of Celebrity Advocacy," *Communication and Critical/Cultural Studies*, 9.1 (2012), 1–21, at 2; Tester, *Humanitarianism and Modern Culture.*

[62] Alison Jaggar discusses "emotional hegemony" as the social constitution of emotion in service of the dominant interests and values of the hierarchical social group. See Alison M. Jaggar, "Love and Knowledge: Emotion in Feminist Epistemology," in Alison M. Jaggar and Susan R. Bordo, *Gender/Body/Knowledge: Feminist Reconstructions of Being and Knowing* (New Brunswick: Rutgers University Press, 1992), pp. 145–171, at p. 159.

Central to my analysis has been an examination of how the emotional dimensions of witnessing a natural catastrophe and its trauma are implicated in mobilizing a distinct, potentially transformative form of political community: a transnational aid community, comprising individuals (survivors and witnesses), governments and NGOs alike. In particular, the chapter focused on unraveling how key visual and verbal media representations helped to evoke humanitarian (and communally constitutive) meanings that were made possible at least in part through audiences' socioculturally embedded emotional receptivity.

To do so, the chapter specifically analyzed dominant media imagery of the 2004 Southeast Asian tsunami. I demonstrated that prominent representations created a context in which the tsunami was perceived as an unprecedented humanitarian catastrophe worthy of some form of compassionate public response. Western representations of the devastation and trauma achieved this by portraying the tsunami in a manner that aligned with established narratives of, and emotions associated with, developing world disaster: they framed the suffering and trauma in a distinctly colonial manner. This colonial framing is significant as it taps into humanitarian meanings that pivot not only on a sense of passivity and powerlessness of developing world victims but also on the notion that Western audiences should feel compassionate emotions – and, potentially foremost, pity – in response.

Two themes were central in constructing such colonial frames and ensuing understandings: first, the disempowerment of local actors through images that hinge upon and perpetuate stereotypical perceptions of the developing world's inherent dependence; and second, the corresponding empowerment of distant viewers through images that portray Westerners bravely and successfully coming to the aid of victims and implicitly position viewers in positions of power and benevolence. Yet, as a consequence of such imagery, not simply was it implied that Western viewers should be emotionally receptive to the suffering at hand but it was additionally insinuated that viewers should conceive of the disaster as one that requires active and immediate humanitarian action, no matter how great or small, how sporadic or enduring. Hence, in this manner, tsunami representations suggested to distant viewers that they should not only feel for, or in some way emotionally identify with, the trauma being depicted but also feel compelled (or at least empowered) to act.

Importantly, representations of the tsunami's devastation and trauma can be seen to have abetted a very unusual global political dynamic. As I have previously argued, representations of trauma often close off communal boundaries. Trauma that ensues from political violence, for instance, tends to reaffirm the very boundaries of community that such violence deconstructs. However, representations of the tsunami can be viewed as a part of a set of mediating and signifying practices that are – in times of human need – able to affectively resonate in ways that disturb the prevailing form of political community in world politics: the nation-state. Put differently, tsunami representations were able to "open up" how individuals situate themselves and their responsibilities in relation to others. Yet also significant to my analysis is an understanding of the kind of community that the media photographs helped to construct: one imbued with power and associated emotional regimes that dictate the need for pity, sympathy and possibly compassion in face of distant others' trauma and pain. In this way, the compassionate emotional "performances" serve a dual purpose: They are constitutive of not only the more expansive transnational aid community but also, paradoxically, the more insular communities – and identities – of those who bear witness.

6 Trauma, grief and political transformation

The previous two chapters examined instances in which the emotional dimensions of representing trauma constituted what are essentially bounded conceptions of political community. In the first case – that of Australian identity and community following the 2002 Bali bombing – ensuing communal attachments were insular in focus, creating a stark inside/outside affective political community.[1] The case of the 2004 Asian tsunami then demonstrated how representations of trauma were implicated in a temporal process of reworking such attachments and concomitant responsibilities. However, while the respective connections directed each community differently, in both cases the trauma was mediated uncritically and primarily through appeals to established, dominant emotional meanings and discourses. What we thus see are two different instances of trauma drawing boundaries around and between identities and communities, as well as attachments and ensuing ethical responsibilities.

The focus of the present chapter lies with a third scenario. It explores the possibility of "working through" trauma and the various associated emotions in a manner that generates transformative communal attachments and political outlooks. Rather than constituting insular, politically bounded and potentially retributive forms of post-trauma community, traumatic events and histories may be conceived of in a manner that encourages critical reflection upon ensuing attachments and political mindsets. More cathartic and less maladaptive, redemptive forms of community may be in turn cultivated.

To this end, I propose an alternative way for communities to deal with and move on after widespread trauma: the possibility and

[1] The most well-known work examining how an "inside/outside" spatial dialectic frames conceptions of political community in world politics is R. B. J. Walker, *Inside/Outside: International Relations as Political Theory* (Cambridge: Cambridge University Press, 1993).

potentials immanent in "grieving" traumatic events and histories. Fundamental in this distinction is the opportunity and, indeed, the necessity of properly mourning trauma and, in so doing, coming to terms with the legacy of past suffering. Where common, reflex-like responses to trauma – particularly when politically instigated – trigger forms of remembering that preclude the possibility of working through painful understandings, a turn to grief recognizes the inherent need for individuals and communities to confront traumatic emotions and memories in order to be free of rather than trapped by past pain.

As natural as the processes of grieving loss after suffering and pain may seem, however, a shift from trauma to grief is not an organic social and political undertaking. A politics of grief would entail an active political commitment. It requires an open space through which individuals and communities can reflect upon and challenge shared representations of trauma and the role they play in maintaining entrenched, frequently politically destructive, and intimately emotional communal configurations. Such reflection would enable traumatized communities to acknowledge and gradually accept their wounding and loss, and work through the spectrum of emotions – from fear, anxiety and anger to humiliation, shame and guilt – that inevitably circulate after trauma. It may also in turn afford communities an opportunity to rethink how their sense of collectivity has been constituted.

The present chapter scrutinizes and empirically illustrates the emotional and communal dynamics at stake in my proposed politics of grief through a study of two historical cases: China and South Africa.

The first part of the chapter focuses on China,[2] which provides a case of historical trauma that has yet to be sufficiently worked through. At issue here is how the 1839–1949 period of Western and Japanese colonialism has generated an entrenched emotional political culture – fueled by various emotions, and foremost by "national humiliation" – through which Chinese identity, nationalism and global aspirations now take shape.[3] Largely singular representations of pivotal traumatic events during this period (from the First Opium War through to the

[2] By "China" I refer to the People's Republic of China (PRC). Unless stated otherwise, from here on "China" refers to the PRC.

[3] I have taken the beginning of the First Opium War (1939) and the end of the civil war (1949) to bracket the "Century of National Humiliation." Some sources take the end of the First Opium war (1842) and also the defeat of the Japanese in World War II (1945) in their place instead.

1937 Nanjing Massacre and following Japanese occupation) have been embraced through history and become what Vamik Volkan calls a "chosen trauma":[4] one that shapes not only China's national community but also its ensuing "quest for dignity."[5] In this sense, the overt politicization of China's traumatic history, together with the absence of other features necessary for working through trauma, has precluded the possibility of grieving and reflecting critically upon the past. Some scholars argue that China's traumatic legacy is reenacted to the point that it not only constitutes national identity and community but also motivates and guides contemporary state behavior.[6]

The second part of the chapter then turns to South Africa, a situation in which a community divided by trauma actively sought to work through the past in order to rebuild. In doing so, I pick up where the examination of China left off, focusing more specifically on the potentials for grieving trauma in a politically transformative manner. In particular, I scrutinize the therapeutic and psychosocial healing processes associated with the Truth and Reconciliation Commission (TRC), focusing on how it sought to create a critical emotional and ethical space through which the legacy and injustices of apartheid could be represented – and, in turn, collectively acknowledged and grieved. Various practices (such as giving testimony, listening, apologizing and making new shared meanings) were employed with the hope of generating "empathic sensibilities" through which individuals and the community as a whole could begin to reflect upon past violence in an effort to move on.[7]

Neither of these cases is of course an ideal scenario. However, it is in part because of this that they so powerfully illuminate the key issues

[4] Vamik Volkan, *Bloodlines: From Ethnic Pride to Ethnic Terrorism* (Boulder, CO: Westview Press, 1997), p. 36.

[5] John Fitzgerald, "China and the Quest for Dignity," *The National Interest*, 55 (1999), 47–59.

[6] See, for instance, William A. Callahan, *China: The Pessoptimist Nation* (Oxford: Oxford University Press, 2010); Manjari Chaterjee Miller, *Wronged By Empire: Post-Imperial Ideology and Foreign Policy in India and China* (Stanford: Stanford University Press, 2013); Zheng Wang, *Never Forget National Humiliation: Historical Memory in Chinese Politics and Foreign Relations* (New York: Columbia University Press, 2012).

[7] Pumla Gobodo-Madikizela, "Empathetic Repair after Mass Trauma: When Vengeance is Arrested," *European Journal of Social Theory*, 11.3 (2008), 331–351, 338.

and complexities at stake. Juxtaposing the two cases as a neglected and then more considered attempt to deal with and move forward from past trauma, China and South Africa together illustrate both the potentials – and, just as significantly – the challenges involved with working through and socially grieving the legacy of trauma, especially politically instigated trauma. Notable here is that both are situations involving political violence, which tends to precipitate the more worrying scenario of communities being fiercely and antagonistically constituted and/or divided through feelings of shared injury. As historical cases different from the previous two empirical chapters, they furthermore demonstrate that trauma has long-term intergenerational effects. Working through trauma is a long and ongoing process, which inevitably takes time. At the same time structurally very different, both cases provide concrete insights into the conditions – and emotional and political processes – required in a turn to grief, and in how we can actively cultivate modes of perceiving and feeling about trauma that can work to rebuild community in more inclusive and politically regenerative ways.

Before I begin, I offer a couple of brief caveats. In focusing on the two historical situations I stress that my accounts do not aim to be comprehensive in their retelling of the respective traumas. Moreover, in assessing dominant representations in each case, I do not claim to be exhaustive of all interpretations. The key purpose in analyzing the dominant historical narratives is, first of all, to explore the potentially deleterious long-term consequences of representing (and failing to work through) historical trauma; and then in turn, and second, to probe the potentials for representing – and for perceiving of and feeling for – trauma differently. At stake in these alternative narratives are, I suggest and demonstrate, ways of conceiving of trauma that promote more successful communal mourning, a crucial precondition for establishing renewed, less emotionally maladaptive and more genuinely cathartic, affective political communities.

China's chosen trauma: enacting the "Century of National Humiliation"

To apprehend the combined emotional and political legacies left by China's collective historical trauma, it is necessary to first delve briefly into China's past, and into stories told about China's past. I focus on events beginning in the mid-nineteenth century, as it is this period that has come to be narrated and perceived of as a particularly troubling time in China's history.

The outbreak of the First Opium War in 1839 is generally considered to signal a turning point in modern Chinese history: the ensuing century – up until the triumph of the Chinese Communist Party (CCP) in the civil war in 1949 – is represented and has overwhelmingly come to be known in China as the "Century of National Humiliation" (*bainian guochi*).[8] Spanning a number of devastating, painful and sometimes shocking events – from the signing of unequal trading treaties to various violent and repressive territorial incursions – Chinese now perceive of this as a period in which they were bullied, harassed, attacked and ultimately subjected to a state of semicolonial rule. Indeed, the dominant "national humiliation" discourse tells of how during this time China was "ruthlessly violated by Japanese and Western imperialism":[9] its riches were plundered, its people pillaged, and its territory and sovereignty forcibly taken.

More than simply painful, however, this "Century" is perceived to be particularly traumatic: prevailing Chinese representations communicate that foreign aggression instigated not only immense suffering but also a profound, worldview-shattering kind of dishonoring. It is thus not the Western and Japanese violence alone that makes this period significant. The semicolonialism belittled Qing China, reducing it to an arena for international competition and to a source of potential revenue.[10] What is now known as the "Century of National Humiliation" thus not simply illuminated China's political and military vulnerabilities, but significantly, in so doing, challenged China's

[8] In Chinese historiography, a distinct separation exists between previous dynastic rulers, some of which had external origins, and the nineteenth-century influx of Western and Japanese colonial powers. American commentator Richard Harris noted this as early as 1959: "The Chinese have one very broad generalization about their own history: they think in terms of 'up to the Opium war' and 'after the Opium war'; in other words, a century of humiliation and weakness to be expunged." See Richard Harris, "China and the World," *International Affairs*, 35 (1959), 161–169, 162. For other accounts, see Peter Hays Gries, *China's New Nationalism: Pride, Politics and Diplomacy* (Berkeley: University of California Press, 2004), pp. 43–53; Miller, *Wronged By Empire*, pp. 10–15; Wang, *Never Forget National Humiliation*, pp. 47–69.

[9] Geremie R. Barmé, "To Screw Foreigners is Patriotic: China's Avant-Garde Nationalists," *The China Journal*, 34 (1995), 209–234, 210.

[10] Miller, *Wronged By Empire*, p. 14.

view of itself – China's "cultural and moral superiority"[11] – and its perceived place in the world. In short, the hundred years of suffering at foreign hands exposed China as "weak" where the then powers-that-be thought they were the strongest of the strong, a "high civilization" beyond all others.[12] For China, each defeat was thus a significant "come down" – hence the now "official" narrative of being nationally humiliated.[13]

To fully appreciate the social, cultural and political significance of this historical period, let us first consider some of the key events that comprise the so-perceived traumatic century. Below is a chronology, together with what has come to be the respective accepted "humiliation" narrative.

While no doubt individually painful and difficult to move on from, when put together these events and the linear "national humiliation" narrative they make up now occupy a central place in the Chinese cultural and political present. Perceptions of collective historical trauma are firmly embedded in China's cultural consciousness.

Many scholars write of the significance of trauma and humiliation discourses in China. A recent study by Manjari Chaterjee Miller examines not only how Western and Japanese colonialism[14] constitutes a collective trauma in China but also how this colonial trauma has far-reaching political implications today. She tells of how the forced foreign incursions disrupted and dramatically transformed social order in China, and were characterized by their "oppression, humiliation and violence."[15] Perceptions of China's recent past are indelibly marked by the recurring, traumatic image of a "glorious civilization" being brutally "brought to its knees."[16] William Callahan also writes extensively

[11] Zheng Wang, "The Chinese Dream: Concept and Context," *Journal of Chinese Political Science*, 19.1 (2014), 1–13, 4.

[12] Alison Adcock Kaufman, "The Century of Humiliation Then and Now: Chinese Perceptions of the International Order," *Pacific Focus*, 105.1 (April 2010), 1–33, 12.

[13] William A. Callahan, "National Insecurities: Humiliation, Salvation, and Chinese Nationalism," *Alternatives: Local, Global, Political*, 29.2 (2004), 199–218, 206.

[14] Miller notes that Mao in fact referred to China during this period as a "semicolony" (*ban zhimin di*). See Miller, *Wronged By Empire*, p. 132.

[15] Miller, *Wronged By Empire*, p. 24.

[16] Manjari Chaterjee Miller, "The Trauma of Colonialism," *New York Times*, August 14, 2013. At www.nytimes.com/2013/08/15/opinion/global/the-trauma-of-colonialism.html?_r=0. Accessed March 4, 2014.

Table 6.1 *Chronology of China's "Century of National Humiliation"*[a]

Date	Event	Source of "National Humiliation"
1839–1842	First Opium War	The beginning of national humiliation. China's first defeat to the British. Forfeiture of sovereignty and territory.
1856–1860	Second Opium War	China goes to war with Western powers (Britain and France, with support of Russia and the US) over similar issues to the First Opium War. A further loss of sovereignty and territory.
1860	Destruction of Yuanming Garden Palace, Beijing	The Second Opium War ends with the ransacking of the Yuanming Garden Palace. Possessing inordinate beauty and treasures, the palace and its gardens were symbolic of the wealth, status and power of China's dynastic rulers. Never having been rebuilt, the ruined gardens stand as a symbol of China's "national wound."
1894–1895	First Sino-Japanese War	China's first defeat to the Japanese, which resulted in the transferal of the Korean Peninsula to Japanese sphere of influence. A further loss of prestige.

Table 6.1 (cont.)

Date	Event	Source of "National Humiliation"
1850s	Ghosts of the Black River	Massacre of Hailanpao and the sixty-four villages of Jiangdon in Manchuria by the Russians. 7,000 Chinese are believed to have been killed. The Qing concede more territory, this time to Russia.
1898–1900	Boxer Uprising and Eight Nation Alliance Invasion	Deep humiliation from the Boxer Uprising, who act in conjunction with eight foreign powers. The foreign Alliance eventually takes control of Beijing, as the empress dowager and the imperial court again retreat.
February 1904–September 1905	Russo-Japanese War	Russia and Japan go to war over Manchuria (and Korea). Japan is victorious. China concedes more territory in Manchuria.
1931	Japanese Invasion	Japanese stage the Mukden Incident (an explosion staged to give a pretext for subsequent invasion) and invade Manchuria, creating the puppet state Manchukuo. China petitioned the then League of Nations for assistance, to little avail. Japanese occupation would not end until the fall of Japan in World War II.

Date	Event	Source of "National Humiliation"
December 13, 1937–September 9, 1945	The Massacre of Nanjing, followed by Second Japanese War	Also known as the "Rape" of Nanjing, the Nanjing Massacre was an episode of mass murder, rape and looting as the Japanese captured Nanjing, the then capital of China. China maintains that 300,000 were killed. While several perpetrators have since been prosecuted for international war crimes, Chinese voices commonly perceive that Japan has never truly repented for their wrongs.

[a] This chronology has been adapted from Zhou Shan and Zhang Chunbo (eds.), *Guochi lu: Tushou Zhonghua bainian* [A Record of National Humiliation: Pictures and Stories of China's Century] (Lanzhou: Gansu Youth Press, 1997), which is used and cited in Callahan, "National Insecurities," 204–205.

on ensuing discourses of Chinese national humiliation. He argues that humiliation has become the "master narrative of modern Chinese history": it "unproblematically dots texts (in both Chinese and English) about Chinese identity and politics" – so much so that it is now "a key part of modern Chinese subjectivity."[17] Peter Hays Gries likewise contends that the hundred years of humiliation is essential to apprehending the nature of modern China. For him, the weight of the PRC's traumatic "Century" is heavy enough to constitute a "foundational" moment in the formation of the contemporary Chinese nation.[18]

The traumas that were collectively experienced and are now perceived of in China are thus clear. But, of course, few nations are free of traumatic experiences and histories. Violence and suffering mar the foundations of so many modern societies. So, what is significant about the relationship between China's history of trauma, ensuing

[17] Callahan, "National Insecurities," 204, 206.
[18] Gries, *China's New Nationalism*, p. 47; also pp. 43–53.

humiliation and the ensuing contemporary political culture? How and why – to what extent, and in what manner – do past traumas live on in China today? Why is it important that we appreciate how exactly collective trauma remains "alive" in modern China, so to speak? And, since so much time has passed since the "Century of National Humiliation," why has it not healed the old wounds?

Zheng Wang's insightful study of historical memory in China leaves us with key insights that help when reflecting upon such questions.[19] He suggests it is helpful to examine the constitutive influence of the suffering endured throughout the "Century of National Humiliation" through the lens of what psychoanalyst Vamik Volkan calls "chosen trauma."[20] Chosen trauma refers to instances when memories of violence and injustice become internalized within a large group's identity such that the ensuing trauma predominantly defines them. Similar to the notion of "cultural trauma"[21] or "national trauma,"[22] central to the concept of chosen trauma is that perceptions (and thus shared representations) of injury and feelings of loss proliferate throughout a large group in the wake of extreme events, instilling a sense of victimization not simply in those who experience the events directly but also in community members who bear witness, either immediately or even

[19] Wang, *Never Forget National Humiliation*; Zheng Wang, "National Humiliation, Historical Education, and the Politics of Historical Memory: Patriotic Education Campaign in China," *International Studies Quarterly*, 52.4 (2008), 783–806.

[20] For Volkan, suggestive in the term is "a large group's unconscious 'choice' to add a past generation's mental representation of an event to its own identity, and the fact that, while groups may have experienced any number of traumas in their history, only certain ones remain alive over centuries." See Vamik D. Volkan, "Transgenerational Transmissions and Chosen Traumas: An Aspect of Large Group Identity," *Group Analysis*, 34.1 (2001), 79–97, at 88. Further discussions of "chosen trauma" can also be found in Volkan, *Bloodlines*, pp. 36–49; Vamik D. Volkan, "Traumatized Societies and Psychological Care: Expanding the Concept of Preventative Medicine," *Mind and Human Interaction*, 11 (2000), 177–194.

[21] Jeffrey C. Alexander, *Trauma: A Social Inquiry* (Cambridge: Polity, 2012), pp. 6–30; Jeffrey C. Alexander, "Toward a Theory of Cultural Trauma," in Jeffry C. Alexander, Ron Eyerman, Bernhard Giesen, Neil J. Smelser and Piotr Stompka, *Cultural Trauma and Collective Identity* (Berkeley: University of California Press, 2004), pp. 1–30; Ron Eyerman, *Cultural Trauma: Slavery and the Formation of African American Identity* (Cambridge: Cambridge University Press, 2001); Piotr Sztompka, "Cultural Trauma: The Other Face of Social Change," *European Journal of Social Theory*, 3.4 (2000), 449–466.

[22] See Chapter 4.

generations later. Following Volkan, Wang's turn to chosen trauma traces how suffering endured during the painful "Century" remains alive in stories told in China today, to the extent that trauma helps China to identify itself, both within itself, as a coherent national political collective, and externally, as an international actor on the world stage.[23]

In sum: past trauma remains a persistent force in China's political present. Such is China's relationship with the past that, as some trauma scholars would put it, it appears even that the Chinese relive, or "reenact,"[24] their injury and pain: the collective suffering is repetitively relived, such that not simply has China as a nation been unable to accept and move beyond it, but moreover that the ensuing trauma has become a defining part of their contemporary national culture, identity and conception of political community.

Representing national humiliation: the celebration of trauma and the emotional inscription of the Chinese nation

To more properly discern how China's traumatic past lives on in the present day, I now turn to and analyze key representations of the traumatic "Century." One short section cannot do justice to the complete humiliation narrative, nor can it articulate how each individual event comprising the history is represented. I must necessarily adopt a narrower focus: I scrutinize the overarching humiliation narrative as well as select representations of key events within the "Century of National Humiliation." In doing so, I demonstrate how the prevailing representation of suffering during this period produces a range of communally constitutive, nationalistic meanings that function to "re-create the nation"[25] by preserving a sense of injury. I focus in particular on the affective dynamics involved, showing how dominant representations

[23] Wang, *Never Forget National Humiliation*, pp. 7–10, 40–69; Wang, "National Humiliation, Historical Education, and the Politics of Historical Memory," 785–788.

[24] The concept of "reenactment" is used to describe situations in which unhealed trauma manifests in social relations through which sufferers internalize and reexperience unresolved pain to the point that it affects their sense of self and also relations with others. See Carolyn Yoder, *The Little Book of Trauma Healing: When Violence Strikes and Community is Threatened* (New York: Good Books, 2006), pp. 32–34.

[25] Callahan, "History, Identity, and Security," 202.

(and interpretations) implicate a spectrum of emotions – most explicitly, humiliation, but also guilt, shame, anger and pride – and concomitant forms of emotional agency that cohere China's national community in powerful ways. So powerful, that the strength and intensely affective nature of ensuing Chinese nationalism is a phenomenon oft commented on, and by some analysts, feared.

Like all histories, China's painful past is shaped by the stories told about it: official stories, approved by the CCP and passed down through various political and media channels, but also stories that people tell themselves; stories told in history textbooks, children's books, in plays, operas and songs, by grandparents, parents and friends. Traumatic memories and those that are ceremoniously commemorated through state-sponsored anniversaries are in this way part of a process of interpretation, abstraction and representation – a process through which certain events are illuminated and made meaningful while others may be cast a blind eye.

The official "Century of National Humiliation" narrative is no different, and is pivotal in this respect. Many scholars have revealed that the historical narrative is a product of such interpretation – appropriation, even. They suggest that it has been carefully and intentionally crafted, with specific "political and cultural, foreign and domestic" aims in sight.[26] Particular events have been kept in while others have been carved out, smoothening the narrative of China's past. As a historiography, the hundred years of humiliation is, as such, a representational artifact, a product of cultural memory and myth, rather than an historical account of how things "really were." As Wang reminds us, "[a] central element to the creation of this narrative is selection of what the people will remember and what they will forget."[27] This is not to dispute that the events comprising the "Century" did not happen; indeed they did. Or that there were not shocking or even in some instances outrages of horrendous proportions. Historians agree they were.[28] It is rather to say that critical voices and visions of history have been silenced; China's modern history has been written, more than all else, as one of suffering not of their own making.

[26] Callahan, "National Insecurities," 205.
[27] Wang, *Never Forget National Humiliation*, p. 10.
[28] For example, see Immanuel C. Y. Hsü, *The Rise of Modern China*, 6th ed. (New York and Oxford: Oxford University Press, 2000).

Consider for instance, as scholars before me lay bare, the selectivity of the overarching narrative. The accepted chronology charts a history of imperialist and foreign aggression in China. Yet all of China's internal, often violent, political struggles have been left out. This includes so-called "dark anniversaries",[29] such as the 1959 Tibetan Uprising, the closing down of the Xidan Democracy Wall in 1979, and the Tiananmen Square tragedy of 1989. The Taiping Rebellion from 1851 to 1864, which, as a civil war, does not fit the humiliation metanarrative, has also been omitted.[30] As have been the considerable physical and psychological wounds incurred through Mao's various violent twentieth-century upheavals, from the Hundred Flowers Campaign (1956) and the Great Leap Forward (1958–1961) to the 1966–1976 Cultural Revolution. The latter are, like events of the traumatic "Century," an intrinsic part of China's national story and have been central to the constitution of the Chinese state. After all, it was through the Mao's "class struggle" and Communist leadership that the now PRC came into being. Efforts have been made to recognize and commemorate the wrongs of China's ruling party,[31] yet the attention afforded China's internal struggles pales in comparison to the trauma/humiliation narratives mobilized against foreign powers. Narratives of suffering at the behest of the West and the Japanese are presented in a singular and omnipresent light: they emphasize repeated foreign exploitation and aggression and mobilize the Chinese people in opposition to it.

An important body of literature that critically probes dominant representations of the PRC's history links it with now prevalent narratives of Chinese victimhood.[32] This research examines the significance of stories about China's history of suffering and trauma by looking

[29] Wang, *Never Forget National Humiliation*, p. 6.

[30] Callahan, "National Insecurities," 205.

[31] One example would be a recently constructed Cultural Revolution Museum constructed in Shantou.

[32] For example, Ian Buruma, "The Joys and Perils of Victimhood," *New York Review of Books*, 46 (1999), 4–8; Edward Friedman, "Raising Sheep on Wolf Milk: The Politics and Dangers of Misremembering the Past in China," *Totalitarian Movement and Political Regimes*, 9.2/3 (2008), 389–409; Neil Renwick and Qing Cao, "China's Political Discourse Towards the 21st Century: Victimhood, Identity, and Political Power," *East Asia*, 17 (1999), 111–143; Jung Tsu, *Failure, Nationalism, and Literature: The Making of Modern Chinese Identity, 1895–1937* (Stanford: Stanford University Press, 2006).

to how discourses of victimization are in fact a recent phenomenon rather than an age-old one. Importantly, scholars tell of how the official version of history shifted from China as "victor" (under the leadership of Mao Zhedong) to that of China as "victim" (from Deng Xiaoping on). To be clear, under Mao the prevailing view of Chinese history glorified the CCP as "victors": the Communist Revolution was represented as having liberated the Chinese people from the feudalism and injustices of a corrupt dynastic system. In this view, China's pre-"Liberation" (pre-1949) sufferings were blamed on the ineptitude of the Qing; the anti-feudal masses were correspondingly valorized for throwing off their class-based chains. However, in the early 1990s (after the Tiananmen protests of 1989) as the attraction of the West grew and appreciation of the Communist Revolution declined, the CCP took a different approach to marshaling the past in order safeguard its political legitimacy. A new "patriotic education policy" was put in place, which saw the "victor" reading of history reframed.[33] Here, the CCP refocused interpretations away from China as "victor" to that of China as "victim."[34] Museum, memorial sites, history textbooks and a range of other exhibitionary cultural activities (such as the performance of operas, songs, speeches, slogans and films) were revised such that accounts shifted away from the CCP's victorious class struggle and toward those dominated by the suffering and oppression China endured under foreign hands.[35]

So where a "victim" status was once a stain to be erased or overlooked, it has come to be a defining aspect of the contemporary Chinese nation. In the past two decades, it has been an important part of guaranteeing a patriotic, unified China. The strategic (and highly political) reworking of history has been hugely effective, both in terms of cohering the Chinese nation and in reinvigorating the one-party rule of the CCP. Neil Renwick and Qing Cao explain that the now deeply embedded narratives of victimhood, suffering and loss – and

[33] William A. Callahan, "History, Identity, and Security: Producing and Consuming Nationalism in China," *Critical Asian Studies*, 38.2 (2006), 179–208, 185–186.

[34] Gries, *China's New Nationalism*, pp. 69–70, 84–85; Wang, *Never Forget National Humiliation*, pp. 95–100.

[35] See also Friedman, "Raising Sheep on Wolf Milk," 396–398; Rana Mitter, "Old Ghosts, New Memories: China's Changing War History in the Era of Post-Mao Politics," *Journal of Contemporary History*, 38.1 (2003), 117–131.

also paradoxically of the PRC's now "heroic"[36] redemption, for which the CCP explicitly credits itself – are central to legitimizing the Chinese political system.[37] Specifically, the post-Mao interpretation of China as "victim" helps to maintain the strength of the CCP's rule by mobilizing a shared history of suffering and, as such, enabling the CCP to proclaim that under its leadership never again will China be oppressed.

It is through such processes of historical representation that the emotional landscape – the nature and boundaries of affect – of the national community are configured.[38] Representations of China's traumatic history do this by appealing to and reconstituting prefigured, historically grounded emotional subjectivities. Put differently, representations tap into social meanings that resonate at least in part due to the shared, culturally embedded forms of feeling that such meanings invoke. The linkages between dominant representations of historical trauma, ensuing meanings, and emotions thus become intrinsic to how the Chinese enact national identity and, in turn, feel communally "attached."

To more fully appreciate the affective dynamics at stake, it is therefore necessary to look closer at the key meanings ensuing from preponderant representations of the past. Two meanings, both denotative and possessing deeper, connotative value, are important.

The first involves the seemingly simple observation that the "humiliation" narrative is itself an explicitly emotive phrase, which has come to signify "the exploitation of China by foreign nations and the righteous anger that such exploitation has aroused in the Chinese

[36] Mitter, "Old Ghosts New Memories," 128. Callahan also writes of national humiliation's "discursive twin": "national salvation," while Wang similarly writes of how China's "chosen glories" are constitutive of Chinese political identity as much as is "chosen trauma." See Callahan, "National Insecurities," 203–204; Wang, *Never Forget National Humiliation*, pp. 41–45.

[37] Renwick and Cao, "China's Political Discourse Towards the 21st Century," 129.

[38] Many scholars discuss and analyze linkages between China's historical trauma, the continuing perception of humiliation, and the present strength of nationalist communal attachments. See, for example, Callahan, *China*, pp. 19–28; Yingjie Guo, *Cultural Nationalism in Contemporary China* (London: Routledge, 2004); Yingjie Guo, "Patriotic Villains and Patriotic Heroes: Chinese Literary Nationalism in the 1990s," *Nationalism and Ethnic Politics*, 4.1–2 (2007), 163–188; Gries, *China's New Nationalism*, p. 48; Tsu, *Failure, Nationalism, and Literature*, pp. 1–8; Wang, *Never Forget National Humiliation*, pp. 12, 26–27, 225–226.

people."[39] China is presented as and perceived to be united, a homogenous whole, joined by the profound, unjust suffering experienced at the hands of others. Put differently, the post-Mao reinterpretation of history focuses understandings of past grievances not as those isolated to a generation, or those that are set within a more complex, nuanced modern history, but as suffering that has been directed against all Chinese. Victimization and suffering incurred throughout the traumatic "Century" in this way become a "badge of honor" for the Chinese people. Past trauma is distinguished as a distinct collective national experience, which exceptionalizes China as a national community.

Like this – and second – the history of trauma and humiliation functions to re-create long-held perceptions about "who" China is and "where" China's belongs in the international system. This is to say, as commentators contend, that the belief that the Chinese civilization is unique and superior is re-created through the veil of their exploitation and dishonoring.[40] Colonial sufferings endured by the Chinese are precisely so traumatic because of the historical (and continuing) perception of China's greatness.[41] Popular understandings of their painful past inculcate a longing to "regain lost status," for China to return to what is viewed as its proper place and "chosen glory."[42]

Popular representations of the historical trauma thus align and resonate with intensely emotional existential dichotomies that commentators suggest have prevailed in China for centuries, as well as the historically engrained, often implicit "structures of feeling" that function to support such dichotomies.[43] Included here are binaries of

[39] Damien Kinney, "Rediscovering a Massacre: The Filmic Legacy of Iris Chang's *The Rape of Nanking*," *Continuum: Journal of Media and Cultural Studies*, 26.1 (2012), 11–23, at 12.

[40] Wang, *Never Forget National Humiliation*, pp. 41, 43; Gries, *China's New Nationalism*, pp. 70.

[41] As the world's heavenly mandated "central" or "middle" kingdom (as linguistically coded in China's name, *Zhong guo*), China, and its people, Wang writes, possess the view "of the Chinese civilization as universal and superior." See Wang, *Never Forget National Humiliation*, pp. 41, 43.

[42] Miller, *Wronged By Empire*, p. 132.

[43] Callahan refers to emotional norms that underpin the Chinese nation as "structures of feeling"; see his *China*, p. 19–28. The term and concept "structures of feeling" was earlier articulated by Raymond Williams, and has been drawn upon in Mabel Berezin, "Secure States: Towards a Political Sociology of Emotion," in Jack Barbalet (ed.), *Emotions and Sociology*

civilized/barbaric, "inside/outside, domestic/foreign, China/West"[44] together with the sources of honor/dishonor pride/humiliation, shame/anger that undergird them. Stories told about the past, together with the ritualized commemorative practices through which such stories are enacted, tie in heavily to conceivably nationalistic emotions – a pride, dignity and love for one's community – while, paradoxically, promoting caution, and even anxiety and anger, toward those outside. Indeed, commemorating the collective historical trauma through official humiliation provides citizens with a constant reminder of their past vulnerability and pain (thus implicating emotions associated with loss and anger), while simultaneously signaling both the greatness of China's rise (pride and dignity) and the need for vigilance in the face of any foreign actions that may diminish it once again (anxiety). Callahan stresses so much. He suggests that the overwhelming emphasis on memorializing the history of foreign brutality has shifted energies away from domestic issues (and protest after Tiananmen) toward the "enemy" outside; it "differentiate[s] Chinese citizens from the foreign other."[45] Rana Mitter too shows how the victimization narrative creates a "common enemy to oppose … regardless of party affiliation and, more controversially, nationality."[46] National identity and community are in this way emotionally constituted around a positive/negative binary, with Chinese community the "positive," set in contrast to the "negative," foreign and hostile outside/other.[47]

Chinese national identity and community can thus be seen to be powerfully constituted through the nationalistic meanings and emotions associated with representations of past suffering and enduring trauma. Within China, cultural trauma and ensuing humiliation have been reinterpreted and represented as strengths; sites where past violence has become the epitome of present-day sovereign control, sites

(Oxford: Blackwell, 2002), pp. 33–52, at p. 39; Jennifer Harding and E. Deidre Pribram, "The Power of Feeling: Locating Emotions in Culture," *European Journal of Cultural Studies*, 5.4 (2002), 407–426, at 416.

44 Callahan, *China*, p. 22.

45 Callahan, "History, Identity, and Security," 186, 202.

46 Mitter, "Old Ghosts, New Memories," 120.

47 Both Western powers and Japan are the sources of such "Othering" identity dynamics. Together with the work of Callahan and Gries, see, for instance, Shogo Suzuki, "The Importance of 'Othering' in China's National Identity: Sino-Japanese Relations as a Stage of Identity Conflicts," *The Pacific Review*, 20.1 (2007), 23–47.

at which communal injuring is celebrated in ways that reproduce historically engrained "structures of feeling" and both distinguish and reconstitute Chinese nationalism, identity, and community.[48]

Unfinished mourning, emotions and the failure to work through trauma

Even though the representation and remembrance of China's traumatic past are highly politicized, the constitutive effects cannot be dismissed on the grounds of being the product of mere government propaganda. As Manjari Miller stresses, the hundred years of humiliation at foreign hands "is seen as a trauma and responded to as a trauma."[49] So prominent is the national trauma culture that within China "[t]he sense of injury is wide-ranging and pervasive";[50] the history of suffering is "exceptionally painful and difficult to overcome."[51] Indeed, the past reaches forward to reflect a community "trapped by the past that wounded them"[52] – rather than, that is, a community that has accepted and, as much as is possible after a prolonged period of violence, suffering and loss, come to terms with its turbulent history.

Having demonstrated, albeit briefly, how past trauma has become collectivized and inscribed, emotionally, into contemporary configurations of Chinese identity and community, the present section critically examines the consequences at stake in doing so. I focus in particular on the potentially deleterious communal and political effects, underlining that dominant modes of representing (and, in turn, remembering) frame the historical trauma in a manner that implicates a range of powerful nationalistic emotions that work against the possibility of coming to terms with the injury. Prevailing representations – politicized as they may be – keep the pain and distressing emotions "fresh" for Chinese nationals, thereby inhibiting opportunities to successfully mourn and work through the trauma. Examining the ensuing political

48 Callahan, *China*, p. 19.
49 Miller, *Wronged By Empire*, pp. 134–135.
50 Miller, *Wronged By Empire*, p. 26.
51 Anne F. Thurston, "Community and Isolation: Memory and Forgetting," in G. Gong (ed.), *Memory and History in East and Southeast Asia* (Washington, DC: CSIS Press, 2001), pp. 149–172, at p. 170.
52 Kate Schick, "Acting Out and Working Through: Trauma and (In)Security," *Review of International Studies*, 37.4 (2011), 1837–1855, at 1842.

dynamics – both for China domestically and in terms of China's rise in global politics – the section demonstrates how less antagonistic and more reflective and regenerative communal configurations depend upon the ability of traumatized communities to confront, grieve and work through trauma and the complex emotions trauma can long proliferate.

I begin by making a simple and now likely obvious point: even though long past, representations of China's trauma have kept ensuing wounds too "fresh" for individuals and the Chinese community as a whole to, together, confront and work through them. Said differently, representations of the "Century of National Humiliation" narrate the trauma in such a way that Chinese nationals are prompted to relive and "act out" the sense of injury and loss, rather than undergo (necessary) adaptive processes that enable the community to come to terms with and move beyond it.

It is in this way, as intimated earlier, that the PRC can be seen as a community constituted, at least in part, by "chosen trauma," or as Johan Galtung similarly puts it, a "chosenness-myth-trauma" syndrome.[53] I reintroduce this concept here because, more than merely descriptive, it helps us to appreciate the aberrant and possibly destructive consequences of memorializing collective trauma in such a manner.

Volkan's work, which first introduced the term "chosen trauma," scrutinizes and worries about such post-trauma communal configurations. Through extensive empirical research into ethnic identity (and conflict) in the Balkans, Middle East and communities in the US, he shows how shared images of historical trauma may not simply delineate group identity but also, in so doing, keep the collective trauma unresolved, irrespective of how far back the "actual" event stretches. Feelings of helplessness and loss persist within the group, as do shame and humiliation due to perceived weakness. However, rather than properly mourning and working through the injury and associated emotions, groups constituted by chosen trauma pursue strategies that seek to compensate for their victimization. This often results in the

[53] Volkan, *Bloodlines*, p. 36–49; Johan Galtung, "The Construction of National Identities for the Cosmic Drama: Chosen-Myths-Trauma (CMT) Syndromes and Cultural Pathologies," in S. P. Udayakumar (ed.), *Handcuffed to History: Narratives, Pathologies and Violence in South-East Asia* (Westport: Praeger, 2001), pp. 61–77.

traumatized community (unconsciously or otherwise) attempting to restore or somehow assert their social position (or dominance), as a counterbalance to feelings of inferiority. Volkan describes this in terms of the development of an exaggerated "entitlement" ideology, which can in turn incite antagonistic belief systems and, at worst, expressions (or even acts) of retribution and revenge.[54]

Galtung, likewise, suggests that a sense of "chosenness" – a feeling of group fate and destiny that is instigated by the perception of shared pain – can be cultivated in response to collective traumas. While binding the group together, this kind of communal "chosenness" can also be a source of the types of cultural myths and "paranoia" that may in some situations have led to violence and trauma in the first place.[55] This would be akin to what Allan Young calls a "pathologic secret," or Richard Wilson, in a slight different vein, a "constitutive violence": these conditions refer to instances when traumatic events and memories are so extreme and disrupting that they become a central organizing principle for life after.[56] Significant here, therefore, is that not merely do chosen traumas frame communal attachments. Chosen traumas motivate group behaviors as well.[57]

Whether knowingly or unknowingly co-opted, communities constituted through trauma and associated unpleasant emotions in this manner can therefore be socially and politically problematic. Grief literatures examine the associated post-trauma dynamics extensively, although, bar a few exceptions, resulting insights have remained largely in the context of individual recovery after trauma. These literatures

[54] Vamik D. Volkan, "Chosen Trauma, The Political Ideology of Entitlement and Violence," paper presented in Berlin, June 10, 2004. At www.vamikvolkan.com/Chosen-Trauma%2C-the-Political-Ideology-of-Entitlement-and-Violence.php/. Accessed June 20, 2014; Volkan, "Transgenerational Transmissions and Chosen Traumas"; Volkan, "Traumatized Societies and Psychological Care," 190.

[55] Galtung, "The Construction of National Identities for the Cosmic Drama," 63–64, 74.

[56] Allan Young, *The Harmony of Illusions: Inventing Post-Traumatic Stress Disorder* (Princeton: Princeton University Press, 1995), pp. 28–30; Richard A. Wilson, "The *Sizwe* Will Not Go Away: The Truth and Reconciliation Commission, Human Rights and Nation-Building in South Africa," *African Studies*, 55.2 (1996), 1–20, at 16.

[57] Vamik Volkan goes as far as to claim, "Adopting a chosen trauma can enhance ethnic pride, reinforce a sense of victimization, and even spur a group to avenge its ancestors' hurts"; see Volkan, *Bloodlines*, p. 78.

refer to this situation as a state of "complicated" or "frozen" grief, meaning that necessary post-trauma mourning processes have been left "unfinished," thereby precluding the possibility for genuine healing and recovery.[58] "Stuck" in a state of perpetual grief, destructive psychological, emotional and social patterns then emerge: sufferers repetitively relive their injuring experience through "acting it out," which in turn prevents the working through of trauma that is necessary to move beyond trauma's most debilitating effects and reengage with normal social life.[59] Rather than learning to accept what has occurred, and to some degree detaching from the trauma, sufferers incorporate the loss into their self such that they become perpetually attached to, dependent upon and constituted by it.[60] Maladaptive strategies of post-trauma survival ensue.

But, just as individuals need to mourn trauma and work through emotions associated with injury and loss, so too do communities. The very patterns identified by Volkan and Galtung are linked to the inability to mourn and move beyond trauma. Some politics and international

[58] Within grief theory, the terms "complicated mourning" or "complicated grief" are typically used to signify that an obstacle has prevented or truncated the necessary processes involved with mourning trauma and loss. This means that the trauma remains unresolved. In cases of unresolved or "un-mourned" trauma, sufferers tend to continually reenact their pain in an unending attempt to come to terms with the injury and loss. Repeated and protracted "acting out" would, for instance, be a product of such "complicated" or unfinished mourning. See, for instance, Robert A. Neimeyer, "Complicated Grief and the Quest for Meaning: A Constructivist Contribution," *Omega: Journal of Death and Dying*, 52.1 (2006), 37–52; J. William Worden, *Grief Counseling and Grief Therapy: A Handbook for the Mental Health Practitioner*, 4th ed. (New York: Springer, 2009), pp. 127–152; Volkan, *Bloodlines*, pp. 37–38. Specifically on how grief can become "frozen," see Pauline Boss, *Ambiguous Loss: Learning to Live with Unresolved Grief* (Cambridge, MA: Harvard University Press, 1999), pp. 9–11.

[59] Judith Lewis Herman, *Trauma and Recovery: From Domestic Abuse to Political Terror* (London: Pandora, 1992), pp. 155–159. See also Vamik D. Volkan and Elizabeth Zintl, *Life After Loss: The Lessons of Grief* (New York: Scribener and Sons, 1993).

[60] Sigmund Freud conceived of this state of unresolved (and unmourned) trauma as "melancholia." Melancholia differs from mourning in that its work is never complete; melancholia is thus, in a sense, unsuccessful or unattempted mourning – what I call in this chapter "unfinished mourning." See Sigmund Freud, "Mourning and Melancholia," in *On Metapsychology: The Theory of Psychoanalysis*, trans. James Strachey, compiled and edited by Angela Richards (Harmondsworth: Penguin, 1991), pp. 247–268.

relations scholars have begun to adapt such understandings of trauma and recovery to global politics. Following the terrorist attacks of September 11, 2001, Jenny Edkins demonstrated how reflex political reactions after trauma seek to restore order by memorializing trauma in ways that "forget" the vulnerability and pain (rather than genuinely heal it).[61] Kate Schick too examines how political trauma is "acted out" through meaning-making narratives that ultimately "gloss over" (rather than critically reflect upon) suffering, and in so doing cordon off community – thus producing aberrant, insecure and potentially belligerent political configurations.[62] The work of K. M. Fierke also reveals a comparable pattern about trauma and political community. Fierke shows that when experienced in a collective context, "defeat, humiliation or betrayal" after trauma can create solipsistic communities inclined toward retaliation and violence.[63] Evelin Lindner also shows how collective humiliation can begin a vicious cycle of violence and vindication: "[w]hen a humiliated mind is left to reflect upon its own destruction, it may become convinced that it must inflict even greater pain on the perpetrator."[64] Scholars that examine the psychology of peace and conflict have also of course for long alluded that it is through the very "impact of trauma" that cultural anxieties and conflict-prone perceptions of "the outer social world" can be formed.[65]

[61] Jenny Edkins, "Forget Trauma? Responses to September 11," *International Relations*, 16.2 (2002), 243–256.

[62] Schick, "Acting Out and Working Through," 1842–1847.

[63] K. M. Fierke, *Critical Approaches to International Security* (London: Polity, 2007), pp. 132–137; K. M. Fierke, "Whereof We Can Speak, Thereof We Must Not Be Silent: Trauma, Political Solipsism and War," *Review of International Studies*, 30.4 (2004), 471–491; Khaled Fattah and K. M. Fierke, "A Clash of Emotions: The Politics of Humiliation and Political Violence in the Middle East," *European Journal of International Relations*, 15.1 (2009), 67–93.

[64] Evelin Linder, *Making Enemies: Humiliation and International Conflict* (Westport, CT: Praeger Security International, 2006), p. xv.

[65] Malvern Lumsden, "Breaking the Cycles of Violence," *Journal of Peace Research*, 34.4 (1997), 377–383, 377. See also Daniel Bar-Tal, "From Intractable Conflict Through Conflict Resolution to Reconciliation: Psychological Analysis," *Political Psychology*, 21.1 (2000), 351–366; Daniel Bar-Tal, Eran Halperin and Joseph De Riveria, "Collective Emotions in Conflict Situations: Societal Implications," *Journal of Social Issues*, 63.2 (2007), 441–460, at 455–456; Timothy Gallimore, "Unresolved Trauma: Fuel for the Cycle of Violence and Terrorism," in Chris E. Stout (ed.), *Psychology of Terrorism: Coping with the Continuing Threat* (Westport: Praeger, 2004), pp. 67–93; Masi Noor, Nurit Shnabel, Samer Halabi and Arie Nadler, "When Suffering Begets Suffering: The Psychology of Competitive Victimhood

Recently, a special issue of *Alternatives*, edited by James Brassett and Nick Vaughan-Williams, has similarly underscored the politics and ethics of "governing traumatic events."[66] Drawing attention to how "responses to 'traumatic events' condition the possibility for particular forms of governance," they suggest that how trauma is "managed," performed and in turn comes to be known is central to understanding the resulting nature of political power – and community.[67]

These dynamics are revealing when it comes to appreciating the case of China. Even though more specialists suggest that the PRC is emerging as a "peace-loving nation,"[68] China's relationship to the past belies a nation fixated on its historical grievances. Mobilized only in the last two and a half decades, representations of the "Century of National Humiliation" have cultivated an intensely emotional trauma culture, which ultimately celebrates collective (national) suffering and associated humiliation for unifying ends. The resulting national cohesion can in this way be seen to have emerged as a consequence of the precise emotions and anxieties that scholars suggest need to be worked through.

It is not difficult to discern of the political consequences of China's trauma-based emotional dynamics. Residues of their history of suffering are evident within the nature of the PRC's domestic and global political relations. Characterizing the legacy is simple: most significant here, both within China and to how the PRC projects itself on the world stage, is the manner in which the sense of national humiliation and shame motivates the PRC to emerge stronger than ever – to avenge past wrongs; to never again be oppressed. It is precisely because the PRC so strongly perceives of its historical abuse and neglect that it

Between Adversarial Groups in Violent Conflicts," *Personality and Social Psychology Review*, 16.4 (2012), 351–374.

[66] James Brassett and Nick Vaughan-Williams (eds.), Special Issue on "Governing Traumatic Events," *Alternatives: Local, Global, Political*, 37.3 (2012), 183–281.

[67] James Brassett and Nick Vaughan-Williams, "Governing Traumatic Events," *Alternatives: Local, Global, Political*, 37.3 (2012), 183–187, 186.

[68] William A. Callahan, "How to Understand China: the Dangers and Opportunities of Being a Rising Power," in the Forum section "The Rise of China," *Review of International Studies*, 31 (2005), 701–714, at 706. My inquiry in this chapter also provides further opportunity to debunk the prominent "China as threat" thesis that has until recently prevailed in Sino-US analysis, and offers fruitful psychosocial and emotional insights that may enhance engagements with China.

now struggles for international recognition, dignity and respect. Mao Zhedong's infamous 1949 "stand up" declaration aptly captures this sentiment still today: "Ours will no longer be a nation subject to insult and humiliation. We have stood up."[69] During his time, Deng Xiaoping also pointed to what had been learned through the previous century. In 1989 he reiterated, "the Chinese people will not be intimidated ... they felt inferior for more than a century, but now ... they have stood up."[70]

Given this, it is not surprising that China's ensuing ontological anxieties play out most acutely on the world stage, manifesting a host of "national insecurities."[71] Going beyond geopolitical theories, great power politics and traditional security analysis, studies underscore the psychological and affective legacies emanating from China's traumatic past, showing how they are visible in a range of China's "emotional and instrumental" political motivations and behaviors.[72]

Significant here is that China's "Century of Humiliation" is seen as key to understanding how and why the PRC emerges on the international scene in the manner it does. William Callahan, David Scott and Manjari Miller all contend, for instance, that the PRC's foreign policy is intimately linked to the symbolic politics associated with representing China's historical trauma. Showing how "the Chinese go to great pains ... to emphasize their colonial history, and even more significantly, their victimization by colonial powers,"[73] Miller argues that past suffering translates into an overarching approach to both the PRC's interstate relations and also particular political priorities. Specifically, Miller proposes that we consider this in terms of a "post-imperial ideology." She identifies – and empirically examines – three broad goals at stake: (1) to inure an overarching sense of victimhood that drives "the subordinate goals of (2) maximizing territorial sovereignty and (3) maximizing status."[74] In this way, Miller links

[69] Mao Zhedong cited in Zhiqun Zhu, "Introduction: The People's Republic of China Today," in Zhiqun Zhu (ed.), *The People's Republic of China Today: Internal and External Challenges* (Singapore: World Scientific Publishing), p. 4.

[70] David Scott, *China and the International System 1840–1949: Power, Presence, and Perceptions in a Century of Humiliation* (Albany: SUNY Press, 2008), p. 294.

[71] Callahan, "National Insecurities."

[72] Gries, *China's New Nationalism*, p. 24.

[73] Miller, *Wronged By Empire*, p. 132.

[74] Miller, *Wronged By Empire*, p. 132. See also pp. 8–10.

the colonial trauma (together with the China's continuing status as a "victim") to the PRC's hyper-vigilance and anxiety in relation to issues involving both any perceived loss of "face" (status and recognition) and more "concrete" policy regarding what the PRC considers the inviolability of state borders. As she puts it, her conception of post-imperial ideology "explains behavior on important foreign policy issues" such as when China "feel[s] their sovereignty is threatened, that borders they consider non-negotiable are at stake, or feel[s] they will suffer a loss of face or decline in prestige."[75]

Callahan delves a little deeper into the linkages between dominant narratives of humiliation, ensuing identity issues and foreign policy. He argues that China's "positive" and "negative" feelings about itself – which Callahan specifies as China's "pride and humiliation," or its "superiority and inferiority complex" arising from the traumatic century – are pivotal to understanding the PRC's rise in global politics.[76] Preoccupied with their suffering and often possessing the perception of continued subjugation and maltreatment, the PRC seeks to "cleanse," "wipe away," "erase" or even "revenge" the nation of its shame.[77] "Beijing's search for respect and status drive the PRC's foreign policy," Callahan argues.[78] So much is the case that at "the heart of Chinese foreign policy thus is not a security dilemma, but an identity dilemma."[79]

Appreciating the emotional and political legacies of China's historical trauma tells us much. It is at least in part why, for instance, incidents such as the 2001 Spy Plane Crisis and the 1999 Belgrade embassy bombing are so difficult for the PRC and the Chinese. They were seen as so much more than tragic accidents. Both incidents tapped into historical memory of Western (and other foreign) "hegemonic behavior"[80] in China and to China's continued sensitivity toward

[75] Miller, *Wronged By Empire*, p. 135.

[76] Callahan, *China*, pp. 9–11.

[77] The quotes "cleanse," "wipe away" and "revenge" are drawn from Callahan, *China*, p. 199; and Callahan, "National Insecurities," 205–206. On the "erasure" of China's humiliation, see Gries, *China's New Nationalism*, pp. 43–44.

[78] Callahan, *China*, p. x.

[79] Callahan, *China*, p. 192.

[80] Joseph Y. S. Cheng and King-Lun Ngok, "The 2001 'Spy' Plan Incident Revisited: The Chinese Perspective," *The Chinese Journal of Political Science*, 9.1 (2004), 63–83.

foreign dominance; they were viewed as clear "assaults on Chinese dignity."[81] In 1999, for instance, the embassy bombing incited the largest protests since Tiananmen ten years earlier, although this time the fury rallied the nation together in China's defense. Protestors wearing white headbands in grief and outrage held up photographs of the three Chinese killed and placards with slogans such as "Down with US Imperialism," "Stop American Aggression," "The Chinese People Cannot Be Bullied." Retaliatory demands also emerged, as some citizens demanded, "Blood debts must be paid back in blood."[82] Notwithstanding the politicization of Japan's crimes, China's "apology politics" with Japan and now strong anti-Japanese sentiment can also be seen an indicator of the unresolved injury and exploitation incurred at the hands of the Japanese.[83] China's unwillingness to let go of disputed territories, and even their clamp-down on dissent in Tibet can also be viewed through the lens of national humiliation.[84] The 2008 Summer Olympic Games also demonstrate both the "chosen trauma" and "chosen glory" mobilized from understandings of the past. Chinese voices heralded the 2008 Summer Olympic Games in Beijing as a symbolic opportunity for the PRC to "show the world its strengths and greatness."[85] While it did largely just this, dazzling the world with the showcase stadiums and ceremonies, the Games were also shadowed by the preceding torch relay protests, which paradoxically also strengthened the narratives of victimization that the Olympics were thought to originally undo.[86]

But all this is not intended to paint a "negative" political or diplomatic picture. To highlight the political consequences of the emotional dynamics at stake is equally not to condone the events that constitute

[81] Gries, *China's New Nationalism*, p. 136.

[82] Tsu, *Failure, Nationalism and Literature*, p. 2.

[83] Shogo Suzuki, "Can Apology Serve as a Security Policy? Responsible Scholarship and Breaking the Chains of Negative History in Sino-Japanese Relations," *Korean Journal of Defense Analysis*, 20.4 (2008), 319–333.

[84] Miller, *Wronged By Empire*, pp. 30–31, 72–77; see also Callahan, "National Insecurities," 205–206; Yinan He, "History, Chinese Nationalism and the Emerging Sino-Japanese Conflict," *Journal of Contemporary China*, 16 (2007), 1–24.

[85] Orville Schell, "China: Humiliation and the Olympics," *New York Review of Books*, 55.13 (2008), 30–33.

[86] See Kingsley Edney, "The 2008 Beijing Olympic Torch Relay: Chinese and Western Narratives," *Journal of Current Chinese Affairs/China aktuell*, 37.2 (2008), 111–125.

the now "Century of Humiliation." Neither is it to condemn China's continuing response to the historical trauma, as overtly political and politicized as it be. I also surely do not mean to incite or imply a need for caution of the PRC and of its international political behavior.[87] Rather, I draw attention to the enduring legacy of China's "Century of National Humiliation" in order to underscore the political effects of representing trauma in a manner that preserves the sense of collective injury, thus inhibiting the possibility of properly mourning and working through the traumatic emotions associated with a painful past.

Traumatic events and histories can have a profound, sometimes dislocating and destructive communal impact. Trauma leaves complex emotional and psychological legacies, which can be easily passed down through generations, shaping communities and their politics long into the future. Haunted by memories of pain and suffering, traumatized communities paradoxically search to "forget" their trauma while simultaneously becoming emotionally fixated, and constituted, by it.[88] In these circumstances a particular emotional politics – centered on the loss, humiliation, fear, anger and even guilt – often binds the community closer together. Emotions such as fear, anger, rage, anxiety, humiliation, shame, and even guilt can proliferate, helping to constitute community in conjunction with the uncertainty, vulnerability and insecurity that inevitably accompanies experiences of injury and pain. Prolonged, and unresolved "acting out" may result, which ritualizes trauma's commemoration rather than promoting practices that enable community members to more genuinely mourn and work through it. Communities are then unable to heal and move on in a forward-looking manner.

No matter what the political context is – authoritarian or democratic, stable or chaotic – numerous problematic scenarios emerge from such affective politics. The most worrying of these is that a political community constituted by emotions such as fear, anger and humiliation can be dragged into new forms of conflict and trauma. This too is unfortunately often the case, as simplistic narratives that demonize others and pursue redemption and revenge can be sought to

[87] Indeed, given the insights provided by an appreciation of China's perception of past trauma, I stress that greater understanding of China's ensuing inhibitions and anxieties is necessary in order to best approach the PRC and its global rise.
[88] Edkins, "Forget Trauma?"

counteract the sense of injury, loss and injustice.[89] Instead of solving the problems at stake, ensuing political attitudes may instead generate new antagonisms that increase rather than reduce the propensity for further violence.

The potentials for working through a traumatic past: toward the possibility of grieving trauma

Thus far my analysis has pointed to the problematic and potentially destructive consequences of failing to work through trauma. Yet, it is not unusual that communities – from the local to the state – are challenged in their capacity to confront and reconcile traumatic pasts. Some commentators speak of so-called intractable conflicts: situations where trauma and ensuing antagonisms have persisted for so long that they have created a vicious cycle of violence.[90] From the Middle East to Afghanistan, from Sri Lanka to Somalia, from East Timor to Iraq and from Rwanda to Kashmir, years and often decades of conflict have left societies deeply divided and traumatized. And this is not to mention the intensely affective politics of identity, community and security that emerged after the more recent terrorist attacks in the West. In all of these situations in one way or another we witnessed the emergence of new forms of violence, which generates new fears, new anxieties and new hatreds.

But the key purpose here is not to label conflicts as intractable, but to instead identify the emotional dynamics that can make it difficult for the respective societies to move on from discourses of fear, anxiety, hatred, dishonor and humiliation.[91] Without unraveling the impact of the various emotions associated with violence and trauma, the often

[89] Schick, "Acting out and Working Through," 1842–1983; Yoder, *The Little Book of Trauma Healing*, pp. 45–47.

[90] Robert D. Kaplan, *Balkan's Ghosts: A Journey Through History* (London: Picador, 2005).

[91] Some scholars find the very notion of intractable conflict problematic. They instead locate the roots of violence not in ancient hatreds but in much more recent political manipulations. See, for instance, David Campbell, *National Deconstruction: Violence, Identity, and Justice in Bosnia* (Minneapolis: Minnesota University Press, 1998); Norman M. Naimark, *Fires of Hatred: Ethnic Cleansing in Twentieth-Century Europe* (Cambridge, MA: Harvard University Press, 2002).

long-standing issues that underlie conflict (and potentially further trauma) remain concealed and unaddressed.

This is where my present argument comes in. An appreciation of the maladaptive processes that can bind community in the wake of trauma provides us with a critical opportunity. Specifically, the prototypical response I have examined is not the only way for societies to move on after experiences of trauma. I propose and explore an alternative, politically transformative response: the potentials involved with "grieving" societal trauma.[92]

A turn to grief recognizes the intensely emotional and dislocating effects of trauma and underscores the need for communities to grieve injury and loss in order not merely to adapt and reconcile life after, but to do so in a way that acknowledges and challenges the types of perceptions that make further violence more likely. It takes shape through the opportunity to critically engage with, and properly mourn, the reality and legacy of trauma and, in so doing, "work through" unpleasant memories, emotions and understandings. Indeed, a politics of grief recognizes the inherent need for individuals and communities to confront intensely painful emotions and meanings in order to be free of rather than trapped by past trauma. By confronting trauma head-on through natural (and necessary) grieving processes, communities could actively reflect upon rather than internalize and co-opt the ensuing trauma. Less maladaptive, redemptive and more reparative, politically transformative and forward-looking forms of community may consequently ensue.

A "politics of grief" can be understood and situated somewhat in distinction to the typical "politics of trauma."[93] Where predominant

[92] Work that has begun to develop the conception of "grieving" political trauma includes: Judith Butler, *Precarious Life: Powers of Mourning and Violence* (London: Verso, 2003); Antoinette Errante, "Peace Work as Grief Work in Mozambique and South Africa," *Peace and Conflict: Journal of Peace Psychology*, 5.3 (1999), 261–279; Fierke, "Whereof We Can Speak, Thereof We Must Not Be Silent"; Richard F. Mollica, *Healing Invisible Wounds: Paths to Hope and Recovery in a Violent World* (Nashville, TN: Vanderbilt University Press, 2009); Brent E. Sasley, "Violence, Grief, and Memory: How Emotions Help Maintain or Resolve Conflict," paper presented at the Annual Convention of the International Studies Association, March 26–29, 2014; Schick, "Acting Out and Working Through"; Edward Weisband, "On the Aporetic Borderlines of Forgiveness: Bereavement as Political Form," *Alternatives: Global, Local, Political*, 34.4 (2009), 359–381.

[93] K. M. Fierke and Jay Winter both draw a similar distinction between trauma and grief; see Fierke, "Whereof We Can Speak, Thereof We Must Not Be

political responses to collective traumas memorialize trauma in ways that preserve the shock, pain and hyper-vigilance for an affected community, a turn to grief involves a search to undergo a range of combined personal and political processes that assist individuals and communities to come to terms with violence, injury and loss. Fierke's work again clarifies; trauma is distinguished by "an inability to mourn or speak" of what has occurred, whereas grief is an emotional response to loss that enables a sufferer to "redefine her place in everyday life" through finding ways of "integrating the experience into a meaningful social world."[94] Grief work does this by promoting the conscious acceptance, processing and reflection upon not only what has happened or changed, but also the associated intensely difficult emotional and psychological effects. A shift to grief would additionally in this way require active political agency after trauma, which sits in contrast to prevailing political (trauma-focused) dynamics. At the same time, however, I urge that trauma and grief exist on a spectrum of possible responses to violence, catastrophe and loss, and can as such be seen as two sides of the same coin: they both shape emotional and communal attachments, although they do so in profoundly different ways.

In a practical sense, an ethos of communal grieving would be distinguished by a range of bereavement processes that are a natural and crucial part of healing. While these would be culturally and contextually distinct, I consider them through a generalizable frame of mourning, and, as some scholars discuss, the "working through" of trauma.[95]

Mourning is an essential part of bereavement processes that ensue after any significant traumatic loss. An acutely painful time laden with many challenging emotions and affects, the mourning process implies a normal response in which a sufferer/bereaved evaluates their relationship to the trauma – whether it is, for example, a concrete trauma such as death, loss of a limb, one's health; an abstract or "symbolic loss";[96]

Silent," 476; Jay Winter, *Sites of Memory, Sites of Mourning: The Great War in European Cultural History* (Cambridge: Cambridge University Press, 1995), pp. 5, 29.

94 Fierke, "Whereof We Can Speak, Thereof We Must Not Be Silent," 472, 476.

95 Dominick LaCapra, *Writing History, Writing Trauma* (Baltimore: Johns Hopkins University Press, 2001), pp. 148–149; and in international relations, see Schick, "Acting Out and Working Through."

96 Such as challenged or loss of social status, honor or prestige. See Katherine Walsh, *Grief and Loss: Theories and Skills for the Helping Professionals*, 2nd ed. (New Jersey: Pearson, 2012), p. 11.

or even the threat of a potential traumatic loss – and learns to accept it, adapt and cope anew.[97] As a process abetting the individual recovery from trauma, to mourn thus involves a coming to terms with, or a kind of reckoning with, what has happened and has been lost.

Sigmund Freud's "Mourning and Melancholia" was the first work to identify mourning as an essential psychic response to traumatic loss.[98] Freud distinguished mourning as a process of grieving through which a sufferer's psychological relationship to trauma reaches a conclusion. Some scholars conceive of Freud's conception of mourning as "normal grieving,"[99] or, as I put it here, "complete" or "successful" mourning. Put in these terms, to have undergone "successful" mourning is to have intellectually and emotionally accepted what has happened, and to have in turn grieved the injury and loss in way that gradually relinquishes or transforms the former bonds (to the lost, loved object or person).[100] Through mourning, the sufferer/s should be less dependent upon the source of injury and upon what or who has been lost; their identity should, in other words, be less "attached" to it.[101] Judith Butler explains that "[O]ne mourns when one accepts that by the loss one undergoes one will be changed, possibly forever ... mourning has to do with agreeing to undergo a transformation."[102] New attachments and meanings should be made possible. For these reasons, mourning

[97] Herman, *Trauma and Recovery*, pp. 175–195; Nini Leik and Marianne Davidsen-Nielsen, *Healing Pain: Attachment, Loss and Grief Therapy* (London and New York: Routledge, 1991), pp. 25–30, 37–38; Linda Machin, *Working with Loss and Grief* (London, Sage, 2009), p. 49; Worden, *Grief Counseling and Grief Therapy*, pp. 39–53.

[98] Sigmund Freud, "Mourning and Melancholia," in *On Metapsychology: The Theory of Psychoanalysis*, trans. James Strachey, compiled and edited by Angela Richards (Harmondsworth: Penguin, 1991), pp. 247–268.

[99] Pauline Boss, *Ambiguous Loss: Learning to Live with Unresolved Grief* (Cambridge, MA: Harvard University Press, 1999), p. 9; Worden, *Grief Counseling and Grief Therapy*, p. 17; Vamik D. Volkan, *Animal Killer: Transmission of War Trauma from One Generation to the Next* (London: Karnac, 2013), p. 64; Volkan and Zintl, *Life After Loss*, pp. 13–14.

[100] Machin, *Working with Loss and Grief*, p. 49; Mollica, *Healing Invisible Wounds*, chapter on "The Trauma Story," pp. 34–61; Worden, *Grief Counseling and Grief Therapy*, pp. 46–49.

[101] Francis MacNab, *Life After Loss: Getting Over Grief and Getting on With Life* (Newtown: Millennium Books, 1989), pp. 44–45; Simon Shimshon Rubin, "Mourning Distinct From Melancholia: The Resolution of Bereavement," *British Journal of Medical Psychology*, 57 (1984), 339–345; Volkan, *Bloodlines*, p. 37.

[102] Butler, *Precarious Life*, p. 21.

is conceived of as a critical part of "the cognitive process of coming to terms with a loss through confronting the loss" and to moving on after, even while recognizing that the ensuing loss with always remain.[103] The terms "normal," "successful" or "complete"[104] merely denote the fact that mourning has taken a natural and healthy course: the bereaved has been able to resolve the loss and move on.

Particularly important to the tasks of mourning is the recognition, expression and eventual transformation of various emotions that can inhibit or impair normal life after. Successful mourning is pivotal in counteracting many of the unpleasant and potentially "destructive"[105] emotions that have been normalized by extreme experiences. As I have underscored throughout my inquiry, traumatic events and histories are so overwhelming in part because they are so intensely and intimately emotional; the deep suffering and rupturing of reality inflicted by trauma stands outside everyday experiences and outside an individual's ability to make cognitive and emotional sense of it. Simultaneously, we crave emotional understanding when so disorientated by trauma. While a strange emotional "numbness" may immediately ensue, shock

[103] Paul C. Rosenblatt, "Grief that Does Not End," in Dennis Klass, Phyllis R. Silverman and Steven L. Nickman (eds.), *Continuing Bonds: New Understandings of Grief* (London and Philadelphia: Taylor and Francis, 1996), pp. 45–58, at p. 52.

[104] By " complete," I do not, however, mean to imply that that mourning is a finite process distinguished by a beginning and an end. Mourning is a long-term, ongoing process, in which the bereaved is constantly rethinking and redefining their attachment to what has happened and to what has been lost. Some scholars in fact dispute the idea that the loss has to be fully relinquished through mourning, maintaining instead that "continuing bonds" with the way things were are often a necessary and normal part of how some trauma sufferers get on after. See Dennis Klass, Phyllis R. Silverman and Steven L. Nickman (eds.), *Continuing Bonds: New Understandings of Grief* (London and Philadelphia: Taylor and Francis, 1996); Mario Mikculincer and Philip R. Shaver, "An Attachment Perspective of Bereavement," in Margaret S. Stroebe, Robert O. Hansson, Henk Schut and Wolfgang Stroebe (eds.), *Handbook of Bereavement Research and Practice: Advances in Theory and Intervention*, pp. 3–25 (Washington, DC: American Psychological Association, 2008).

[105] Some scholars refer to these as "negative" emotions, citing emotions such as shame, humiliation, anger and rage. I consciously chose not to do so, both as after trauma these emotions are completely normal, and because (as I stress in this chapter) it is critical that they are acknowledged, spoken of and understood. Pejoratively labeling them "negative" implicitly implies a certain wrongdoing for feeling them, which I believe works against this.

and denial quickly produce feelings of anxiety and fear. Then, with the gradual realization of what has happened (and on the political level), a community may feel collectively angered, humiliated, shamed, embarrassed, despairing and even guilty from their losses.[106] For a therapeutically orientated approach, the full spectrum of emotions is normal, yet such an approach also stresses that it is critical that all painful emotions and memories are recognized and worked through. Grief literatures even go as far as to suggest that "mastering"[107] one's emotions after trauma is central to recovery.

Learning to recover and "sit with" traumatic memories and express associated feelings is in this respect vital, and key to successful mourning.[108] Psychologist Robert Weiss suggests that the practices of bereavement are in this way emotionally "ameliorative."[109] Significant here are a range of concrete (and, as I show, representational) tasks, potentially including giving testimony or truth-telling, bearing witness and listening (and doing so often over and over again), which enable sufferers as well as whole communities to accept and in one sense "make real" what has happened, reconnect with the social world and create new forward-looking meanings from their pain. In other words, allowing people to speak of their experiences, thoughts and emotions can be therapeutic. Richard Mollica explains that speaking out about traumatic experiences in such a manner is an important part of mourning: telling one's "trauma story" begins the process of transforming destructive emotions that have been conditioned through excessive violence.[110] Judith Lewis Herman also insists on the need to gradually open up – both verbally and emotionally – to prevent painful memories and feelings from plunging traumatized individuals

[106] Yoder, *The Little Book of Trauma Healing*, p. 35.

[107] Volkan and Zintl, *Life After Loss*, p. 59; Worden, *Grief Counseling and Grief Therapy*, p. 42.

[108] Herman, *Trauma and Recovery*, pp. 188–189; Martha Minow, "The Hope for Healing: What Can Truth Commissions Do?" in Robert I. Rotberg and Dennis Thompson (eds.), *Truth V. Justice: The Morality of Truth Commissions* (Princeton: Princeton University Press, 2010), pp. 241–242.

[109] Robert S. Weiss, "The Nature and Causes of Grief," in M. S. Stroebe, R. O. Hansson, H. Schut and W. Stroebe (eds.), *Handbook of Bereavement Research and Practice* (Washington D.C.: American Psychological Association, 2008), pp. 29–44.

[110] Mollica, *Healing Invisible Wounds*, p. 234. See also James W. Pennebaker, *Opening Up: The Healing Power of Expressing Emotions* (New York: Guilford, 1990).

and communities into a state of hyperarousal, from which retributive, revenge-orientated thoughts and practices often ensue.[111]

It is in this manner that grief and recovery literatures frequently employ the notion of "working through": while the stages abetting recovery and reconstruction are widely debated and contested, working through is in this sense seen to encompass grieving practices that enable a sufferer to process and come to terms with both "the literal physical pain that many people experience *and* the emotional and behavioral pain associated with loss" – to, quite literally, consciously "work through" what has occurred.[112] Situated at the other end of the spectrum to "acting out," working through is part of the mourning process through which traumatized individuals confront a changed reality and transform their attachment to trauma "into a memory that no longer eclipses all other thoughts."[113]

So valuable is the concept of working through that a range of scholars have adapted and extended it to conceiving of recovery after large-scale, communal traumas. For these studies, the basic principles of what it means to "work through" trauma remain the same: to work through is still to undergo natural grieving processes that enable the expression and acceptance of loss. But it is also more than this: for politics studies in particular, "working through" includes the further capacity to critically reflect upon what has happened and upon the conditions that enabled the particular events in the first place. As Dominick LaCapra explains, working through should involve "a discourse of mourning that involves critique – critique is another form of working through."[114] Implicit here, for LaCapra, is that working through plainly "requires going back to problems, working them over, and perhaps transforming the understanding of them."[115] Kate Schick similarly employs the notion of working through, suggesting it should result in the cultivation of "critical judgment."[116] Critical judgment is a vital aspect of communal grieving in so far that it incorporates an element of "soul-searching" and, ultimately, "[r]eflection and insight into those practices that facilitate violence."[117] Like LaCapra, the objective

[111] Herman, *Trauma and Recovery*, pp. 176–181, 189.
[112] Worden, *Grief Counseling and Grief Therapy*, pp. 43–44. Emphasis Added.
[113] Volkan, *Bloodlines*, p. 37.
[114] LaCapra, *Writing History, Writing Trauma*, p. 178.
[115] LaCapra, *Writing History, Writing Trauma*, p. 148.
[116] Schick, "Acting Out and Working Through," 1848.
[117] Schick, "Acting Out and Working Through," 1852.

for Schick is to obtain an "enhanced understanding" of the circumstances through which conflict occurs and in turn "be able to challenge the damaging knee-jerk reactions" after trauma that preserve patterns of violence.[118]

Conceptualized in *both* a therapeutic and more explicitly political sense, "working through" can therefore be seen as an ideal type of personal yet also political, and communal response to trauma – particularly in the case of widespread societal trauma that has been inflicted at the hands of another, when "rushed" reactions that seek to restore political order by "forgetting" trauma often take over.[119] It encompasses the crucial grieving practices trauma sufferers require in order to reconnect with the social world and heal, whilst also pressing for the type of reflection and open-endedness that political theorists suggest are key to deconstructing cycles of violence in the intensely emotional aftermath of collective pain.[120] Working through is thus very much an active political process, focused not at passively "moving on" individuals and communities after trauma but at bringing suffering and its memory into focus in a way that prompts a questioning of the very mindsets and structures (of power, exclusion and injustice, inside/outside, and so on) that may have facilitated violence in the first place.[121] Of course, the assumption implicit in this political conception is that such questioning will prompt not merely consideration of existing social and communal configurations but also a revision of those that may prove problematic.

To grieve and more fully "work though" communal trauma would thus be highly desirable. Communities that work through trauma

118 Schick, "Acting Out and Working Through," 1852.

119 Jenny Edkins, "The Rush to Memory and the Rhetoric of War," *Journal of Political and Military Sociology*, 31.2 (2003), 231–251; Edkins, "Forget Trauma?" Judith Butler also cites the response of President Bush after the terrorist attacks of September 11, 2001 to be one that feared the possibility of grief. Butler writes of how as early as September 21, 2001 – a mere ten days after – the US president claimed that the nation had "finished grieving" and that they had reached "the time for resolute action to take the place of grief." "When grief is feared," continues Butler, "our fears can give rise to resolve it [trauma and loss] quickly, to banish it in the name of an action invested with the power to restore the loss or return the world to a former order, or to reinvigorate a fantasy that the world formerly was orderly." See her *Precarious Life*, pp. 29–30.

120 Butler, *Precarious Life*, pp. 19–49; Jenny Edkins, *Trauma and the Memory of Politics* (Cambridge: Cambridge University Press, 2004).

121 See also Schick, "Acting Out and Working Through," pp. 1852–1853, 1854.

(present or historical) in such a reflective manner would resist the impulse to memorialize trauma in ways that "gloss over"[122] and preserve the pain and associated emotions, and might consequently be constituted more through the process of grieving (and in turn healing, emotional and otherwise) than through a persistent image of the traumatic encounter itself. Judith Butler argues that grief can in this way be "a resource for politics": it can shift communities away from a passive and powerless turn to fear and retaliation, toward an active engagement with suffering and the enduring emotions that inhibit peaceful resolution of conflict.[123] Grief can be, in short, an "opportunity for growth."[124] Butler even goes further to suggest that grieving may illuminate mutual humanly vulnerability. By facilitating "a point of identification with suffering," a principle of responsibility "by which we vow to protect others from the kinds of violence we have suffered" might emerge.[125]

But while insightful conceptual work has been undertaken to theorize grief, less has been said on how a politics of grief plays out in practice. Few studies, if any, have articulated how individuals together with their community are to push beyond the seemingly overwhelming "emotionally numbing" aspects of trauma in order to reach the self- and communally conscious reflection required to properly mourn and work through trauma.[126] Political examinations of grief and, specifically, of how communities are to realize these transformative emotional and communal dynamics can thus be taken some steps further. How might we promote or cultivate a politics (and ethics) of grief and "working

[122] Schick, "Acting Out and Working Through," 1854.
[123] Butler, *Precarious Life*, p. 30.
[124] Leik and Davidsen-Nielsen, *Healing Pain*, p. 21.
[125] Butler, *Precarious Life*, p. 30.
[126] In this sense, "working through" must foremost entail the conscious recognition that even though trauma sufferers often try to emotionally distance themselves from their traumatic past, relinquishing it to the dark confines of memory, they need to confront it in order to prevent destructive narratives or closures from taking shape. Saul Friedlander articulates this paradox insightfully in "Trauma, Transference and 'Working Through' in Writing the History of the 'Shoah,'" *History and Memory*, 4.1 (1992), 39–59, at 51–53. Some politics and international relations studies have similarly acknowledged this paradox and the need to conceptualize ways around it. See, for instance, Butler, *Precarious Life*, 19–49; Edkins, *Trauma and the Memory of Politics*; Fierke, "Whereof We Can Speak, Thereof We Must Not Be Silent."

through" within and between traumatized communities in world politics? What specifically would it entail? Can practices of representing trauma – that is, how we collectively narrate and conceive of past injury and loss, despite a perceived inexpressibility – help to promote more genuine attempts to grieve pain and work through the affectively charged, often antagonistic mindsets that can prevail after trauma?

The next section begins to address these questions. It does so by turning to one case in which a community divided by prolonged animosity, conflict and trauma sought to put an end to violence, heal and rebuild: South Africa.

South Africa and the struggle over apartheid: the TRC as an attempt to grieve and heal societal trauma

Postapartheid South Africa is one of the most prominent cases of an attempt to work through – and to both individually and collectively mourn – societal trauma. Literally meaning "apartness" or separateness in Afrikaans, apartheid was an enforced segregation policy that separated South African people by race. It was introduced by the Afrikaner-dominated National Party government in 1948 and remained official practice until the first democratic elections on April 27, 1994.[127] Apartheid affected every aspect of life: where people were to live, go to school, work, whom they could marry and where they were buried when they died. It was a time of extraordinary oppression and was fraught with increasing civil tension, conflict, violence and injustice. The government forcibly repressed those who resisted or spoke out against the policy. Anti-separatists still fought back violently. In the 1980s, South Africa eventually disintegrated into a form of civil war, with both parties to the conflict sharing responsibility for suffering.

The apartheid era has in this way been seen as an outstanding trauma that characterized the lives of all South Africans.[128] The people of South Africa – black and white – possessed in some cases decades of

[127] Apartheid was abandoned in a series of negotiations in the early 1990s; however, it was not formally renounced until the first democratic election, in 1994. See Nancy L. Clark and William H. Worger, *South Africa: The Rise and Fall of Apartheid*, 2nd ed. (Harlow: Pearson, 2011), pp. 3–6.

[128] For research that focuses on the apartheid era specifically as a societal trauma, see Christopher J. Colvin, "'Brothers and Sisters, Do Not Be Afraid of Me': Trauma, History and the Therapeutic Imagination in the New South Africa," in Katharine

unacknowledged violent encounters, to themselves and to their loved ones. Moreover, the decades of structural and physical violence had profound emotional and psychological impact on the wider population, creating deep societal divisions and animosities that South Africa's 1993 Interim Constitution explicitly characterized as "a legacy of hatred, fear, guilt and revenge."[129] The task of uniting South Africa after therefore required more than the repudiation of the apartheid policy: individuals and the community as a whole required catharsis.

And, yet, the immediate postapartheid reconciliation process has come to be distinguished precisely because it took the need to remember, acknowledge and mourn past trauma seriously. From the very beginning of the reconciliation process this objective took shape through the invocation of a range of informal and also formalized discourses that prioritized national unity through both individual and collective healing. It has even been said that discourses of healing became the "hallmark"[130] of the reconstruction process: they provided a frame through which the divided community could connect around meanings that shifted away from conflict and toward those that recognized, and prompted the community to begin to collectively recover from, the outstanding trauma. South African reconciliation has in this way been characterized as a political conflict that was, in a sense, therapeutically managed; reconstructing the postapartheid state became a moment through which individuals scarred by trauma could come together by giving voice, bearing witness to, and making new – collective and forward-looking – meanings out of each other's pain. The "the culture of silence" surrounding injustice was broken.[131]

Hodgkin and Susannah Radstone (eds.), *Contested Pasts: The Politics of Memory* (London and New York: Routledge, 2003), pp. 153–167; Merle Friedman, "The Truth and Reconciliation Commission in South Africa as an Attempt to Heal a Traumatized Society," in A. Y. Shalev, Rachel Yehuda and Alexander C. McFarlane (eds.), *International Handbook of Human Response to Trauma* (New York: Kluwer, 2000), pp. 399–411.

129 "National Unity and Reconciliation," Constitution of the Republic of South Africa Act 200 of 1993, p. 147. At https://peaceaccords.nd.edu/site_media/media/accords/Constitution_of_South_Africa_Act_200_of_1993.pdf. Accessed July 30, 2014.

130 Claire Moon, "Healing Past Violence: Traumatic Assumptions and Therapeutic Interventions in War and Reconciliation," *Journal of Human Rights*, 8.1 (2009), 71–91, at 79.

131 Terry Dowdall, "Psychological Aspects of the Truth and Reconciliation Commission," in H. Russel Botman and Robin M. Petersen (eds.), *To*

Victims could finally be heard. For only through giving voice to and acknowledging suffering and the wrongs committed could individuals and the community properly grieve the past, emotionally repair, and try to heal.

The task of unifying South Africans and reconciling their traumatic past was specifically assigned to the TRC. The TRC was established in 1995 through negotiations aimed at averting further violence and healing wounds.[132] Its method has drawn worldwide attention for how it dealt with atrocities committed and has been largely applauded, although numerous debates have since been waged about how successful it really was.[133] In what follows, I engage a range of literature on South African reconciliation and specifically the TRC. However, I do so against the backdrop of my turn to a politics of grief: I focus on how the TRC sought to facilitate collective healing through encouraging the society to come to terms with what had happened under apartheid and work through the trauma. Specifically, I examine how the TRC's workings are reflective of, and help to underline, some of the emotional, social and political processes that traumatized communities must undergo in order to grieve and work through trauma in a transformative fashion. Doing so enables me to articulate more closely what a turn to grief after trauma may entail, and, crucially, how traumatized societies searching to form more ameliorative, reflective and ultimately regenerative attachments and political outlooks may be able to arrive there.

While the TRC can be seen to have fulfilled various specific therapeutic functions, there is one aspect that underpins its contribution to the type of societal grieving I advocate: the TRC South Africa sought to foster the conditions through which the articulation of past trauma

Remember and Heal: Theological and Psychological Reflections on Truth and Reconciliation (Cape Town: Human and Rousseau, 1996), p. 34.

132 For a thorough account of the background and work of the TRC, see Alex Boraine, *A Country Unmasked: Inside South Africa's Truth and Reconciliation Commission* (Oxford: Oxford University Press, 2001).

133 Critical discussions of the truth and reconciliation process include: James L. Gibson and Amanda Gouws, "Truth and Reconciliation in South Africa: Attributions of Blame and the Struggle over Apartheid," *American Political Science Review*, 93.3 (1999), 501–517; Aletta J. Norval, "Memory, Identity and the (Im)possibility of Reconciliation: The Work of the Truth and Reconciliation Commission in South Africa," *Constellations*, 5.2 (1998), 250–265.

could contribute to the transformation of relations between citizens in order to inclusively rebuild South African community. To achieve this, the TRC set out to provide an official forum through which the wounds left by apartheid could be represented, formally acknowledged, and, in the societal realm at least, laid to rest. The three committees through which it operated – the Committee on Human Rights Violations, the Amnesty Committee, and the Reparation and Rehabilitation Committee – were key: they offered a public space through which, on one hand, victims could formally give voice to their abuse and suffering, and, on the other hand, perpetrators could repent, ask forgiveness and, on the condition of full disclosure of the actions they committed, apply for amnesty. While this formal expression and recognition of suffering and injustice was of important therapeutic value to victims, it also performed an imperative social role: it brought South Africa's painful past out into the open, for acknowledgment and understanding. In other words, the TRC became, as Stanley Cohen would put it, the key site for "the symbolic recognition of what is already known but was officially denied."[134] It provided a communal context through which private or widely assumed but invalidated knowledge about all the horrific things that happened under apartheid was made public. Painful memories and emotions that had for long kept the society divided could be begun to be worked through. Victims, perpetrators and the wider community as bystanders could try to come to terms with their roles in the past and together search for closure.

Three more specific processes help us to appreciate how the TRC's approach contributed to the regeneration of South African community. While distinct they are also interrelated – together, they prompted South Africa to face up to the past in order to begin to properly grieve the trauma and, in turn, collectively rethink and rebuild the future.

The first involves a consideration of the therapeutic significance of survivor testimony within the context of the TRC and the role it played in nation building. When conceptualizing the TRC, the National Unity and Reconciliation Act of 1995 recognized that to pursue a form of prosecutorial justice would be problematic. In a society ravaged by such profuse and systemic violence, fear and hatred, it was perceived

[134] Stanley Cohen, *States of Denial: Knowing About Atrocities and Suffering* (Cambridge: Polity Press, 2001), p. 13.

that the full prosecution of crimes would only continue to divide the nation and make it impossible to move forward. What was needed was a way of accounting for human rights violations that unified and healed the traumatized society. To this end, the TRC focused on starting a process of dialogue between former enemies. Formally mediated and recorded by the TRC, the dialogue was to be founded on processes frequently perceived as key to recovery after trauma, including survivor testimony or "truth telling," listening and the official acknowledgment of past suffering and injustice.

The TRC's testimony or "truth telling" method was therefore central to appreciating how South Africa attempted to grieve and heal. TRC Chair Archbishop Desmond Tutu's opening address at an HRV Committee submission in May 1996 reflects the emphasis the committee placed on societal healing by way of telling "truths" about one's suffering and/or the wrongs one has committed. Introducing the aims of the TRC, he famously proclaimed,

> We are charged to unearth the truth about our dark past, to lay the ghosts of that past so that they will not return to haunt us and that will thereby contribute to the healing of the traumatised and wounded people for all of us in South Africa are wounded people. And in this manner to promote national unity and reconciliation.[135]

In this statement we can see the extent to which the TRC emphasized the significance of individuals' physical and emotional pain, and of how the unearthing of that pain was considered vital in order for victims, as well as the entire nation, to come to terms with the past and heal. Former President Nelson Mandela also described the work of the TRC in a such manner. He explained that "Only by knowing the truth can we hope to heal the terrible wounds of the past that are the legacy of apartheid. Only the truth can put the past to rest."[136] Later the TRC further reported on the perceived need to "open" such wounds so that

[135] Truth and Reconciliation Commission South Africa, *Human Rights Violations Hearings* (East London, May 15, 1996). At www.justice.gov.za/trc/hrvtrans%5Chrvel1/mohape.htm. Accessed July 23, 2014.

[136] Nelson Mandela cited in Pumla Gobodo-Madikizela, "Transforming Trauma in the Aftermath of Gross Human Rights Abuses," in Arie Nadler, Thomas E. Malloy and Jeffrey D. Fisher (eds.), *The Social Psychology of Intergroup Reconciliation* (Oxford: Oxford University Press, 2008), pp. 57–75, at p. 60.

they "must not be allowed to fester."[137] The underlying premise of the commission here is borrowed from trauma studies, which professes the "restorative power of truth-telling" in the face of extreme, inexplicable events, that to "[k]now the truth will set you free; expose the terrible secrets of a society and heal that society."[138] Truth-telling was such a medium through which "the pain of past might be transformed and purged;" it was "the key therapy" by which South Africa simultaneously addressed both individual and collective national trauma.[139]

The TRC can, I thus suggest, be seen as operating as a type of cathartic space or medium by which individuals and society more generally could acknowledge and begin to mourn trauma. Formally testifying to past suffering enabled victims together with perpetrators and the wider community to fully apprehend and come to terms with wrongs that were committed. While the broad focus on "unearthing" and "healing" wounds was crucial, other more specific recovery processes were also at play. Specifically, the testimonial approach facilitated a range of bereavement practices that help victims to rekindle a form of normality after trauma, including as telling (and retelling), safely reexperiencing the events in an attempt to better comprehend them, being listened to and having one's experiences (and their impact) formally acknowledged. Many studies have affirmed the therapeutic significance of the TRC's method. The approach the TRC took allowed those who had suffered to tell their stories in a structured, affirming, sensitive and respectful environment. Many who testified are said to have found the process to be a positive and cathartic experience.[140] Testifiers told of how, when speaking before the TRC, they felt the committee was a group of people who, for the first time, seemed to believe and understand the pain they had endured for so long, and that in this recognition they at last felt dignified.[141] Having past experiences recognized

137 Truth and Reconciliation Commission South Africa, *Report Volumes 1–5* (Cape Town: Truth and Reconciliation Commission, 1998), p. 1 (1) 27.

138 Martha Minow, *Between Vengeance and Forgiveness: Facing History after Genocide and Mass Violence* (Boston: Beacon Press, 1998), p.66.

139 Moon, "Healing Past Violence," 79.

140 W. Orr, "PTSD and the Truth and Reconciliation Commission," *Continuing Medical Education Journal*, 16 (1998), 142.

141 See Dumia B. Ntsebeza, "The Uses of Truth Commissions: Lessons for the World," in Rotberg and Thompson (eds.), *Truth V. Justice*, pp. 158–168, at p. 160.

and validated through the TRC made survivors feel respected again as human beings.

The second specific contribution involves what is termed the process of "rehumanization": bearing witness to each other's (previously incompatible) stories through testimony started the process of rehumanizing individuals and groups that had been demonized.

Peace and conflict literatures have shown that in situations of heighted social tension, negative typecasting overwhelms intergroup relations. Groups view each other pejoratively and attach negative traits to each other, inspiring perceptions of irresolvable difference and "otherness." Political psychologists such as Daniel Bar-Tal, Neta Oren and Ervin Staub argue that negative stereotyping functions to "delegitimize" or "devalue" each group in the eyes of the other.[142] Groups view each other as depersonalized and homogeneous actors, which objectifies and leads to the attribution of meanings and motives that may be at least in part imaginative constructs produced by each other's fears.[143] In such adversarial social relations, emotional discourses and patterns that intensify antagonisms become normal. Groups quickly become "enemies." Moral obligations too become a matter of "us" versus "them," which means boundaries are drawn around whose suffering matters. Violence becomes legitimated; and the others' pain erased. Elaine Scarry famously showed that when victims are dehumanized their pain becomes "invisible, inaudible."[144] Perpetrators may either choose not to see, or simply be blind to, the other's suffering. A "competitive victimhood" spiral may prevail, in which opposing groups both represent and perceive of their own past as having involved greater injustice.[145] A basis for maintaining conflict ensues.

Reconciling social relations in the wake of mass violence is thus in part a question of how to "reverse" these dehumanizing dynamics such that groups divided by years of conflict can perceive of each

[142] Neta Oren and Daniel Bar-Tal, "The Detrimental Dynamics of Delegitimization in Intractable Conflicts: The Israeli–Palestinian Case," *International Journal of Intercultural Relations*, 31.1 (2007), 111–126; Ervin Staub, *Overcoming Evil: Genocide, Violent Conflict and Terrorism* (Oxford: Oxford University Press, 2011), pp. 327–330.

[143] See also K. M. Fierke, "Emotion and Intentionality," *International Theory*, 6.3 (2014), 563–567.

[144] Elaine Scarry, *The Body in Pain: The Making and Unmaking of the World* (Oxford: Oxford University Press, 1985), p. 44.

[145] Noor et al., "When Suffering Begets Suffering."

other anew, possibly even from the unique perspective of the other.[146] Both victims and perpetrators need be returned of the humanity that has been taken from them; they need to be "rehumanized" in order to deconstruct the depersonalized stereotypes that intensify antagonisms and confound the ability to empathize and see things from the other's perspective.

The TRC's focus on victims *and* perpetrators was in this respect important. As a context for both groups to tell their stories, the TRC sought to facilitate mutual understanding. Crucially, the TRC did so through cultivating empathic connections between victim and perpetrator. Victims' testimony of the pain and traumatic legacies wrought by violence, together with the direct witnessing and accounting for that violence by perpetrators, prompted recognition of the very real human impact that had previously been denied. Likewise, perpetrators' accountability and apologies for past actions in many cases made way for forgiveness. Writing of the importance of empathy in processes of reconciliation, Jodi Halpern and Harvey Weinstein contend that such encounters facilitated through the TRC promoted in some cases "emotional resonance" between victim and perpetrator: through hearing each other's stories the TRC encouraged victim and perpetrator to recognize and empathize with the distinct (and personalized) experiences and perspectives of the other.[147] Pumla Gobodo-Madikizela further describes how it was this empathic character of the TRC encounters that made them rehumanizing. Through the asking and offering of empathy, perpetrators felt with and alongside victims; they were "touched" to identify and respond, and often so with remorse.[148] It was then through this emotional exchange that humanity was returned to both parties. Recognition of individual suffering validated the victim's pain and in doing so restored them of dignity – and their humanity. As a response to victims' pain, remorse likewise reconnected perpetrators with their own humanness – the humanly ability to feel at the sight of the body in pain. But these dynamics are by no means intended to excuse or exonerate perpetrators of their crimes. Nor does it imply, as Martha Minow

[146] Jodi Halpern and Harvey M. Weistein, "Rehumanizing the Other: Empathy and Reconciliation," *Human Rights Quarterly*, 26 (2004), 561–583, at 567.

[147] Halpern and Weinstein, "Rehumanizing the Other," 574.

[148] Pumla Gobodo-Madikizela, "Remorse, Forgiveness, and Rehumanization: Stories from South Africa," *Journal of Humanistic Psychology*, 42.1 (2002), 7–32, at 22–23.

cautions, "turning the other cheek or forgetting what happened."[149] What it does do, however, is foster the compassion, humility and even sense of affinity – the "humane connections" – that are necessary to deconstruct the stereotypical mindsets that lead to further violence and inhibit healing in deeply divided post-trauma societies.[150]

Third and finally is an appreciation of how the TRC orientated the reconstruction process away from a disabling (and communally dividing) vision of the traumatic past and toward the future. This is to say that the TRC negotiated the trauma in a manner that made new (shared) forward-looking and communally regenerative meanings out of past pain.

Significant here is that the TRC's search for reconciliation was underpinned by restorative rather than retributive visions of justice. Indeed, evident from the very beginning was the TRC's emphasis on reparation rather than retaliation, and on forgiveness, not vengeance. A well-known passage from the 1993 Interim Constitution symbolizes this objective at the outset. It recognized that to put an end to violent conflict and unite all South African citizens, "there is a need for understanding but not for vengeance, a need for reparation but not for retaliation, a need for ubuntu but not for victimisation."[151] To be clear, "ubuntu" here refers to an African tradition of "restoring evildoers to the community rather than punishing them."[152] Desmond Tutu's explanation of ubuntu is particularly revealing:

> Ubuntu says I am human only because you are human. If I undermine your humanity I dehumanize myself. You must do what you can to maintain this great harmony, which is perpetually undermined by resentment, anger, desire for vengeance. That's why African jurisprudence is restorative rather than retributive.[153]

[149] Minow, *Between Vengeance and Forgiveness*, p. 146.

[150] Gobodo-Madikizela, "Remorse, Forgiveness, and Rehumanization," 13–14.

[151] "National Unity and Reconciliation," Constitution of the Republic of South Africa Act 200 of 1993, p. 147. At https://peaceaccords.nd.edu/site_media/media/accords/Constitution_of_South_Africa_Act_200_of_1993.pdf. Accessed July 30, 2014.

[152] Lyn S. Graybill, "South Africa's Truth and Reconciliation Commission: Ethical and Theological Perspectives," *Ethics and International Affairs*, 12 (1998), 43–62, at 47.

[153] Desmond Tutu cited in Graybill, "South Africa's Truth and Reconciliation Commission," 47.

Thus rather than interpreting past violence in a manner that creates further inflammatory emotional discourses, the TRC provided a restorative frame that forced the nation to "sit with" and reflect upon what had happened. The TRC was, as such, able to "calm" the situation and bring past trauma into focus through the shared/collective objective of individual and social repair.

The work of the TRC – specifically, truth recovery and acknowledgment – was therefore not just about unearthing the troubling past, but moreover about doing so in order to be able to look collectively to the future, and to do so in a way that united and rebuilt South African society. Some scholars have examined this attribution of new, shared meanings to the South African nation. Some contend that much of the relative success in reconstructing the community had to do with the manner in which individual suffering and national suffering were conflated so as to harmonize the society around shared pain and to in turn restore unity.[154] These scholars show and argue that individual and national suffering were conjointly articulated with reference to a range of psychotherapeutic metaphors and practices, including "the wounds of the past," the "traumatized," "wounded people" of South Africa.[155] Hence, not only was individual suffering projected onto a collective, national frame, but also the nation was "conceived of as a physical body" – and, at that, "[a] sick one."[156] "Healing the nation" thus became "the popular idiom for building the nation."[157]

Scrutinizing victim testimony to the TRC, discourse-focused research also argues that if the expression of apartheid trauma did serve a transformative purpose it did so because it was in part a guided process. When testifying, victims were directed to reflect upon the past with a view to a reconciled future. Annelies Verdoolaege examines, for instance, how the testimony process was a "strictly regulated and controlled discourse," focused on creating "new realities, new truths" from which the "new South Africa" could take shape. Committee

[154] Claire Moon, *Narrating Political Reconciliation: South Africa's Truth Commission* (Plymouth: Lexington, 2008), pp. 115–138; Moon, "Healing Past Violence," 78–79; Richard A. Wilson, *The Politics of Truth and Reconciliation in South Africa: Legitimizing the Post-Apartheid State* (Cambridge: Cambridge University Press, 2001), pp. 14–15.

[155] See especially Moon, "Healing Past Violence," 78–80.

[156] Wilson, *The Politics of Truth and Reconciliation in South Africa*, p. 14.

[157] Wilson, *The Politics of Truth and Reconciliation in South Africa*, pp. 14–15.

members frequently framed questions to testifiers in terms of how their testimony was important for resolving conflict, and specifically what needed to be done to achieve "peace." If the perpetrators come and tell the full truth and express remorse, would forgiveness be granted? And, was that enough for "reconciliation"?[158] In such a line of questioning and truth-telling, the aim of national unity and healing through reparation and understanding is clear. Whereas this kind of negotiating of testimony was not intended to alter the precise telling of abuses endured, it does force the individual victims/testifiers to contemplate their own suffering through the lens of collective, political healing and reconciliation rather than through frames that search for closure through retribution.

To underline the healing and communally rebuilding dynamics at stake is not, however, to unconditionally applaud the work of the TRC. A number of scholars critique the TRC's approach. One of the most prominent concerns involves the claim that the TRC prioritized the social realm over the individual; that the TRC's emphasis on social harmony came at the cost of truly recognizing the enduring and very personal psychological effects of individual trauma. Richard Wilson, for example, targets the therapeutic, medicalized model implicit in the TRC's conceptualization of national healing (and reconciliation). He suggests that it insufficiently addresses the real pain suffered by victims of human rights abuses. "Individual psychological processes cannot be reduced to national process," he argues.[159] Other scholars have similarly questioned the intersection between individual and communal recovery in the context of the TRC. Some are skeptical of the long-term consequences of the one-off retelling of trauma that was facilitated.[160] Drawing from literature on processes required for successful trauma recovery, these scholars question whether a one-time testimony can effectively address the individual traumas endured and the ongoing process of reckoning that trauma requires. Consequently,

[158] See Annelies Verdoolaege, "Dealing with a Traumatic Past: The Victim Hearings in the South African Truth and Reconciliation Commission and their Reconciliation Discourse," *Critical Discourse Studies*, 6.4 (2009), 297–309, 300.

[159] Wilson, *The Politics of Truth and Reconciliation in South Africa*, p. 15.

[160] Colvin, "Brothers and Sisters, Do Not Be Afraid of Me," 164; Phulma Gqola, "Defining People: Analysing Power, Language and Representation in Metaphors of the New South Africa," *Transformation*, 47 (2001), 94–106.

like Wilson they fear that the testimony and amnesty process created "an opportunity to rewrite the past and install a new national myth" at the expense of personal recovery.[161] Admittedly, too, not all has been smooth since the "new" South Africa was rebuilt in the 1990s. Significant structural inequities remain, causing ongoing inopportunity, racial discrimination and injustice. And although from the outset this was not explicitly something the TRC was mandated to address, some suggest that perhaps it should have been considered along with the immediate rebuilding process that was facilitated.

Acknowledging the limitations and challenges faced by the TRC, and also after, for a lasting conception of South Africa reconciliation is important. Certainly these need to be tackled if South Africa is to overcome structural inequalities and prosper into the truly inclusive society that was envisaged after apartheid. However, to focus solely on the continuing problems with this one case is to neglect crucial broader insights. As I show next, the grieving and recovery processes employed in postapartheid South Africa can help us to appreciate the types of social and political mindsets and measures that can be enacted after trauma to help wounded communities recognize and work through the painful traumatic realities, memories and emotions.

Emotions and a global politics of grief

At first glance, South Africa may appear to be a unique case rather than one containing wider, global political insights. After all, post-apartheid South Africa was a rare occasion when an almost natural "space" or "turning point" had formed in conflict, through which the ensuing trauma could be considered, reframed and worked through. South Africa is moreover an example of a prolonged struggle within a nation-state, rather than between states and other international or transnational actors. The political and emotional dynamics at stake may therefore appear less complex than the geo-politically and strategically charged environments that constrain states in the aftermath of the massive traumas associated with, for instance, acts of war or terrorism. So, what broader political insights can be gleaned from the

[161] Aletta J. Norval, "'No Reconciliation Without Redress': Articulating Political Demands in Post-Transitional South Africa," *Critical Discourse Studies*, 6.4 (2009), 311–321, at 311.

case of South Africa for the realm of world politics? Can we transpose lessons learnt from the search to reconstruct South African community onto interstate relations after the traumas of war, genocide or terrorism? Can an appreciation of South Africa's palpable shift from a traumatized to a grieving community help us to consider a "global politics of grief"?

This final section examines the broader insights revealed through the case of South Africa with a view to demonstrating how a politics of grief bears out in the global political arena. In this respect, there are compelling intersections with a range of emerging international relations literatures, such as those on the politics of apology, forgiveness and reconciliation.[162] However, at the same time I underscore that grief, as I conceive of it, is an important – and precursory – post-trauma political practice. A conception of grief adds to scholarly as well as policy-orientated understandings of how traumatized societies are to psychologically and emotionally heal in order for formal acts of contrition and reconciliation to be more successful. The key point I thus stress ultimately concerns crucial, "bigger picture" questions of how aggrieved, traumatized communities can promote a shift away from emotional patterns that perpetuate violence toward those required to undergo grieving and healing. Grief in this sense would be a crucial requirement for achieving social relations that are conducive to successful crisis resolution and reconciliation.

The reconstruction of South Africa after the trauma of apartheid illuminates two factors, or preconditions, that I argue are critical in facilitating a turn from societal trauma to grief. First is a necessary attentiveness to the affective legacies that can be left by past trauma. Shared emotional wounds and legacies can play a key role in shaping the nature, values and political priorities of communities after pivotal

[162] For example, P. E. Digeser, *Political Forgiveness* (Ithaca: Cornell University Press, 2001); Mark Gibney, Rhoda E. Howard-Hassman, Jean-Marc Coicaud and Nicklaus Steiner (eds.), *The Age of Apology: Facing Up to the Past* (Philadelphia: University of Pennsylvania Press, 2008); Yinan He, (Cambridge: Cambridge University Press, 2009); Jennifer Lind, "Apologies in International Politics," *Security Studies*, 18.3 (2009), 517–556; Jennifer Lind, *Sorry States: Apologies in International Politics* (Ithaca: Cornell University Press, 2008); Nava Löwenheim, "A Haunted Past: Requesting Forgiveness for Wrongdoing in International Relations," *Review of International Studies*, 35.3 (2009), 531–555.

traumatic occurrences. Second is then an appreciation of the pivotal role representations can play in initiating, perpetuating and, importantly, transforming such legacies, thereby paving the way for communities to be reconstituted more through the collective attempt to grieve, heal and even potentially reconcile with perceived adversaries.

While the intense, disorientating emotions and even emotionally "numbing" character of individual trauma cannot be disputed, at the collective level emotions can, through the representations that allow trauma to be collectively enacted and become socially meaningful, often seem to "take over." Emotions such as humiliation and shame, particularly when they go unacknowledged, can lead to anger and orientate communal attachments around disingenuous, antagonistic perceptions of others and the world "outside."[163] Emotional legacies left by trauma can moreover remain and be transmitted intergenerationally through collective performances that ritualize the mourning process rather than enable its successful completion. In this way, emotions, together with the representations and ensuing discourses through which collective emotions and affects are manifest, are central to the development of patterns of violent interactions between groups, whether internal to a state, or between states and other global actors.

Yet, practices of representation are politically significant not only because they can generate or perpetuate collective anxieties after trauma. The political power, and potential, of representations likewise lies in their ability to shift how we think and feel. Rather than making social and emotional meaning through memorializing trauma in ways that preserve the sense of injury and, in turn, hyper-vigilant or even retaliatory mindsets, communities can actively harness – or "reclaim" – the potentials immanent in practices of representation. To do so would require a different conception of agency than is usual after trauma: it would require conscious reflection upon the stories we tell and types of emotional meanings and political mindsets and behaviors that are implicated. But through such reflection, wounded communities – whether it be through the media, in politics and even between individuals and their family and friends – can decide to tell a different story about violence, pain and their memory.[164] They can choose to narrate trauma differently.

[163] Thomas J. Scheff and Suzanne M. Retzinger, *Emotions and Violence: Shame and Rage in Destructive Conflicts* (Lexington, 1991), esp. p. 68.

[164] See also Schick, "Acting Out and Working Through," pp. 1849–1851.

The narration of South Africa's collective trauma through the TRC provides inroads to understanding how these transformative potentials of representing trauma can be realized. Through processes of formal acknowledgment, collective reflection and the development of a shared experience and history around the establishment of mutual "truths," the TRC demonstrates that societal trauma can be mediated in an alternative manner. Trauma that once violently divided can be reframed so as to acknowledge the deep suffering endured while simultaneously dissolving divisions and steering the community away from further animosity toward the type of collective reckoning, reflection and mourning that characterizes political grieving. Representations can in this way work to enable the type of critical space and agency required for communities to reflect upon trauma in such a way that the painful and potentially destructive emotions associated with shared trauma stand a greater chance of being worked through. Through representations, therefore, societal trauma *can* be consciously and purposively "reclaimed."

Just as representations and subsequent social discourses can instigate emotional patterns that lead to violence, they can then also unsettle such patterns. Significant in this respect is that the way past trauma is spoken of, written of or visualized can help to orientate a community toward the type of emotional recognition and expression required to shift communities away from destructive emotional patterns after pain. Consider, once again, the case of South Africa and the TRC. The reconciliation process and TRC were of critical importance in recognizing and, in turn, conceiving of past trauma in a manner that pushed the South African national community away from further conflict and toward a simultaneous need to acknowledge and "work through" the painful emotions and memories that had helped to keep society divided. Previously divisive affective attachments (and detachments) were deconstructed and, through the process of mutual reflection and grief, emotionally and politically reconstituted. Thus, somewhat paradoxically, just as violence and trauma had for long kept the community divided it became a core part of cohering the "new" South Africa.

Representations can in this way enact the type of conscious "emotion work" that sociologist Arlie Russell Hochschild suggests is central to maintaining the well-being of social relations.[165] Hochschild

[165] Arlie Russell Hochschild, *The Managed Heart: The Commercialization of Human Feeling* (Berkeley: University of California Press, 1983).

conceives of different forms of emotional work, or, as she first conceived, "emotional labor." The conception I invoke highlights the social and political processes through which the ways we feel take shape; it is suggestive of an "awareness of manipulating attitudes, thoughts, or behaviors in the service of feelings."[166] Key here is that emotions are social phenomena that are managed and governed – through recognizing the social stimuli, values and beliefs that shape the ways we feel, we can take back control of our emotions. We can ourselves instigate emotional – and social – change.

Allow me to elaborate in relation to the "emotional work" implicated in the narration of trauma. The typical "politics of trauma" pivots on representations that rely on and preserve a "prefigured emotional landscape" – one in which political responses to trauma suggest that emotional responses of shock, fear, anxiety, humiliation, anger and rage are automatic and inevitable.[167] Preponderant representations and political responses to them in turn solidify these emotions, keeping them largely "fixed" with no space to move forward through them. Communities can then be emotionally constituted in insular, antagonistic ways, such as was arguably the case after the Bali bombing, or even in the present case of China. However, by reflecting upon how we choose to represent trauma, we can inspire the collective mindfulness necessary to enact a different type of emotional politics. Communities can encourage the type of conscious "emotion work" that holds hope for the more successful mourning and healing necessary to confront violence rather than perpetuate it. Specifically, rather than emotionally enacting trauma in ways that perform and constitute collective identity and community bound by trauma's debilitation, individuals and their communities would search to undergo proper grieving processes that allow for the working through and, as much as is possible, the conscious acceptance of trauma.

[166] Hochschild referenced in Thomas J. Scheff, *Catharsis in Healing, Ritual, and Drama* (Berkeley: University of California Press, 1979), p. 7. To elaborate further, Hochschild uses the term primarily to denote the social conditioning or regulation of emotions. While this often takes place in unconscious and inaudible ways, emotion work can also be cultivated consciously in service of particular ends.

[167] Andrew A. G. Ross, *Mixed Emotions: Beyond Fear and Hatred in International Conflict* (Chicago: University of Chicago Press, 2014), pp. 18–19.

It may still appear too large a leap from the role of representations in framing and reframing internal state processes after trauma to the seemingly more global political arena. However, the significance of representational processes remains the same across a range of different communal contexts, irrespective of the size of the community at issue. All communities, after all, simply comprise individuals, and as such the social processes through which communities are structured differ only by scale. Of course, this is not to paint a picture of the respective community as homogenous or static or without fissures of dissent – or without elements that may from time to time transgress the very community boundaries being imposed by typical understandings of trauma. It is merely to say that the emotional dimensions of representing trauma play a central role in cohering – and can thereby also transform – the contours of political communities, from familial structures, to ethnic communities and to those at, or even above, the level of the state.

Understanding this co-constitutive relationship between emotions and representing trauma thus offers untold insights for the practice of everyday world politics. It offers an opportunity to think anew about current and enduring historical conflicts, where they emerge from and how to better deal with ensuing traumatic legacies. Foremost here is the need to resist the impulse to narrate injury and loss through frames that truncate communal mourning in an effort to foreclose the political space – the uncertainty – that the trauma has opened. And while individual and shared losses associated with trauma will always in one sense remain, the grieving processes I advocate would instigate the type of acceptance and critical evaluation that enables traumatic emotions to be processed and worked through. This would prevent the kind of overt politicization of trauma from which reflex-like retributive post-trauma practices ensue. And it would make both emotional and political healing possible. Collective injury and loss could, in other words, be integrated into normality in a positive manner thereby enabling the community to look forward.

Summary: from emotionally enacting trauma to reclaiming trauma through grief

This chapter has comprised the third and final chapter of my empirical engagement into how the emotional dimensions of representing trauma can abet the constitution of community in world politics. Different to the previous two cases I examined (Chapters 4 and 5), however, the present chapter has examined the transformative possibilities that can be realized after trauma. Specifically, the chapter scrutinized how trauma can be perceived of and represented in ways that help to acknowledge and reconfigure emotional meanings, attachments and legacies that orientate communities negatively after violence, injury and loss. Key to doing so, I argued, is a turn away from the reflex-like, "knee jerk" political responses that so often proliferate after trauma toward the potentials immanent in a politics of grief.

A turn to grief contributes toward a regenerative emotional and political order after trauma by facilitating practices necessary for individuals and a wider community to properly mourn injury and loss, and to in turn work through numerous painful emotions. Doing so is crucial, for, as history shows us, trauma can leave social and emotional legacies that are passed on through generations, constituting and reconstituting communities that are bound by (old or new) hatreds and antagonisms. In such circumstances, emotional discourses that validate one's own community while stigmatizing others often ensue. A "chosen trauma" type phenomenon can develop, whereby communities become emotionally constituted in ways that consciously or unconsciously motivate them around compensating for, or retaliating in response to, their perceived losses. A process of communal grieving is intended to counter these emotional dynamics. Grief would be a regenerative and genuinely transformative political process, focused on coming to terms with trauma in a way that enables collective reflection upon the emotional mindsets and insecurities that prevent communities from moving forward, and finding peace, after violence.

Practices of representation are fundamental to whether a community turns to trauma or grief after collective injury. Representations of traumatic events and histories tend to mediate the injury and pain in an uncritical manner that preserves the sense of loss as well as the difficult, potentially destructive emotions that accompany loss, particularly when such loss is politically motivated. This was the case following recent traumas such as the US community following the terrorist attacks of September 11, 2002, and the Australian community following the 2002 Bali bombing. Centuries-old historical traumas such as that of Bosnia – culminating in the breakup of Yugoslavia in the 1990s – are also illustrative. In these instances shared representations of immediate and lengthy historical trauma implicate a collective sense of anxiety, insecurity, fear and outrage that paved the way for retaliatory forms of violence. Alternative modes of representing trauma are therefore necessary. Critical in this respect are ways of representing – speaking, giving testimony, pictorializing, and memorializing – that prompt a community to critically reflect upon trauma and the meanings that are, in spite of trauma's isolation and even meaninglessness, nonetheless ascribed to it.

I have demonstrated the transformative potentials of grief by examining two different instances of historical trauma. First I examined the case of China, and, second, South Africa.

China is an interesting case as it helps us to appreciate the difficulties involved with grieving and working through trauma in a politically transformative manner. Shared representations of the "Century of National Humiliation" have come to be a site through which the Chinese national community is emotionally inscribed and reconstituted. While various alternative or competing historical narratives could be voiced, a history of trauma and victimization at foreign hands has come to be widely accepted and, as such, immensely powerful. Historical trauma has come to shape not only Chinese identity and community but also the nature of China's rise in global politics. China thus reflects a community that has neglected to come to terms with its past. Through representations, trauma remains unresolved.

My analysis of South Africa then demonstrated a situation in which a society searched to consciously grieve and work through the past in order to repair and rebuild a community torn apart by violence. Rather than representing past trauma through discourses that heighten injury and fuel a sense of unabated injustice, discourses of healing and reparation were evident and prioritized from the very beginning of the reconciliation process: the language of trauma, hidden suffering, wounding, truth-telling, forgiveness and catharsis became axiomatic to state reconstruction. This is important because such discourses provided a shared representational frame (and, specifically, a language) through which the community could both understand the effects of the violent conflict and focus individual and societal responses to it. Significantly, such discourses also set the scene for the TRC's emergence, as well as its relative successes. Through the TRC, victims could come face-to-face with perpetrators, giving testimony to violence against them and the enduring psychological and emotional effects. Acknowledgment of this trauma, and of casting ill-feelings aside irrespective of forgiveness, was the cornerstone and a crucial accomplishment of the TRC. This is not to say that individuals did not continue to suffer from the past, but that the political meanings and emotional significance ascribed to the violence changed.

A turn to grief thus provides a fresh perspective upon trauma that would be invaluable in many enduring historical and contemporary local and global conflicts. Yet, at the same time, I stress that the process of communal grieving is not intended to provide an instant quick "fix." Grief cannot force communities to promptly forget what they have gone through and look on rosily to the future. Working through trauma takes time. It is also a contextually specific process, which may – unlike the case of South Africa that I examined – require still more complex mechanisms of formal judicial justice. Different culturally distinct customs and practices of bereavement – a culturally salient version of what it means, how trauma victims "work through" and recovery – may also be necessary in different global situations. My point in this chapter has thus been more simple, and precursory: to show that grieving processes are an essential precondition for traumatized communities to work through the types of emotions and mindsets that inhibit the resumption of nonviolent politics and even reconciliation after trauma. But as such they offer untold potentials, and may provide practical tools we can look to in order to try to transform entrenched crises. In particular, the need for grief brings the way we represent and remember violence and suffering to the fore. A turn to grief helps us to see that the narration of suffering is central to how individuals and communities can be actively aided to turn from a politics of trauma to that of grief – and away from harmful, potentially conflict-perpetuating emotions and toward those that facilitate combined emotional and political reconciliation.

Conclusion

Affective communities and emotional cultures in international relations

This book has investigated the relationship between trauma, emotion and the construction of political community. It has done so by examining how practices of representation can make seemingly individual, inimitable experiences of trauma meaningful in ways that help to constitute wider forms of political community.

Part I connected a range of interdisciplinary literatures into the nature of trauma, emotions and the representational processes that prompt individuals to make sense of trauma in a shared and, in some instances, collectivizing manner. Part II then empirically illustrated this dynamic by examining dominant representations of very different but equally pivotal contemporary and historic traumatic events: the 2002 Bali bombing, the December 2004 Southeast Asian tsunami, China's history of colonial trauma and "national humiliation" and, finally, the legacy of apartheid in South Africa. These chapters show how such representations signal and can mobilize a range of socially embedded emotional meanings about the respective trauma and suffering, meanings that can be recognized, understood, accepted and potentially reflected upon in a particular communal environment.

My inquiry has shown that representations are inextricably linked to the different types of emotional and communal responses that can ensue after widespread trauma. Three distinct communal formations are important. Each can be distinguished by the differing emotional orientations and attachments through which they are enacted, enabled and constituted. At issue with the case of the Bali bombing was the constitution of an insular and parochial sense of Australian nationalism and corresponding form of national political community. The tsunami, in contrast, demonstrated the transgressive possibilities of representing trauma: it showed that traumatic events, particularly at the global level, may be able to produce the shared meanings and sense of common purpose required to constitute political community beyond the nation-state. The cases of China and South Africa then revealed the challenges and possibilities of transforming communities bound by painful and potentially destructive emotions associated with historical trauma. Whereas China's persistent representation of its colonial trauma produces meanings that cohere the national community by perpetuating traumatic emotions, postapartheid South Africa reflects an active attempt to represent trauma and work through associated emotions in order to transform and unite a community divided by decades of violent conflict.

One objective in particular has structured my conceptual and empirical investigation: the need to better understand the pivotal but relatively neglected role that emotions play in the processes through which trauma can constitute political communities. Be it a natural catastrophe or some form of political violence, be it experienced as a direct witness or observed from a safe distance, emotions are central to experiences of trauma. During times of widespread catastrophe emotions also become publicly pronounced, illuminating the social-therapeutic and intensely political discourses that so often follow public tragedy. Emotions thus inevitably help to shape perceptions and responses to such trauma. However, there has been relatively little scholarly engagement with how the emotional nature of traumatic events can influence the configuring of society and politics. This is particularly the case in international relations. This book has sought to address this shortcoming by examining how emotions associated with trauma can – through practices of representation – help to constitute the shared meanings that are intrinsic to the formation of political communities.

In this concluding chapter, I reflect on insights gleaned from my combined conceptual and empirical inquiry. I outline the broader significance of this study for how scholars, politicians and other practitioners think about not only disciplinary international relations but also the state and practice of world politics more generally.

I start off by expanding on the most fundamental contribution of my study: the conceptualization of emotions as important social and political forces, which are inevitably intertwined with the social processes constitutive of identity and community in world politics. Drawing from both the theoretical and empirical insights of my inquiry, I argue that the production of social, collective forms of emotion can in particular circumstances constitute "affective communities": communities produced or preserved at least in part by a host of emotional representations that either implicitly or explicitly preference particular ways of feeling and perceiving of the world.

Unlike existing theorizations of emotions in world politics, this conceptualization brings representational practices to the forefront. This is to say that I not only draw attention to the socially or culturally bounded nature of emotion, but also situate representations as mediating forces that contribute to the articulation and rearticulation of emotions and emotional meanings. Representations enable particular emotions and affective dispositions to be performed after trauma. Considering the politics of emotion in this manner is significant as it takes existing international relations-based theorizations a step further: it enables scholars to consider not simply how emotions themselves act as social and political forces but also how the these very forces in turn shape the emotional predispositions of individuals and collectives.

The issue of power inevitably comes into play when one explores linkages between representation, emotions and politics. As responses to representations, emotions can be produced in ways that serve entrenched interests. The reverse of this is that representations, together with prevailing modes of interpretation, inevitably preference particular historically and socioculturally constituted ways of feeling. This is to say that, in signifying particular meanings (and helping to mobilize particular discourses), representations inevitably highlight and legitimize some forms of emotional receptivity over others. This is why an appreciation of the relationship between emotions and power is critical to a more considered understanding of the roles emotions play in world politics. At the very least, understanding these linkages enables scholars to comprehend the dynamics of identity and community better: how the combined cultural and political nature of emotions can both limit and potentially transgress established forms of community and responsibility.

Finally, theorizing emotions in this manner opens inroads into understanding the importance of emotions in international relations more broadly. The final section maps these – and in doing so concludes with an opening for future research. Specifically, I underscore how this conceptualization of political emotions and the production of such emotional cultures is central to attaining a more holistic appreciation of not only a range of important empirical and normative debates in world politics but also the shifting nature and potentials for transnational communities and their politics.

Communities of feeling: how representations can configure boundaries of affect

My inquiry has conceptually and empirically explored how practices of representation can depict individual experiences of trauma in ways that socially situate traumatic occurrences within a wider community of others. It has demonstrated that representations help to "share" trauma, prompting individuals to "make sense" of their experiences in particular cooperative manners. Often, such representations draw attention to the harrowing nature of traumatic events: they signify shock, vulnerability and confusion. Victims and witnesses strive to comprehend what they are experiencing, being affected by emotional responses and drawing upon prevailing discourses and symbols to make sense of what they see and feel. In this way, seemingly individual traumatic, catastrophic events are enacted in manners that in fact possess social significance and meaning, thereby enabling trauma to be perceived as a collective experience. In turn, through sharing and in illuminating a distinct collective meaning, representations can renew or reshape important social connections and be instrumental to the constitution of political community.

I have also shown that emotions play a key role in shaping the shared meanings that are needed to constitute community after trauma. Emotions are bound up in how trauma is experienced and witnessed. They are also embedded within the representations used to communicate trauma and, in turn, the messages that such representations convey. Emotions are an inherent part of the perceptive and interpretive processes that allow one to "make sense" of representations of trauma. During a time of crisis, emotions can additionally illuminate ostensibly private trauma in very public ways. As my analysis has demonstrated, representations of trauma can be perceived to cultivate social or collective forms of emotion – forms of feeling that appear at least through the media and in politics as shared and, as a consequence, of unique value in constituting a socially recognized (and widely held) understanding of a particular traumatic event or traumatic history.

Social forms of emotions can therefore be seen as particularly important to appreciating the linkages between trauma and political community. Social emotions are collective manifestations of culturally and historically cultivated and, to an extent, socially normalized and accepted forms of feeling. Social emotions are as such relational;

they are, as Jonathan Mercer puts it, "a feeling that has intrinsic importance to an actor in some relationship to an entity."[1] I have suggested that one way to consider the collectivizing possibilities of emotion (that is, the mobilization of social emotions) is to think of emotions as phenomena that can, because of their social nature, be "pulled upon," both by one's own experiences and events seemingly external to them. The mediation of distant trauma provides a helpful illustration. Witnessing trauma through the mediations of photographers, journalists and politicians can "steer" an audience's emotions; mediations can, in other words, "pull" individuals and prompt emotional receptivity (and a wider affective resonance) in this or that way depending on what is seen. While such mediations may not go so far as to explicitly tell viewers what to think and how to feel, they do ground one's understanding by making particular aspects of the trauma visible – and, of course, others invisible. Key here is that representations act as the lens through which individuals see, perceive and feel. Representations "frame" traumatic events.[2] By showing part of the picture, part of the trauma, representations appeal to particular historically and culturally grounded ways of knowing and feeling. Hence effectively "pulling" victims' and witnesses' emotions in historically embedded, culturally sensitive manners. Patterns of words and images are therefore a mechanism through which individual and distant experiences of trauma can resonate with and affectively appeal to a wider society, to a community linked by shared patterns of emotionality and feeling.

Representations of trauma can in this way, in particular circumstances, abet the construction of what I term "affective communities": communities temporally drawn together by shared emotional understandings of the respective event or series of them. The solidarity and strength of community after both the Bali bombing and Southeast Asian tsunami, as well as in the enduring wake of collective historical traumas such as in mainland China, provide cases in point.

Consider first the Bali bombing. Multiple emotional meanings are imbricated in various political discourses that effectively constrained,

[1] Jonathan Mercer "Feeling Like a State: Social Emotion and Identity," *International Theory*, 6.3 (2014), 515–535, at 516.

[2] Kimberly Gross and Lisa D'Ambrosio, "Framing Emotional Response," *Political Psychology*, 25.1 (2004), 1–29.

or limited, the boundaries of identity and political community. Representations of the bombing were, I illustrated, key to the dissemination of such discourses as well as to guiding the emotions felt in response. Through the media, Australian viewers were presented with images of death and situations of tragic survival, of families in mourning and political figures solemn yet determined to formulate an adequate policy response. Textual representations moreover drew explicitly upon discourses that prioritized nationalist imagery, cultural icons and political-security concerns. These dominant representations produced meanings consonant with the trauma being a distinctly national tragedy of significance for not only victims in Bali but also the entire nation. The trauma became a national trauma, an event both defying public belief and irrevocably fracturing (and paradoxically remaking) the national community and its values and priorities. And, as depicted by the media, a corresponding unique sense of national cohesiveness emerged.

So strong was Australian solidarity after the bombing that linkages have been drawn between the emergent cohesiveness and newfound strength of community and security policy. Matt McDonald, for instance, argues that the bombing and its memory were instrumental in garnering public support for the priority of the then government to join the Coalition of the Willing to intervene militarily in Iraq.[3] The Australian prime minister even went as far as to explicitly invoke public memory of the Bali bombing in relation to the forthcoming Iraq war: "Australians should 'bear [the events of Bali] in mind if we become involved in conflict in Iraq,'" the prime minister urged.[4] Defense analysts similarly perceived of the bombing as a new-world threat to Australian "sovereignty and way of life," and thus a trigger for a raft of more active globally focused security policy changes.[5] Here, it can be seen that widely recognized emotionally charged social discourses came not only to frame dominant understandings of the

[3] Matt McDonald, "Constructing Insecurity: Australia Security Discourse and Policy Post-2001," *International Relations*, 19.3 (2005), 297–320; Matt McDonald, "'Lest We Forget': The Politics of Memory and Australian Military Intervention," *International Political Sociology*, 4.3 (2010), 287–302.

[4] Prime Minister John Howard cited in Matt McDonald, "Perspectives on Australian Foreign Policy, 2004," *Australian Journal of International Affairs*, 59.2 (2005), 153–168, at 160.

[5] Alan Dupont, "Transformation or Stagnation? Rethinking Australia's Defence," *Australian Journal of International Affairs*, 57.1 (2003), 55–76, at 55.

bombing and its trauma but also to constitute communal – and in turn political, and security-focused – agency.

Situations of collective historical trauma illuminate similar affective and communal dynamics. As I examined, the strength of Chinese nationalism and political community can, for instance, be seen to have been made possible in part through representations of a shared painful past, and this even while acknowledging that other dynamics important to a one-party state are at play. Dominant representations of the various traumatic events that now comprise the "Century of National Humiliation" create meanings that not simply keep the sense of injury and loss fresh, but also, in so doing, perpetuate emotional discourses (and ensuing structures of feeling) that distinguish and exceptionalize mainland Chinese from all those "outside." Ironically, where once such nationalism was based around an interpretation of the Chinese as "victors" in the face of Western and Japanese oppression, new narratives reinterpret past trauma through the lens of the Chinese citizens as distinct "victims."[6] Representing collective trauma in this manner is important as the ensuing culture of humiliation has significant implications for the nature of Chinese domestic and foreign politics: Chinese political identity and community are cohered around an ensuing search to regain international recognition and status, as well as through a pride and unwillingness to ever again be dishonored or oppressed.[7] In this sense, Chinese community is constituted narrowly and negatively; as a collective, the PRC is ontologically determined in opposition to an external, foreign other.[8]

The response to the Southeast Asian tsunami, however, enables an appreciation of very different yet equally compelling emotional dynamics. Indeed, that the tsunami generated a community that was not previously there has made it a particularly interesting case through which to examine the relationship between trauma, emotions and political community.

[6] See, for instance, Peter Hays Gries, *China's New Nationalism: Pride, Politics, and Diplomacy* (Berkeley: University of California Press, 2004), pp. 43–53, 69–85.

[7] See Manjari Chaterjee Miller, *Wronged By Empire: Post-Imperial Ideology and Foreign Policy in India and China* (Stanford: Stanford University Press, 2013).

[8] See William A. Callahan, *China: The Pessoptimist Nation* (Oxford: Oxford University Press, 2010).

Although temporal in nature, the tsunami united victims with distant donors, aid organizations and governments in a very substantial transnational community committed to the immediate and longer-term outreach of aid and more general humanitarian responsibilities. Key to this response is the recognition that representations can open up how one thinks about one's attachments to others. Representations of the tsunami helped to disturb the prevailing configuration of community in world politics; they prompted individuals to reconsider how they conceptualize their connections and responsibilities. After the tsunami, the powers that ordinarily maintain community – a national community – momentarily turned outwards, making way for the reworked sense of attachment that representations of the trauma helped to produce.

Representations of the tsunami can therefore be interpreted to have enabled – reconfigured – boundaries of political community. This is particularly important to how we appreciate the existence of community in world politics. Ordinarily, representations of trauma – which tend to comprise the trauma of war, terrorist attacks and, on occasion, natural catastrophe – reinstate power structures traditional to the nation-state. They close off communal boundaries; they tend to silence alternative discourses through which new configurations of community can be generated. Yet, the tsunami imagery I examined can be seen to have produced humanitarian discourses that to some extent broke down distinctions between "us" and "them," discourses that were made meaningful in part through one's emotional inclinations and receptivity toward images of suffering.

This is not to argue, however, that the type of community that was mobilized after the tsunami is without its problems. As my analysis of media images demonstrates, the transnational connections were to at least some degree constituted through traditional, hierarchical perceptions of non-Western helplessness and need. Many images of the catastrophe and trauma were inherently colonial representations, stressing the passivity and dependence of victims rather than their resilience. These attributes are important to how we can consider the transnational communal linkages and response that ensued. Not only does the presentation of abject and dehumanizing images of non-Western cultural others align with historical trends in imaging distant (non-Western) suffering, but also numerous literatures have found that emotions of sympathy, pity, compassion and empathy are key to linking such images with humanitarian intentions and actions.[9] And, yet, while such emotions may have been significant in driving donations and thus the corresponding sense of transnational community, they do prompt important ethical questions concerning the exact nature of such a community. While its actions were undoubtedly humanitarian in intension, it forces one to wonder if, rather than being revolutionary, the transnational aid community may at least partially resemble (and thus perpetuate) existing hierarchies of power, domination and ultimately even the subjugation of the developing world.

Thinking less critically, however, it may also seem commonsensical that if trauma is to foster solidarity and communal attachments some emotional elements must be present – whether it be emotions of "fellow feeling" or those associated with more stereotypical depictions of human need. Of course, community cannot exist without solidarity or some form of shared sentiment or common bond and purpose. However, international relations only recently begun to truly consider emotions as a basis for social and political behavior. To add to this, some literatures that examine the linkages between representations (and, in particular, images) of suffering and emotions have argued that emotions are in fact of little consequence. Susan Moeller, for instance, suggests that emotions once thought to pervade the experience of witnessing trauma (such as compassion or sympathy) are now passive in the face of the challenge to procure a willingness to respond to human suffering.[10] Scholars are also reticent about the idea of empathy.[11] Some even consider empathy an

[9] For instance, Lilie Chouliaraki, "Post-Humanitarianism: Humanitarian Communication Beyond a Politics of Pity," *International Journal of Cultural Studies*, 13.2 (2010), 106–126; Birgitta Höijer, "The Discourse of Global Compassion: The Audience and Media Reporting of Human Suffering," *Media, Culture & Society*, 26.4 (2004), 513–531; Juha Käpylä and Denis Kennedy, "Cruel to Care? Investigating the Governance of Compassion in the Humanitarian Imagery," *International Theory*, 6.2 (2014), 255–292.

[10] Susan D. Moeller, *Compassion Fatigue: How the Media Sells Disease, Famine, War and Death* (New York: Routledge, 1999). See also Stanley Cohen, *States of Denial: Knowing About Atrocities and Suffering* (Cambridge: Polity, 1993); Arthur Kleinman and Joan Kleinman, "The Appeal of Experience; The Dismay of Images: Cultural Appropriations of Suffering in Our Times," *Daedalus*, 125.1 (1996), 1–25; Keith Tester, *Compassion, Morality and the Media* (Milton Keynes: Open University Press, 2001).

[11] Carolyn J. Dean, "Empathy, Pornography, and Suffering," *Differences: A Journal of Feminist and Cultural Studies*, 14.1 (2003), 88–124; E. Ann Kaplan, *Trauma Culture: The Politics of Loss in Media and Literature* (New Brunswick: Rutgers University Press, 2005).

"impossibility,"[12] an "empty"[13] liberal emotional ideal that is thwarted by the inability to truly step outside of one's own feelings and experiences and see the world from the unique perspective of another. Still other scholars have argued that the task of representing human suffering and trauma will inevitably entail significant ethical dilemmas.[14] However, many scholars are also still hopeful. Recent studies have returned to the idea that feelings of indignation, sympathy, compassion, empathy and even anger might help to replace the selectivity with which we approach catastrophe and suffering with a more ingenuous, human-needs-based response.[15]

Notwithstanding the ethical value of such debates, these debates obscure the broader insight that my research reveals: representations of trauma can help to constitute community by creating socially and, importantly, emotionally meaningful understandings of trauma and its loss and pain. In this process, such representations tap into or mobilize particular socially embedded emotions, in turn uniting individuals around the common purpose and bonds that ensue. Viewers thus need to be able to recognize, understand, and feel for the suffering before them if they are to subsequently pull together – whether it is to reach out to help, offer collective condolences, or to rebuild or transform existing configurations of community for the better. For my primary argument, the precise shape of the emotions felt in response is thus not necessarily what is important. What is important is the recognition that, after trauma, emotions can be critical social and political forces, helping to constitute and reconstitute the social discourses as well as the concomitant wider shared meanings needed to either confine or expand the boundaries of community in world politics.

[12] Patricia Molloy, "Face to Face with the Dead Man: Ethical Responsibility, State-Sanctioned Killing, and Empathetic Impossibility," *Alternatives: Social Transformation and Humane Governance*, 22.4 (1997), 467–492.

[13] Kaplan, *Trauma Culture*, pp. 21, 93–94.

[14] Elizabeth Dauphinée, "The Politics of the Body in Pain: Reading the Ethics of Imagery," *Security Dialogue*, 38.2 (2007), 139–155.

[15] See, for instance, Jodi Halpern and Harvey M. Weinstein, "Rehumanizing the Other: Empathy and Reconciliation," *Human Rights Quarterly*, 26.3 (2004), 561–583; Käpylä and Kennedy. "Cruel to Care?" 283–286; Martha C. Nussbaum, "Compassion: The Basic Social Emotion," *Social Philosophy and Policy*, 13.1 (1996), 27–58; Carolyn Pedwell, "Economies of Empathy: Obama, Neoliberalism, and Social Justice," *Environment and Planning D: Society and Space*, 30 (2012), 280–297; Maureen Whitebrook "Compassion as a Political Virtue," *Political Studies*, 50.3 (2002), 529–554.

Emotions as social and political forces

Emotions thus clearly matter. Emotions are a pervasive element of individual and social life, and can be important political forces. Yet, while this view of emotions has become meanwhile more and more established across the social sciences, my inquiry has also traced how, within international relations – where power politics and traumas of war have (ironically) plagued humankind for centuries – there is a long history (and a continuing legacy) of expunging emotions from scholarly analysis.

The traditional neglect of emotions has much to do with their status in Western philosophy and thought more generally.[16] Very few phenomena would seem at first glance as personal and thus individual as emotions. Emotions seem natural, not cultural; private, not public; inchoate and ephemeral, rather than concrete and susceptible to the scrutiny of social science. Such views about emotions have dictated how they are considered – and, indeed, whether emotions are considered – not only in disciplinary international relations but also in much broader Western modes of thought. Consider how words such as "fear," "disgust" and "love" are invoked when speaking about one's self, and the private, yet are discouraged and rarely observed within official political responses to key social issues or events. Emotions in this sense are not simply devalued – cast as the irrational, the vulnerable and the female – but their pervasive presence in social and political life is marginalized and neglected. As a consequence, Western thinking (and social and political analysis more specifically) has been concerned with how to go about eliminating, or at best "controlling" emotions and creating a passionless space where "good," reason-filled judgment takes place.

This line of thought has meant that the emotional underpinnings of society and politics have received insufficient scholarly attention. And while studies in broader social science and cultural studies have begun to rectify this shortcoming, the difficulties associated with accepting emotions in politics have set a trend that stretches far into the study and practice of international relations. The dominance of rational,

[16] See Roland de Sousa, *The Rationality of Emotion* (Cambridge, MA: MIT Press, 1987); Jon Elster, *Alchemies of the Mind: Rationality and the Emotions* (Cambridge: Cambridge University Press, 1999).

structure-bound and organizational models of conceptualizing world politics has led to a general subordination of emotion.[17] Even some recent studies on affect and emotion within international relations that seek to deconstruct the myth of an emotionless political rationality often wind up perpetuating the cognitive, technical idea of rationality that they seek to displace.

My inquiry has sought to address this gap: it has highlighted that emotions are necessary and indeed important social and political forces that must be taken seriously in international relations scholarship.

Two key shifts are important to cultivating the types of scholarly mindsets necessary to do so.

First, scholars must heed calls to cease to consider emotions in opposition to rationality.[18] One way to examine emotions in world politics is to consider them as forms of appraisal, as a pervasive part of the interpretative, perceptive tools individuals use to situate themselves and make the social world meaningful. Conceiving of emotions in such a manner is often aligned with a cognitive approach to understanding human emotion. However, the stance I purport here is intended merely to invoke the idea that emotions are a necessary – and therefore telling – part of how individuals respond to the world around them. Emotions help to shape responses to particular political events and stimuli. As such, they cannot be divorced from social structures and political processes, or simply wished away. Instead, this view purports that it is entirely rational to feel in particular ways, in the sense that emotions inevitably help to motivate subsequent beliefs and actions.[19] Robert Solomon and Martha Nussbaum are two theorists

[17] Neta C. Crawford, "The Passion of World Politics: Propositions on Emotions and Emotional Relationships," *International Security*, 24.4 (2000), 116–136, at 117; Jonathan Mercer, "Rationality and Psychology in International Politics," *International Organization*, 59.1 (2005), 77–106.

[18] Feminist studies were among the first to debunk traditional dichotomies of mind/body and reason/emotion. Of scholars who specifically examine emotions in world politics, the work of Neta Crawford and Jonathan Mercer also stands out as early attempts to problematize the opposition of emotions and rationality. See Crawford, "The Passion of World Politics"; Jonathan Mercer, "Approaching Emotion in International Politics," paper presented at the annual meeting of the International Studies Association, San Diego, CA, April 25, 1996.

[19] J. M. Barbalet, *Emotion, Social Theory and Social Structure: A Macrosociological Approach* (Cambridge: Cambridge University Press, 2001), pp. 45–49.

who stress that emotions are important forms of knowledge and evaluative thought.[20] They also both fiercely defend the proposition that emotions tell us certain things, providing insights and pointers that could be of use in our attempts to both understand and address social and political challenges. This line of thinking is critical as it elevates an understanding of emotion as a pervasive and indeed valuable resource in political decision-making processes. It stresses not only the public but also the scholarly value of emotion.

Second is the recognition that emotions and emotionality are not individual achievements but are instead deeply cultural and social phenomena. Emotions are formed and structured within particular social and cultural environments. They are constituted and embodied in relation to culturally specific traditions, such as language, habits and memories. This means not only that emotions are conceived within a predominant sociocultural environment, but also that individuals gain an understanding of what it means to feel in particular ways from within the same social and cultural surroundings.[21] Simply put, one's emotionality is dependent upon a culturally grounded set of meanings to both inspire feelings and to in turn provide a basis for their interpretation. It consequently can be seen that shared forms of emotional expression and meaning are necessary for individuals to make sense of the world in the context of a wider community. As Anthony Giddens once put it, "[e]motional attunement is necessary to the interpretative understanding upon which interpersonal communication depends."[22] Consider, for instance, how in order experience feelings such as anger, love, happiness, lust or frustration, one must be grounded in a cultural context that makes anger, love, happiness, lust

[20] Robert C. Solomon, *Not Passions Slave: Emotions and Choice* (Oxford: Oxford University Press, 2003); Martha C. Nussbaum, "Rational Emotions," in her *Poetic Justice: The Literary Imagination and Public Life* (Boston: Beacon, 1995), pp. 53–78; Martha C. Nussbaum, *Upheavals of Thought: The Intelligence of Emotions* (Cambridge: Cambridge University Press, 2001).

[21] See Rom Harré (ed.), *The Social Construction of Emotion* (New York: Basil Blackwell, 1986); Catherine A. Lutz, *Unnatural Emotions: Everyday Emotions on a Micronesian Atoll and their Challenge to Western Theory* (Cambridge: Cambridge University Press, 1988).

[22] Anthony Giddens, "Foreword," in Thomas J. Scheff (ed.), *Microsociology: Discourse, Emotion, and Social Structure* (Chicago: University of Chicago Press, 1990), p. xii.

or frustration meaningful (and in turn determines a response to that emotion – whether it is something to be proud of, ashamed of, etc.). Emotions are therefore not only formed in a social setting but also find meaning (even if such meaning is open to change) in particular social and cultural environments.

However, this is not to imply that emotions and one's sense of emotionality cannot shift and change. It actually means the precise opposite: that emotions are "de-essentialized," as anthropologist Catherine Lutz puts it.[23] No longer are emotions conceptualized as internal, individual, private or innate psychobiological factors; rather, emotions are mediated by cultural and social relations, and they are used to both enact, sustain and potentially transform those settings over time.

Emotions are in this way both private and public, individual and collective. Expressed in a more general way: emotions have a history and also, importantly, future. Particular emotional dispositions can be passed down, helping to form and reform not only social attachments and communities but also the political decisions and behaviors that such attachments and communities help to enable.

Emotion, the state and international relations

Throughout this book I have alluded to – and at times directly engaged – the new and burgeoning literature on emotions and world politics. Such is the now state of the field that few scholars would challenge the idea that emotions play a political role. Recent studies from various theoretical positions either explicitly acknowledge or refer to the powerful roles that emotions play in international political life.[24]

[23] Lutz, *Unnatural Emotions*, p. 5.

[24] A sample of some, and as drawn upon in Chapter 2, includes: Roland Bleiker and Emma Hutchison, "Fear No More: Emotions and World Politics," *Review of International Studies*, 34 (2008), 115–135; Khaled Fattah and K. M. Fierke, "A Clash of Emotions: The Politics of Humiliation and Political Violence in the Middle East," *European Journal of International Relations*, 15.1 (2009), 67–93; K. M. Fierke, *Political Self-Sacrifice: Agency, Body and Emotion in International Relations* (Cambridge: Cambridge University Press, 2012); Jacques E. C. Hymans, *The Psychology of Nuclear Proliferation: Identity, Emotions, and Foreign Policy* (Cambridge: Cambridge University Press, 2006); Rose McDermott, "The Feeling of Rationality: The Meaning of Neuroscientific Advances for Political Science," *Perspectives of Politics*, 2.4 (2004), 691–706; Jonathan Mercer, "Emotional Beliefs," *International Organization*, 64.1

Accompanying this recognition is the broader idea that emotions are a vital component of a more holistic understanding of the international; that emotions do not, in fact, exist in opposition to rationality but are instead an intrinsic part of the cognitive processes that enable political understanding. Emotions are in one way or another embedded within all political perceptions, standpoints, behaviors and even policies.

My ambition was not to offer a systematic engagement with this body of literature on emotions and world politics. Another type of book – a more survey-oriented one – would be necessary for this endeavor. I have merely thought to draw on existing insights and develop some of them a step further. The key issue here revolves around how to theorize and empirically investigate collective emotions.

Existing international relations literature on collective emotions focuses mostly on understanding the actions of states. Of central influence here have been constructivist investigations into state emotions that draw on a tradition of theorizing the "state as person." Alexander Wendt played a key role in initiating suggestions (albeit with some skepticism) that states can be considered meta-physical organisms. If one does so, then states can be attributed with qualities normally characteristic of individuals, including the capacity for common knowledge, collective consciousness and, by extension, the ability to have emotions.[25] Although the anthropomorphic notion of a state as person is debated and contested[26] it has provided scholars with new ways to

(2010), 1–31; Dominique Moïsi, "The Clash of Emotions." *Foreign Affairs*, 86.1 (2007), 8–12; Andrew A. G. Ross, *Mixed Emotions: Beyond Fear and Hate in International Conflict* (Chicago: Chicago University Press, 2014); Andrew A. G. Ross, "Coming in from the Cold: Constructivism and Emotions," *European Journal of International Relations*, 12.2 (2006), 197–222, at 212–213; Brent Sasley, "Affective Attachments and Foreign Policy: Israel and the 1993 Oslo Accords," *European Journal of International Relations*, 16.4 (2010), 687–709; Ty Solomon, "The Affective Underpinnings of Soft Power," *European Journal of International Relations*, 20.3 (2014), 720–741.

25 Alexander Wendt, "The State as Person in International Theory," *Review of International Studies*, 30.2 (2004), 289–316, at 311–314; Alexander Wendt, *Social Theory of International Politics* (Cambridge: Cambridge University Press, 1999), pp. 215–224.

26 In *Social Theory and International Politics*, Wendt suggests that anthropomorphizing the state remains "problematic" in so far that states comprise more complex social structures than individuals and as such possess different forms of agency and behavioral options. See pp. 221–224. For

theorize emotions at the level of the state. Jonathan Mercer, for instance, provocatively questions the extent to which individuals can "feel like a state" in order to examine whether group emotions can be conceived of at the state level.[27] Showing that emotions are more than the sum of the bodily feelings they emerge from, Mercer turns to beliefs and identities as sources of emotional attribution.[28] Feelings can in this way be sources of identification at the state level, even though states themselves do not possess an organic, physical body. Brent Sasley likewise draws on traditional psychology-based intergroup emotions theory to explore the possibility that a group as large as the state can itself be a receptacle of "intergroup emotions."[29] The assumption of the original theoretical model is that the more people associate with a particular social identity the more they share emotions. Sasley then applies this model to the state and explores the extent to which a "sense of belonging to the state means that citizens of the state, including decision makers, share in their psychological-emotional identification with the group."[30] Ultimately for Sasley, though, and for others who pursue similar approaches, a state may experience emotions in so far that the state is essentially a group constituted by individuals that cultivate, share and identify with each other emotionally.[31]

But, of course, not all scholars agree that emotional attributes can – or at least can so seamlessly – be transposed on to states. States, some argue, are "ontologically incapable of having feelings."[32] This is not to deny that emotions and affective dispositions play an important role at the level of collectives. But difficult questions remain largely unanswered. Who is a state and how exactly are its emotions formed and expressed? How can they be understood and theorized? Whose emotional attachments are

debate on the concept of "state as person," see Patrick Thaddeus Jackson, "Forum Introduction: Is the State a Person? Why Should We Care?" *Review of International Studies*, 30.2 (2004), 255–258.

27 Mercer, "Feeling Like a State."

28 Mercer, "Feeling Like a State"; Mercer, "Emotional Beliefs."

29 Brent E. Sasley, "Theorizing States' Emotions," *International Studies Review*, 13.3 (2011), 453–476, at 465.

30 Sasley, "Theorizing States' Emotions," 460.

31 Similar conceptualizations include Lucille Eznack, "Crises as Signals of Strength: The Significance of Affect in Close Allies' Relationships," *Security Studies*, 20.2 (2011), 238–265; Oded Löwenheim and Gadi Heimann, "Revenge in International Politics," *Security Studies*, 17.4 (2008), 685–724.

32 Paul Digeser, "Friendship Between States," *British Journal of Political Science*, 39.2 (2009), 323–344, at 327–328.

representative of the state? Is it those of key representative actors, such as heads of states or foreign ministers, or is it the larger discursive regime that makes up statehood and its values?

The challenge ahead lies in translating a commonsensical position on the importance of collective emotions into a more thorough understanding of how exactly emotions matter at the level of the state. Doing so cuts to the core of the existence of "collective emotions." If theoretical approaches fail to account for how exactly individual, seemingly inimitable emotions are transcribed into that of a wider community, how, then, do we know collective forms of feeling exist at all? Approaches that reflect upon and account for the possibility of shared emotions and emotional meanings are therefore needed.

Some scholars have started to address the issues at stake. Andrew Ross searched for ways to effectively "capture" the collective significance of emotions.[33] He concluded that while constructivism is uniquely placed to incorporate emotion in its scope of analysis, it might require some rethinking in order to grasp the nonmaterial, affective dimensions of emotion. In particular, Ross stresses the need to "resist the idea that *either* material *or* ideational forces are causally determinative in a given situation."[34] For Ross, constructivism has thus far failed to account for the "nonconscious processes" through which emotions are produced and transmitted to create meanings. He notes here the need to recognize and better understand the symbolic origins and power of emotions.[35] Janice Bially Mattern takes Ross' concerns a step further.[36] For her existing approaches to theorizing emotion in world politics are problematic in that they "flatten" emotion: they reduce multilayered and complex emotional experiences to a fraction of their constitutive components. This compression of emotion highlights their material dimensions but to the detriment of understanding how emotions are socially formed through the complex interplay of structure and agency.

[33] Ross, *Mixed Emotions*; Ross, "Coming in from the Cold."

[34] Ross, "Coming in from the Cold," 208. Emphasis in original.

[35] Andrew A. G. Ross, "Why They Don't Hate Us: Emotion, Agency and the Politics of 'Anti-Americanism,' " *Millennium: Journal of International Studies*, 39.1 (2010), 109–125, at 110.

[36] Janice Bially Mattern, "A Practice Theory of Emotion for International Relations," in Emanuel Adler (ed.), *International Practices* (Cambridge: Cambridge University Press, 2011), pp. 63–86.

Challenges and disputes will undoubtedly remain an integral part of theorizing state emotions. Once one begins to investigate emotions as nonmaterial social forces, a whole set of new problems, particularly of a methodological nature, begin to emerge. Add to this a series of more general critiques of constructivist approaches, most notably that their state-centric and often piece-meal focus marginalizes important other realms where collective emotions operate more diffusely, yet just as prominently.

Representations as the link between private and public emotions

I have thought to advance existing debates on the nature and role of collective emotions by drawing attention to – and empirically investigating – one particular and in my view particularly important issue: the role of representations.[37]

Representations are the language and imagery through which meanings are produced and disseminated throughout societies. In the past two decades, numerous international relations scholars have uncovered how representations – and ensuing interpretative processes – are key to making meanings from which knowledge and understandings about world politics as well as global political relations are constructed.[38] But few if any of these insights have yet to be connected to our understanding of collective emotions. Thus far, these studies have

[37] In doing so I draw upon previous single- and co-authored work; see Emma Hutchison, "A Global Politics of Pity? Disaster Imagery and the Emotional Construction of Solidarity after the 2004 Asian Tsunami," *International Political Sociology*, 8.1 (2014), 1–19; Emma Hutchison and Roland Bleiker, "Theorizing Emotions in World Politics," *International Theory*, 6.3 (2014), 491–514; Roland Bleiker and Emma Hutchison, "Fear No More: Emotions and World Politics," *Review of International Studies*, 34 (2008), 115–135.

[38] For example, see Roland Bleiker, *Aesthetics and World Politics* (New York: Palgrave, 2009); David Campbell, *Writing Security: United States Foreign Policy and the Politics of Identity*, 2nd ed. (Minneapolis: University of Minnesota Press, 1998); François Debrix and Cynthia Weber (eds.), *Rituals of Mediation: International Politics and Social Meaning* (Minneapolis: University of Minnesota Press, 2003); Roxanne Lynn Doty, *Imperial Encounters: The Politics of Representation in North–South Relations* (Minneapolis: University of Minnesota Press, 1996); Janice Bially Mattern, *Ordering International Politics: Identity, Crisis, and Representational Force* (New York: Routledge, 2005); Michael J. Shapiro, "Strategic Discourse/Discursive Strategy: The Representation of 'Security Policy' in the Video Age," *International Studies Quarterly*, 34.3 (1990), 327–340; Lene Hansen, *Security as Practice: Discourse*

shown that by promoting particular ways of understanding issues and events, representations inevitably illuminate some perspectives – only to silence others. And in doing so they tell us how to think about the world. Representations are thus not merely political in the sense that they are central to the constitution of social and collective actions, processes and configurations; their capacity to prioritize particular meanings makes them political sites in and of themselves.

Yet, our ability to make sense and meaning out of representations is not all about a classical "cognition." Making sense of representations is also about affect, feelings and emotions, about how individuals are emotionally constituted by and thus are situated within and attached to the world around them. There is in fact a cyclical process at play. Emotions help individuals to make sense of representations, while over time representations also help to shape and reshape individual emotions.

Representations are the foundational building blocks in the constitution of collective forms of emotion. As such, they are central to examining the individual and collective politics of emotion. Representations enable detailed studies into emotions, since, as constitutive and discursive approaches of emotions contend, representations inevitably stand for or embody particular contextually bound forms of feeling.[39] Important here is that not simply do practices of representing reality give meaning to the world around us, but crucially that in doing so representations inevitably "say something" emotionally.[40] Indeed, they preference particular ways of feeling (and knowing) by tapping into established sociocultural customs of affect and emotion, which in turn helps to shape how one perceives of and belongs in the world. It is through representations, therefore, that emotions can be embodied, transmitted and interpreted in ways that elicit particular sociocultural meanings, values and beliefs.[41]

Analysis and the Bosnian War (London: Routledge, 2006); Cynthia Weber, *Simulating Sovereignty: Intervention, the State, and Symbolic Exchange* (Cambridge: Cambridge University Press, 1995); Jutta Weldes, *Constructing National Interests: The United States and the Cuban Missile Crisis* (Minneapolis: University of Minnesota Press, 1999).

39 Nussbaum, *Upheavals of Thought*, pp. 151–169.

40 Stuart Hall, "Introduction," in Stuart Hall (ed.), *Representations: Cultural Representations and Signifying Practices* (London: Sage in association with the Open University, 1997), pp. 1, 5.

41 Nico H. Frijda, Antony S. R. Manstead and Sacha Bem, "The Influence of Emotions on Beliefs," in Nico H. Frijda, Antony S. R. Manstead and

My inquiry has demonstrated the significance of representations for study the collective politics of emotion by examining the role emotions may play in the formation of community after trauma. I showed not only that representations of trauma can tap into or help to mobilize discourses seemingly constitutive of a community of individuals (who either feel or identify with trauma's pain in similar ways), but also that such representations and ensuing discourses do so through appealing to community in widely recognized (socially and culturally constituted) emotional ways. Other scholars have also employed trauma to demonstrate the public and political potentials of emotion. Indeed, a widely perceived traumatic event is a time when private emotions are arguably the most publicly pronounced.[42] But catastrophe is of course not the only condition through which emotions can be politically influential. Emotions play a central role at all times.

Conceptualizing emotions alongside the politics of representation in this manner is therefore profitable in two distinct ways. First, it provides a promising starting point for international relations-based emotions scholars seeking to bridge the complex conceptual divide between individual and collective (public) emotions; and second, and important for international relations scholars more generally, it adds to existing contributions that underline the instrumental role representations play in creating the social meanings on which international relations are based.[43]

In sum, a focus on representations underlines that emotions play a crucial role in producing the meanings that are key to the constitution (and reconstitution) of political perceptions, policies, actions and actors, whilst simultaneously providing an object for scholarly analysis into the processes through which emotions are imbued within international relations.

Emotions, power and world politics

Recognizing the centrality of representations to understanding the collective dynamics of emotion consequently enables us to consider

Sacha Bem (eds.) *Emotions and Beliefs: How Feelings Influence Thoughts* (Cambridge: Cambridge University Press, 2000), pp. 1–9; Mercer, "Emotional Beliefs," 2.

42 Crawford, "The Passion of World Politics," 130; Ross, "Coming in From the Cold," 211–214; Zehfuss, *Wounds of Memory*, pp. 240–242.

43 See footnote 38.

how emotions are implicated in the play of power. Indeed, since emotions and emotional responses are inevitably produced by the arrangement of signs and codes (concealed within forms of representation), it becomes clear that emotions can be produced in ways that serve particular entrenched interests. While this kind of "production" of emotions may be an intentional strategy, the conscious (political) manipulation of emotions is not my primary argument. Nor is it necessarily the case. More to the point is the recognition that while representations provide the mediums through which emotions can be shared, they can at the same time be sites of power through which emotions and emotional meanings are articulated (and also potentially rearticulated) and prioritized.

To reiterate, power in this sense is not intended to imply the traditional international relations sense, in terms of the instrumental "hard" (military, force-based) or "soft" (economic or otherwise) forms of coercion. Rather, it is power in the Foucauldian sense, which shifts away from the analysis of strong-arming actors and institutions toward the idea that "power is everywhere."[44] Power is diffused in the knowledge, discourses and "regimes of truth" that have been developed over time through the media, politics, education and so on. The element of power per se then emerges from the notion that such discourses and truths consequently inform perceptions and set the parameters of what constitutes appropriate behavior in particular sociocultural contexts.

Numerous international relations scholars have of course now undertaken Foucauldian and similar deconstructionist analyses of world politics, although to date few if any have done so in relation to the politics of emotion. Of those who do, very few take emotions as the primary object of their scholarly analysis.[45]

Within the social sciences, it is sociologists and anthropologists that have shown most interest in understanding the role that social order and thus power play in the emergence of emotions. While such

[44] Michel Foucault, *History of Sexuality: The Will to Knowledge* (London: Penguin, 1998), p. 63.

[45] Work by Jenny Edkins, Karin Fierke and Maja Zehfuss incorporates emotion from such a perspective and is helpful in setting the agenda for further studies that situate emotions at the center of analysis. Recent article-length inquiries that have questioned the relationship between emotion, affect and power include: Simon Koschut, "Emotional (Security) Communities: The Significance of Emotions Norms in Inter-Allied Conflict Management," *Review of International Studies*, 40.3 (2014), 533–558; Solomon, "The Affective Underpinnings of Soft Power."

contributions are diverse in scope and focus, their emphasis on the social and cultural aspects of emotion have led broadly to studies that suggest that power relations play a key role in determining what can, cannot, should or even must be said about the self and one's emotions. They take prevailing social discourses as their mode for analyzing emotions, showing not only how such discourses are inseparable from changing power relations in social life but also how emotions are both implicated in the maintenance of, as well as produced as a consequence of, the discourses on which such power relations (and attendant social hierarchies) are based.[46] Rom Harré, for instance, famously argues that "local moral orders" produce emotional cultures that dictate appropriate affective responses to certain stimuli.[47] Arguments concerning the social construction of emotions are in this view taken a step further; emotional responses are considered at least in part a response to how individuals are expected to feel in particular circumstances. Arlie Russell Hochschild's well-known analysis additionally suggests that emotions are governed by local "feeling rules," which are essentially the normative expectations of how to feel in different social contexts.[48] Such rules determine how individuals should feel at, say, the birth of a child, the death of a grandparent, one's university graduation, confrontation with a cancer diagnosis and so on – all the way

[46] See, for instance, Lila Abu-Lughod and Catherine A. Lutz, "Introduction: Emotion, Discourse, and the Politics of Everyday Life," in Catherine A. Lutz and Lila Abu-Lughod (eds.), *Language and the Politics of Emotion* (Cambridge: Cambridge University Press, 1990), pp. 1–23; Maruška Svašek, "Introduction: Emotions in Anthropology," in Kay Milton and Maruška Svašek (eds.), *Mixed Emotions: Anthropological Studies in Feeling* (Oxford: Berg, 2005), pp. 1–24.

[47] Harré, *The Social Construction of Emotions*, p. 6. In a similar vein on the definition and development of "emotional regimes" that bind communities, see also William Reddy, *The Navigation of Feeling: A Framework for the History of Emotions* (Cambridge: Cambridge University Press, 2001), pp. 124–126, 129, 330–333. Almost three decades ago Peter N. Stearns and Carol Z. Stearns also put forward the notion of "emotionology," which also implies that "the attitudes or standards of a society" legitimize what constitutes appropriate emotional expression. See their "Emotionology: Clarifying the History of Emotions and Emotional Standards," *American Historical Review*, 90.4 (1985), 813–836.

[48] Arlie Russell Hochschild, "Emotion Work, Feeling Rules and Social Structure," *American Journal of Sociology*, 85.3 (1979), 551–575; Arlie Russell Hochschild, *The Managed Heart: The Commercialization of Human Feeling* (Berkeley: University of California Press, 1983).

through, of course, to how one experiences and should feel for various representations of suffering and trauma. Hence, just as Foucault said power relations create sexuality and its disciplining, local social power structures too can create discourses that constitute emotions and emotionality.

Recent studies have sought to further underscore the political and more specific communal implications of this line of argument. Cultural theorist Sara Ahmed and historian Barbara Rosenwein forward different yet equally telling inquiries into the linkages between emotions, social structure and community.[49] For Ahmed, communities – particularly national communities – are upheld through such rules to the extent that such regimes are constitutive of an "affective economy."[50] Significant here, like cultural anthropologists before Ahmed, is an understanding of particular emotions as dependent upon social norms for their existence and circulation. In the same vein as Lutz contends that "[t]he meaning of emotion is sensitive to the context, and particularly the social relations, within which its use occurs,"[51] Ahmed clarifies that "emotions do things, and they align individuals with communities – or bodily space with social space – through the very intensity of their attachments."[52] In examining affective economies and how particular emotions circulate and become attached to particular people and objects, Ahmed examines how various emotions (such as fear) and norms concerning boundaries of citizenship are mutually constitutive. "Citizenship works as a way to police the boundaries of neighbourhoods," she argues, which for her means that the affective attachments are themselves built into the "values, truths and norms" through which the respective society is governed.[53] For Ahmed, such relativistic yet normative social prescriptions shape communal attachments and identity, in turn influencing prevailing emotional (and in turn political) responses to issues that challenge boundaries of citizenship and responsibility, such as refugees and terrorism.

[49] Sara Ahmed, *The Cultural Politics of Emotion* (Edinburgh: Edinburgh University Press, 2004); Barbara H. Rosenwein, *Emotional Communities in the Early Middle Ages* (Ithaca: Cornell University Press, 2006).
[50] Sara Ahmed, "Affective Economies," *Social Text*, 79.2 (2004), 117–139.
[51] Lutz, *Unnatural Emotions*, p. 58.
[52] Ahmed, "Affective Economies," 119.
[53] Ahmed, "Affective Economies," 134.

Historical inquiries such as that of Rosenwein come to similar conclusions, albeit taking a different route to arrive there. Stressing the social and relational nature of emotions, Rosenwein proposes that throughout history people have lived in "emotional communities": "groups in which people adhere to the same norms of emotional expression and value," which are "created and reinforced by ideologies, teachings and common presuppositions."[54] Rosenwein continues to stress that this Foucauldian social disciplining of emotions has a regulatory function that both shapes conventions of feeling in specific circumstances and paradoxically provides for fissures of dissent through which people can emotionally adapt.[55] Emotions are in this sense a key part of our perpetually changing social history. William Reddy's concept of "emotives" is also poignant in this respect. Emotives can be conceived of as the conscious external expression of emotions, which is importantly a performative act through which emotions are shaped.[56] The links to power here for Reddy are clear:

> If we conceive of community conventions as stipulating styles of emotional control that exploit the capacity of emotives to shape emotions, then power, politics, and liberation regain their meaning. Emotional control is the real site of the exercise of power: politics is just a process of determining who must repress as illegitimate, who must foreground as valuable, the feelings and desires that come up for them in given contexts and relationships.[57]

In this understanding, emotions and emotionality therefore function to position individuals within structures of domination and relations of power.[58] And while not ruling out the prospect of communities' ability to emotionally change, it does stress the inextricable and

[54] Rosenwein, *Emotional Communities in the Early Middle Ages*, pp. 2, 25.
[55] Rosenwein, *Emotional Communities in the Early Middle Ages*, pp. 18–25, 197–200.
[56] William M. Reddy, "Against Constructionism: The Historical Ethnography of Emotions," *Current Anthropology*, 38.3 (1997), 327–351.
[57] Reddy, "Against Constructionism," 335.
[58] See also Alison M. Jaggar's concept of "emotional hegemony" in her "Love and Knowledge: Emotion in Feminist Epistemology," in Alison M. Jaggar and Susan R. Bordo, *Gender/Body/Knowledge: Feminist Reconstructions of Being and Knowing* (New Brunswick, NJ: Rutgers University Press, 1989), pp. 145–171.

"extensive" role that power plays even when it comes to such communal transformation.[59]

While the push to examine emotions in relation to discourse and the play of social power is not without critics,[60] I suggest that it provides a useful starting place for considering the convergence between emotions and world politics. Significantly, it adds a crucial dimension to existing theoretical discussions by providing a framework for understanding how emotions can undergird – that is, limit and as well as potentially transform – prevailing social, political and communal structures, from the local, the nation-state and the global.

While today the nation-state is certainly not the only form of community existing in world politics, its dominance does provide a useful example to flesh out the intersection of emotions, power and how together they help to configure political communities. Indeed, since entrenched social interests and emotions are to some extent mutually constitutive, and since the interests of nation-state to a considerable degree bind identity and community, must emotions (of belonging and associated responsibility) be adhered within – and potentially determined by – conceptions of national community?

Examining once again the linkages between media representations and prevailing political discourses of the Bali bombing demonstrates how the confluence of emotion and prevailing social structures (and thus power) can shape political agency and community. Textual and pictorial representations of the event and its aftermath produced a range of meanings associated with national trauma: through popular discourse the bombing was depicted to have struck at the core of the Australian national community, its values and its way of life, yet to have also simultaneously summoned an incredible collective strength and communal resilience. Discourses associated with notions of collective shock, grief, anger, fear and insecurity consequently prevailed – and then soon after gave way to those tinged with the antagonism of retribution and revenge. These and other emotional discourses and meanings situate the bombing as an event damaging traditional power structures of the nation-state, and while the fact of the tragedy

[59] Reddy, "Against Constructionism," 333.

[60] The emphasis on studying emotion in relation to discourse and power has to some degree been met with the counter-emphasis on studying emotion as an embodied, sensory and affective experience. I examined conceptions as well as some critiques of emotion as a bodily experience in Chapter 2.

challenges sovereign power such meanings then in turn reinstate the very power that is disrupted.[61] Simply put, emotional renderings of representations strengthened preexisting sovereign interests by guiding individual emotions in ways that promote an understanding of, and reckoning with, a collective trauma. Dominant representations produced emotional discourses and meanings that remade community and restored political control along national lines.

In international relations, discourses of fear and associated emotions (such as anxiety) have been of course largely singled out as crucial aspects of the discursive practices that maintain the sovereign power of the nation-state. Like the situation following the Bali bombing, such discourses tend to come from top-down efforts aimed at restoring order and cultivating affective support for ensuing political policies.[62] But representations of such events – often trauma, and particularly politically motivated violence – tend to promote antagonistic political affiliations and allegiances. In the push to overcome uncertainty and restore order after violence and its trauma, communities become centered around disingenuous inside/outside dichotomies.[63] Energies and resources are spent keeping perceived "dangers" at bay. Defensive, militaristic security policies are frequently privileged. Hence the emotions and in turn the solidarity that are generated after trauma can reinstate a conservative, insular vision of political community. Established, often stereotypical and exclusionary boundaries of identity and political community – whether these are racial, ethnic or those of a nation-state – may be reinforced.

While the fear and insecurity associated with representations of the Bali bombing can be interpreted to have been both partially produced by and also affirming of power structures traditional to the nation-state, defining the same processes after the Southeast Asian

[61] See Jenny Edkins, "Forget Trauma? Responses to September 11," *International Relations*, 16.2 (2002), 243–256; Kate Schick, "Acting Out and Working Through: Trauma and (In)Security," *Review of International Studies*, 37.4 (2011), 1837–1855, at 1838.

[62] Jack Holland and Ty Solomon examine such efforts in the context of the US garnering public support for military action after 9/11. See Jack Holland and Ty Solomon, "Affect is What States Make of It: Articulating Everyday Experiences of 9/11," *Critical Studies on Security*, 2.3 (2014), 262–277.

[63] See R. B. J Walker, *Inside/Outside: International Relations as Political Theory* (Cambridge: Cambridge University Press, 1993).

tsunami is not nearly so clear-cut. Indeed, representations and ensuing solidarity discourses of the Southeast Asian tsunami could be read in one of three ways: as temporally transgressing national boundaries (and thus state power); at once affirming the very emotional cultures that bind national community (thus keeping with the state as the locus of power); and finally, as sites of resistance and contestation that tug bit-by-bit at communitarian conceptions of self/other, community/responsibility and work toward breaking down notions of "us" and "them" through long-term change (thus part of a long-term process that erodes state power and autonomy).

Consider first the idea that the response to the tsunami reflects a fundamental transformation or redescription of community in world politics. Representations of the tsunami and subsequent emotional discourses and meanings transgressed the nationally bounded sentiments that tend to delimit community as well as coordinated international action. It would seem, in other words, that dominant conceptions of power – in the form of the predominance of the sovereign state and concomitant form of national community – were momentarily subverted. And perhaps in some ways they were. But then consider – and second – the types of ethical issues and questions that my reading of dominant tsunami imagery raises. Yes, Western donors gave, but they did so prompted by essentialized notions of the developing world. The developing world was depicted as passive, vulnerable and needy, thereby producing disingenuous stereotypes that tap into the kind of "common sense"[64] (historically conditioned) pity with which the West so often approaches non-Western disaster. In this sense, power was not subverted but, rather, prevailing constellations of Western power and autonomy were again reinforced. This is to say that while subsequent discourses of pity, sympathy and possibly compassion no doubt abetted the constitution of the transnational aid community, at the same time they also served to reinforce boundaries of identity and community (and privilege) in the West. Complicit in this critique is the additional notion that after the tsunami wealthy nations responded so swiftly and so generously not simply because of humanitarian concerns, but moreover because of an assessment of classic realpolitik: being perceived as generous has now too become

[64] Keith Tester, *Humanitarianism and Modern Culture* (University Park: Pennsylvania State University Press, 2010), p. ix.

part of the national interest.[65] Charitable, humanitarian giving thus becomes a medium to celebrate a national character and image.[66] It consolidates the boundaries of the state. So, in terms of power perhaps very little was really changed.

The third reading is the most optimistic, however. Following sociocultural constitutive and discursive accounts of emotion, it can also be argued that the kind of emotional receptivity witnessed after the tsunami is precisely what is required in order to open up and potentially reshape emotional attachments to others. The emotions evoked in response to witnessing the tsunami's devastation through imagery may as such play a small part in a longer-term project of eroding and transforming existing linkages between emotions, power and community in world politics. Indeed, I argue that the nonmaterial and continually emerging affective dimensions of social life may be part of what is key to moving beyond, or at minimum recognizing, the multiple, shifting, overlapping forms of community in world politics.

Even if not as altruistic in motivations as it appears at first glance, the transnational community mobilized after the tsunami did nonetheless disrupt how individuals and governments consider their commitments. Importantly, representations of the tsunami opened individuals – particularly distant audiences in the West – to others in a manner that worked toward empathetic engagements with the others' trauma. Such empathy may be the key to breaking down boundaries where necessary; it may be crucial in cultivating the "transformation of community"[67] that is required for nation-states to come together around pivotal instances of suffering in world politics, not only when

[65] David Kennedy, *The Dark Side of Virtue: Reassessing International Humanitarianism* (Princeton: Princeton University Press, 2004), p. xvii; Brent Steele, *Defacing Power: The Aesthetics of Insecurity in Global Politics* (University of Michigan Press, 2010), p. 94.

[66] See Brad West and Ruthie O'Reilly, "National Humanitarianism and the 2004 Indian Ocean Tsunami," *Journal of Sociology* (OnlineFirst, 2014).

[67] Andrew Linklater, *The Transformation of Political Community: Ethical Foundations of a Post-Westphalian Era* (Cambridge: Polity, 1998). On the potentials and limits of empathy in the global community, see Jill Bennett, "The Limits of Empathy and the Global Politics of Belonging," in Judith Greenberg (ed.), *Trauma At Home: After 9/11* (Lincoln and London: University of Nebraska Press, 2003), esp. pp. 132–138; Neta Crawford, "Institutionalizing Passion in World Politics: Fear and Empathy," *International Theory*, 6.3 (2014), 535–557.

spontaneous, crippling disasters such as the tsunami strike, but also during times when human hardship and trauma are caused incrementally. Significantly, too, such compassionate, potentially empathetic emotional configurations may be critical markers of changes in the underlying power hierarchies that structure (in this case global) social relations.[68]

It is much in this light that my third and final empirical inquiry enters the picture. With this appreciation that emotions shift and change and can help to disrupt prevailing social orders, I examined the possibility and processes involved with actively procuring lasting emotional and communal transformation. I focused specifically on how representational practices can help to unsettle destructive emotional patterns that prevail in communities that have endured extensive or prolonged historical trauma. Of significance here, I argued, is a need for communities to consciously and fully grieve trauma: individuals and community as a whole need time and space to properly mourn injury and loss and, critically, to work through painful emotions and memories. But arriving at this kind of sociotherapeutic "grief" is not an organic undertaking. As I as well as others before me show, the reflex reaction of political elites to trauma is to "secure through a failure to secure,"[69] to use the very site of injury and uncertainty as a point to securitize and reassert sovereign authority and control. Of course, therein lies the dilemma: it is precisely in doing this – in "rushing" to memorialize and "forget" trauma and its insecurity[70] – that emotions such as anxiety, fear, resentment and humiliation prevail and can become collectively entrenched. This is why South Africa and the Truth and Reconciliation Commission (TRC) presented an insightful study. The processes employed by the TRC illuminate the power of alternative narratives in diffusing conflict and helping to transform collective emotions. It shows that by acknowledging, mourning and taking time to reflect upon historical trauma, individuals and communities divided

[68] Mika Aatola also discusses humanitarian mobilizations as potential places for a redescription of power in global politics. See Mika Aaltola, *Western Spectacle of Governance and the Emergence of Humanitarian World Politics* (New York: Palgrave, 2009), p. 15.

[69] Charlotte Heath-Kelly, "Securing Through a Failure to Secure? The Ambiguity of Resilience at the Bombsite," *Security Dialogue* 46.1 (2015), 69–85.

[70] Edkins, "Forget Trauma?"; Jenny Edkins, "The Rush to Memory and the Rhetoric of War," *Journal of Political and Military Sociology*, 31.2 (2003), 231–250.

by pain can begin to work through divisive emotions and attempt to rebuild communal attachments in a more harmonious and inclusive manner.

Emotions – and, in particular, emotions that either move communities away from practices of exclusion during times of human need, or away from antagonisms and violence – can therefore in this reading be reflected upon as sites of contestation and resistance. Or to put it more accurately, emotions can help to fuel or motivate practices of collective resistance and political protest, and in turn help to constitute the kinds of transformative forms of political agency needed to cultivate more inclusive forms of community. Key once again here – like after the Southeast Asian tsunami, and like the attempts to acknowledge and grieve South Africa's legacy of historical trauma – are the processes involved with the representation and interpretation of political issues and phenomena. Representations and ensuing wider emotional discourses can not only affirm social power structures but can also challenge prevailing power structures and in doing so act as forms of communal dissent – and, crucially, transformation. In this respect, global media and communication technologies would play a key role in mediating beyond the status quo. They would be responsible for understandings that shift forms of feeling that maintain orthodox boundaries toward emotions that enable engagements between others that can in turn lead to alternative, emergent communities.

The emotional roots of such transformative political engagements are, however, not easily pinned down. Nor can they be easily – or readily – procured. There is no "quick fix" to how we may activate emotions or cultivate broader "affective energies" in ways that promote positive change.[71] Even harnessing the transformative potentials of trauma through a politics of grief, as I suggest, is a difficult process, which often must balance the need to work through painful emotions and memories with the need for mechanisms of formal apology or justice. But what is clear is that representations play a critical role in prompting particular emotive, political discourses, which can then help to make forms of collective identity, agency and community possible. Being attentive to this may in turn promote a critical ethos that promotes challenging the status quo through representations that

[71] Andrew A. G. Ross, *Affective States: Rethinking Passion in World Politics*, PhD Dissertation, Johns Hopkins University, 2005, p. 10.

encourage us to rethink worldviews and corresponding conceptions of community, security and responsibility.

Emotional cultures in world politics

While a type of empathetic emotional engagement – as well as the ensuing "boundless" type of community – may still be a distant ideal, the communal distinctions I have drawn so far do suggest the presence of what I call "emotional cultures" in international relations. In this final section, I conclude by considering the meaning and significance of such cultures, focusing on how the notion of emotional cultures may help scholars to better understand the limits and potentials of community in international relations, and by extension how emotions and emotionality can play a pivotal role in constituting various forms of action and interaction in world politics.

Thus far, the term emotional cultures has only largely gained broad salience in literature on organizational behavior and the sociology of management.[72] It is generally used to describe the culture of smaller (or sometimes not so small) enterprises and how sensitive, responsive and "emotionally intelligent" organizations are for those who comprise them. However, I suggest that the term may be useful in a broader social and political sense: it can help us to appreciate the ebbs and flows of emotions and emotionality in world politics.

The term "emotional cultures" is suggestive of the particular context-bound conditions through which emotions are continually constituted and how, as such, emotional dispositions help to define the core values, principles, behavioral norms and moral standards of respective societies. Put differently, a particular "emotional culture" implies the emotional (or broader affective) conditions that help to regulate and shape interaction within societies and their politics. So in this sense it is similar to Hochschild's work on "feeling rules."

[72] For example, Sigal G. Barsade and Donald E. Gibson, "Why Does Affect Matter in Organizations?" *Academy of Management Perspectives*, 21.1 (2007), 36–59; Stephen Fineman, "Organizations as Emotional Arenas," in Stephen Fineman (ed.), *Emotion in Organizations* (Thousand Oaks, CA: Sage, 1993), pp. 9–35; Nicky James, "Emotional Labour: Skill and Work in the Social Regulation of Feelings," *The Sociological Review*, 37.1 (1989), 15–42; John Van Maanen and Gideon Kunda, "'Real Feelings': Emotional Expression and Organizational Culture," *Research in Organizational Behavior*, 11 (1989), 43–103.

Established through tradition and time – and by no means static – cultures of emotion influence how individuals and communities interpret political issues and events. Think of emotional cultures as the historical by-product of what Ross calls "affective energies": cultivated and affirmed over time, affective energies, which incorporate feelings, concrete emotions and even moods and sentiments, circulate and can come to constitute a widely held emotional regime.[73] Such emotional cultures in turn influence how, and indeed whether, a community responds to particular political issues and events; certainly such a culture would partially shape responses to near or distant trauma. Indeed, the idea of an emotional culture incorporates combined classic and discursive constructionist understandings of emotion in order to appreciate how the sociocultural and historical constitution of emotions paradoxically binds but can also help to change acceptable social behaviors and, by extension, political standpoints and policies.

Various intersecting, interconnecting and at times incommensurable or contradictory emotional cultures are, I argue, at play in everyday international relations. Visible so far through my analysis are at least two, although in examining inroads into emotionally instigated political change I see an inkling of three. The first consists of the emotional conditions through which the nation-state is created and reproduced. Implicated here is a wide spectrum of emotions, from the "warm" feelings (for e.g. of love) associated with nationalism, to the anxiety and fear that has been found to position a protective and insular nation-state in opposition to a dangerous and threatening world outside. The second then involves emotions typically associated with humanitarian actions beyond state borders: the pity, sympathy, compassion and possible empathy with which we engage with others' suffering and trauma. But these two cultures are intertwined: just as fear and insecurity are emotional mechanisms (and part of a wider cultivated culture) formed over time as reflex attempts to protect us, it is pity and sympathy that too keep us looking in. Pity and sympathy for distant suffering allow us to feel sorry, maybe to give, and then to silently look away. These cultures have, I suggest, come to constitute and bind identity and community and associated privilege in the West. Even though such emotions are directed toward somebody or toward a particular political phenomena or issue, they are more about – that

[73] Ross, *Mixed Emotions*.

is, they are indicative and constitutive of – Western dispositions, Western subjectivities. They (partially) define Western identities and ensuing engagements with others. In this scenario, these seemingly widespread emotional dispositions – and ensuing cultures – paradoxically both enable and limit engagements with others. For instance – and with respect to the former – such emotions do frequently help to mobilize humanitarian relief actions, which go on to make significant achievements in contributing to the alleviation of distant suffering.[74] However – and with respect to latter – it is the very same emotions that seem to have helped create a more entrenched culture that fosters an indifference or an inability to respond – or an uncertainty about how to respond – to others' suffering. This not compassion fatigue, but a far deeper form of despondence.

It is through such cultures, therefore, that emotions of sympathy, pity and compassion just as much as fear, anxiety and anger frame the artificial – or "imagined"[75]– construction of political identity and community in international relations.

But this is not to argue that particular emotional cultures will prevail permanently. Neither is it to suggest that forms of "emotional dissent" do not exist within such cultures. As I hope to have conveyed, emotional cultures are conditional: they can and would shift and change together with changes in predominant societal expectations and values. Moreover, due to the rapid progress of globalization and in particular the speed and transnational nature of contemporary communications, it could also be seen that the emotional cultures that bind and support communities and their attitudes and behaviors are indeed destined to change, eventually, in one way or another, in what may seem either for better or for worse.

This is one reason why I have steered my inquiry toward emergent possibilities for cultivating potentially transformative emotional cultures. A more peaceful world politics depends upon greater recognition of the centrality and importance of emotions in shaping communities and their politics. Understanding that emotions lie, often inaudibly,

[74] See also Michael Barnett, *The Empire of Humanity: A History of Humanitarianism* (Ithaca: Cornell University Press, 2011), pp. 224–226; Aaltola, *Western Spectacle of Governance and the Emergence of Humanitarian World Politics*, pp. 15–38.

[75] Benedict Anderson, *Imagined Communities: Reflections on the Origins and Spread of Nationalism* (London and New York: Verso, 2006 [1983]).

at the core of all human (and thus political) interaction enables us to reflect upon the constitutive role of feelings, and why is it that we feel in the ways that we do. And, importantly, we can contemplate and ask how might our others feel and why. Emotions tell us too much to be left out of the political picture. In stark contrast to how they were once perceived, emotions offer unique insight into how political rationality is constructed. An appreciation of how emotions – and socially constituted emotional cultures – function in different ways to perform and reconstitute identities and communities also offers endless possibilities for progressive social change. Just as emotions can only enhance our explanatory understanding, they can also be part of political solutions: they can help us to unmuddle situations – of conflict and crisis – that seem intractable and they provide a key piece of the puzzle when considering how thorny problems may be best addressed.

Understanding both the constitution and influence of such emotional cultures is therefore important as it points to significant potentials associated with emotions and emotionality in world politics. Foremost, appreciating how particular widely held social emotional dispositions are cultivated, sustained and indeed can shift and change helps us to understand the affective dimensions of a broad range of political behaviors and also how particular communities become attached and committed to the types of political actions and policies that they do. Key here is not merely that emotional cultures help to bind political community and ensuing notions of solidarity and responsibility. The prevalence of such cultures (together with the potentials for such cultures to change) has implications for a wide range of empirical and normative debates in world politics. A more complete understanding of a range of scholarly and practical endeavors in international relations ensues, from understanding the motives and behaviors of nation-states and other key actors in international relations, inquiries into terrorism, international security, alliance building and cooperation to engagements with more normative issues, such as humanitarian intervention, international justice and the politics of reconciliation.

Considering emotional cultures as a shifting social and political affective phenomenon may also help us to appreciate the somewhat changing landscape of world politics. More and more it can be seen that transnational media has the capacity to emotionally empower and mobilize communities – such as those formed along ethnic, religious or humanitarian lines – that transgress sovereign power. These communities may not be formally legitimized and they may be temporary; however, the emotional cultures that bind them can be powerful motivators underpinning shared meanings, beliefs, identities and actions. The transnational potentials of emotions and for the constitution of emotional cultures beyond the boundaries of the nation-state therefore present distinct potentials. Specifically, respective emotional cultures could play a critical role in enabling and limiting various differently motivated, emergent transnational communities and ensuing social and political priorities. An attentiveness to how such possibilities emerge – through the representational practices that possess power to give meaning and value to the world, and in doing so shape (and reshape) corresponding cultures of emotion – may thus be critical to creating less exclusionary communities and more reflective, compassionate local and global political practices.

Bibliography

Aaltola, Mika, *Western Spectacle of Governance and the Emergence of Humanitarian World Politics* (New York: Palgrave, 2009).

Abu-Lughod, Lila and Catherine A. Lutz, "Introduction: Emotion, Discourse and the Politics of Everyday Life," in Catherine A. Lutz and Lila Abu-Lughod (eds.), *Language and the Politics of Emotion*, pp. 1–23 (Cambridge: Cambridge University Press, 1990).

Agamben, Giorgio, *Homo Sacer: Sovereign Power and Bare Life*, trans. Daniel Heller-Roazen (Stanford: Stanford University Press, 1998).

Means Without Ends, trans. Vincenzo Binetti and Cesare Casarino (Minneapolis: University of Minnesota Press, 2000).

Åhäll, Linda and Thomas A. Gregory (eds.), "Security, Emotions, Affect," *Critical Studies on Security*, 1.1 (2013), 117–140.

Ahmed, Sara, *The Cultural Politics of Emotion* (Edinburgh: Edinburgh University Press, 2004).

"Affective Economies," *Social Text*, 79.2 (2004), 117–139.

Alcoff, Linda and Laura Gray, "Survivor Discourse: Transgression or Recuperation?" *Signs: Journal of Women in Culture and Society*, 18.2 (1993), 260–290.

Alexander, Jeffrey C., *Trauma: A Social Theory* (Cambridge: Polity, 2012).

"Toward a Theory of Cultural Trauma," in Jeffrey C. Alexander, Ron Eyerman, Bernard Gieson, Neil J. Smelser and Piotr Sztompka (eds.), *Cultural Trauma and Collective Identity*, pp. 1–30 (Berkeley: University of California Press, 2004).

Alexander, Jeffrey C., Ron Eyerman, Bernard Gieson, Neil J. Smelser and Piotr Sztompka, *Cultural Trauma and Collective Identity* (Berkeley: University of California Press, 2004).

Anderson, Benedict, *Imagined Communities: Reflections on the Origins and Spread of Nationalism* (London: Verso, 1991).

Antze, Paul and Michael Lambek (eds.), *Tense Past: Cultural Essays in Trauma and Memory* (London: Routledge, 1996).

Aradau, Claudia, "The Perverse Politics of Four-Letter Words: Risk and Pity in the Securitisation of Human Trafficking," *Millennium: Journal of International Studies*, 33.2 (2004), 251–277.

Arendt, Hannah, *On Revolution* (London: Penguin, 1990 [1963]).

Arnold, Wayne, "At the Epicenter, Tales of Death And of Stubborn Fights for Life," *The New York Times*, 29 December 2004, p. 1.

"Australians United Share the Sorrow of Bali," *The Australian*, 19 October 2002, p. 18.

Baer, Ulrich, *Spectral Evidence: The Photography of Trauma* (Cambridge, MA: The MIT Press, 2002).

Bal, Mieke, Jonathon Crewe and Leo Spitzer (eds.), *Acts of Memory: Cultural Recall in the Present* (Hanover: University Press of New England, 1999).

Ball, Michael S. and Gregory W.H. Smith, *Analyzing Visual Data*, Qualitative Research Methods Series, Vol. *24* (Newbury Park: Sage, 1992).

Balzacq, Thierry and Robert Jervis, "Logics of Mind and International System: A Journey with Robert Jervis," *Review of International Studies*, 30.4 (2004), 559–582.

Barbalet, Jack M., *Emotion, Social Theory and Social Structure: A Macrosociological Approach* (Cambridge: Cambridge University Press, 2001).

Barbalet, Jack M. (ed.), *Emotions and Sociology* (Oxford: Blackwell, 2002).

Barmé, Geremie R., "To Screw Foreigners is Patriotic: China's Avant-Garde Nationalists," *The China Journal*, 34 (1995), 209–234.

Barnett, Michael, *The Empire of Humanity: A History of Humanitarianism* (Ithaca: Cornell University Press, 2011).

Barnett, Michael and Raymond Duvall, "Power in International Politics," *International Organization*, 59.1 (2005), 39–75.

Barnett, Michael and Thomas G. Weiss, *Humanitarianism Contested: Where Angels Fear to Tread* (Milton Park: Routledge, 2011).

Barsade, Sigal G., and Donald E. Gibson, "Why Does Affect Matter in Organizations?" *Academy of Management Perspectives*, 21.1 (2007), 36–59.

Barsalou, Lawrence W., "Grounded Cognition," *Annual Review of Psychology*, 59 (2008), 617–645.

Bar-Tal, Daniel, "From Intractable Conflict Through Conflict Resolution to Reconciliation: Psychological Analysis," *Political Psychology*, 21.1 (2000), 351–366.

Bar-Tal, Daniel, Eran Halperin and Joseph De Riveria, "Collective Emotions in Conflict Situations: Societal Implications," *Journal of Social Issues*, 63.2 (2007), 441–460.

Barthes, Roland, *Elements of Semiology*, trans. Annette Lavers and Colin Smith (New York: Farrar, Giroux and Strauss, 1967).

Image, Music, Text, trans. Stephen Heath (London: Fontana, 1977).

Batty, Nancy Ellen, "'We are the World, We are the Children': The Semiotics of Seduction in International Children's Relief Efforts," in Roderick

McGillis (ed.), *Voices of the Other: Children's Literature and the Postcolonial Context*, pp. 17–38 (New York: Routledge, 2000).
Bellamy, Christopher, *Knights in White Armour: The New Art of War and Peace* (London: Hutchinson, 1997).
Berger, John, *Ways of Seeing* (London: Penguin, 1972).
Berlant, Lauren, "The Subject of True Feeling: Pain, Privacy, Politics," in Jodi Dean (ed.), *Cultural Studies and Political Theory*, pp. 42–62 (Ithaca: Cornell University Press, 2000).
Bell, Duncan S. A., "Mythscapes: Memory, Mythology, and National Identity," *British Journal of Sociology*, 54.1 (2003), 63–81.
(ed.), *Memory, Trauma and World Politics: Reflections on the Relationship Between the Past and the Present* (Basingstoke: Palgrave Macmillan, 2006).
"Introduction: Memory, Trauma and World Politics," in Duncan S. A. Bell (ed.), *Memory, Trauma and World Politics: Reflections on the Relationship Between the Past and the Present*, pp. 1–29 (Basingstoke: Palgrave Macmillan, 2006).
Bendelow, Gillian and Simon J. Williams (eds.), *Emotions and Social Life: Critical Themes and Contemporary Issues* (London: Routledge, 1998).
Bennett, Jill, "The Limits of Empathy and the Global Politics of Belonging," in Judith Greenberg (ed.), *Trauma at Home: After 9/11*, pp. 132–138 (Lincoln and London: University of Nebraska, 2003).
Empathic Vision: Affect, Trauma and Contemporary Art (Stanford, CA: Stanford University Press, 2005).
Berezin, Mabel, "Emotions and Political Identity: Mobilizing Affection for the Polity," in Jeff Goodwin, James M. Jasper and Francesca Polletta (eds.), *Passionate Politics: Emotions and Social Movements*, pp. 83–98 (Chicago: University of Chicago Press, 2001).
"Secure States: Towards a Political Sociology of Emotion," in Jack M. Barbalet (ed.), *Emotions and Sociology*, pp. 33–52 (Oxford: Blackwell, 2002).
Bhabha, Homi, "The Other Question: Reconsidering the Stereotype in Colonial Discourse," *Screen*, 24.6 (1983), 18–36.
Bhatia, Michael V., "Fighting Words: Naming Terrorists, Bandits, Rebels and other Violent Actors," *Third World Quarterly*, 26.1 (2005), 5–22.
Bially Mattern, Janice, *Ordering International Politics: Identity, Crisis, and Representational Force* (New York: Routledge, 2005).
"Why 'Soft Power' Isn't So Soft: Representational Force and the Sociolinguistic Construction of Attraction in World Politics," *Millennium: Journal of International Studies*, 33.3 (2005), 583–612.

"A Practice Theory of Emotion for International Relations," in Emanuel Adler and Vincent Pouliot (eds.), *International Practices*, pp. 63–86 (Cambridge: Cambridge University Press, 2011).

"On Being Convinced: An Emotional Epistemology of International Relations," *International Theory*, 6.3 (2014), 589–594.

Biro, Matthew, "Representation and Event: Anselm Kiefer, Joseph Beuys, and the Memory of the Holocaust," *The Yale Journal of Criticism*, 16.1 (2003), 113–146.

Blackman, Lisa and Couze Venn (eds.), Special Issue on "Affect," *Body & Society*, 16.1 (2010), 7–230.

Blanchot, Maurice, *The Writing of Disaster*, trans. Ann Smock (Lincoln and London: University of Nebraska Press, 1995).

Bleiker, Roland, "Give it the Shade? Paul Celan and the Politics of Apolitical Poetry," *Political Studies*, 47.4 (1999), 661–676.

"The Aesthetic Turn in International Political Theory," *Millennium: Journal of International Studies*, 30.3 (2001), 503–539.

Aesthetics and World Politics (New York: Palgrave, 2009).

Bleiker, Roland and Emma Hutchison, "Fear No More: Emotions and World Politics," *Review of International Studies*, 34.1 (2008), 115–135.

Bleiker, Roland and Emma Hutchison (eds.), "Forum section on 'Emotions and World Politics'," *International Theory*, 6.3 (2014), 491–594.

Bleiker, Roland and Amy Kay, "Representing HIV/AIDS in Africa: Pluralist Photography and Local Empowerment," *International Studies Quarterly*, 51.1 (2007), 139–163.

Boltanski, Luc, *Distant Suffering: Morality, Media and Politics*, trans. Graham Burchell (Cambridge: Cambridge University Press, 1999).

Booth, Ken and Nicholas J. Wheeler, *The Security Dilemma: Fear, Cooperation, and Trust in World Politics* (Basingstoke: Palgrave Macmillan, 2007).

Booth, W. James, "Communities of Memory: On Identity, Memory, and Debt," *American Political Science Review*, 93.2 (1999), 249–263.

Boraine, Alex, *A Country Unmasked: Inside South Africa's Truth and Reconciliation Commission* (Oxford: Oxford University Press, 2001).

Bordo, Susan R., *Unbearable Weight: Feminism, Western Culture, and the Body* (Berkeley: University of California Press, 1994).

Boss, Pauline, *Ambiguous Loss: Learning to Live with Unresolved Grief* (Cambridge, MA: Harvard University Press, 1999).

Bouson, J. Brooks, *Quiet as It's Kept: Shame, Trauma and Race in the Novels of Toni Morrison* (Albany: State University of New York Press, 2000).

Bracken, Patrick J., *Trauma: Culture, Meaning and Philosophy* (London: Whurr, 2002).

Brassett, James, "Cosmopolitan Sentiments after 9/11? Trauma and the Politics of Vulnerability," *Journal of Critical Globalisation Studies*, 2 (2010), 12–29.

Trauma and Global Ethics: The Politics of Vulnerability, unpublished manuscript (University of Warwick).

Brassett, James and Nick Vaughan-Williams, "Governing Traumatic Events," *Alternatives: Local, Global, Political*, 37.3 (2012), 183–281.

(eds.), Special Issue on "Governing Traumatic Events," *Alternatives: Local, Global, Political*, 37.3 (2012), 180–281.

Brauman, Rony, "Global Media and the Myths of Humanitarian Relief: The Case of the 2004 Tsunami," in Richard Ashby Wilson and Richard D. Brown (eds.), *Humanitarianism and Suffering: The Mobilization of Empathy*, pp. 108–117 (New York: Cambridge University Press, 2009).

Brison, Susan J., *Aftermath: Violence and the Remaking of the Self* (Princeton: Princeton University Press, 2002).

Bronfen, Elisabeth, "Reality Check: Image Affects and Cultural Memory," *differences: A Journal of Feminist Cultural Studies*, 17.1 (2006), 20–46.

Brook, Donald, "On Non-Verbal Representation," *British Journal of Aesthetics*, 37.3 (1997), 232–245.

Bronfen, Elisabeth, "Reality Check: Image Affects and Cultural Memory," *differences: A Journal of Feminist Cultural Studies*, 17.1 (2006), 20–46.

Brown, Wendy, *States of Injury: Power and Freedom in Late Modernity* (Princeton: Princeton University Press, 1995).

"Wounded Attachments: Oppositional Political Attachments in Late Modern Democracy," *Political Theory*, 21.3 (1993), 390–410.

Bruner, Jerome, "The Narrative Construction of Reality," *Critical Inquiry*, 18.1 (1991), 1–21.

Brydon-Brown, Sarah, "Four Mates Drink in the Sari Bar, Moments Later Three of Them Are Dead," *The Australian*, 18 October 2002, p. 1.

Burke, Anthony, *Fear of Security: Australia's Invasion Anxiety*, 2nd edition (Port Melbourne: Cambridge University Press, 2008).

Burkitt, Ian, *Social Selves: Theories of the Social Formation of Personality* (London: Sage, 1991).

"Social Relationships and Emotions," *Sociology*, 31.1 (1997), 37–55.

"Powerful Emotions: Power, Government and Opposition in the 'War on Terror'," *Sociology*, 39.4 (2005), 679–695.

Burman, Erica, "Innocents Abroad: Western Fantasies of Childhood and the Iconography of Emergencies," *Disasters*, 18.3 (1994), 238–253.

Buruma, Ian, "The Joys and Perils of Victimhood," *New York Review of Books*, 46.6 (1999), 4–8.

Bush, George W, "You are either with us or against us," *CNN*, 6 November 2001.

Butler, Judith, "Performative Acts and Gender Constitution: An Essay in Phenomenology and Feminist Theory," *Theatre Journal*, 40.4 (1988), 519–531.

Precarious Life: The Powers of Mourning and Violence (London: Verso, 2004).

Giving an Account of Oneself: A Critique of Ethical Violence (New York: Fordham University Press, 2005).

Frames of War: When is Life Grievable? (London: Verso, 2008).

Calhoun, Craig, "Nationalism, Political Community and the Representation of Society; Or, Why Feeling at Home is not a Substitute for Personal Space," *European Journal of Social Theory*, 2.2 (1999), 217–231.

Callahan, William A., "National Insecurities: Humiliation, Salvation, and Chinese Nationalism," *Alternatives: Local, Global, Political*, 29.2 (2004), 199–218.

"How to Understand China: the Dangers and Opportunities of Being a Rising Power," *Review of International Studies*, 31 (2005), 701–714.

"History, Identity, and Security: Producing and Consuming Nationalism in China," *Critical Asian Studies*, 38.2 (2006), 179–208.

"Trauma and Community: The Visual Politics of Chinese Nationalism and Sino-Japanese Relations," *Theory and Event*, 10.4 (2007).

China: The Pessoptimist Nation (Oxford: Oxford University Press, 2010).

Cameron, Deborah, *Working with Spoken Discourse* (London: Sage, 2001).

Campbell, David, *National Deconstruction: Violence, Identity, and Justice in Bosnia* (Minneapolis: University of Minnesota Press, 1998).

"MetaBosnia: Narratives of the Bosnian War," *Review of International Studies*, 24 (1998), 261–281.

Writing Security: United States Foreign Policy and the Politics of Identity, 2nd edition (Minneapolis: University of Minnesota Press, 1998).

"The Deterritorialization of Responsibility: Levinas, Derrida, and Ethics After the End of Philosophy," in David Campbell and Michael J. Shapiro (eds.), *Moral Spaces: Rethinking Ethics and World Politics*, pp. 29–56 (Minneapolis: University of Minnesota Press, 1999).

"Time is Broken: The Return of the Past in the Response to September 11," *Theory & Event*, 5.2 (2002).

"Atrocity, Memory, Photography: Imaging the Concentration Camps of Bosnia," Parts 1 and 2, *Journal of Human Rights*, 1.1/2 (2002), 1–33, 143–772.

"Horrific Blindness: Images of Death in Contemporary Media," *Journal for Cultural Research*, 8.1 (2004), 55–74.

"Geopolitics and Visuality: Sighting the Darfur Conflict," *Political Geography*, 26.4 (2007), 357–382.

Imaging Famine. Available at www.imaging-famine.org. Accessed February 8, 2015.

Campbell, David and Michael J. Shapiro (eds.), *Moral Spaces: Rethinking Ethics and World Politics* (Minneapolis: University of Minnesota Press, 1999).

Campbell, David and Michael J. Shapiro, "Guest Editor's Introduction," in David Campbell and Michael J. Shapiro (eds.), Special Issue on "Securitization, Militarization and Visual Culture in the Worlds of Post-9/11," *Security Dialogue*, 38. 2 (2007), 131–137.

Campbell, David and Michael J. Shapiro (eds.), Special Issue on "Securitization, Militarization and Visual Culture in the Worlds of Post-9/11," *Security Dialogue*, 38.2 (2007), 131–288.

Caruth, Cathy (ed.), *Trauma: Explorations in Memory* (Baltimore: Johns Hopkins University Press, 1995).

"Recapturing the Past: Introduction," in Cathy Caruth (ed.), *Trauma: Explorations in Memory*, pp. 151–157 (Baltimore: Johns Hopkins University Press, 1995).

Unclaimed Experience: Trauma, Narrative, History (Baltimore: Johns Hopkins University Press, 1996).

"Traumatic Awakenings," in Hent de Vries and Samuel Weber (eds.), *Violence, Identity, and Self-Determination*, pp. 208–222 (Stanford: Stanford University Press, 1997).

Cheng, Joseph Y. S., and Ngok, King-Lun, "The 2001 'Spy' Plan Incident Revisited: The Chinese Perspective," *The Chinese Journal of Political Science*, 9.1 (2004), 63–83.

Chouliaraki, Lilie, *The Spectatorship of Suffering* (London: Sage, 2006).

"The Aestheticization of Suffering on Television," *Visual Communication*, 5.3 (2006), 261–285.

"Mediation as Moral Education," *Media, Culture & Society*, 30.5 (2008), 831–847.

"Post-Humanitarianism: Humanitarian Communication Beyond a Politics of Pity," *International Journal of Cultural Studies*, 13.2 (2010), 107–126.

"The Theatricality of Humanitarianism: A Critique of Celebrity Advocacy," *Communication and Critical/Cultural Studies*, 9.1 (2012), 1–21.

The Ironic Spectator: Solidarity in the Age of Post-Humanitarianism (Cambridge: Polity, 2013).

Chouliaraki, Lilie and Norman Fairclough, *Discourse in Late Modernity: Rethinking Critical Discourse Analysis* (Edinburgh: Edinburgh University Press, 1999).

Chow, Rey, "Postmodern Automatoms," in Judith Butler and Joan W. Scott (eds.), *Feminists Theorize the Political*, pp. 101–117 (New York: Routledge, 1992).

Christie, Michael, "Flags Lowered as Australia Digests Its Own September 11," *Reuters News*, 15 October 2002.

Clark, Nancy L. and William H. Worger, *South Africa: The Rise and Fall of Apartheid*, 2nd edition (Harlow: Pearson, 2011).

Clore, Gerard L. and Jeffrey R. Huntsinger, "How the Object of Affect Guides Its Impact," *Emotion Review* 1.1 (2009), 39–54.

Clore, Gerard L. and Andrew Ortony, "Cognition in Emotion? Always, Sometimes or Never?" in Richard D. Lane and Lynn Nadel (eds.), *Cognitive Neuroscience of Emotion*, pp. 24–61 (New York: Oxford University Press, 2000).

Coan, James A., "Emergent Ghosts of the Emotion Machine," *Emotion Review*, 2.3 (2010), 274–285.

"What We Talk About When We Talk About Emotion," *Emotion Review*, 2.3 (2010), 292–293.

Cohen, Stanley, *States of Denial: Knowing About Atrocities and Suffering* (Cambridge: Polity, 1993).

Colvin, Christopher J., "'Brothers and Sisters, Do Not Be Afraid of Me': Trauma, History and the Therapeutic Imagination in the New South Africa," in Katharine Hodgkin and Susannah Radstone (eds.), *Contested Pasts: The Politics of Memory*, pp. 153–167 (London and New York: Routledge).

Connerton, Paul, *How Societies Remember* (Cambridge: Cambridge University Press, 1989).

Connolly, William E., *Why I Am Not A Secularist* (Minneapolis: University of Minnesota Press, 1999).

"Suffering, Justice, and the Politics of Becoming," in David Campbell and Michael J. Shapiro (eds.), *Moral Spaces: Rethinking Ethics and World Politics*, pp. 125–153 (Minneapolis: University of Minnesota Press, 1999).

Identity|Difference: Democratic Negotiations of Political Paradox, 2nd edition (Minneapolis: University of Minnesota Press, 2002).

Neuropolitics: Thinking, Culture, Speed (Minneapolis: University of Minnesota Press, 2002).

Conroy, John, *Unspeakable Acts, Ordinary People: The Dynamics of Torture* (Berkeley: University of California Press, 2000).

Constitution of the Republic of South Africa, "National Unity and Reconciliation," Act 200, 1993. Available at https://peaceaccords.nd.edu/site_media/media/accords/Constitution_of_South_Africa_Act_200_of_1993.pdf. Accessed July 30, 2014.

Cosgrave, John, *Synthesis Report: Expanded Summary. Joint Evaluation of the International Response to the Indian Ocean Tsunami* (London: Tsunami Evaluation Coalition, 2007).

Crane, Susan, "Writing the Individual Back into Collective Memory," *The American Historical Review*, 102.5 (1997), 1372–1385.
Crary, Jonathon, *Suspensions of Perception: Attention, Spectacle, and Modern Culture* (Cambridge, MA: MIT Press, 1999).
Crawford, Neta C., "The Passion of World Politics: Propositions on Emotions and Emotional Relationships," *International Security*, 24.4 (2000), 116–136.
"Emotions and International Security: *Cave! Hic Libido*," *Critical Studies on Security*, 1.1 (2013), 121–123.
"Institutionalizing Passion in World Politics: Fear and Empathy," *International Theory*, 6.3 (2014), 535–557.
Culbertson, Roberta, "Embodied Memory, Transcendence, and Telling: Recounting Trauma, Re-establishing Self," *New Literary History*, 26.1 (1995), 169–195.
Damasio, Antonio, *Descartes' Error: Emotion, Reason and the Human Brain* (London: Vintage, 2006 [1994]).
The Feeling of What Happens: Body and Emotion in the Making of Meaning (London: Vintage, 2000).
Darby, Philip, "Security, Spatiality and Social Suffering," *Alternatives: Global, Local, Political*, 31.4 (2006), 453–473.
Dauber, Cori, "Image as Argument: The Impact of Mogadishu on U.S. Military Intervention," *Armed Forces and Society*, 27.2 (2001), 205–229.
Dauphinée, Elizabeth, "The Politics of the Body in Pain: Reading the Ethics of Imagery," *Security Dialogue*, 38.2 (2007), 139–155.
D'Costa, Bina D., *The Gendered Construction of Nationalism: From Partition to Creation*, PhD Dissertation (Canberra: The Australian National University, 2003).
Dean, Carolyn J., "Empathy, Pornography, and Suffering," *differences: A Journal of Feminist and Cultural Studies*, 14.1 (2003), 88–124.
Dean, Jodi (ed.), *Cultural Studies and Political Theory* (Ithaca: Cornell University Press, 2000).
Debrix, François and Cynthia Weber (eds.), *Rituals of Mediation: International Politics and Social Meaning* (Minneapolis: University of Minnesota Press, 2003).
Delbo, Charlotte, *Auschwitz and After*, trans. Rosette C. Lamont (New Haven: Yale University Press, 1995).
Days and Memory, trans. Rosette C. Lamont (Malboro: Malboro Press, 1985).
Demertzis, Nicholas (ed.), *Emotions in Politics: The Affect Dimension in Political Tension* (Basingstoke: Palgrave Macmillan, 2013.
Derrida, Jacques, "Structure, Sign and Play in the Discourse of the Human Sciences," in Rick Rylance (ed.), *Debating Texts: A Reader in*

Twentieth Century Literary Theory and Method, pp. 123–136 (Milton Keynes: Open University Press, 1987).
de Sousa, Roland, *The Rationality of Emotion* (Cambridge, MA.: MIT Press, 1987).
Didion, Joan, *The Year of Magical Thinking* (London: Fourth Estate, 2005).
Digeser, P. E., *Political Forgiveness* (Ithaca: Cornell University Press, 2001).
"Friendship Between States," *British Journal of Political Science*, 39.2 (2009), 323–344.
Dimsdale, J. E. (ed.), *Survivors, Victims, and Perpetrators: Essays on the Nazi Holocaust* (Washington, D.C.: Hemisphere, 1980).
Di Prete, Laura, *"Foreign Bodies": Trauma, Corporeality, and Textuality in Contemporary American Culture* (New York: Routledge, 2006).
"DeLillo's *The Body Artist*: Performing the Body, Narrating Trauma," *Contemporary Literature*, 46.1 (2005), 483–510.
Dixon, Thomas, *From Passions to Emotions: The Creation of a Secular Psychological Category* (Cambridge: Cambridge University Press, 2003).
Dodson, Louise, "The week the PM felt a nation's pain," *The Age*, 18 October 2002, p. 17.
Donini, Antonio, "The Far Side: The Meta Functions of Humanitarianism in a Globalised World," *Disasters*, 34.S2 (2010), 220–237.
Doty, Roxanne Lynn, *Imperial Encounters: The Politics of Representation in North–South Relations* (Minneapolis: University of Minnesota Press, 1996).
Dowdall, Terry, "Psychological Aspects of the Truth and Reconciliation Commission," in H. Russel Botman and Robin M. Petersen (eds.), *To Remember and Heal: Theological and Psychological Reflections on Truth and Reconciliation* (Cape Town: Human and Rousseau, 1996).
Dupont, Alan, "Transformation or Stagnation? Rethinking Australia's Defense," *Australian Journal of International Affairs*, 57.1 (2003), 55–76.
Easterly, William Russell, *White Man's Burden: Why the West's Efforts to Aid the Rest Have Done So Much Ill and So Little Good* (New York: Penguin, 2006).
Eccleston, Roy, Don Greenlees and Megan Saunders, "World Alert: Season of Terror," *The Weekend Australian*, October 19–20, 2002, p. 1.
Edkins, Jenny, "Forget Trauma? Responses to September 11," *International Relations*, 16.2 (2002), 243–256.
Trauma and the Memory of Politics (Cambridge: Cambridge University Press, 2003).
"The Rush to Memory and the Rhetoric of War," *Journal of Political and Military Sociology*, 31.2 (2003), 231–251.

"Ground Zero: Reflections on Trauma, In/distinction and Response," *Journal for Cultural Research*, 8.3 (2004), 247–270.

"Exposed Singularity," *Journal for Cultural Research*, 9.4 (2005), 359–386.

"Remembering Relationality: Trauma Time and Politics," Duncan S. A. Bell (ed.), *Memory, Trauma and World Politics: Reflections on the Relationship Between the Past and the Present*, pp. 99–115 (Basingstoke: Palgrave Macmillan, 2006).

Edkins, Jenny and Adrian Kear (eds.), *International Politics and Performance: Critical Aesthetics and Creative Practice* (Milton Park and New York: Routledge, 2013).

Edney, Kingsley, "The 2008 Beijing Olympic Torch Relay: Chinese and Western Narratives," *Journal of Current Chinese Affairs/China aktuell*, 37.2 (2008), 111–125.

Egeland, Jan, "Foreword," in Michael Barnett and Thomas G. Weiss, *Humanitarianism Contested: Where Angels Fear to Tread* (Milton Park: Routledge, 2011).

Elster, Jon, *Alchemies of the Mind: Rationality and the Emotions* (Cambridge: Cambridge University Press, 1999).

Eng, David L., "The Value of Silence," *Theatre Journal*, 54.1 (2002), 85–94.

Errante, Antoinette, "Peace Work as Grief Work in Mozambique and South Africa," *Peace and Conflict: Journal of Peace Psychology*, 5.3 (1999), 261–279.

Erikson, Kai, *A New Species of Trouble: Explorations in Disaster, Trauma, and Community* (New York: W.W. Norton, 1994).

"Notes on Trauma and Community," in Cathy Caruth (ed.), *Trauma: Explorations in Memory*, pp. 183–200 (Baltimore: Johns Hopkins University Press, 1995).

Eyerman, Ron, *Cultural Trauma: Slavery and the Formation of African American Identity* (Cambridge: Cambridge University Press, 2001).

"The Past in the Present: Culture and the Transmission of Memory," *Acta Sociologica*, 47.2 (2004), 159–169.

Eznack, Lucile, "Crises as Signals of Strength: The Significance of Affect in Close Allies' Relationships," *Security Studies*, 20.2 (2011), 238–265.

"The Mood Was Grave: Affective Dispositions and States' Anger Related Behaviour", *Contemporary Security Policy*, 34.3 (2013), 552–580.

Fassin, Didier, *Humanitarian Reason: A Moral History of the Present*, trans. Rachel Gomme (Berkeley: University of California Press, 2012).

Fassin, Didier and Richard Rechtman, *The Empire of Trauma: An Inquiry into the Condition of Victimhood*, trans. Rachel Gomme (Princeton: Princeton University Press, 2009).

Fattah, Khaled and K.M. Fierke, "A Clash of Emotions: The Politics of Humiliation and Political Violence in the Middle East," *European Journal of International Relations*, 15.1 (2008), 67–93.

Fentress, James and Chris Wickham (eds.), *Social Memory* (London: Blackwell, 1992).

Ferguson, Kathy, *The Man Question: Visions of Subjectivity in Feminist Theory* (Berkeley: University of California Press, 1993).

Fierke, K.M., "Links Across the Abyss: Language and Logic in International Relations," *International Studies Quarterly*, 46.3 (2002), 331–354.

"The Liberation of Kosovo: Emotion and the Ritual Reenactment of War," *Focaal: European Journal of Anthropology*, 39 (2002), 93–113.

"Whereof We Can Speak, Thereof We Must Not Be Silent: Trauma, Political Solipsism and War," *Review of International Studies*, 30 (2004), 471–491.

"Bewitched by the Past: Social Memory, Trauma and International Relations," in Duncan Bell (ed.) *Memory, Trauma and World Politics: Reflections on the Relationship Between the Past and the Present*, pp. 116–134 (Basingstoke: Palgrave Macmillan, 2006).

Critical Approaches to International Security (Cambridge: Polity, 2007).

Political Self-Sacrifice: Agency, Body and Emotion in International Relations (Cambridge: Cambridge University Press, 2012).

"Emotion and Intentionality," *International Theory*, 6.3 (2014), 563–567.

Fineman, Stephen, "Organizations as Emotional Arenas," in Stephen Fineman (ed.), *Emotion in Organizations*, pp. 9–35 (Thousand Oaks, CA: Sage, 1993).

Fitzgerald, John, "China and the Quest for Dignity," *The National Interest*, 55 (Spring 1999), 47–59.

Fontan, Victoria, "Polarization Between Occupier and Occupied in Post-Saddam Iraq: Colonial Humiliation and the Formation of Political Violence," *Terrorism and Political Violence*, 18.2 (2006), 217–238.

Foucault, Michel, *The Archaeology of Knowledge*, trans. A. M. Sheridan Smith (London: Routledge, 2002).

History of Sexuality: The Will to Knowledge (London: Penguin, 1998).

Frank, Arthur W., *The Wounded Story-Teller: Body, Illness, Ethics* (Chicago: University of Chicago Press, 1995).

Freud, Sigmund, "Mourning and Melancholia," trans. James Strachey, in Angela Richards (ed.), *On Metapsychology: The Theory of Psychoanalysis*, pp. 247–268 (Harmondsworth: Penguin, 1991),

Friedman, Edward, "Raising Sheep on Wolf Milk: The Politics and Dangers of Misremembering the Past in China," *Totalitarian Movement and Political Regimes* 9.2/3 (2008), 389–409.

Friedman, Merle, "The Truth and Reconciliation Commission in South Africa as an Attempt to Heal a Traumatized Society," in A. Y. Shalev et al. (eds.), *International Handbook of Human Response to Trauma*, pp. 399–411 (Dordrecht, The Netherlands: Kluwer, 2000).

Friedlander, Saul, "Trauma, Transference and 'Working Through' in Writing the History of the 'Shoah'," *History and Memory*, 4.1 (1992), 39–59.

Frijda, Nico H., *The Emotions* (Cambridge: Cambridge University Press, 1986).

Frijda, Nico H., Antony S. R. Manstead and Sacha Bem, "The Influence of Emotions on Beliefs," in Nico H. Frijda, Antony S. R. Manstead and Sacha Bem (eds.) *Emotions and Beliefs: How Feelings Influence Thoughts*, pp. 1–9 (Cambridge: Cambridge University Press, 2000).

Gallimore, Timothy, "Unresolved Trauma: Fuel for the Cycle of Violence and Terrorism," in Chris E. Stout (ed.), *Psychology of Terrorism: Coping with the Continuing Threat*, pp. 67–93 (Westport: Praeger, 2004).

Galtung, Johan, "The Construction of National Identities for the Cosmic Drama: Chosen-Myths-Trauma (CMT) Syndromes and Cultural Pathologies," in Udayakumar (ed.), *Handcuffed to History: Narratives, Pathologies and Violence in South-East Asia*, pp. 61–77 (Westport: Praeger, 2001).

Gammon, Earl, "Affect and the Rise of the Self-Regulatory Market," *Millennium: Journal of International Studies*, 37.2 (2008), 251–278.

Gedi, Noa and Yigal Elam, "Collective Memory – What Is It?" *History and Memory*, 8.1 (1996), 30–50.

George, Alexander L. and Juliette L. George, *Presidential Personality and Performance* (Boulder, CO.: Westview Press, 1998).

Gibney, Mark, Rhoda E. Howard-Hassman, Jean-Marc Coicaud and Nicklaus Steiner (eds.), *The Age of Apology: Facing Up to the Past* (Philadelphia: University of Pennsylvania Press, 2008).

Gibson, James L. and Gouws, Amanda, "Truth and Reconciliation in South Africa: Attributions of Blame and the Struggle over Apartheid," *American Political Science Review*, 93.3 (1999), 501–517.

Giddens, Anthony, "Foreword," in Thomas J. Scheff, *Microsociology: Discourse, Emotion, and Social Structure* (Chicago: University of Chicago Press, 1990).

Gillis, John, "Memory and Identity: The History of a Relationship," in John Gillis (ed.), *Commemorations: The Politics of National Identity* (Princeton: Princeton University Press, 1994).

Gilmore, Leigh, *The Limits of Autobiography: Trauma and Testimony* (Ithaca: Cornell University Press, 2001).

Gobodo-Madikizela, Pumla, "Remorse, Forgiveness, and Rehumanization: Stories from South Africa," *Journal of Humanistic Psychology*, 42.1 (2002), 7–32.

"Empathetic Repair after Mass Trauma: When Vengeance is Arrested," *European Journal of Social Theory*, 11.3 (2008), 331–351.

"Transforming Trauma in the Aftermath of Gross Human Rights Abuses," in Arie Nadler, Thomas E. Malloy and Jeffrey D. Fisher (eds.), *The Social Psychology of Intergroup Reconciliation*, pp. 57–75 (Oxford: Oxford University Press, 2008).

Goodwin, Jeff, James M. Jasper and Francesca Polletta, "Introduction: Why Emotions Matter," in Jeff Goodwin, James M. Jasper and Francesca Polletta (eds.), *Passionate Politics: Emotions and Social Movements*, pp. 1–26 (Chicago: University of Chicago Press, 2001).

Gqola, Phulma, "Defining People: Analysing Power, Language and Representation in Metaphors of the New South Africa," *Transformation: Critical Perspectives on Southern Africa*, 47 (2001), 94–106.

Graham, Sarah Ellen, "Emotion and Public Diplomacy: Dispositions in international Communications, Dialogue and Persuasion," *International Studies Review*, 16.4 (2014), 522–539.

Graybill, Lyn S., "South Africa's Truth and Reconciliation Commission: Ethical and Theological Perspectives," *Ethics and International Affairs*, 12 (1998), 43–62.

Greenberg, Judith, "The Echo of Trauma and the Trauma of Echo," *American Imago*, 55.3 (1998), 319–347.

Greenlees, Don, "Terror Hits Home," *The Australian*, October 14, 2002, p. 1.

Gries, Peter Hays, *China's New Nationalism: Pride, Politics and Diplomacy* (Berkeley: University of California Press, 2004).

Gross, Kimberly and Lisa D'Ambrosio, "Framing Emotional Response," *Political Psychology*, 25.1 (2004), 1–29.

Guo, Yingjie, *Cultural Nationalism in Contemporary China* (London: Routledge, 2004).

"Patriotic Villains and Patriotic Heroes: Chinese Literary Nationalism in the 1990s," *Nationalism and Ethnic Politics*, 4.1–2 (2007), 163–188.

Haas, Aaron, *In the Shadow of the Holocaust: The Second Generation* (Ithaca: Cornell University Press, 1990).

Halbwachs, Maurice, *On Collective Memory*, trans. Lewis A. Coser (Chicago: University of Chicago Press, 1992 [1925]).

Hall, Cheryl, *The Trouble with Passion: Political Theory Beyond the Reign of Reason* (New York: Routledge, 2005).

Hall, Stuart (ed.), *Representation: Cultural Representations and Signifying Practices* (London: Sage and The Open University, 1997).

"Introduction," in Stuart Hall (ed.), *Representation: Cultural Representations and Signifying Practices*, pp. 1–12 (London: Sage and The Open University, 1997).

"The Work of Representation," in Stuart Hall (ed.), *Representation: Cultural Representations and Signifying Practices*, pp. 13–74 (London: Sage in association with The Open University, 1997).

Hall, Todd, "We Will Not Swallow This Bitter Fruit: Theorizing a Diplomacy of Anger," *Security Studies*, 20.4 (2011), 521–555.

Halpern, Jodi and Harvey M. Weinstein, "Rehumanizing the Other: Empathy and Reconciliation," *Human Rights Quarterly*, 26.3 (2004), 561–583.

Harding, Jennifer and E. Deidre Pribram, "The Power of Feeling: Locating Emotions in Culture," *European Journal of Cultural Studies*, 5.4 (2002), 407–426.

Hariman, Robert and John Louis Lucaites, "Public Identity and Collective Memory in U.S. Iconic Photography: The Image of the Accidental Napalm," *Critical Studies in Media Communication*, 20.1 (2003), 35–66.

No Caption Needed: Iconic Photographs, Public Culture, and Liberal Democracy (Chicago: Chicago University Press, 2007).

Harré, Rom, "Emotions as Cognitive-Affective-Somatic Hybrids," *Emotion Review*, 1.4 (2009), 294–301.

(ed.), *The Social Construction of Emotions* (Oxford: Blackwell, 1986).

Harré, Rom and W. Gerrod Parrot (eds.), *The Emotions: Social, Cultural and Biological Dimensions* (London: Sage, 1996).

Harris, Richard, "China and the World," *International Affairs*, 35 (1959), 161–169.

Hansen, Lene, *Security as Practice: Discourse Analysis and the Bosnian War* (London: Routledge, 2006).

Hayner, Priscilla B., *Unspeakable Truths: Confronting State Terror and Atrocity* (New York: Routledge, 2001).

Hayward, Clarissa Ryle, *De-Facing Power* (New York: Cambridge University Press, 2000).

He, Yinan, "History, Chinese Nationalism and the Emerging Sino-Japanese Conflict," *Journal of Contemporary China*, 16.50 (2007), 1–24.

The Search for Reconciliation in Sino-Japanese and German-Polish Relations since World War II (Cambridge: Cambridge University Press, 2009).

Heaney, Jonathan G., "Emotions and Nationalism: A Reappraisal," in Nicholas Demertzis (ed.), *Emotions in Politics: The Affect Dimension in Political Tension*, pp. 243–263 (Basingstoke: Palgrave Macmillan, 2013).

"Emotions and Power: A Bifocal Prescription to Cure Theoretical Myopia," *Journal of Political Power*, 6.3 (2013), 355–362.

"Emotions and Power: Reconciling Conceptual Twins," *Journal of Political Power*, 4.2 (2011), 259–277.

Heard, Barry, *Well Done, Those Men: Memoirs of a Vietnam Veteran* (Carlton, Victoria: Scribe Books, 2005).

Heath-Kelly, Charlotte, "Securing through the Failure to Secure? The Ambiguity of Resilience at the Bombsite," *Security Dialogue*, 46.1 (2015), 69–85.

Herman, Judith Lewis, *Trauma and Recovery: From Domestic Abuse to Political Terror* (London: Basic Books, 1992).

Hewett, Jennifer, "Amid a Nation's Pain, a Call to Stand Together," *Sydney Morning Herald*, October 18, 2002, p. 1.

Higgins, Ean, "Father of Bali Bombing Victim Reflects on his Constant Struggle," *The Australian*, October 13, 2013. Available at www.theaustralian.com.au/in-depth/terror/father-of-bali-bombing-victim-reflects-on-his-constant-struggle/story-fnpdbcmu-1227088093916. Accessed November 10, 2014.

Hill, Christopher, *The Changing Politics of Foreign Policy* (Basingstoke: Palgrave Macmillan, 2003).

Hirsch, Marianne, "Surviving Images: Holocaust Photographs and the Work of Postmemory," *The Yale Journal of Criticism*, 14.1 (2001), 5–37.

"I Took Pictures: September 2001 and Beyond," in Judith Greenberg (ed.) *Trauma at Home: After 9/11*, pp. 69–88 (Lincoln and London: University of Nebraska, 2003).

Hochschild, Arlie Russel, "Emotion Work, Feeling Rules and Social Structure," *American Journal of Sociology*, 85.3 (1979), 551–575.

The Managed Heart: The Commercialization of Human Feeling (Berkeley: University of California Press, 1983).

Hoffmaster, Barry, "Fear of Feeling," *The Hastings Center Report*, 33.1 (2003), 45–57.

Holland, Jack and Ty Solomon, "Affect is What States Make of It: Articulating Everyday Experiences on 9/11," *Critical Studies on Security*, 20.3 (2014), 262–277.

Höijer, Birgitta, "The Discourse of Global Compassion: The Audience and Media Reporting of Human Suffering," *Media, Culture & Society*, 26.4 (2004), 513–531.

Holmes, Marcus, "Believing This and Alieving That: Theorizing Affect and Intuitions in International Politics," *International Studies Quarterly*, 59.4 (2015), 706–720.

Howell, Alison, *Madness in International Relations: Psychology, Security, and the Global Governance of Mental Health* (London and New York: Routledge, 2011).

Hsü, C. Y., *The Rise of Modern China*, 6th Edition (New York and Oxford: Oxford University Press, 2000).

Hughes, Dominic, "Australians in Shock After Bali attack," *BBC News*, international edition, October 13, 2002. Available at http://bbc.co.uk/2/hi/asia-pacific/2324261.stm. Accessed September 25, 2012.

Hughes, Rachel, "The Abject Artefacts of Memory: Photographs from Cambodia's Genocide," *Media, Culture & Society*, 25.1 (2003), 23–44.

Humphrey, Michael, "From Terror to Trauma: Commissioning Truth for National Reconciliation," *Social Identities*, 6.1 (2000), 7–27.

The Politics of Atrocity and Reconciliation: From Terror to Trauma (London: Routledge, 2002).

Hungerford, Amy, *The Holocaust of Texts: Genocide, Literature and Personification* (Chicago: University of Chicago Press, 2003).

Hutchison, Emma, "A Global Politics of Pity? Disaster Imagery and the Emotional Construction of Solidarity after the 2004 Asian Tsunami," *International Political Sociology*, 9.1 (2014), 1–19.

Hutchison, Emma and Roland Bleiker, "Theorizing Emotions in World Politics," *International Theory*, 6.3 (2014), 491–514.

Hymans, Jacques E. C., *The Psychology of Nuclear Proliferation: Identity, Emotions, and Foreign Policy* (Cambridge: Cambridge University Press, 2006).

Jackson, Marni, *Pain: The Science and Culture of Why We Hurt* (London: Bloomsbury, 2003).

Jackson, Patrick Thaddeus, "Forum Introduction: Is the State a Person? Why Should We Care?" *Review of International Studies*, 30.2 (2004), 255–258.

Jackson, Sally and Stephen Brook, "Death in Bali – How Australia's Media Reacted When Terror Hit Our Doorstep," *The Australian*, October 17, 2002.

Jacoby, Tami Amanda, "A Theory of Victimhood: Politics, Conflict and the Construction of Victim-Based Identity," *Millennium: Journal of International Studies*, 43.2 (2015), 511–530.

Jaggar, Alison M., "Love and Knowledge: Emotion in Feminist Epistemology," in Susan R. Bordo and Alison M. Jaggar (eds.), *Gender/Body/Knowledge: Feminist Reconstructions of Being and Knowing*, pp. 145–171 (New Brunswick, NJ: Rutgers University Press, 1989).

James, Nicky, "Emotional Labour: Skill and Work in the Social Regulation of Feelings," *The Sociological Review*, 37.1 (1989), 15–42.

James, William, "What is an Emotion?" *Mind*, 9 (1884), 188–205.
"The Physical Basis of Emotion" *Psychological Review*, 1.5 (1894), 516–529.
Jameson, Frederic, *The Political Unconscious: Narrative as Socially Symbolic Act* (Ithaca: Cornell University Press, 1981).
Jeffery, Renée, "Reason, Emotion and the Problem of World Poverty: Moral Sentiment Theory and International Ethics," *International Theory*, 3.1 (2011), 143–178.
Reason and Emotion in International Ethics (Cambridge: Cambridge University Press, 2014).
Jervis, Robert, *Perception and Misperception in International Politics* (Princeton: Princeton University Press, 1976).
Johnson, Nuala C., "Cast in Stone: Monuments, Geography and Nationalism," *Environment and Planning D: Society and Space*, 13 (1995), 51–65.
Jones, Amelia, *Body Art/Performing the Subject* (Minneapolis: University of Minnesota Press, 1998).
Jones, Gail, "Surviving a Bootprint," *The Australian Literary Review*, May 2, 2007, pp. 24–25.
Kansteiner, Wulf, "Finding Meaning in Memory: A Methodological Critique of Collective Memory Studies," *History and Theory*, 41.2 (2002), 179–197.
Kaplan, E. Ann, "A Camera and A Catastrophe: Reflections on the Trauma and the Twin Towers," in Judith Greenberg (ed.), *Trauma at Home: After 9/11*, pp. 95–106 (Lincoln and London: University of Nebraska, 2003).
Trauma Culture: The Politics of Loss in Media and Literature (New Brunswick, NJ: Rutgers University Press, 2005).
Kaplan, Robert D., *Balkan's Ghosts: A Journey Through History* (London: Picador, 2005).
Käpylä, Juha and Denis Kennedy, "Cruel to Care? Investigating the Governance of Compassion in the Humanitarian Imagery," *International Theory*, 6.2 (2014), 255–292.
Kaufman, Alison Adcock, "The Century of Humiliation Then and Now: Chinese Perceptions of the International Order," *Pacific Focus*, 105.1 (2010), 1–33.
Kearney, Richard, "Narrative and the Ethics of Remembrance," in Richard Kearney and Mark Dooley (eds.), *Questioning Ethics: Contemporary Debates in Philosophy*, pp. 18–32 (London: Routledge, 1999).
On Stories (London: Routledge, 2002).
Kennedy, Denis, "Selling the Distant Other: Humanitarianism and Imagery – Ethical Dilemmas of Humanitarian Action," *The Journal of Humanitarian Assistance* (2009). Available at http://sites.tufts.edu/jha/archives/411. Accessed November 2, 2014.

Kinney, Damien, "Rediscovering a Massacre: The Filmic Legacy of Iris Chang's *The Rape of Nanking*," *Continuum: Journal of Media and Cultural Studies*, 26.1 (2012), 11–23.

Kinnvall, Caterina, "Trauma and the Politics of Fear: Europe at the Crossroads," in Nicholas Demertzis (ed.), *Emotions in Politics: The Affect Dimension in Political Tension*, pp. 143–166 (Basingstoke: Palgrave Macmillan, 2013).

Kirmayer, Laurence J., "Landscapes of Memory: Trauma, Narrative, and Dissociation," in Paul Antze and Michael Lambek (eds.), *Tense Past: Cultural Essays in Trauma and Memory*, pp. 173–198 (London: Routledge, 1996).

Klass, Dennis, Silverman, Phyllis R. and Nickman, Steven L. (eds.), *Continuing Bonds: New Understandings of Grief* (London and Philadelphia: Taylor & Francis, 1996).

Kleber, Rolf J., Charles R. Figley and Berthold P. R. Gersons (eds.), *Beyond Trauma: Cultural and Societal Dynamics* (New York and London: Plenum Press, 1995).

Kleinman, Arthur, *The Illness Narratives: Suffering, Healing and the Human Condition* (New York: Basic Books, 1989).

Kleinman, Arthur and Joan Kleinman, "The Appeal of Experience; The Dismay of Images: Cultural Appropriations of Suffering in Our Times," *Daedalus*, 125.1 (1996), 1–24.

Kleinman, Arthur, Veena Das and Margaret Lock (eds.), *Social Suffering* (Berkeley: University of California Press, 1997).

Kofman, Sarah, *Smothered Words*, trans. Madaleine Dobie (Illinois: Northwestern University Press, 1998).

Korf, Benedikt, "Antinomies of Generosity: Moral Geographies and Post-Tsunami Aid in Southeast Asia," *Geoforum*, 38.2 (2007), 366–378.

Koschut, Simon, "Emotional (Security) Communities: The Significance of Emotion Norms in Inter-Allied Conflict Management," *Review of International Studies*, 40.3 (2014), 533–558.

Kristeva, Julia, *Desire in Language: A Semiotic Approach to Literature and Art* (New York: Columbia University Press, 1980).

Powers of Horror: An Essay in Abjection, trans. Leon S. Roudiez (New York: Columbia University Press, 1982).

"New Maladies of the Soul," in Kelly Oliver (ed.), *The Portable Kristeva* (New York: Columbia University Press, 1997).

LaCapra, Dominick, *Writing History, Writing Trauma* (Baltimore: Johns Hopkins University Press, 2001).

Lahr, John, "Down and Out: Twenty-Seven Characters in Search of Play," *The New Yorker*, May 31, 2004, p. 92.

Lambek, Michael and Paul Antze, "Introduction: Forecasting Memory," in Paul Antze and Michael Lambek (eds.), *Tense Past: Cultural Essays in Trauma and Memory*, pp. xi–xxxviii (New York: Routledge, 1996).

Langer, Lawrence L., *Holocaust Testimonies: The Ruins of Memory* (New Haven and London: Yale University Press, 1991).

"The Alarmed Vision: Social Suffering and Holocaust Atrocity," *Daedalus*, 125.1 (1996), 47–66.

Larkin, Michael, "Deciding on an Emotion-Laden Photograph for Page One," *Nieman Reports*, 56.3 (2002), 77.

Laub, Dori, "Truth and Testimony: The Process and the Struggle," in Cathy Caruth (ed.), *Trauma: Explorations in Memory*, pp. 61–75 (Baltimore: Johns Hopkins University Press, 1995).

"September 11, 2001 – An Event Without a Voice," in Judith Greenberg (ed.), *Trauma at Home: After 9/11*, pp. 204–215 (Lincoln and London: University of Nebraska, 2003).

Lebow, Richard Ned, "Reason, Emotion and Cooperation," *International Politics*, 42.3 (2005), 283–313.

"Fear, Interest and Honour: Outlines of a Theory of International Relations," *International Affairs*, 82.3 (2006), 431–448.

LeDoux, Joseph E., "Emotion: Clues From the Brain," *Annual Review of Psychology*, 46 (1995), 209–235.

Leep, Matthew Coen, "The Affective Production of Others: United States Foreign Policy Towards Israeli–Palestinian Conflict," *Cooperation and Conflict*, 45.3 (2010), 331–352.

Leik, Nini and Marianne Davidsen-Nielsen, *Healing Pain: Attachment, Loss and Grief Therapy* (London and New York: Routledge, 1991).

Leuder, Ivan, Victoria Marsland and Jiří Nekvapil, "On Membership Categorization: 'Us,' 'Them' and 'Doing Violence' in Political Discourse," *Discourse & Society*, 15.2–3 (2004), 243–266.

Lewis, Jeff, "Paradise Defiled: The Bali Bombings and the Terror of National Identity," *European Journal of Cultural Studies*, 9.2 (2006), 223–242.

Lewis, Jeff and Sonya de Masi, "Unholy Wars: Media Representations of the First Bali Bombings and their Aftermath," *Media International Australia, Incorporating Culture and Policy*, 122 (2007), 59–72.

Leys, Ruth, *Trauma: A Genealogy* (Chicago: University of Chicago Press, 2000).

"The Turn to Affect: A critique," *Critical Inquiry*, 37.4 (2011), 434–472.

Lind, Jennifer, *Sorry States: Apologies in International Politics* (Ithaca: Cornell University Press, 2008).

"Apologies in International Politics," *Security Studies*, 18.3 (2009), 517–556.

Lindner, Evelin, *Making Enemies: Humiliation and International Conflict* (Westport: Praeger Security International, 2006).

Lingis, Alfonso, *The Community of Those Who Have Nothing in Common* (Indiana: Indianapolis University Press, 1994).

Linklater, Andrew, *The Transformation of Political Community: Ethical Foundations of a Post-Westphalian Era* (Cambridge: Polity, 1998).

The Problem of Harm in World Politics: Theoretical Investigations (Cambridge: Cambridge University Press, 2011).

"Anger and World Politics: How Collective Emotions Shift Over Time," *International Theory*, 6.3 (2014), 574–578.

Lipton, Eric, "Even at Charity Used to Aiding, It's a Scramble," *The New York Times*, December 31, 2004, p. 1.

Lisle, Debbie, "Gazing at Ground Zero: Tourism, Voyeurism and Spectacle," *Journal for Cultural Research*, 8.1 (2004), 3–21.

Little, Graham, *The Public Emotions: From Mourning to Hope* (Sydney: Australian Broadcasting Commission, 1999).

Lock, Margaret, "Cultivating the Body: Anthropology and Epistemologies of Bodily Practice and Knowledge," *Annual Review of Anthropology*, 22 (1993), 133–155.

Loseke, Donileen R., "Examining Emotion as Discourse: Emotion Codes and Presidential Speeches Justifying War," *The Sociological Quarterly*, 50.3 (2009), 497–524.

Löwenheim, Nava, "A Haunted Past: Requesting Forgiveness For Wrongdoing in International Relations," *Review of International Studies*, 35.3 (2009), 531–555.

Löwenheim, Oded and Gadi Heimann, "Revenge in International Politics," *Security Studies*, 17.4 (2008), 685–724.

Luke, Steven, "Power and the Battle for Hearts and Minds," *Millennium: Journal of International Studies*, 33.3 (2005), 477–493.

Lumsden, Malvern, "Breaking the Cycles of Violence," *Journal of Peace Research*, 34.4 (1997), 377–383.

Lupton, Deborah, *The Emotional Self: A Socio-Cultural Exploration* (London: Sage, 1998).

Lutz, Catherine A., *Unnatural Emotions: Everyday Sentiments on a Micronesian Atoll and their Challenge to Western Theory* (Chicago: University of Chicago Press, 1988).

"Engendered Emotion: Gender, Power, and the Rhetoric of Emotional Control in American Discourse,' in Rom Harré and W. Gerrod Parrot (eds.), *The Emotions: Social, Cultural and Biological Dimensions*, pp. 151–170 (London: Sage, 1996).

Lutz, Catherine A. and Lila Abu-Lughod, "Introduction: Emotion, Discourse, and the Politics of Everyday Life," in Catherine A. Lutz and Lila Abu-Lughod (eds.), *Language and the Politics of Emotion*, pp. 1–24 (Cambridge: Cambridge University Press, 1990).

Lutz, Catherine A. and Lila Abu-Lughod (eds.), *Language and the Politics of Emotion* (Cambridge: Cambridge University Press, 1990).

Lyon, Margot L., "Missing Emotion: The Limitations of Cultural Constructivism in the Study of Emotion," *Cultural Anthropology*, 10.2 (1995), 244–263.

"The Material Body, Social Processes and Emotion: 'Techniques of the Body' Revisited," *Body & Society*, 3.1 (1997), 83–101.

"Emotion and Embodiment: The Respiratory Mediation of Somatic and Social Processes," in Alexander Laban Hinton (ed.), *Biocultural Approaches to Emotion*, pp. 182–212 (Cambridge: Cambridge University Press, 1999).

Machin, Linda, *Working with Loss and Grief* (London: Sage, 2009).

Malkki, Liisa H., "Speechless Emissaries: Refugees, Humanitarianism, and Dehistoricization," *Cultural Anthropology*, 11.3 (1996), 377–404.

Mamadouh, Virginie, "After Van Gogh: The Geopolitics of the Tsunami Relief Effort in the Netherlands," *Geopolitics*, 13.2 (2008), 205–231.

Manzo, Kate, "Imaging Humanitarianism: NGO Identity and the Iconography of Childhood," *Antipode*, 40.4 (2008), 632–657.

Marcus, George E., "Emotions in Politics," *Annual Review of Political Science*, 3 (2002), 221–250.

Martin, J. R., "Mourning: How We Get Aligned," *Discourse & Society*, 15.2–3 (2004), 321–344.

Martin, Roger, "Howard Weeps at 'Cruel View of Humanity'," *The Weekend Australian*, October 19–20, 2002, p. 1.

Massumi, Brian, *Parables for the Virtual: Movement, Affect, Sensation* (Durham, NC: Duke University Press, 2002).

Maxwell, Anne, *Colonial Photography and Exhibitions: Representations of the "Native" and the Making of European Identities* (London and New York: Leicester University Press, 1999).

Mayo, James M., "War Memorials as Political Landscape," *Geographical Review*, 78.1 (1988), 62–75.

MacNab, Francis, *Life After Loss: Getting Over Grief and Getting on With Life* (Newtown: Millennium Books, 1989).

McDermott, Rose, "The Feeling of Rationality: The Meaning of Neuroscientific Advances for Political Science," *Perspectives on Politics*, 2.4 (2004), 691–706.

"The Body Doesn't Lie: A Somatic Approach to the Study of Emotion in World Politics," *International Theory*, 6.3 (2014), 557–562.

McDonald, Matt, "Constructing Insecurity: Australian Security Discourse and Policy Post-2001," *International Relations*, 19.3 (2005), 297–320.

"Perspectives on Australian Foreign Policy, 2004," *Australian Journal of International Affairs*, 59.2 (2005), 153–168.

"Lest We Forget: The Politics of Memory and Australian Military Intervention," *International Political Sociology*, 4.3 (2010), 287–302.

McIlveen, Luke, "Day of Mourning on Sunday," *The Australian*, October 15, 2002, p. 2.

McNally, Richard, *Remembering Trauma* (Cambridge, MA: Harvard University Press, 2003).

Megill, Allan, "History, Memory, Identity," *History of the Human Sciences*, 11.3 (1998), 37–62.

Mercer, Jonathan, "Approaching Emotion in International Politics," paper presented at the Annual Meeting of the International Studies Association, San Diego, California, April 25, 1996.

"Rationality and Psychology in International Politics," *International Organization*, 59 (2005), 77–106.

"Emotional Beliefs," *International Organization*, 64.1 (2010), 1–31.

"Emotion and Strategy in the Korean War," *International Organization*, 67.2 (2013), 221–252.

"Feeling Like a State: Social Emotion and Identity," *International Theory*, 6.3 (2014), 515–535.

Metherell, Mark, "Sprig of Wattle for Mourning," *Sydney Morning Herald*, October 18, 2002, p. 2.

Mikculincer, Mario and Philip R. Shaver, "An Attachment Perspective of Bereavement," in Margaret S. Stroebe, Robert O. Hansson, Henk Schut and Wolfgang Stroebe (eds.), *Handbook of Bereavement Research and Practice: Advances in Theory and Intervention*, pp. 3–25 (Washington, D.C.: American Psychological Association, 2008).

Miller, Manjari Chaterjee, *Wronged By Empire: Post-Imperial Ideology and Foreign Policy in India and China* (Stanford: Stanford University Press, 2013).

"The Trauma of Colonialism", *New York Times*, August 14, 2013. Available at www.nytimes.com/2013/08/15/opinion/global/the-trauma-of-colonialism.html?_r=0. Accessed March 4, 2014.

Miller, Nancy K., "'Portraits of Grief': Telling Details and the Testimony of Trauma," *differences: A Journal of Feminist Cultural Studies*, 14.3 (2003), 112–135.

Miller, Nancy K. and Jason Tougaw (eds.), *Extremities: Trauma, Testimony, and Community* (Illinois: University of Illinois Press, 2002).

Milliken, Jennifer, "The Study of Discourse in International Relations: A Critique of Research and Methods," *European Journal of International Relations*, 5.2 (1999), 225–254, 229.

Milton, Kay, "Afterword," in Kay Milton and Maruška Svašek (eds.), *Mixed Emotions: Anthropological Studies in Feeling* (Oxford: Berg, 2005).
Milton, Kay and Maruška Svašek (eds.), *Mixed Emotions: Anthropological Studies in Feeling* (Oxford: Berg, 2005).
Minow, Martha, "Surviving Victim Talk," *UCLA Law Review*, 40 (1993), 1411–1445.
Between Vengeance and Forgiveness: Facing History after Genocide and Mass Violence (Boston: Beacon Press, 1998).
"The Hope for Healing: What Can Truth Commissions Do?" Robert I. Rotberg and Dennis Thompson (eds.), *Truth V. Justice: The Morality of Truth Commissions*, pp. 235–260 (Princeton: Princeton University Press, 2010).
Mitchell, William J.T., *Picture Theory: Essays on Verbal and Visual Representation* (Chicago: Chicago University Press, 1994).
"The Unspeakable and the Unimaginable: Word and Image in a Time of Terror," *ELH: Journal of English Literary History*, 72 (2005), 291–308.
Mitter, Rana, "Old Ghosts, New Memories: China's Changing War History in the Era of Post-Mao Politics," *Journal of Contemporary History*, 38.1 (2003), 117–131.
Misztal, Barbara A., "The Sacralization of Memory," *European Journal of Social Theory*, 7.1 (2004), 67–84.
Moeller, Susan D., *Compassion Fatigue: How the Media Sell Disease, Famine, War and Death* (New York: Routledge, 1999).
Moïsi, Dominique, "The Clash of Emotions," *Foreign Affairs*, 86.1 (2007), 8–12.
The Geopolitics of Emotions: How Cultures of Fear, Humiliation and Hope are Reshaping Our World (New York: Doubleday, 2009).
Moldoveanu, Mihnea and Nitin Nohria, *Master Passions: Emotion, Narrative, and the Development of Culture* (Cambridge, MA: The MIT Press, 2002).
Möller, Frank, "Rwanda Revisualized: Genocide, Photography, and the Era of the Witness," *Alternatives: Global, Local, Political*, 35.2 (2010), 113–136.
Mollica, Richard F., *Healing Invisible Wounds: Paths to Hope and Recovery in a Violent World* (Nashville, TN: Vanderbilt University Press, 2009).
Molloy, Patricia, "Face to Face with the Dead Man: Ethical Responsibility, State-Sanctioned Killing, and Empathetic Impossibility," *Alternatives: Social Transformation and Humane Governance*, 22.4 (1997), 467–492.
Moon, Claire, *Narrating Political Reconciliation: South Africa's Truth Commission* (Plymouth: Lexington, 2008).

"Healing Past Violence: Traumatic Assumptions and Therapeutic Interventions in War and Reconciliation," *Journal of Human Rights*, 8.1 (2009), 71–91.

Moore, M., Dodson, L. and Gray, D., "Dozens of Australians Feared Dead. PM Brands Act 'Barbaric'," *The Age*, October 14, 2002, p.1.

Morgan, David, "Pain: The Unrelieved Condition of Modernity," *European Journal of Social Theory*, 5.3 (2002), 307–322.

Morris, David B., *The Culture of Pain* (Berkeley: University of California Press, 1993).

"About Suffering: Voice, Genre and Moral Community," *Daedalus*, 125.1 (1996), 25–45.

Morrison, Toni, *Beloved* (New York: Penguin, 1987).

"Nobel Lecture," lecture presented December 7, 1993, Available at http://nobelprize.org/nobel_prizes/literature/laureates/1993/morrison-lecture.html. Accessed October 8, 2006.

Muldoon, Paul, "The Moral Legitimacy of Anger," *European Journal of Social Theory*, 11.3 (2008), 299–314.

Mulvey, Laura, *Visual and Other Pleasures* (London: Macmillan, 1989).

Mydans, Seth, "Amid Chaos, Sri Lankans Struggle to Survive," *The New York Times*, December 30, 2004, p. 1.

Naimark, Norman M., *Fires of Hatred: Ethnic Cleansing in Twentieth-Century Europe* (Cambridge, MA: Harvard University Press, 2002).

Nair, Sheila, "Governance, Representation and International Aid," *Third World Quarterly*, 34.4 (2013), 630–652

Nash, Kate, "Cosmopolitan Political Community: Why Does It Feel So Right?" *Constellations: International Journal of Critical and Democratic Theory*, 10.4 (2003), 506–518.

National Geographic, "The Deadliest Tsunami in History?" Available at http://news.nationalgeographic.com/news/2004/12/1227_041226_tsunami.html. Accessed November 2, 2014.

Naylor, Tristen, "Deconstructing Development: The Use of Power and Pity in the International Development Discourse," *International Studies Quarterly*, 55.1 (2011), 177–197.

Neimeyer, Robert A., "Complicated Grief and the Quest for Meaning: A Constructivist Contribution," *Omega: Journal of Death and Dying*, 52.1 (2006), 37–52.

Neimeyer, Robert A., Holly G. Prigerson and Betty Davis, "Mourning and Meaning," *American Behavioral Scientist*, 46.2 (2002), 235–251.

Noor, Masi, Nurit Shnabel, Samer Halabi and Arie Nadler, "When Suffering Begets Suffering: The Psychology of Competitive Victimhood Between Adversarial Groups in Violent Conflicts," *Personality and Social Psychology Review*, 16.4 (2012), 351–374.

Norton, Anne, *Reflections on Political Identity* (Baltimore: Johns Hopkins University Press, 1988).

Norton, Matthew, "Narrative Structure and Emotional Mobilization in Humanitarian Representations: The Case of the Congo Reform Movement," *Journal of Human Rights*, 10.3 (2011), 311–338.

Norval, Aletta J., "Memory, Identity and the (Im)possibility of Reconciliation: The Work of the Truth and Reconciliation Commission in South Africa," *Constellations*, 5.2 (1998), 250–265.

"'No Reconciliation Without Redress': Articulating Political Demands in Post-Transitional South Africa," *Critical Discourse Studies*, 6.4 (2009), 311–321.

Novick, Peter, *The Holocaust and Collective Memory* (London: Bloomsbury, 1999).

Ntsebeza, Dumia B., "The Uses of Truth Commissions: Lessons for the World," in Robert I. Rotberg and Dennis Thompson (eds.), *Truth V. Justice: The Morality of Truth Commissions*, pp. 158–168 (Princeton: Princeton University Press, 2010).

Nussbaum, Martha C., *Loves Knowledge: Essays on Philosophy and Literature* (New York: Oxford University Press, 1990).

"Emotions and Women's Capabilities," in Jonathon Glover and Martha Nussbaum (eds.), *Women, Culture and Development*, pp. 360–395(New York: Oxford University Press, 1995).

Poetic justice: The Literary Imagination and Public Life (Boston: Beacon, 1995).

"Compassion: The Basic Social Emotion," *Social Philosophy and Policy*, 13.1 (1996), 27–58.

Upheavals of Thought: The Intelligence of Emotions (Cambridge: Cambridge University Press, 2001).

"Compassion and Terror," *Daedalus*, 132.1 (2003), 10–26.

Nussbaum, Martha C. and Jonathon Glover (eds.), *Women, Culture and Development* (New York: Oxford University Press, 1995).

Olick, Jeffrey K., "Collective Memory: The Two Cultures," *Sociological Theory*, 19.3 (1999), 333–348.

Olson, David R., "Thinking About Narrative," in Bruce K Britton and A. D. Pelligrini (eds.), *Narrative Thought and Narrative Language*, pp. 99–112 (New York and London: Psychology Press, 1990).

Oren, Neta and Daniel Bar-Tal, "The Detrimental Dynamics of Delegitimization in Intractable Conflicts: The Israeli–Palestinian Case," *International Journal of Intercultural Relations*, 31.1 (2007), 111–126.

Orford, Anne, *Reading Humanitarian Intervention: Human Rights and the Use of Force in International Law* (Cambridge: Cambridge University Press, 2003).

Orr, W., "PTSD and the Truth and Reconciliation Commission," *Continuing Medical Education Journal*, 16 (1998), 142–143.

Owens, Patricia A., "Xenophilia, Gender, and Sentimental Humanitarianism," *Alternatives: Global, Local, Political*, 29.3 (2004), 285–305.

Pain, Rachel and Susan J. Smith (eds.), *Fear: Critical Geopolitics and Everyday Life* (Aldershot: Ashgate, 2008).

Panksepp, Jaak, *Affective Neuroscience: The Foundations of Human and Animal Emotions* (Oxford: Oxford University Press, 1998).

Pedwell, Carolyn, "Economies of Empathy: Obama, Neoliberalism, and Social Justice," *Environment and Planning D: Society and Space*, 30.2 (2012), 280–297.

Pennebaker, James W., *Opening Up: The Healing Power of Expressing Emotions* (New York: Guilford, 1990).

Perlez, Jane, "From Heart of Indonesia's Disaster, A Cry for Help," *The New York Times*, January 2, 2005, p. 1.

Perlmutter, David D., *Photojournalism and Foreign Policy: Icons of Outrage in International Crises* (Westport: Praeger, 1998).

Petersen, Roger, *Understanding Ethnic Violence: Fear, Hatred and Resentment in Twentieth-Century Eastern Europe* (Cambridge: Cambridge University Press, 2002).

Phelps, Elizabeth A., "Emotion and Cognition: Insights from Studies of the Human Amygdala," *Annual Review of Psychology*, 57 (2006), 27–53.

Philipose, Liz, "The Politics of Pain and the End of Empire," *International Feminist Journal of Politics*, 9.1 (2007), 60–81.

Philpott, Simon, "A Controversy of Faces: Images from Bali to Abu Ghraib," *Journal for Cultural Research*, 9.3 (2005), 227–244.

Prager, Jeffrey, *Presenting the Past: Psychoanalysis and the Sociology of Misremembering* (Cambridge, MA: Harvard University Press, 1998).

Prinz, Jesse J., *Gut Reactions: A Perceptual Theory of Emotion* (Oxford: Oxford University Press, 2004).

Prosser, Jay, *Light in the Dark Room: Photography and Loss* (Minneapolis: University of Minnesota Press, 2005).

Pupavac, Vanessa, "Misanthropy Without Borders: The International Children's Rights Regime," *Disasters*, 25.1 (2001), 95–112.

"Therapeutic Governance: Psycho-social Intervention and Trauma Risk Management," *Disasters*, 25.4 (2001), 358–372.

"Pathologizing Populations and Colonizing Minds: International Psychosocial Programs in Kosovo," *Alternatives: Global, Local, Political*, 27 (2002), 489–511.

"War on the Couch: The Emotionology of the New International Security Paradigm," *European Journal of Social Theory*, 7.2 (2004), 149–170.

Radley, Alan, "Portrayals of Suffering: On Looking Away, Looking At, and the Comprehension of Illness Experience," *Body & Society*, 8.3 (2002), 1–23.

Radley, Alan and Marie Kennedy, "Picturing Need: Images of Overseas Aid and Interpretations of Cultural Difference," *Culture & Psychology*, 3.4 (1997), 435–460.

Ragg, Mark, "The Numbers No-one Wants to Figure Out," *Sydney Morning Herald*, October 17, 2002, p. 5.

Randall, William L., *The Stories We Are: An Essay on Self-Creation* (Toronto: University of Toronto Press, 1995).

Rathbun, Brian C., *Trust in International Cooperation: International Security Institutions, Domestic Politics and American Multilateralism* (Cambridge: Cambridge University Press, 2012).

Ray, Larry, "Mourning, Melancholia and Violence," in Duncan S. A. Bell (ed.), *Memory, Trauma and World Politics: Reflections on the Relationship Between the Past and the Present*, pp. 135–156 (Basingstoke: Palgrave Macmillan, 2006).

Reddy, William M., "Against Constructionism: The Historical Ethnography of Emotions," *Current Anthropology*, 38.3 (1997), 327–351.

"Emotional Liberty: Politics and History in the Anthropology of Emotions," *Cultural Anthropology*, 14.2 (1999), 256–288.

The Navigation of Feeling: A Framework for the History of Emotions (Cambridge: Cambridge University Press, 2001).

Renwick, Neil and Qing Cao, "China's Political Discourse Towards the 21st Century: Victimhood, Identity, and Political Power," *East Asia*, 17.4 (1999), 111–143.

Resende, Erica and Dovile Budryte (eds.), *Memory and Trauma in International Relations: Theories, Cases and Debates* (London and New York: Routledge, 2014).

Ricoeur, Paul, "The Creativity of Language," in Richard Kearney (ed.), *Dialogues With Contemporary Continental Thinkers: The Philosophical Heritage: Paul Ricoeur, Emmanuel Levinas, Herbert Marcuse, Stanislas Breton, Jacques Derrida*, pp. 17–35 (Manchester: Manchester University Press, 1984).

"On Narrative Imagination: On Life-Stories," in Richard Kearney (ed.), *Debates in Continental Philosophy: Conversations in Continental Thinkers*, pp. 330–337 (New York: Fordham University Press, 2004).

Risse, Thomas, "'Let's Argue!': Communicative Action in World Politics," *International Organization*, 54.1 (2000), 1–39.

Rorty, Richard R., *Contingency, Irony, and Solidarity* (Cambridge: Cambridge University Press, 1989).

Rosaldo, Michelle Z., *Knowledge and Passion: Ilongot Notions of Self and Social Life* (Cambridge: Cambridge University Press, 1980).

"Toward an Anthropology of Self and Feeling," in Richard A. Shweder and Robert A. LeVine (eds.), *Culture Theory: Essays on Mind, Self and Emotion*, pp. 137–157 (Cambridge: Cambridge University Press, 1984).

Rose, Gillian, *Visual Methodologies: An Introduction to the Interpretation of Visual Materials* (London: Sage, 2001).

Rosenblatt, Paul C., "Grief that Does Not End," in Dennis Klass, Phyllis R. Silverman and Steven L. Nickman (eds.), *Continuing Bonds: New Understandings of Grief*, pp. 45–58 (London and Philadelphia: Taylor and Francis, 1996).

Rosenwein, Barbara H., *Emotional Communities in the Early Middle Ages* (Ithaca: Cornell University Press, 2006).

"Worrying About Emotions in History," *The American Historical Review*, 107.3 (2002), 821–845.

Ross, Andrew A. G., *Affective States: Rethinking Passion in World Politics*, PhD Dissertation (Baltimore: Johns Hopkins University, 2005).

"Coming in from the Cold: Constructivism and Emotions," *European Journal of International Relations*, 12.2 (2006), 197–222.

"Why They Don't Hate Us: Emotion, Agency and the Politics of 'Anti-Americanism'," *Millennium: Journal of International Studies*, 39.1 (2010), 109–125.

Mixed Emotions: Beyond Fear and Hatred in International Conflict (Chicago: Chicago University Press, 2014).

Ross, Susan Dente, "Introduction," in Susan Dente Ross and Paul Martin Lester (eds.), *Images that Injure: Pictorial Stereotypes in the Media*, 3rd edition (Westport: Praeger, 2011).

Roudometof, Victor, "Beyond Commemoration: The Politics of Collective Memory," *Journal of Political and Military Sociology*, 31.2 (2003), 161–170.

Rubin, Simon Shimshon, "Mourning Distinct From Melancholia: The Resolution of Bereavement," *British Journal of Medical Psychology*, 57.4 (1984), 339–345.

Sasley, Brent E., "Affective Attachments and Foreign Policy: Israel and the 1993 Oslo Accords," *European Journal of International Relations*, 16.4 (2010), 687–709.

"Theorizing States' Emotions," *International Studies Review*, 13.3 (2011), 453–476.

"Violence, Grief, and Memory: How Emotions Help Maintain or Resolve Conflict," paper presented at the Annual Convention of the International Studies Association, March 26–29, 2014.

Sassen, Saskia, "Women's Burden: Counter Geographies of Globalization and the Feminization of Survival," *Nordic Journal of International Law*, 71.2 (2002), 255–274.

Saurette, Paul, "You Dissin me? Humiliation and Post 9/11 Global Politics," *Review of International Studies*, 32.3 (2006), 495–522.

Scarry, Elaine, *The Body in Pain: The Making and Unmaking of the World* (New York: Oxford University Press, 1985).

Resisting Representation (New York: Oxford University Press, 1994).

Scheer, Monique, "Are Emotions a Kind of Practice?" *History and Theory*, 51.2 (2012), 193–220.

Scheff, Thomas J., *Catharsis in Healing, Ritual, and Drama* (Berkeley: University of California Press, 1979).

Microsociology: Discourse, Emotion, and Social Structure (Chicago: University of Chicago Press, 1990).

"Emotions and Identity: A Theory of Ethnic Nationalism," in Craig Calhoun (ed.), *Social Theory and the Politics of Identity*, pp. 277–303 (Oxford: Blackwell, 1994).

Bloody Revenge: Emotions, Nationalism and War (Boulder, CO: Westview Press, 1994).

Scheff, Thomas J. and Suzanne M. Retzinger, *Emotions and Violence: Shame and Rage in Destructive Conflicts* (Lexington, MA: Lexington Books, 1991).

Schell, Orville, "China: Humiliation and the Olympics," *New York Review of Books*, 55.13 (2008). Available online at www.nybooks.com/articles/2008/08/14/china-humiliation-the-olympics/. Accessed December 24, 2015.

Schick, Kate, "Acting Out and Working Through: Trauma and (In)security," *Review of International Studies*, 37.4 (2011), 1837–1855.

Schmemann, Serge, "The Anniversary of World War II is an Invitation to Continue Fighting," *The New York Times*, March 22, 2005.

Schwartz, Murray, "Locating Trauma: A Commentary on Ruth Ley's *Trauma: A Genealogy*," *American Imago*, 59.3 (2002), 367–384.

Schwarz, Norbert, "Emotion, Cognition and Decision Making," *Cognition and Emotion*, 14.4 (2000), 433–440.

Scott, David, *China and the International System 1840–1949: Power, Presence, and Perceptions in a Century of Humiliation* (Albany, NY: SUNY Press, 2008).

Seale, Clive, *Constructing Death: The Sociology of Dying and Bereavement* (Cambridge: Cambridge University Press, 1998).

Shalev, Ariel Y., "PTSD: A Disorder of Recovery?" in Laurence J. Kirmayer, Robert Lemelson and Mark Barad (eds.), *Understanding Trauma: Integrating Biological, Clinical, and Cultural Perspectives*, pp. 207–223 (New York: Cambridge University Press, 2007).

Shan, Zhou and Zhang Chunbo (eds.), *Guochi lu: Tushou Zhonghua bainian [A Record of National Humiliation: Pictures and Stories of China's Century]* (Lanzhou: Gansu Youth Press, 1997).
Shapiro, Michael J., *Language and Political Understanding: The Politics of Discursive Practices* (New Haven: Yale University Press, 1981).
(ed.), *Language and Politics* (Oxford: Blackwell, 1984).
The Politics of Representation: Writing Practices in Biography, Photography, and Policy Analysis (Madison: University of Wisconsin Press, 1988).
"Warring Bodies and Bodies Politic: Tribal Warriors Versus State Soldiers," in Michael J. Shapiro and Hayward R. Alker (eds.), *Challenging Boundaries: Global Flows, Territorial Identities*, pp. 455–480 (Minneapolis: University of Minnesota Press, 1996).
Violent Cartographies: Mapping Cultures of War (Minneapolis: University of Minnesota Press, 1997).
Methods and Nations: Cultural Governance and the Indigenous Subject (New York: Routledge, 2004).
Shapiro, Michael J. and Hayward R. Alker (eds.), *Challenging Boundaries: Global Flows, Territorial Identities* (Minneapolis: University of Minnesota Press, 1996).
Shaw, Martin, *Civil Society and Media in Global Crises: Representing Distant Violence* (London: Pinter, 1996).
Shepherd, Laura, "Visualising Violence: Legitimacy and Authority in the 'War on Terror'," *Critical Studies in Terrorism*, 1.2 (2008), 213–226.
Shepperd, Taryn, *Sino-US Relations and the Role of Emotion in State Action: Understanding Post-Cold War Crisis Interactions* (Basingstoke: Palgrave Macmillan, 2013).
Sheridan, Greg, "A Threat We Ignore at Our Peril," *The Australian*, October 14, 2002, p. 11.
Shlaim, Avi, *The Iron War: Israel and the Arab World* (London: Penguin, 2001).
Simpson, David, *9/11: The Culture of Commemoration* (Chicago: University of Chicago Press, 2006).
Smith, Debbie James, "Big-Eyed, Wide-Eyed, Sad-Eyed Children: Constructing the Humanitarian Space in Social Justice Documentaries," *Studies in Documentary Film*, 3.2 (2009), 159–175.
Smith, Mick, Joyce Davidson, Laura Cameron and Liz Bondi (eds.), *Emotions, Place and Culture* (Surrey: Ashgate, 2009).
Solomon, Jeffrey L., "Modes of Thought and Meaning Making: The Aftermath of Trauma," *Journal of Humanistic Psychology*, 44.3 (2004), 299–319.
Solomon, Robert C., *The Passions: Emotions and the Meaning of Life*, 2nd edition (Indianapolis: Hackett, 1993).
Not Passion's Slave: Emotions and Choice (Oxford: Oxford University, 2003).

The Joy of Philosophy: Thinking Thin Versus the Passionate Life (Oxford: Oxford University Press, 2003).

Solomon, Ty, "'I Wasn't Angry Because I Couldn't Believe it was Happening': Affect and Discourse in Responses to September 11," *Review of International Studies*, 38.4 (2012), 907–928.

"The Affective Underpinnings of Soft Power," *European Journal of International Relations*, 20.3 (2014), 720–741.

Staub, Ervin, *Overcoming Evil: Genocide, Violent Conflict and Terrorism* (Oxford: Oxford University Press, 2011).

Steele, Brent, "Making Words Matter: The Asian Tsunami, Darfur, and 'Reflexive Discourse' in International Politics," *International Studies Quarterly*, 51.4 (2007), 901–925.

Defacing Power: The Aesthetics of Insecurity in Global Politics (Ann Arbor: University of Michigan Press, 2010).

Stearns, Peter N. and Carol Z. Stearns, "Emotionology: Clarifying the History of Emotions and Emotional Standards," *American Historical Review*, 90.4 (1985), 813–836.

Sturken, Maria, "The Wall, the Screen and the Image: The Vietnam Veteran's Memorial," *Representations*, 35 (1991), 118–142.

Tangled Memories: The Vietnam War, The Aids Epidemic and the Politics of Remembering (Berkeley: University of California Press, 1997).

Summerfield, Derek, "Addressing Human Response to War and Atrocity: Major Challenges in Research and Practices and the Limitations of Western Psychiatric Models," in Rolf J. Kleber, Charles R. Figley and Berthold P. R. Gersons (eds.), *Beyond Trauma: Cultural and Societal Dynamics* (New York and London: Plenum Press, 1995).

Suski, Laura, "Children, Suffering and the Humanitarian Appeal," in Richard Ashby Wilson and Richard D. Brown (eds.), *Humanitarianism and Suffering: The Mobilization of Empathy*, pp. 202–222 (New York: Cambridge University Press, 2009).

Suzuki, Shogo, "The Importance of 'Othering' in China's National Identity: Sino-Japanese Relations as a Stage of Identity Conflicts," *The Pacific Review*, 20.1 (2007), 23–47.

"Can Apology Serve as a Security Policy? Responsible Scholarship and Breaking the Chains of Negative History in Sino-Japanese Relations," *Korean Journal of Defense Analysis*, 20.4 (2008), 319–333.

Svašek, Maruška, "Introduction: Emotions in Anthropology," in Kay Milton and Maruška Svašek (eds.), *Mixed Emotions: Anthropological Studies in Feeling*, pp. 1–24 (Oxford: Berg, 2005).

Sylvester, Christine, "The Art of War/The War Question in (Feminist) IR," *Millennium: Journal of International Studies*, 33.3 (2005), 855–878.

Sznaider, Natan, "The Sociology of Compassion: A Study in the Sociology of Morals," *Cultural Values* (now *Journal for Cultural Research*), 2.1 (1998), 117–139.

Sztompka, Piotr, "Cultural Trauma: The Other Face of Social Change," *European Journal of Social Theory*, 3.4 (2000), 449–466.

Tagg, John, *The Burden of Representation: Essays in Photographies and Histories* (Basingstoke: Palgrave Macmillan, 1988).

Tester, Kieth, *Compassion, Morality and the Media* (Milton Keynes: Open University Press, 2001).

Humanitarianism and Modern Culture (University Park: Pennsylvania State University Press, 2010).

Thein, Deborah, "After or Beyond Feeling? A Consideration of Affect and Emotion in Geography," *Area*, 37.4 (2005), 450–456.

Thrift, Nigel, "Intensities of Feeling: Towards a Spatial Politics of Affect," *Geografiska Annaler: Series B, Human Geography*, 86.1 (2004), 57–78.

Non-Representational Theory: Space, Politics, Affect (New York: Routledge, 2008).

Thurston, Anne F., "Community and Isolation: Memory and Forgetting," in G. Gong (ed.), *Memory and History in East and Southeast Asia*, pp. 149–172 (Washington, D.C.: CSIS Press, 2001).

Todorov, Tzvetan, *Hope and Memory: Lessons from the Twentieth Century*, trans. David Bellos (Princeton: Princeton University Press, 2003).

Truth and Reconciliation Commission South Africa, Report Volumes 1–5 (Cape Town: Truth and Reconciliation Commission, 1998).

"Human Rights Violations Hearings," May 15, 1996. Available at www.justice.gov.za/trc/hrvtrans%5Chrvel1/mohape.htm. Accessed July 23, 2014.

Tsu, Jung, *Failure, Nationalism, and Literature: The Making of Modern Chinese Identity, 1895–1937* (Stanford, CA: Stanford University Press, 2006).

Tsunami Evaluation Coalition, "The Boxing Day Tsunami in Numbers." Available at www.alnap.org/pool/files/tsunami-stats-facts.pdf. Accessed November 2, 2014.

Tuathail, Gearóid Ó., "'Just Out Looking for a Fight': American Affect and the Invasion of Iraq," *Antipode*, 35.5 (2003), 856–870.

Turner, Jonathon H. and Jan E. Stets, *The Sociology of Emotions* (Cambridge: Cambridge University Press, 2005).

"Twelfth Anniversary of Bali Bombings to be Marked with Quiet Reflection in Kuta, Australia." Available at www.news.com.au/world/twelfth-anniversary-of-bali-bombings-to-be-marked-with-quiet-reflection-in-kuta-australia/story-fndir2ev-1227087719623. Accessed November 10, 2014.

van Fraassen, Bas C., *Scientific Representation: Paradoxes of Perspective* (Oxford: Oxford University Press, 2008).

Van Maanen, John and Gideon Kunda, "'Real Feelings': Emotional Expression and Organizational Culture," *Research in Organizational Behavior*, 11 (1989), 43–103.

Verdoolaege, Annelies, "Dealing with a Traumatic Past: The Victim Hearings in the South African Truth and Reconciliation Commission and their Reconciliation Discourse," *Critical Discourse Studies*, 6.4 (2009), 297–309.

Vice, Sue, "Yellowing Snapshots: Photography and Memory in Holocaust Literature," *Journal for Cultural Research*, 8.3 (2004), 293–315.

Volkan, Vamik D., *Bloodlines: From Ethnic Pride to Ethnic Terrorism* (Boulder, CO: Westview Press, 1997).

"Traumatized Societies and Psychological Care: Expanding the Concept of Preventative Medicine," *Mind and Human Interaction*, 11 (2000), 177–194.

"Transgenerational Transmissions and Chosen Traumas: An Aspect of Large Group Identity," *Group Analysis*, 34.1 (2001), 79–97.

"Chosen Trauma, The Political Ideology of Entitlement and Violence," paper presented in Berlin, June 10, 2004. Available at www.vamikvolkan.com/Chosen-Trauma%2C-the-Political-Ideology-of-Entitlement-and-Violence.php/. Accessed June 20, 2014.

Animal Killer: Transmission of War Trauma from One Generation to the Next (London: Karnac, 2013).

Volkan, Vamik D. and Elizabeth Zintl, *Life After Loss: The Lessons of Grief* (New York: Scribener and Sons, 1993).

Wajnryb, Ruth, *The Silence: How Tragedy Shapes Talk* (Crows Nest, New South Wales: Allen and Unwin, 2001).

Walden, Amy, "Motherless and Childless, An Indian Villages Toll," *The New York Times*, December 31, 2004, p. A12.

Walker, R. B. J., *Inside/Outside: International Relations as Political Theory* (Cambridge: Cambridge University Press, 1993).

Walsh, Katherine, *Grief and Loss: Theories and Skills for the Helping Professionals*, 2nd edition (New Jersey: Pearson, 2012).

Walter, Tony, *On Bereavement: The Culture of Grief* (Buckingham: Open University Press, 1999).

Wang, Zheng, "National Humiliation, Historical Education, and the Politics of Historical Memory: Patriotic Education Campaign in China," *International Studies Quarterly* 52.4 (2008), 783–806.

Never Forget National Humiliation: Historical Memory in Chinese Politics and Foreign Relations (New York: Columbia University Press, 2012).

"The Chinese Dream: Concept and Context," *Journal of Chinese Political Science*, 19.1 (2014), 1–13.

Warinski, Christopher, "'Post-Heroic Warfare' and Ghosts – The Social Control of Dead American Soldiers in Iraq," *International Political Sociology*, 2.2 (2008), 113–127.

Warner, Daniel, "Searching for Responsibility/Community in International Relations," in David Campbell and Michael J. Shapiro (eds.), *Moral Spaces: Rethinking Ethics and World Politics*, pp. 1–28 (Minneapolis: University of Minnesota Press, 1999).

Weber, Cynthia, "Performative States," *Millennium: Journal of International Studies*, 27.1 (1998), 77–95.

Simulating Sovereignty: Intervention, the State, and Symbolic Exchange (Cambridge: Cambridge University Press, 1995).

Weine, Steven M., *Lives and Memories of Ethnic Cleansing in Bosnia-Herzegovina* (New Brunswick, NJ: Rutgers University Press, 1991).

Weisband, Edward, "On the Aporetic Borderlines of Forgiveness: Bereavement as a Political Form," *Alternatives: Global, Local, Political*, 34.4 (2009), 359–381.

Weiss, Robert S., "The Nature and Causes of Grief," in Margaret S. Stroebe, Robert O. Hansson, Henk Schut and Wolfgang Stroebe (eds.), *Handbook of Bereavement Research and Practice*, pp. 29–44 (Washington D.C.: American Psychological Association, 2008).

Weldes, Jutta, Mark Laffey, Hugh Gusterson and Raymond Duvall (eds.), *Cultures of Insecurity: States, Communities, and the Production of Danger* (Minneapolis: University of Minnesota Press, 1999).

Wendt, Alexander, "Anarchy is What States Make of It: The Social Construction of Power Politics," *International Organization*, 46.2 (1992), 391–425.

Social Theory of International Politics (Cambridge: Cambridge University Press, 1999).

"The State as Person in International Theory," *Review of International Studies*, 30.2 (2004), 289–316.

West, Brad, "Collective Memory and Crisis: The 2002 Bali Bombing, National Heroic Archetypes and the Counter Narrative of Cosmopolitan Nationalism," *Journal of Sociology*, 44.4 (2008), 337–353.

West, Brad and Ruthie O'Reilly, "National Humanitarianism and the 2004 Indian Ocean Tsunami," *Journal of Sociology*, OnlineFirst, forthcoming.

Wheeler, Nicholas J., "Beyond Waltz's Nuclear World: More Trust May Be Better," *International Relations*, 23.3 (2009), 428–445.

White, Hayden, *The Content of the Form: Narrative Discourse and Historical Representation* (Baltimore: Johns Hopkins University Press, 1987).

Whitebrook, Maureen, *Identity, Narrative, and Politics* (London: Routledge, 2001).

"Compassion as a Political Virtue," *Political Studies*, 50.3 (2002), 529–554.

Widmaier, Wesley W., "Emotions Before Paradigms: Elite Anxiety and Populist Resentment from the Asian to Subprime Crises," *Millennium: Journal of International Studies*, 39.1 (2010), 127–144.

Wierzbicka, Anna, *Emotions Across Languages and Cultures: Diversity and Universals* (Cambridge: Cambridge University Press, 1999).

Williams, Michael C., "Words, Images, Enemies: Securitization and International Politics," *International Studies Quarterly*, 47.4 (2003), 511–531.

Williams, Simon J. and Gillian A. Bendelow, "Introduction: Emotions in Social Life," in Gillian Bendelow and Simon J. Williams (eds.), *Emotions in Social Life: Critical Themes and Contemporary Issues*, pp. xv–xxx (London and New York: Routledge, 1998).

"The 'Emotional' Body," *Body & Society*, 2.3 (1996), 125–139.

Wilson, Richard A., "The *Sizwe* Will Not Go Away: The Truth and Reconciliation Commission, Human Rights and Nation-Building in South Africa," *African Studies*, 55.2 (1996), 1–20.

The Politics of Truth and Reconciliation in South Africa: Legitimizing the Post-Apartheid State (Cambridge: Cambridge University Press, 2001).

Winter, Jay, *Sites of Memory, Sites of Mourning: The Great War in European Cultural History* (Cambridge: Cambridge University Press, 1995).

Winterson, Jeanette, *The Passion* (London: Vintage, 2004 [1987]).

Sexing the Cherry (New York: Grove Press, 1989).

Wood, Nancy, *Vectors of Memory: Legacies of Trauma in Postwar Europe* (Oxford: Berg, 1999).

Worden, William J., *Grief Counseling and Grief Therapy: A Handbook for the Mental Health Practitioner*, 4th edition (New York: Springer, 2009).

Wright, Sarah, "Emotional Geographies of Development," *Third World Quarterly*, 33.6 (2012), 1113–1127.

Wright-Neville, David and Debra Smith, "Political Rage: Terrorism and the Politics of Emotion," *Global Change, Peace and Security*, 21.1 (2009), 85–98.

Yoder, Carolyn, *The Little Book of Trauma Healing: When Violence Strikes and Community is Threatened* (New York: Good Books, 2006).

Young, Allan, *The Harmony of Illusions: Inventing Post-Traumatic Stress Disorder* (Princeton: University of Princeton Press, 1997).

"Suffering and the Origins of Traumatic Memory," in Arthur Kleinman, Veena Das and Margaret Lock (eds.), *Social Suffering*, pp. 245–260 (Berkeley: University of California Press, 1997).

Zehfuss, Maja, "Forget September 11," *Third World Quarterly*, 24.3 (2003), 513–528.

Wounds of Memory: The Politics of War in Germany (Cambridge: Cambridge University Press, 2007).

"Hierarchies of Grief and the Possibility of War: Remembering UK Fatalities in Iraq," *Millennium: Journal of International Studies*, 38.2 (2009), 419–440.

Zaretsky, Eli, "Trauma and Dereification: September 11 and the Problem of Ontological Security," *Constellations*, 9.1 (2002), 98–105.

Zelizer, Barbie, *Remembering to Forget: Holocaust Memory Through the Camera's Lens* (Chicago: University of Chicago Press, 1998).

"Death in Wartime: Photographs and the 'Other War' in Afghanistan," *Harvard International Journal of Press/Politics*, 10.3 (2005), 26–55.

Zerubavel, Eviatar, *Time Maps: Collective Memory and the Shape of the Past* (Chicago: University of Chicago Press, 2003).

Zhu, Zhiqun. "Introduction: The People's Republic of China Today," in Zhiqun Zhu (ed.), *The People's Republic of China Today: Internal and External Challenges* (Singapore: World Scientific Publishing).

Index

CAMBRIDGE STUDIES IN INTERNATIONAL RELATIONS

128 Michael G. Findley, Daniel L. Nielson and J. C. Sharman
Global shell games
Experiments in transnational relations, crime, and terrorism

127 Jordan Branch
The cartographic state
Maps, territory, and the origins of sovereignty

126 Thomas Risse, Stephen C. Ropp and Kathryn Sikkink (eds.)
The persistent power of human rights
From commitment to compliance

125 K. M. Fierke
Political self-sacrifice
Agency, body and emotion in international relations

124 Stefano Guzzini
The return of geopolitics in Europe?
Social mechanisms and foreign policy identity crises

123 Bear F. Braumoeller
The great powers and the international system
Systemic theory in empirical perspective

122 Jonathan Joseph
The social in the global
Social theory, governmentality and global politics

121 Brian C. Rathbun
Trust in international cooperation
International security institutions, domestic politics and American multilateralism

120 A. Maurits van der Veen
Ideas, interests and foreign aid

119 Emanuel Adler and Vincent Pouliot
International practices

118 Ayşe Zarakol
After defeat
How the East learned to live with the West

117 Andrew Phillips
War, religion and empire
The transformation of international orders

116 Joshua Busby
Moral movements and foreign policy

115 Séverine Autesserre
The trouble with the Congo
Local violence and the failure of international peacebuilding

114 Deborah D. Avant, Martha Finnemore and Susan K. Sell
Who governs the globe?

113 Vincent Pouliot
International security in practice
The politics of NATO–Russia diplomacy

112 Columba Peoples
Justifying ballistic missile defence
Technology, security and culture

111 Paul Sharp
Diplomatic theory of international relations

110 John A. Vasquez
The war puzzle revisited

109 Rodney Bruce Hall
Central banking as global governance
Constructing financial credibility

108 Milja Kurki
Causation in international relations
Reclaiming causal analysis

107 Richard M. Price
Moral limit and possibility in world politics

106 Emma Haddad
The refugee in international society
Between sovereigns

105 Ken Booth
Theory of world security

104 Benjamin Miller
States, nations and the great powers
The sources of regional war and peace

103 Beate Jahn (ed.)
Classical theory in international relations

102 Andrew Linklater and Hidemi Suganami
The English School of international relations
A contemporary reassessment

101 Colin Wight
Agents, structures and international relations
Politics as ontology

100 Michael C. Williams
The realist tradition and the limits of international relations

99 Ivan Arreguín-Toft
How the weak win wars
A theory of asymmetric conflict

98 Michael Barnett and Raymond Duvall
Power in global governance
97 Yale H. Ferguson and Richard W. Mansbach
Remapping global politics
History's revenge and future shock
96 Christian Reus-Smit
The politics of international law
95 Barry Buzan
From international to world society?
English school theory and the social structure of globalisation
94 K. J. Holsti
Taming the sovereigns
Institutional change in international politics
93 Bruce Cronin
Institutions for the common good
International protection regimes in international security
92 Paul Keal
European conquest and the rights of indigenous peoples
The moral backwardness of international society
91 Barry Buzan and Ole Wæver
Regions and powers
The structure of international security
90 A. Claire Cutler
Private power and global authority
Transnational merchant law in the global political economy
89 Patrick M. Morgan
Deterrence now
88 Susan Sell
Private power, public law
The globalization of intellectual property rights
87 Nina Tannenwald
The nuclear taboo
The United States and the non-use of nuclear weapons since 1945
86 Linda Weiss
States in the global economy
Bringing domestic institutions back in
85 Rodney Bruce Hall and Thomas J. Biersteker (eds.)
The emergence of private authority in global governance
84 Heather Rae
State identities and the homogenisation of peoples
83 Maja Zehfuss
Constructivism in international relations
The politics of reality
82 Paul K. Ruth and Todd Allee
The democratic peace and territorial conflict in the twentieth century

81 Neta C. Crawford
Argument and change in world politics
Ethics, decolonization and humanitarian intervention

80 Douglas Lemke
Regions of war and peace

79 Richard Shapcott
Justice, community and dialogue in international relations

78 Phil Steinberg
The social construction of the ocean

77 Christine Sylvester
Feminist international relations
An unfinished journey

76 Kenneth A. Schultz
Democracy and coercive diplomacy

75 David Houghton
US foreign policy and the Iran hostage crisis

74 Cecilia Albin
Justice and fairness in international negotiation

73 Martin Shaw
Theory of the global state
Globality as an unfinished revolution

72 Frank C. Zagare and D. Marc Kilgour
Perfect deterrence

71 Robert O'Brien, Anne Marie Goetz, Jan Aart Scholte and Marc Williams
Contesting global governance
Multilateral economic institutions and global social movements

70 Roland Bleiker
Popular dissent, human agency and global politics

69 Bill McSweeney
Security, identity and interests
A sociology of international relations

68 Molly Cochran
Normative theory in international relations
A pragmatic approach

67 Alexander Wendt
Social theory of international politics

66 Thomas Risse, Stephen C. Ropp and Kathryn Sikkink (eds.)
The power of human rights
International norms and domestic change

65 Daniel W. Drezner
The sanctions paradox
Economic statecraft and international relations

64 Viva Ona Bartkus
The dynamic of secession

63 John A. Vasquez
The power of power politics
From classical realism to neotraditionalism

62 Emanuel Adler and Michael Barnett (eds.)
Security communities

61 Charles Jones
E. H. Carr and international relations
A duty to lie

60 Jeffrey W. Knopf
Domestic society and international cooperation
The impact of protest on US arms control policy

59 Nicholas Greenwood Onuf
The republican legacy in international thought

58 Daniel S. Geller and J. David Singer
Nations at war
A scientific study of international conflict

57 Randall D. Germain
The international organization of credit
States and global finance in the world economy

56 N. Piers Ludlow
Dealing with Britain
The Six and the first UK application to the EEC

55 Andreas Hasenclever, Peter Mayer and Volker Rittberger
Theories of international regimes

54 Miranda A. Schreurs and Elizabeth C. Economy (eds.)
The internationalization of environmental protection

53 James N. Rosenau
Along the domestic-foreign frontier
Exploring governance in a turbulent world

52 John M. Hobson
The wealth of states
A comparative sociology of international economic and political change

51 Kalevi J. Holsti
The state, war, and the state of war

50 Christopher Clapham
Africa and the international system
The politics of state survival

49 Susan Strange
The retreat of the state
The diffusion of power in the world economy

48 William I. Robinson
Promoting polyarchy
Globalization, US intervention, and hegemony

47 Roger Spegele
Political realism in international theory

46 Thomas J. Biersteker and Cynthia Weber (eds.)
State sovereignty as social construct

45 Mervyn Frost
Ethics in international relations
A constitutive theory

44 Mark W. Zacher with Brent A. Sutton
Governing global networks
International regimes for transportation and communications

43 Mark Neufeld
The restructuring of international relations theory

42 Thomas Risse-Kappen (ed.)
Bringing transnational relations back in
Non-state actors, domestic structures and international institutions

41 Hayward R. Alker
Rediscoveries and reformulations
Humanistic methodologies for international studies

40 Robert W. Cox with Timothy J. Sinclair
Approaches to world order

39 Jens Bartelson
A genealogy of sovereignty

38 Mark Rupert
Producing hegemony
The politics of mass production and American global power

37 Cynthia Weber
Simulating sovereignty
Intervention, the state and symbolic exchange

36 Gary Goertz
Contexts of international politics

35 James L. Richardson
Crisis diplomacy
The Great Powers since the mid-nineteenth century

34 Bradley S. Klein
Strategic studies and world order
The global politics of deterrence

33 T. V. Paul
Asymmetric conflicts
War initiation by weaker powers

32 Christine Sylvester
Feminist theory and international relations in a postmodern era

31 Peter J. Schraeder
US foreign policy toward Africa
Incrementalism, crisis and change

30 Graham Spinardi
From Polaris to Trident
The development of US Fleet Ballistic Missile technology

29 David A. Welch
Justice and the genesis of war

28 Russell J. Leng
Interstate crisis behavior, 1816–1980
Realism versus reciprocity

27 John A. Vasquez
The war puzzle
26 Stephen Gill (ed.)
Gramsci, historical materialism and international relations
25 Mike Bowker and Robin Brown (eds.)
From Cold War to collapse
Theory and world politics in the 1980s
24 R. B. J. Walker
Inside/outside
International relations as political theory
23 Edward Reiss
The strategic defense initiative
22 Keith Krause
Arms and the state
Patterns of military production and trade
21 Roger Buckley
US–Japan alliance diplomacy 1945–1990
20 James N. Rosenau and Ernst-Otto Czempiel (eds.)
Governance without government
Order and change in world politics
19 Michael Nicholson
Rationality and the analysis of international conflict
18 John Stopford and Susan Strange
Rival states, rival firms
Competition for world market shares
17 Terry Nardin and David R. Mapel (eds.)
Traditions of international ethics
16 Charles F. Doran
Systems in crisis
New imperatives of high politics at century's end
15 Deon Geldenhuys
Isolated states
A comparative analysis
14 Kalevi J. Holsti
Peace and war
Armed conflicts and international order 1648–1989
13 Saki Dockrill
Britain's policy for West German rearmament 1950–1955
12 Robert H. Jackson
Quasi-states
Sovereignty, international relations and the third world
11 James Barber and John Barratt
South Africa's foreign policy
The search for status and security 1945–1988
10 James Mayall
Nationalism and international society

9 William Bloom
Personal identity, national identity and international relations

8 Zeev Maoz
National choices and international processes

7 Ian Clark
The hierarchy of states
Reform and resistance in the international order

6 Hidemi Suganami
The domestic analogy and world order proposals

5 Stephen Gill
American hegemony and the Trilateral Commission

4 Michael C. Pugh
The ANZUS crisis, nuclear visiting and deterrence

3 Michael Nicholson
Formal theories in international relations

2 Friedrich V. Kratochwil
Rules, norms, and decisions
On the conditions of practical and legal reasoning in international relations and domestic affairs

1 Myles L. C. Robertson
Soviet policy towards Japan
An analysis of trends in the 1970s and 1980s

Lightning Source UK Ltd.
Milton Keynes UK
UKOW06n1340310817
308308UK00014B/158/P

9 781107 095014